COMPUTERS
A VISUAL ENCYCLOPEDIA

Written by

Sherry Kinkoph

Jennifer Fulton

Kelly Oliver

Illustrated by

Katherine Hanley

alpha books

A Division of Macmillan Computer Publishing
201 West 103rd Street, Indianapolis, Indiana 46290 USA

International Standard Book Number: 1-56761-464-7
Library of Congress Catalog Card Number: 93-74398

96 95 94   8 7 6 5 4 3 2 1

Interpretation of the printing code: the rightmost number of the second series of numbers is the number of the book's printing. For example, a printing code of 94-1 shows that the first printing of the book occurred in 1994.

Printed in the United States of America

Publisher: *Marie Butler-Knight*

Managing Editor: *Elizabeth Keaffaber*

Product Development Manager: *Faithe Wempen*

Acquisitions Manager: *Barry Pruett*

Development Editor: *Seta Frantz*

Manuscript Editor: *Audra Gable*

Book Designer: *Barbara Webster*

Layout Designers: *Nathan Clement and Carol Stamile*

Cover Design: *Jay Corpus*

Index: *Jennifer Eberhardt*

Production: *Gary Adair, Brad Chinn, Kim Cofer, Meshell Dinn, Mark Enochs, Stephanie Gregory, Jenny Kucera, Beth Rago, Marc Shecter, Kris Simmons, Greg Simsic, Kevin Spear, Robert Wolf, and Alyssa Yesh.*

Special thanks to Margaret Colvin for ensuring the technical accuracy of this book.

Contents

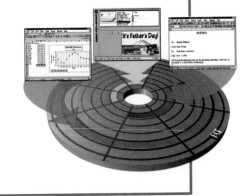

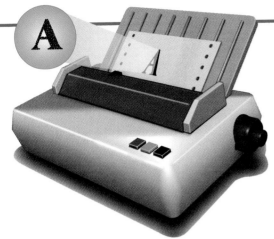

Contents

Q-R

S

P

T-U

V

W-X-Y-Z

Computers—An Overview

Computers are found in all areas of everyday life, from the corner grocery store to the hospital operating room. In spite of their widespread use, most people are unfamiliar with where computers came from, how they work, what tasks they might perform, and what they can be used for in the future.

This book offers insights into all of these areas. *Computers: A Visual Encyclopedia* is an illustrated collection of information about the world of computers, including its inner workings, the types of computer software and hardware, and new technologies. Simply turn the pages and visually explore this fascinating machine known as the *computer*.

This book is written for people of all ages who want to learn more about the basics and history of computers. Each computer topic is alphabetically arranged and can easily be looked up. Each entry also gives further topical references to help the reader learn about related terms, as well as brief definitions of computer words used in conjunction with a particular topic. Scattered throughout the topics are special **How Does It Work** boxes that offer additional insights about the inner workings of the computer's components and programs. Finally, this introduction contains a brief look at computers themselves, how they are used, their history, and a glimpse into their future.

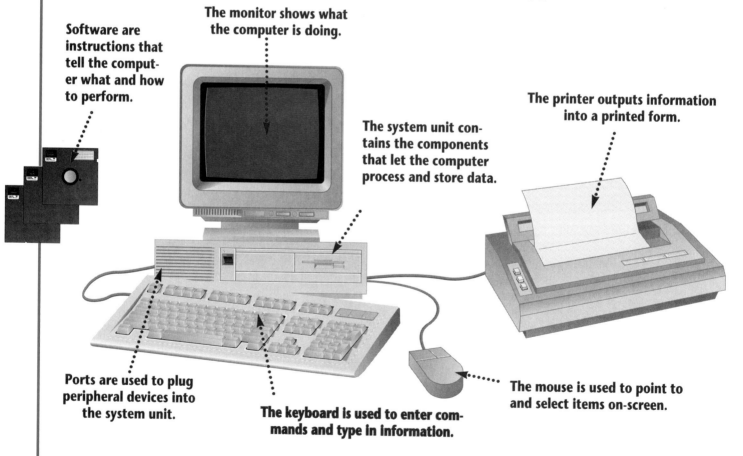

Software are instructions that tell the computer what and how to perform.

The monitor shows what the computer is doing.

The printer outputs information into a printed form.

The system unit contains the components that let the computer process and store data.

Ports are used to plug peripheral devices into the system unit.

The keyboard is used to enter commands and type in information.

The mouse is used to point to and select items on-screen.

How Does It Work?

Basically, the computer accepts information (data), processes it, and then creates output. This sequence begins when the user types in commands at the computer's keyboard. These commands are deciphered by the computer's *operating system*—a special program that coordinates all the computer's tasks. The command instructions are then stored in the computer's random access memory (RAM) chips where they can quickly be manipulated. Next, the instructions are moved into the computer's central processing unit or CPU—the brains of the computer. It is here that the CPU analyzes and processes each instruction and performs the task requested. Any output created by the processing sequence is displayed on the monitor, or perhaps printed out on the printer.

What Is a Computer?

A computer is an electronic machine that enables a user to input, manipulate, store, and output information. Computers perform a variety of tasks that range from creating written

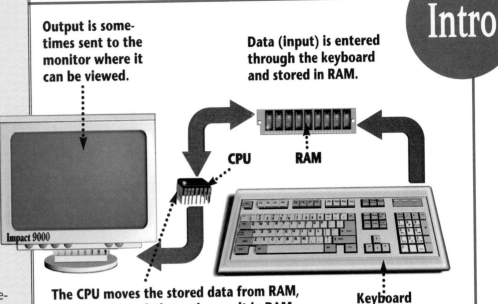

Output is sometimes sent to the monitor where it can be viewed.

Data (input) is entered through the keyboard and stored in RAM.

CPU   RAM

Impact 9000

The CPU moves the stored data from RAM, processes it, and places the result in RAM.

Keyboard

documents to producing slick multimedia presentations containing video, graphics, and sound. Computers calculate complex formulas, organize large lists of data, and provide entertainment. Computers are used in medicine, business, the arts, and education around the globe and in space. They are destined to be an integral part of mankind's future existence.

A computer is made up of three basic parts: the system unit, the monitor, and the keyboard. The system unit contains all the components that store and process data. The monitor displays information. The keyboard allows the user to enter typed commands and information (data). Other peripherals, such as the mouse (a device which allows the user to select items on-screen) and the printer (which prints data) are attached to the computer through the system unit. As the computer processes information (data), it moves that information in

and out of memory. Memory (RAM) is a place inside the system unit where the computer can store data temporarily. When the computer is shut off, everything that was in RAM is erased. So how does the computer ever remember anything? Where does the letter go after it is typed? Well, while the computer is still on (before memory is erased), the user gives the computer a command to copy data from RAM onto the computer's hard drive or onto a floppy disk. The hard drive is a permanent storage area located inside the system unit. A floppy disk is a miniature version of a hard drive, except that it stores a lot less data and it can be transported from place to place. Both the hard drive and the floppy disk contain materials that store data until it is erased. This makes them different from RAM, which can only maintain its data while electricity is sent through it (i.e. while the computer is turned on).

The History of Computers

The first mechanical calculating device was invented by French mathematician Blaise Pascal in 1642. It was constructed with gears and pulleys that had to be turned by hand to operate. In 1801, an automatic weaving loom was invented by Joseph-Marie Jacquard. The loom used a series of punched cards to program weaving patterns for fabrics.

In the 1820s in England, Charles Babbage developed an idea for an "Analytical Engine" that could be programmed to perform any calculation. However, the building of this machine proved too difficult for the artisans of his time. Yet, Babbage's original idea (that a machine could receive variable data or input, process it, and produce a result or output) eventually found its way into the design of modern programmable computers.

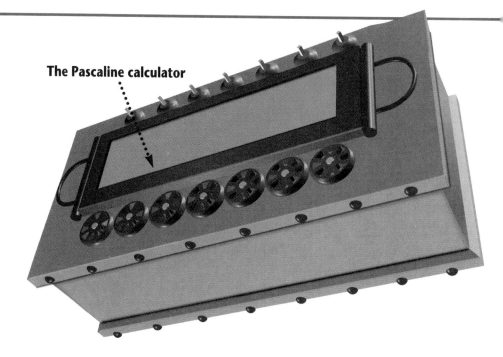

The Pascaline calculator

The Analytical Engine model

With the advent of vacuum tubes in the early 20th century, computer technology shifted to electronics. Gears and pulleys were no longer needed. Instead, electrical switches could achieve the same results using a binary language, where data and instructions were reduced to a series of 1's and 0's (represented within the computer by a series of vacuum tubes which were either on or off). While certainly an improvement over mechanical gears and pulleys, vacuum tube computers were laboriously slow, noisy, and took up large amounts of space, sometimes filling an entire room.

The Atanasoff-Berry Computer, invented in the United States in 1939, was the first to utilize the new vacuum tube technology, although it was designed to perform a single task: the calculation of long mathematical tables. In 1941, the first programmable computer was created by Konrad Zuse in Germany. Called the Z3, it performed various logical operations. The Z3 was programmed by switching electrical relays by hand. A few years later in the United States, the International Business Machines company (IBM) developed a sequence-controlled calculator, called the Mark I.

Vacuum tubes took a considerable amount of power to operate, but they were more efficient than gears and pulleys.

A microprocessor chip

system that mimics old-style vacuum tubes, each tiny transistor within a microchip acts as a single "on" or "off" switch (the 1's and 0' of the computer's binary language).

Since the 1950s, computers have become smaller, faster, and more complex. Inventors and scientists have been able to cram more and more functions onto a single semiconductor chip. The lumbering mainframe computers of the 1950s and 1960s gave way to personal computers in the mid 1970s, which comfortably fit on desktops in the home or at the office. In 1983, there were approximately 2 million personal computers in the United States. By 1993, there were 91 million.

Mainframe computers vary in size: some are the size of a car; others fill an entire room.

In 1946, the first completely electronic computer, ENIAC (Electronic Numerical Integrator and Computer), was designed. Two years later, John von Neumann designed the first computer that was programmed electronically, and not by hand. Created by a team of scientists working for Bell Laboratories, transistor technology entered the scene in 1947. Transistors were as fast as vacuum tubes, but used considerably less power and were smaller in size. However, it was not until the early '70s that transistor technology could be miniaturized, with multiple transistors placed on a tiny microchip. Modern day microchips are constructed of semiconductor material, which provides precise control over the flow of electricity. Yet, in a

An example of an early IBM PC (1981)

IBM AND APPLE

In the early years of personal computers, there were many companies producing their own models, only some of which attained lasting success. In the mid 1970s, the Apple Computer company began selling the first commercially successful personal computer, called the Apple II. The Apple II featured built-in sound and graphics and BASIC (a programming language). In 1981, IBM released its version of a personal computer, called the IBM PC. Because of IBM's size and worldwide marketing expertise, the IBM PC and its clones (similar computers compatible with the IBM technology) began to dominate the computer market. In 1984, Apple introduced the Macintosh, which has become the single best selling brand of personal computer (of which there are no clones.) Today, however, the IBM PC and its clones far outnumber any other type of computer, including the Macintosh. World wide, there are approximately 120 million PC users versus 11 million Macintosh users. The PC and Apple Macintosh computers use two distinctly different operating systems. The PC uses a text-command interface based on the most popular operating system of its time, MS-DOS (Microsoft Disk Operating System). DOS requires the user to type in commands at an on-screen command prompt to perform tasks.

The Macintosh uses a graphical user interface (GUI) instead of a command prompt. A GUI is an interface that relies on graphics, or pictures, instead of typed-in text commands. Users can select on-screen pictures to perform certain tasks. In 1991, System 7, Apple's operating system for the Macintosh, improved on the original system and added true multitasking (the ability to run more than one program at a time), virtual memory, and scalable fonts. In 1985, Microsoft introduced Windows, a GUI interface that operated on top of the text-based DOS. Windows didn't really become popular until version 3 was released in 1990. Windows is now quickly becoming an industry

standard, providing a Mac-like environment for the PC. Currently there are approximately 30 million Windows users world wide, and the number is growing. For comparison, the Macintosh was first released in 1984; it took Microsoft until 1990 to come up with something similar enough to make the GUI popular on the PC. And yet Windows is still not yet as powerful or as fully incorporated into the computer's operating system as the Macintosh GUI. It's also

Apple Macintosh

interesting to remember that the idea behind the GUI wasn't even Apple'–credit for that goes to some researchers over at the Palo Alto Research Center (PARC).

Computers Now

Today, computers are commonplace in schools, homes, and the workplace. They are used in every area of science, medicine, education, entertainment, and industry[md]and especially communications. Computers have improved the way in which people work. They have helped simplify large tasks, and have generally made life a little less difficult.

The personal computer comes in many sizes and shapes, and is used for a variety of purposes. It can sit on a desk, fit into a briefcase, or rest in the palm of the hand. It is used to analyze numbers, write novels, illustrate books, and keep track of a warehouse full of parts and gadgets. Children use it to learn the basics of language and math. Adults use it to tap into bulletin board services or balance a checkbook. Thousands sit and stare into the screen playing endless games. Despite the reservations of those who resist change, computers are here to stay.

Impact 9000

Impact 9000

IBM PC

Computers Tomorrow

Computer science and development is rapidly changing from day to day, bringing engineering advances, new applications, and greater challenges. The future of new technologies, such as virtual reality, robots, cybernetics, artificial intelligence, and other innovative concepts will undoubtedly change today's perspective on computers and how they are used. This book will introduce many of these future technologies through terms like fractals, morphing, personal digital assistants, and voice recognition, just to name a few.

The computers of tomorrow will only be limited to the imagination of man. Understanding what computers are and their potential to benefit mankind opens up a world of exciting challenges and mind-boggling possibilities. It is our sincerest hope that this book helps to do just that.

TRADEMARKS

All terms mentioned in this book that are known to be trademarks have been appropriately capitalized. Alpha Books cannot attest to the accuracy of this information. Use of a term in this book should not be regarded as affecting the validity of any trademark or service mark.

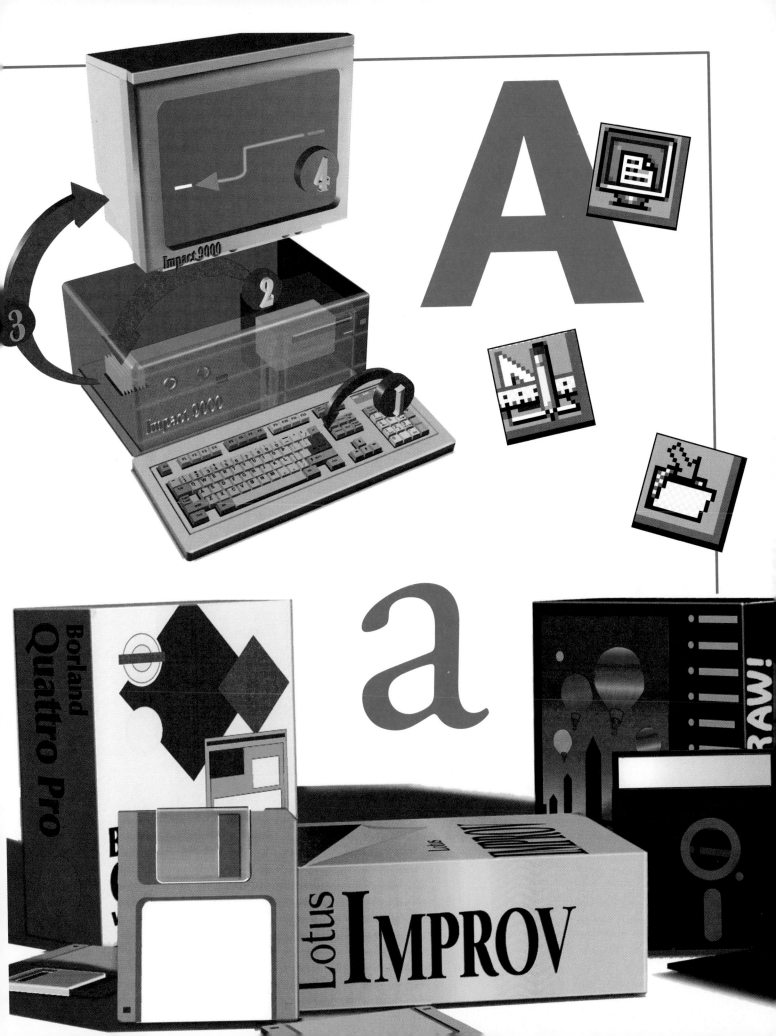

Access

Access is a popular database program developed by Microsoft Corporation. A database is an organized collection of related information, such as a listing of a store's merchandise, each item's price, its internal stocking code, and the number currently on-hand. An address book is also a database: a collection of related names, addresses, and phone numbers. The information in a database is made available through a database management system, such as Microsoft Access.

Released in 1993, Access is designed specifically for use with Microsoft Windows, a graphical user interface (GUI) program that runs on top of the computer's disk operating system (DOS). Access features quick menus (which let the user select commands without moving the mouse out of the area of the screen in which he is working), toolbars (which provide tiny "buttons" representing often used commands, such as saving a file), and an AutoSort command (which allows the user to sort through any column of data with a click of a mouse). Suitable for beginners and expert database users, Access provides simple yet sophisticated methods for locating information stored in database tables. Also see Approach, Database, dBASE, Microsoft, and Windows.

Toolbars and pull-down menus make it simple to use Access commands.

How Does It Work?

Access stores database information in tables that are made up of rows (records) and columns (fields). For example, a customer's record might include the customer's name, company name, address, and phone number, each stored in a separate field within the single customer record.

Microsoft Access is a relational database management system (RDBMS) because data is stored in individual databases (called tables), and is then retrieved based on relationships that are defined by the user. For example, one database table might contain a list of customer names and addresses, and another table might have product IDs and prices. A report can be created that pulls a customer's name and address from the first table, and pulls the items purchased and their prices from the second table to make an invoice.

FIELD

In Access, fields are stored in columns. Each field is a part of a larger record. For example, an item's name, stock number, and price are all fields stored in that item's record.

Field

Table: Customers

Customer ID	Company Name	Contact Name	Contact Title	Address
FRANK	Frankenversand	Peter Franken	Marketing Manager	Berliner Platz 43
FRANR	France restauration	Carine Schmitt	Marketing Manager	54, rue Royale
FRANS	Franchi S.p.A.	Paolo Accorti	Sales Representative	Via Monte Bianco 34

Record

Associate one record in the Customers table...

RECORD

In Access, records are stored in rows. Each record contains pieces of information about a person, a thing, or an event. For example, all of the information about one person (such as his name, title, address, and phone number) would be contained in a single record.

Table: Products

Product ID	Supplier ID	Category ID	Product Name	English Name	Quanti
1	1	1	Chai	Dharamsala Tea	10 boxe
2	1	1	Chang	Tibetan Barley Beer	24 - 12
3	1	2	Aniseed Syrup	Licorice Syrup	12 - 550
4	2	2	Chef Anton's Cajun Seasoning	Chef Anton's Cajun Seasoning	48 - 6 o
5	2	2	Chef Anton's Gumbo Mix	Chef Anton's Gumbo Mix	36 boxe
6	3	2	Grandma's Boysenberry Spread	Grandma's Boysenberry Spread	12 - 8 o
7	3	7	Uncle Bob's Organic Dried Pears	Uncle Bob's Organic Dried Pears	12 - 1 lb
8	3	2	Northwoods Cranberry Sauce	Northwoods Cranberry Sauce	12 - 12
9	4	6	Mishi Kobe Niku	Mishi Kobe Beef	18 - 500
10	4	8	Ikura	Fish Roe	12 - 200
11	5		Queso Cabrales	Cabrales Cheese	1 kg pk

...with another record in the Products table.

Orders

Bill To: Franchi S.p.A.	Ship To: Franchi S.p.A.
Franchi S.p.A.	Via Monte Bianco 34
Frankenversand	
Furia Bacalhau e Frutos do Mar	Torino 10100
Galería del gastrónomo	Italy

Salesperson: Suyama, Michael   Ship Via: ☐ Speedy ☒ United ☐ Federal

Order ID: 10000 Order Date: 10-May-91 Required Date: 07-Jun-91 Shipped Date: 15-May-91

Prod ID:	Product:	Unit Price:	Quantity:	Discount:	Extended Price:
17	Alice Mutton	$27.00	4	0%	$108.00
10	Ikura	$31.00	1	0%	$31.00
*		$0.00	1	0%	

Record: 1 of 2

NORTHWIND

Subtotal:	$139.00
Freight:	$4.45
Total:	$143.45

Record: 1 of 1078

...to create an invoice.

TABLE

A table stores the data in the Access program. Each table holds information about a different subject (for example, an inventory table, an address table, or a client table).

Ami Pro

Ami Pro is one of the most popular word processing programs for Windows. It can be used to create letters, memos, newsletters, résumés, and all other types of written materials. Word processing software does just what its name implies, it allows the user to work with words and the composition of written documents. Of all the software purchased for computers today, word processing applications are the most popular. What distinguishes Ami Pro from other word processors is its ability to handle both text and graphics (pictures) in the creation of newsletters, brochures, sales pamphlets, illustrated reports, and so on. Of all the Windows word processors, Ami Pro is the best at desktop publishing (and the easiest to use). Originally developed by Samna Corporation, a small firm that placed its hopes on the development of the first high-powered Windows word processor, Ami Pro was soon purchased by Lotus and developed into one of the top three Windows word processing programs. Ami Pro is a powerful, high-end product that features all the tools necessary for both word processing and desktop publishing chores. Ami Pro comes with a grammar and spell checker, index and table of contents creators, charting and drawing tools, Fast Format (which allows the user to copy text formatting quickly), and customizable SmartIcons sets, which provide quick access to commonly used commands. Also see Word for Windows, WordPerfect, and Word Processing.

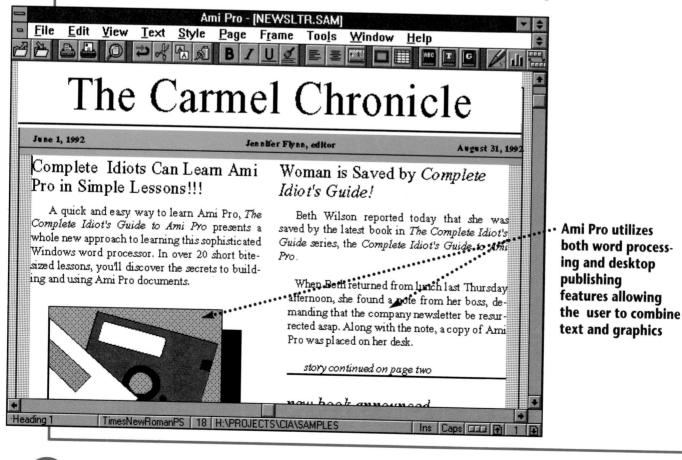

Ami Pro utilizes both word processing and desktop publishing features allowing the user to combine text and graphics

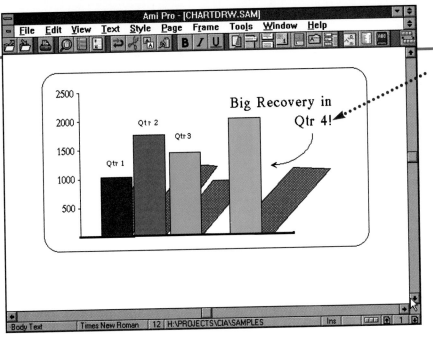

Chart

DESKTOP PUBLISHING

A special type of software program that allows the user to manipulate text and graphics on a single page to create brochures, newsletters, and other illustrated documents. Although most desktop publishing programs don't allow the user to do much with text (such as spell checking), Ami Pro combines the best qualities of a word processor with those of a desktop publishing program.

CHART

Sometimes known as a graph. Graphical representation of columns of related numbers. For example, if the sales figure for March was larger than that for April, the column (or bar) representing March on a chart would also be larger. The larger sales figure for March could also be represented by a larger portion of a pie, or a higher line.

DRAWING

A picture consisting of separate objects, such as rectangles, circles, lines, and squares. For example, a drawing of a PC might consist of two squares (one inside the other), placed on top of a large rectangle with several lines and circles representing buttons and disk drives.

SMARTICONS

Graphical buttons that carry out a task or command. SmartIcons are organized into logical sets that provide quick access to frequently used commands. For example, the Long Documents SmartIcon set contains buttons for commands used to create and modify long, complex documents (as opposed to simple two-page letters). A SmartIcon set is similar to a toolbar or button bar found in other programs. SmartIcons are found in all Lotus programs.

GRAMMAR CHECKER

A program that checks for grammatical errors in documents, and which is usually included as a mini-program within word processors, such as Ami Pro. Grammar checkers check for incomplete sentences, passive voice, awkward phrases, and other grammar problems, and also determines the difficulty of the written material.

SPELL CHECKER

A program that checks the spelling of words in a document. Like grammar checkers, a spell checker is usually included as a mini-program within word processors. Comparing words in the document to words contained in the spell checker's dictionary, the spell checker can help proofread a document. Spell checkers also find duplicate words (such as "the the") that were repeated by mistake, as well as mistakes in capitalization (such as beginning a sentence with a lowercase letter).

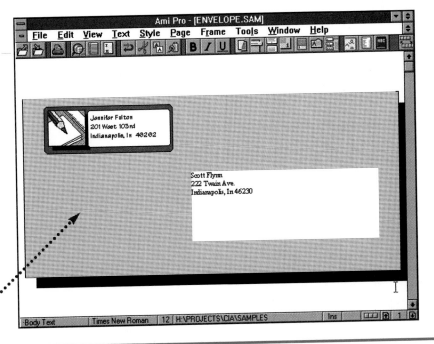

Creating envelopes is easy with AmiPro

ANSI

ANSI stands for the American National Standards Institute, a government agency that was founded to develop standards of function, appearance, and applicability for any item the U.S. Government might buy or sell. ANSI standards currently exist for vast numbers of such seemingly unrelated items as refrigerators, industrial carpet, mayonnaise, and computer parts, among others.

Formed in 1918, this agency is perhaps best known for its efforts in coordinating voluntary standards among public and private industries for computers (floppy disks, magnetic tapes, and other computer parts), video, and programming languages. In particular, the standardization of computer languages, such as COBOL, FORTRAN, and C, has helped to enhance productivity in American industries and increase American competitiveness in the global market.

ANSI released a standard set of computer codes in the late 1950's, known as the "ANSI code." The ANSI code is a listing of computer characters (such as the letter A, the question mark, and the comma) with a number code assigned to each one. The ANSI code also includes characters that control the cursor. These control characters include such things as end-of-line (a character that moves the cursor to the next line), Backspace, Delete, Home (which moves the cursor to the left side of the screen), End (which moves the cursor to the right side of the screen), and Insert. The ANSI code lists only 128 total characters. The original purpose of the ANSI code was to prevent U.S. manufacturers from creating new codes for every little thing. The Pentagon wanted to purchase computer equipment from multiple suppliers, and in order to ensure that the characters generated by one supplier's equipment would be correctly received and translated by another supplier's equipment, the ANSI agency asked manufacturers to submit a standard listing of characters they could all agree upon. They submitted ASCII (or American Standard Code for Information Interchange), the standard list that IBM had developed, which was then adopted by ANSI with a few modifications. Also see ANSI.SYS, ASCII, and Programming.

An example of ANSI code

ANSI.SYS

A driver file used by MS-DOS and OS/2, ANSI.SYS tells the computer how to display information based on the standard codes adopted by the American National Standards Institute (ANSI). Each code in the ANSI table represents either a character (like the letter S) or a number (such as the number 5), and other keys found on the keyboard (such as the Enter key).

Some codes in the table are not found on the keyboard, but programs use them for specific purposes (such as making the PC beep, or moving the cursor to the next line on-screen).

The ANSI.SYS file contains the instructions for displaying each of the characters found on the keyboard (such as the S or the 5). In addition, it contains instructions for moving the cursor when appropriate (when the Backspace key is pressed, for example), and for sending signals to other devices (like the signal indicating when to sound the beep, or when to move the paper in the printer). Most of the control codes in the ANSI table were designed for old style terminals, so a small section of the ANSI table is no longer used. However, some programs adhere to the ANSI standard and require the ANSI.SYS file. Therefore, some computer programs require that the statement, DEVICE=C:\DOS\ANSI.SYS be included within a system configuration file called CONFIG.SYS. When the computer is booted, this statement loads the driver file ANSI.SYS into memory, where its instructions can be accessed by any program.Also see ANSI, CONFIG.SYS, DOS, and OS/2.

4 The code's instructions are executed (in this case, the cursor is moved down one line on-screen).

2 A program issues a command, which references an ANSI code.

3 That code is found in memory.

DRIVER FILE

A special program that helps the computer send or receive data to and from an optional PC device, such as a mouse, a printer, or a joystick. A driver file is also used by the PC to access unused areas of memory or to perform other functions for which the PC was not originally built. Driver files provide additional instructions that enhance the computer's abilities. At startup, a driver file is loaded into memory (RAM), where its instructions can be used by any program that needs them.

1 The user presses the Enter key.

Apple Computers

pple Computer, Inc., is a manufacturing company responsible for creating the widely successful line of Apple and Macintosh computers. Founded in 1976 by Steve Jobs, an ex-Hewlett Packard employee, and Steve Wozniak, a computer hobbyist and concert promoter who co-founded Woodstock (shown below), Apple has grown from a personal computer pioneer to the largest independent manufacturer of non-IBM compatible computers. Apple is a recognized leader in the development of graphical user interfaces (GUIs).

Apple began its rise in 1977 with the Apple II personal computer. This innovative computer, equipped with sound and color graphics, quickly became popular with schools, businesses, and homes. The Apple II was the first computer to include an expansion bus as standard equipment. An expansion bus is a standard connector through which peripherals (optional devices such as a mouse, sound card, printer, etc.) can be attached to a computer. In response, third-party vendors developed a vast assortment of adapters and add-on peripherals

that users could attach to the Apple II through an expansion bus. This expanded the capabilities of the Apple II, and further increased its success. Programmers were encouraged by the success of the Apple II, and started writing programs just for it. VisiCalc, the first electronic spreadsheet program, was developed for the Apple II.

In 1980, the Apple III was released. Unfortunately, this new version had lots of problems, especially with incompatibility (it couldn't run most of the software that was designed for the Apple II), which damaged the company's reputation. It was during this lull in Apple's history that IBM stepped into the marketplace with the IBM PC.

Courtesy of Apple Computer, Inc.

Founders Steve Jobs and Steve Wozniak holding Apple 1 Board.

Courtesy of Apple Computer, Inc.

The Apple IIE

selling brand of computers in the world, and is widely used by people in the fields of advertising, design, publishing, and communications. Also see GUI, IBM, IBM PC, Macintosh, and Spreadsheet.

GUI

Graphical User Interface. A graphically based screen design that allows the user to select commands and manage programs and files by manipulating small pictures called icons (a graphical representation of the command, program, or file).

EXPANSION BUS

A special connector within a computer through which peripherals (such as graphics accelerators, modems, network adapters, memory expansion boards, and printers) can be connected.

PERIPHERALS

Additional hardware connected to the computer. Typical peripherals include the printer, mouse, keyboard, monitor, and modem.

In 1983, Steve Jobs' development team released an innovative (but expensive) new computer, called the Lisa. However, the IBM PC by that time was pretty widely accepted (especially for business use). The Lisa could not compete against IBM's lower price, so it was dropped in 1985. Despite its failure, the Lisa pioneered the graphical user interface (GUI) technology originally developed by a team of engineers and computer scientists at Xerox's Palo Alto Research Center (PARC). A GUI allows the user to issue commands by selecting pictures (icons) that represent an action. This idea was way ahead of its time since IBM (and all other PCs) required the user to type actual words to get the computer to do something. With the Lisa, a new device (called a mouse) was used to point to things on-screen and get things done. So although the Lisa didn't sell very well, it was important because it led to the Macintosh (the single best selling computer in the world today) and to Windows (although Microsoft will probably never admit it). So despite the failure of the Lisa, Apple kept trying, and in 1984, released the Macintosh.

Because it is graphical (picture oriented) in nature, the Macintosh has achieved great success in the areas of desktop publishing and graphic design. Subsequent releases of improved Macintosh products have continued to make Apple a recognized player in the personal computer marketplace, yet they have not been able to overcome the dominance of the IBM PC and its clones. However, the Macintosh remains the single best-

Courtesy of Apple Computer, Inc.

The Macintosh computer by Apple

Application

An application is software with a specific use, such as writing, dealing with numbers, organizing large amounts of data, etc. Popular types of applications include word processors, database managers, spreadsheets, graphics applications, money managers, and games. Other types of computer software include utilities (programs designed to tune the performance of the computer), and system software (basic programs, such as DOS, which are required to operate the PC).

Applications are created with the help of a programming language (such as BASIC or C). A program is a set of instructions that tells the computer how to perform a task. Most programs look somewhat like broken English; the actual words and the structure of each instruction depends on which programming language is being used. Following the rules of a particular programming language, a programmer writes the step-by-step instructions that tell the computer exactly what to do. Anyone can write a program, but he must learn the rules of a particular programming language first. Although most applications are written by teams of people working for

Example Applications

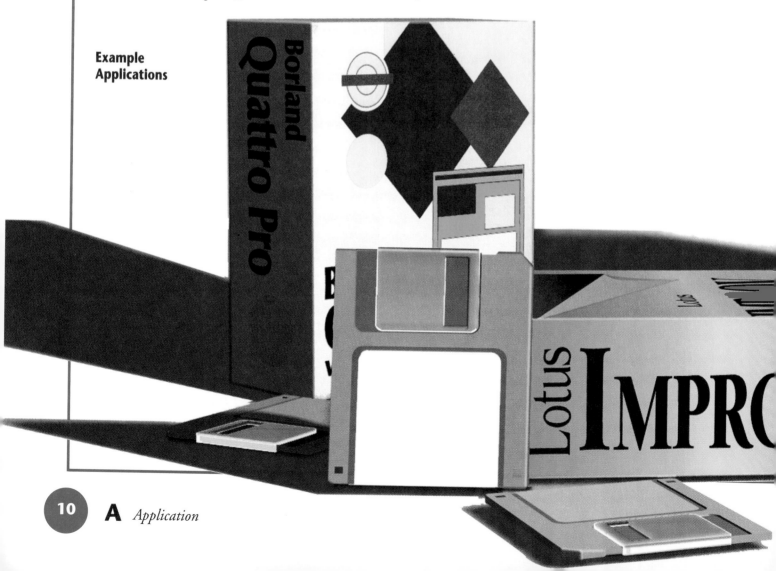

big companies like Microsoft, there is still room for the tinkerer who writes programs at home in his or her spare time. For example, in 1978, Dan Bricklin, a Harvard Business School student, developed an idea for a type of program that could easily be used to perform complex business analyses. With his partner, Bob Frankston, he created the first "spreadsheet" program called VisiCalc. Actually, by most accounts, VisiCalc was the first modern computer application *ever*. Early applications were very complicated to use and required a thorough knowledge of their comands to perform even simple tasks. Today's applications are much easier to use, very intuitive in operation, and friendly to the eye. The total number of commercial applications now available is well into the thousands. However, some large and small companies still write their own private applications to handle all types of jobs, including payroll, personnel, security, facilities management, and accounting. Also see Database, Games, Graphics, Programming, Spreadsheets, and Word Processing.

GAMES PROGRAMS

A program designed purely for fun. A variety of games exist, including action/adventure, flight simulation, role-playing, and computerized versions of real games such as chess, backgammon, and solitaire.

WORD PROCESSING PROGRAM

An application that allows the user to manipulate text to create letters, memos, re[ac]sume[ac]s, manuscripts, and other written documents.

SPREADSHEET PROGRAM

A special application designed for accounting purposes. Spreadsheet programs can manipulate numbers, perform calculations, handle mathematical formulas, and organize data. Spreadsheets enable the user to perform various business analyses and forecasts on complex data.

DATABASE PROGRAM

An application written to organize large quantities of data. Database programs are commonly used to compile address lists, inventory and pricing lists, and patient records.

GRAPHICS PROGRAM

A program created for designing and drawing on the computer. Graphics programs can create art for a myriad of uses, including brochures, letterheads, and other promotional materials.

Approach

Approach is a relational database program from Lotus Development Corporation designed for the Windows platform. Originally developed by Approach Software Corporation, Approach was purchased by Lotus in 1992.

Database programs are designed to organize large quantities of data, such as address lists, merchandise records, and payroll information. In a database, data can quickly be sorted and retrieved, as well as presented in reports.

One key feature that makes Approach stand out is its use of View files. View files are constructed from data files, and they control how data is viewed and manipulated within the Approach program. By separating data from the program itself, Approach can easily use existing databases created with other database programs (such as dBASE, FoxPro, or Paradox), without converting that data into some "Approach-type" format. (Most programs have unique methods of storing data, and when the user tries to use that data in another program, the conversion process results in a loss of information; but this is not so with Approach.) In addition, Approach is so easy to use and understand that it's ideally suited as a "front-end" or "go-between" for more complex database programs: the user can create new databases with Approach and save them in any popular format (dBASE, FoxPro, etc.).

Approach can perform calculations, structure data into an unlimited number of categories, and easily pinpoint important data with query commands. The program also features a built-in forms designer, a report writer, and SmartIcon buttons that provide quick access to the most commonly used database commands. Also see Access, Database, dBASE, and Paradox.

Data can quickly be organized and sorted based on categories called fields.

How Does It Work?

Approach is a relational database management system, which means that information is stored in logical units and then "related" to other units through key fields. Relational databases allow separate database files to exchange data and create new files. For example, one file may contain a list of client names, and another file may have inventory prices. A key field, such as the item number, can be used to relate a particular customer's name from the first file to a particular item and its price from the second file to create an invoice.

FIELD

In Approach, a field is stored in a column. Each field makes up a part of a larger record. For example, an item's name, stock number, and price are all fields stored in that item's record.

By relating this item number to a customer, an invoice is created.

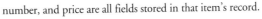

```
Lotus Approach - [C:\APPROACH\EXAMPLES\PRODUCTS.VEW:Data Entry]
File  Edit  View  Records  Design  Objects  Style  Window  Help

                                            Products
DATE
10/5/91
ITEM              PART_NO
IB1001            1234
DESCRIP
Cola, 12 oz/6
CATEGORY
Cola
COST      QTY
$1.45     24000
RESTOCK
Yes

Data Entry    Browse        Record 1      Found 20 of 20
```

SMARTICONS

Graphical buttons that carry out a task or command. SmartIcons are organized into logical sets, which provide quick access to frequently used commands. They are found within the Lotus suite of products, and are similar to toolbars or button bars found in other programs.

RECORD

In Approach, a record is stored in a row. Each record contains pieces of information about a person, a thing, or an event. For example, all of the information about one person (such as his name, title, address, and phone number) would be contained in a single record.

FULTON
7362 EAST 121ST
INDIANAPOLIS IN
BATES AGNEY ADAMS

CUSTOMERS

Artificial Intelligence

Artificial intelligence programs, called AI for short, analyze data and draw conclusions in a way that makes them appear to be "intelligent." Now of course, computers can't think or do anything without being told what to do. So AI programs use complex formulas which attempt to arrive at an answer in a method similar to how a human might do it.

Some AI programs attempt to simulate the way humans think, while others try to mimic an expert with years of experience. Two AI categories that deal with the way humans think are *fuzzy logic* and *neural networks*. Fuzzy logic programs take into account the fact that input is not always precise—sometimes input requires a judgment. For example, an average traffic light turns red or green for a given period of time, regardless of the traffic flow. However, if the traffic light contained an AI computer using fuzzy logic, it could judge when to change the light based on the flow of traffic. The AI computer would not make a decision based on *exactly* how many cars were passing through the intersection, but rather, on whether that traffic was considered "heavy" or "light." Because traffic flow varies, the AI computer would examine the changing number of cars and make a judgment on when to change the light.

Neural networks are almost the complete opposite of fuzzy logic systems. Neural networks, modeled after the neurons and synapses of the human brain, are programmed to reach a "best guess" conclusion based on concrete data (data that doesn't change). By comparing all the data it has, a neural network can draw a fairly accurate prediction of the future. Neural networks have been used in studying economic and financial trends, as well as the stock market.

An example of Artificial Intelligence used in traffic lights

But the most popular AI programs today are not those that simulate human thought patterns, but those that mimic "experts." An expert system contains all the "rules of thumb" normally acquired through years of experience. With its vast database of knowledge, an expert system can analyze a present situation and offer a possible solution based on all the "rules" that it has learned. AI is still in its infancy, as scientists learn more and more about the way humans think. AI programs are useful in many ways, from controlling the temperature in a building (making a judgment as to what's comfortable) to predicting the stock market. In the future, AI programs could be used to pilot a plane, control a car, or design the perfect city. Robots with complex AI programs could perform specific tasks, such as housekeeping, farming, or policing a city—but they will never be like humans.

Computers are great at analyzing data at incredible speeds, but even with advances in AI technology, computers will never be terrifically good at independent judgment or handling unexpected or new situations. Also see Programming.

NEURAL NETWORKS

A system which reaches a "best guess" conclusion by adjusting its analyses until it reaches the most probable answer.

FUZZY LOGIC

A system which reaches a result by assigning half values to impecise input and "weighing them".

EXPERT SYSTEMS

Also called inference engines, expert systems contain a large knowledge base of acquired "rules," based on the experience of experts in a given field. Expert systems can make suggestions based on a given set of circumstances and this pool of collected "rules".

ASCII

Pronounced "ask-kee," this stands for American Standard Code for Information Interchange. The ASCII standard of representing computer characters was established to ensure the accurate transfer of data between different computing devices.

The ASCII code table consists of 128 characters, which are basically the same 128 characters found in the ANSI code table. The first 32 characters of the ASCII table are control codes (such as delete, escape, and carriage return), and the last 96 characters are upper- and lowercase letters, numbers, and special symbols (such as the dollar sign, the percent sign, and the asterisk). On top of that, IBM PC-compatible computers have an extended set of an additional 128 characters, which includes foreign language accent marks and other characters (such as the degree symbol). This extra set of ASCII characters is called the Extended ASCII Set. Part of the ASCII table was adopted as part of the ANSI (American National Standards Institute) Standard PC table in the late '50s. The ANSI standard table of code for use with PCs. Also see ANSI, Binary, and Memory.

BINARY

The simple 1 or 0 upon which all digital computers are based. Input is converted into binary numbers made up of 1's and 0's. The computer stores these binary numbers through the presence or absence of an electrical charge (think of a 1 as being "on," and a 0 as being "off"). Groups of these binary numbers are then translated into character form, based on the ASCII table.

An example of ASCII code

BIT

Stands for **b**inary dig**it**. A single digit in a binary number. Binary numbers are either 1's or 0's. A bit is equivalent to one binary digit.

BYTE

A byte is composed of eight separate binary digits (bits). A byte is used by a computer to store a single character. For example, the binary code 01100100 is the letter d, based on the ASCII table.

Standard ASCII Codes

Decimal	Binary	Character	Description
0	00000000	NUL	Null
1	00000001	SOH	Start of heading
2	00000010	STX	Start of text
3	00000011	ETX	End of text
4	00000100	EOT	End of transmit
5	00000101	ENQ	Enquiry
6	00000110	ACK	Acknowledgment
7	00000111	BEL	Audible bell
8	00001000	BS	Backspace
9	00001001	HT	Horizontal tab
10	00001010	LF	Line feed
11	00001011	VT	Vertical tab
12	00001100	FF	Form feed
13	00001101	CR	Carriage return
14	00001110	SO	Shift out
15	00001111	SI	Shift in
16	00010000	DLE	Data link escape
17	00010001	DC1	Device control 1
18	00010010	DC2	Device control 2
19	00010011	DC3	Device control 3
20	00010100	DC4	Device control 4
21	00010101	NAK	Neg. acknowledge
22	00010110	SYN	Synchronous idle
23	00010111	ETB	End trans. block
24	00011000	CAN	Cancel
25	00011001	EM	End of medium
26	00011010	SUB	Substitution
27	00011011	ESC	Escape
28	00011100	FS	Figures shift
29	00011101	GS	Group separator
30	00011110	RS	Record separator
31	00011111	US	Unit separator
32	00100000	SP	Spacebar/blank space

AUTOEXEC.BAT

DOS PROMPT

A symbol that indicates DOS is ready for the next command. The DOS prompt generally looks like C:\>, but it can be changed by commands in AUTO.EXEC.BAT.

T he AUTOEXEC.BAT is a configuration file containing DOS commands. The AUTOEXEC.BAT is so called because it is automatically executed (run) when the computer is turned on or restarted. An AUTOEXEC.BAT file might contain commands to change the default DOS prompt, or to tell the computer what directories to search when looking for executable files. The user places these commands in the AUTOEXEC.BAT file so that DOS will carry them out each time the computer is turned on or restarted. Without the AUTOEXEC.BAT file, these commands would have to be entered manually every time the computer was booted. Also see Boot, CONFIG.SYS, and DOS.

BATCH FILE

A type of executable file that contains a "batch" or listing of DOS commands to be executed in order, as if the user had typed each one in separately. One example of a batch file is the AUTOEXEC.BAT, whose instructions are executed whenever the system is booted.

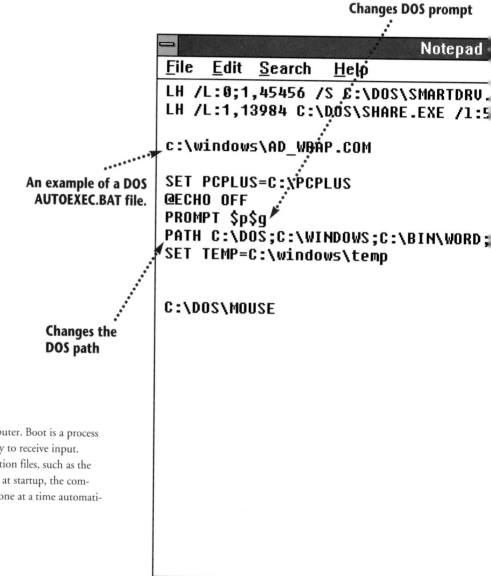

Changes DOS prompt

An example of a DOS AUTOEXEC.BAT file.

Changes the DOS path

BOOT

The process of starting or restarting a computer. Boot is a process that the computer goes through to get ready to receive input. During this boot process, certain configuration files, such as the AUTOEXEC.BAT, are used. For example, at startup, the commands in AUTOEXEC.BAT are executed one at a time automatically, without the user typing them in.

EXECUTABLE FILES

Files that contain computer instructions, as opposed to data files, which contain information (data) to act upon. Executable files end with the extension .EXE, .COM, or .BAT. Examples include files that start programs (such as WINWORD.EXE, which starts the Microsoft Word for Windows program, and AUTOEXEC.BAT, which is a batch file).

Loads two programs into memory

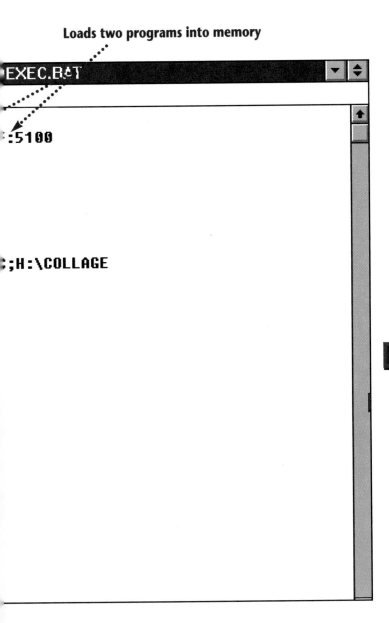

CONFIGURATION FILE

Special files that help to define the current operating environment of the computer. For example, configuration files tell the PC what the DOS prompt should look like, what peripheral devices are currently attached, and what parts of memory (RAM) are available.

CONFIG.SYS

Special configuration file which changes the system defaults to other values.

DOS

Disk Operating System. A software program that tells the computer how to execute its basic tasks (such as displaying a prompt, keeping track of files, and performing commands). DOS acts as the computer's manager, directing tasks and overseeing the different activities requested of the computer.

PATH

The route that DOS travels to locate a file. It's kind of like telling a friend how to find a local shopping center. First he has to start from a known point (DOS calls this the root directory), and then he needs to know the twists and turns to get to the correct street. These "twists and turns" make up the path to a particular file.

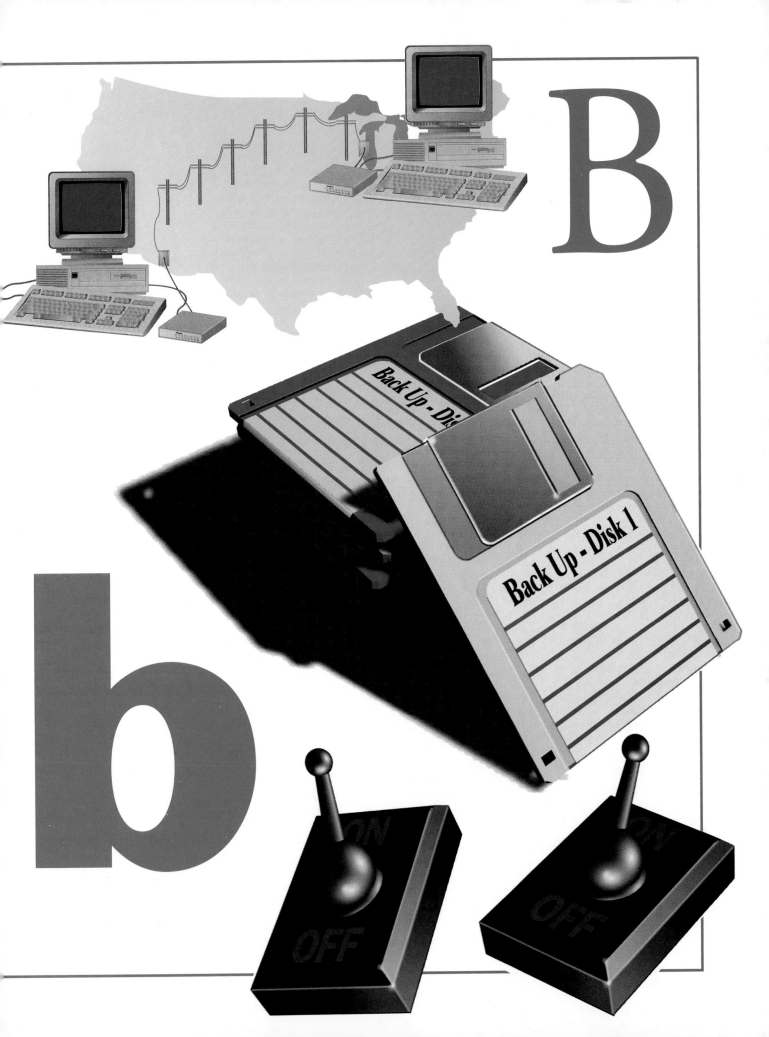

Backup

Backing up a hard disk involves copying its files to a floppy disk or backup tape. Because hard disks inevitably fail, taking some or all of the saved data with them, backups are necessary in case the original files become damaged. Lost data can be restored from the duplicates that were placed on backup disks or tapes. It's also a good practice to make backup copies of program disks and use the copies instead of the originals. This way the original disks can be stored in a safe place and easily retrieved in case something goes wrong with the copies.

Operating systems, such as DOS, OS/2, and Macintosh System, have specific commands for backing up files. For example, in DOS, users can type in the command BACKUP to back up a hard disk. The backup programs provided by the operating system can be used to perform regular backups, or a separate backup utility (which is often faster and easier to use) can be purchased and used instead. For example, with DOS versions prior to version 6.0, backing up files with DOS was very difficult and clumsy. Beginning with DOS 6.0, an easier-to-use backup utility was introduced; but it is not capable of performing timed backups or backups to tape. Whether the user uses the backup command that comes with the operating system, or a separate backup utility, he should keep this in mind: each backup utility program uses its own compression and sequencing routine. Therefore, in order to restore the backed up files, the restore routine associated with the original backup program must be used.

Important files to backup include configuration files (such as AUTOEXEC.BAT and CONFIG.SYS) and data files (such as an important spreadsheet file or word processing document).

How Does It Work?

The process of backing up files is more complex than simply copying those files onto a disk. If files are simply copied to a disk, they may fill the disk until there is no more room for the next file (however, a small amount of unused space may exist). However, if files are backed up onto disks (using a backup program), one part of a file may be copied to a disk (in order to fill the disk entirely), while the rest of the file is copied onto the next disk in the backup set. If these backup files are restored to the hard disk at a later time (because the originals become damaged somehow), they are restored in their original sequence so that the "pieces" of a split file are put back together.

In addition, the backup process typically compresses the files so that the data they contain requires less room to store. That way, more files are placed on a disk than is possible in the normal copying process.

Write-protect tab

Write-protect notch

It is not necessary to backup the program files themselves, unless the original disks have been lost. For example, if a hard disk drive contains WordPerfect (a popular word processing program), it is only necessary to keep backup files of the documents that have been created while using WordPerfect, and not the entire WordPerfect application. If the program files become damaged, simply reinstall WordPerfect from its original disks.

DOS, along with many backup utilities, offers a choice in the type of backup the user performs. For example, with DOS 6.X, he can perform a Full backup (backing up all selected files), a Differential backup (backing up new files or files that have changed since the last Full backup), or an Incremental backup (backing up new files or files that have changed since the last time the user did any kind of backup). These options allow the user to back up only what he feels is necessary, and save time. Also see AUTOEXEC.BAT, CONFIG.SYS, Data Storage, File, Floppy Disk, Hard Disk Drive, and WordPerfect.

WRITE-PROTECT

Another way to prevent data from being lost on a floppy disk is to write-protect the disk. A 5 1/4-inch disk has a write-protect notch that can be covered with a small piece of tape to prevent any files from being changed or written over. A 3 1/2-inch disk has a write-protect tab that can be slid open to protect the disk.

COMPRESSION

A process by which a file is stored in a smaller amount of space than normal.

BASIC

BASIC, a programming language, stands for Beginner's All-Purpose Symbolic Instruction Code. BASIC was created in 1964 by two professors at Dartmouth College: John G. Kemeny and Thomas E. Kurtz. Their idea was to create a simple programming language for beginners. Because it is so simple, BASIC is almost always the first programming language a programmer learns. BASIC is even taught at the grade school and high school levels.

A program is a set of instructions that tells the computer how to perform a task. Most programs look some-what like broken English; the actual words and the structure of each instruction depends on which programming language is being used. Following the rules of a particular programming language, a programmer writes the step-by-step instructions that tell the computer exactly what to do.

After these instructions are written, they are converted into a language the computer can understand, called machine language. Machine language is a series of 1's and 0's based on a binary numbering system, which all computers use. With most versions of BASIC, the programming instructions are converted into machine language using a special program called an interpreter.

Every time an interpreted program is run, it is converted into machine language. An alternative is to compile the program, which permanently converts it into machine language. This eliminates the need for the interpreter and allows the program to run faster. (A compiled program is converted into machine language and stored permanently in a file, which is then reused anytime the program is run.)

A BASIC program looks almost like English.

```
GW-BASIC 3.23
(C) Copyright Microsoft 1983,1984,1985,1986,1987,1988
(C) Copyright American Research Corporation. 1988,1989
60300 Bytes free
Ok
2 PRINT TAB(34);"LIFE"
4 PRINT TAB(15);"CREATIVE COMPUTING   MORRISTOWN, NEW JERSEY"
6 PRINT: PRINT: PRINT
8 PRINT "ENTER YOUR PATTERN:"
9 X1=1: Y1=1: X2=24: Y2=70
10 DIM A(24,70),B$(24)
20 C=1
30 INPUT B$(C)
40 IF B$(C)="DONE" THEN B$(C)="": GOTO 80
50 IF LEFT$(B$(C),1)="." THEN B$(C)=" "+RIGHT$(B$(C),LEN(B$(C))-1)
60 C=C+1
70 GOTO 30
80 C=C-1: L=0
90 FOR X=1 TO C-1
100 IF LEN(B$(X))>L THEN L=LEN(B$(X))
110 NEXT X
120 X1=11-C/2
130 Y1=33-L/2
140 FOR X=1 TO C
1LIST  2RUN←  3LOAD"  4SAVE"  5CONT←  6,"LPT1 7TRON← 8TROFF← 9KEY   0SCREEN
```

Example of GWBASIC

Example of QBasic.

A program can be stopped while it's being interpreted and then certain values can be tested to make sure they are still correct.

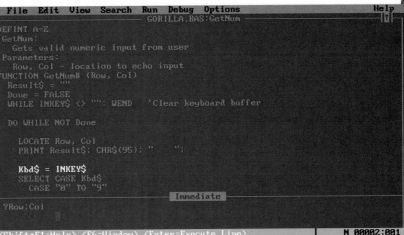

```
     File   Edit   View   Search   Run   Debug   Options                    Help
                        GORILLA.BAS:GetNum
 DEFINT A-Z
 'GetNum:
 '   Gets valid numeric input from user
 'Parameters:
 '   Row, Col - location to echo input
 FUNCTION GetNum% (Row, Col)
   Result$ = ""
   Done = FALSE
   WHILE INKEY$ <> "": WEND      'Clear keyboard buffer

   DO WHILE NOT Done

     LOCATE Row, Col
     PRINT Result$; CHR$(95); "  ";

     Kbd$ = INKEY$
     SELECT CASE Kbd$
       CASE "0" TO "9"
                                        ┌─── Immediate ───┐
 ?Row;Col

 <Shift+F1=Help>  <F6=Window>  <Enter=Execute Line>          N 00002:001
```

Because most BASIC programs are interpreted and not compiled, BASIC is a good language for a programmer who wants to test his program quickly. After writing sections of the program, those sections can be tested right away, without going through the lengthy process of recompiling them. If an error is found, the program instruction can be changed and immediately retested. On the downside, a program written with BASIC wastes computer time because the program's instructions must be interpreted (converted into machine language) each time someone runs the program. In addition, the program is slower because the computer has to do two things at once: interpret each instruction, and then carry it out. Also see Binary, C, Pascal and Programming.

VISUAL BASIC

A version of BASIC created by Microsoft. Visual Basic comes in two versions, one designed for writing DOS applications, and the other designed for Windows applications. Visual Basic makes it easier for the programmer to create things that the user sees, such as dialog boxes, menus, and messages.

QBASIC

A version of BASIC that includes a programming interface with menus and a help system. The interface makes it easier to write and correct a BASIC program. QBasic replaced an earlier version of BASIC called GWBASIC.

COMPILER

Converts a program's instructions into machine language and stores the result in a file. That file can then be used over and over, each time the program is run.

READY-TO-USE PROGRAM FILE

INTERPRETER

Each time an program (like BASIC) is run, it is converted into machine language by an interpreter. This is unlike a compiled program, which is converted into machine language only once.

LOW-LEVEL PROGRAMMING LANGUAGE

A programming language that is similar to machine language—just one level removed from the binary language of 1's and 0's—and is, therefore, difficult for the programmer to understand and work with.

Batch Files

A batch file is a collection of DOS commands. A batch file, such as WP.BAT, ends with the letters .BAT. When the user types in the name of a batch file and presses Enter at the DOS prompt, the commands in that batch file are performed one at a time—with no additional instructions from the user. For example, if the user typed WP and pressed Enter, WordPerfect (a popular word processing program) would start.

A user can create a batch file to perform any routine task. For example, a batch file could be created to prepare a disk for use (a process called formatting). Because the commands are in a batch file, the user doesn't have to type them herself, or even remember what they are—all the user would have to do is type the name of this batch file to format a disk.

The most important batch file is the AUTOEXEC.BAT. This file contains commands that are performed automatically each time the PC is turned on or restarted. Typical AUTOEXEC.BAT commands include those which change the system prompt, display the current date and time, and set the directories in which DOS looks for files.

Batch files were very important before Windows came along, when everyone had to deal with DOS (the PC's operating system). DOS required the user to type everything in—which made each task tedious and easy to make mistakes. Batch files eliminated mistakes because the user no longer typed in the command, just the name of the batch file. With Windows, there is little typing involved in issuing commands. Instead, the user selects commands from a list called a menu, or he selects an icon that represents the command he wants performed. Automation is still desirable in Windows, but instead of saving a list of typed

commands, the user records his actions and saves them in a macro. A macro is like a batch file; when it's activated, the actions recorded in the macro are carried out. Also see AUTO EXEC. BAT, DOS, and Windows.

Name of batch file.

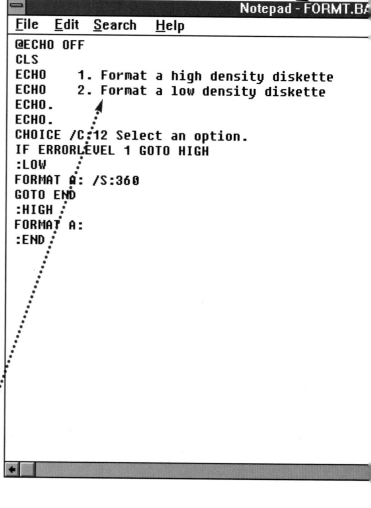

```
Notepad - FORMT.BA
File   Edit   Search   Help
@ECHO OFF
CLS
ECHO      1. Format a high density diskette
ECHO      2. Format a low density diskette
ECHO.
ECHO.
CHOICE /C:12 Select an option.
IF ERRORLEVEL 1 GOTO HIGH
:LOW
FORMAT A: /S:360
GOTO END
:HIGH
FORMAT A:
:END
```

This batch file allows the user to format different types of disks.

PATH

The listing of directories DOS normally searches for files. The default path can be changed by commands in the AUTOEXEC. BAT

DOS
\WORD
\WORD\DOCS
\MEMO.DOC

EDIT

A utility that comes with DOS, which can be used to create text files such as batch files. EDIT replaced an older editor called EDLIN.

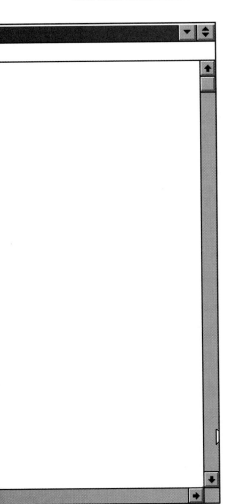

DOS

Short for Disk Operating System, the most popular operating system in use today. The operating system manages the processes of the PC.

HIGH-LEVEL PROGRAMMING LANGUAGE

A programming language that is easy for programmers to understand because it is written more closely to English than to the rudimentary 1's and 0's of machine language.

AUTOEXEC. BAT

A special file containing DOS commands which are automatically performed each time the PC is turned on or restarted. Typical AUTOEXEC. BAT commands change the system prompt, display the current date and time, and set search directories.

SYSTEM PROMPT

The default prompt, which lets the user know that the computer is ready. The DOS prompt typically looks like C>. Commands in the AUTOEXEC. BAT can be used to change the default prompt.

C:\\>

BBS

A BBS (Bulletin Board System) is a special communications program that acts as a kind of electronic bulletin board. A BBS allows multiple people to use it at the same time in order to exchange ideas, offer help with software problems, and converse (through typed conversations) with other users currently connected to the BBS. Users connect their PC to a BBS through a modem, a device that transmits data through ordinary telephone lines. While connected to a BBS, a user can share information with other computer users, leave messages, and upload and download programs. One polpular BBS is the Boston Computer Exchange, a place where members can buy, sell, or trade computers. Pay-for-use information services, such as CompuServe, Prodigy, and Internet are like BBS, but much larger. There are thousands of other BBSs across the globe offering a variety of topics and interests ranging from software support to dating services. To communicate with other computers, a modem is necessary. A modem (MOdulator/DEModulato) changes the computer's digital (binary based) data into an analog (sound based) signal that can be transmitted over a phone line. When a message is received, a modem changes the incoming analog signal (from the phone line) back into a digital signal the computer can understand.

A communications program, such as ProComm Plus, manages the actual transmission process between two computers,

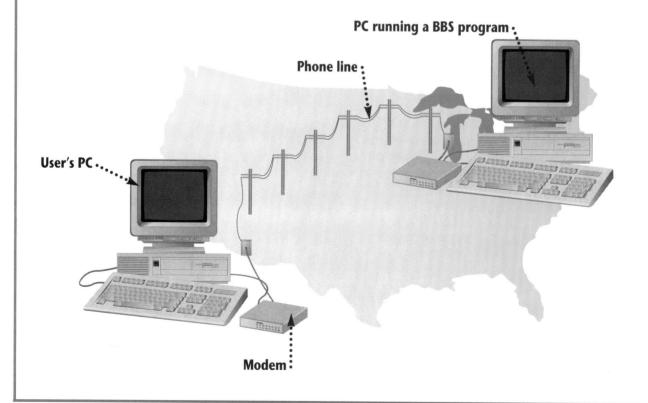

PC running a BBS program

Phone line

User's PC

Modem

determining when to send a character and if a character has been received correctly. The communications program organizes the data to be sent, and then passes that data to the modem, which then converts it to analog signals. In addition, the communications program tells the modem what number to dial, and when to initiate or terminate the call. It's through the communications program that the user can issue commands to the BBS to upload or download a file, or can type the words for a conversation with another user. Also see Communications and Modem.

EXTERNAL MODEM

External modems are self-contained units placed outside of the PC itself. External modems function in the same way as internal modems, but they require their own power source. Since they are separate from the PC, external modems can be easily moved from PC to PC and shared.

UPLOAD

To copy files from your PC to a BBS (or another PC).

DOWNLOAD

To copy files to your PC from a BBS (or another PC).

External modem

SERIAL PORT

A connector on a PC that transfers data one bit at a time (it takes eight bits to represent a single character such as the letter "A" or the number "5"). Serial devices such as a modem, a mouse, or a serial printer are connected to a PC through a serial port.

INTERNAL MODEM

Modems can be internal or external. Internal modems are circuit boards inserted into the system unit. Internal modems function in the same way as external modems, but they do not need a separate power source since they are part of the computer itself.

DIGITAL

Data stored in a computer is made up of tiny digital bits, equal to a 1 or a 0.

ANALOG

A modem transmits sound waves, which is an analog signal. Analog is the opposite of digital.

Binary

Binary numbers are the basis for computer storage. Input into the computer is changed into binary numbers that the computer can store and manipulate. A binary numbering system uses a series of 1's and 0's to represent any number. Non-numbers (such as the letter D) or characters (such as a question mark) are assigned an eight digit binary number so that they too can be represented within the computer.

Binary numbers can also represent decisions and results. For example, a yes (or true) can be represented by a 1, and a no (or false) can be represented by a 0. Using this method, the computer can compare two numbers and, if they are equal, make the result equal to 1. If they are not equal, the result would be 0. In addition, the computer can take further action based on this comparison. For example, if the result was true (1), a certain series of commands could be performed. If the result were false (0), a different set of commands could be performed.

The 1's and 0's of a computer's binary system are represented by two electronic states: ON (high voltage electrical current) or OFF (low current). Quite simply, the 1's and 0's are like little ON/OFF switches inside the computer. Basing an electronic system on the binary system that uses just two numbers is much easier and less expensive than using the decimal system (which has to differentiate between 10 different states: 0, 1, 2, 3, 4, 5, 6, 7, 8, and 9).

Binary data is stored as bits, each bit equal to a 0 or a 1. Eight bits equal one byte of information (a single character, such as the letter S or the number 4). For example, the binary number for the letter A is 01000001. Also see ASCII, Bit, Byte, Data Storage, and Memory.

BYTE

A group of eight bits, equivalent to a single alphanumeric character.

BIT

A binary digit representing an on or off state. A 1 is on, and a 0 is off.

KILOBYTE

Roughly one thousand bytes; a kilobyte is equal to 1,024 bytes

ASCII TABLE

A built-in table which contains the binary sequence of bits for all upper and lower case letters, single-digit numbers, and special symbols.

BIOS

BIOS stands for Basic Input-Output System. BIOS is a set of instructions that tell the computer how to handle the flow of information between the computer and its peripherals, such as the keyboard (input) or the printer (output). The largest part of BIOS, ROM BIOS, is permanently stored in the computer's read-only memory (ROM) chips, which are located on the computer's motherboard inside the system unit. Since the ROM BIOS instructions are read-only memory, they cannot be changed. In an operating system such as DOS (Disk Operating System), the other part of the Basic Input Output System is provided through a special file called IO.SYS. Together, IO.SYS and ROM BIOS manage all of the computer's input or output requests. Because one part of the Basic Input Output System is software (IO.SYS), it can be updated from time to time, thereby improving the overall computer system.

Read-only memory (ROM) chips

One function that BIOS performs happens only when the computer is turned on or restarted (booted). ROM BIOS checks out the computer by performing the power on self test (POST). The computer reads these instructions each time it is turned on and performs a self check of the computer and its components. Also see Central Processing Unit and ROM.

OPERATING SYSTEM

The program that manages a computer's functions.

ROM

Short for Read Only Memory. ROM chips are special chips which permanently store the basic information a computer needs to operate.

INPUT

Data entered into the computer through such devices as the keyboard, mouse, or scanner.

POST

Power on self test. A test the computer performs each time it is turned on to make sure everything is connected properly.

continues

BIOS continued

IO. SYS

One of the three files which comprise DOS. IO. SYS works with ROM BIOS to manage all input and output functions.

PERIPHERALS

Additional hardware connected to the computer. Typical peripherals include the printer, mouse, keyboard, monitor, and modem.

OUTPUT

Data that comes out of the computer, such as information displayed on the monitor or printed on the printer.

POST

Power on self test. A test the computer performs each time it is turned on to make sure everything is connected properly.

MOTHERBOARD

The main circuit board of a computer. All of the PC's components connect to the motherboard.

BOOTABLE DISK

A disk on which a copy of the operating system has been placed. Such a disk can be used to boot (start) a computer when the hard drive is malfunctioning.

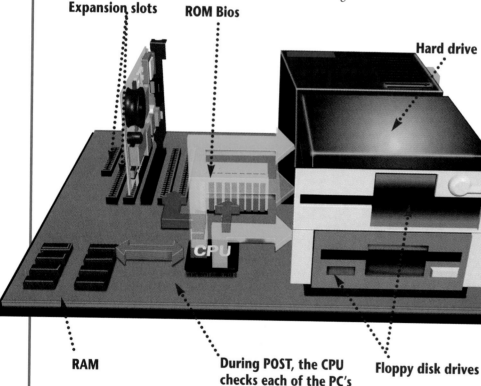

Expansion slots **ROM Bios**

Hard drive

CPU

RAM **During POST, the CPU checks each of the PC's components.** **Floppy disk drives**

How Does It Work?

When the computer is booted, the CPU activates the ROM BIOS chips. ROM BIOS then begins a series of system checks, called the power on self test (POST). The POST tells the CPU to check the bus (a series of connections that link all of the PC's components), the memory (RAM), the peripherals (keyboard, mouse, etc.), and the disk drives. This system check is fast and not very thorough. The POST determines whether everything is connected properly, but it does not check to see if everything is functioning perfectly.

After the POST check is complete, the computer is ready to load the computer's operating system. At this point, a user may notice that the light in drive A comes on again as the CPU checks to see whether a bootable disk has been placed in the drive. If it does not find the operating system software there, the CPU continues to the hard drive, where it copies the operating system into memory so it is ready to go.

Bit

Bit is short for Binary digIT. A bit is a single digit, either a 1 or a 0, and it is the basic unit of information used by computers. Binary numbers (bits) are stored within a computer's microchips by turning an electrical current "on" or "off"; a 1 is represented by an "on" or high voltage current, and a 0 is represented by an "off" or low current.

A group of eight bits is called a byte. It takes a byte to store a single alphanumeric character within a PC. For example, the letter A is stored by saving the eight bits, 01000001.

Because bits are so small, they are rarely referred to as units of storage. However, bytes, kilobytes (roughly a thousand or 1,024 bytes), megabytes (roughly a million or 1,048,576 bytes), and gigabytes (roughly a thousand megabytes or 1,073,741,824 bytes) are more commonly used.

Of course, all of these are based on the humble bit. The size of a file, the storage capacity of a disk, or the amount of computer memory can all be measured in bits. Also see ASCII, Binary, Bitmap, Byte, Communications, Data Storage, and Memory.

BIT MAP

A series of bits stored in memory which form an image when displayed on-screen.

BYTE

A group of eight bits, equal to a single character (a letter of the alphabet, a number, or symbol such as ?).

KILOBYTE

Roughly one thousand bytes, a kilobyte is equal to 1,024 bytes.

MEGABYTE

Roughly one million bytes (1,048,576 bytes). A megabyte is equivalent to 500 double-spaced pages of text.

GIGABYTE

Roughly one thousand megabytes (1,073,741,824 bytes). A gigabyte is equivalent to a half-million double-spaced pages of text.\

BPS

Short for bits per second. BPS is a measurement used to compare the speed of various modems, a device used to transmit data over telephone lines.

Bit Map

A computer screen is made up of thousands of dots of light, called pixels (short for picture elements). A single pixel is composed of up to three rays of light, red, blue, and green, blended into a single dot on-screen. By combining these rays and changing their intensity, virtually any color can be displayed on-screen.

The number of bits required to display a single pixel on-screen varies by the total number of colors a particular monitor can display. The larger the number of possible colors, the larger the number of bits required to describe the exact color needed. Regardless of the actual number of bits

required, a bit map is a series of these bits stored in memory, which form a pattern when read left to right, top to bottom. When decoded by the computer and displayed as pixels on-screen, this pattern forms the image of a picture.

Pixel on   **Pixel off**

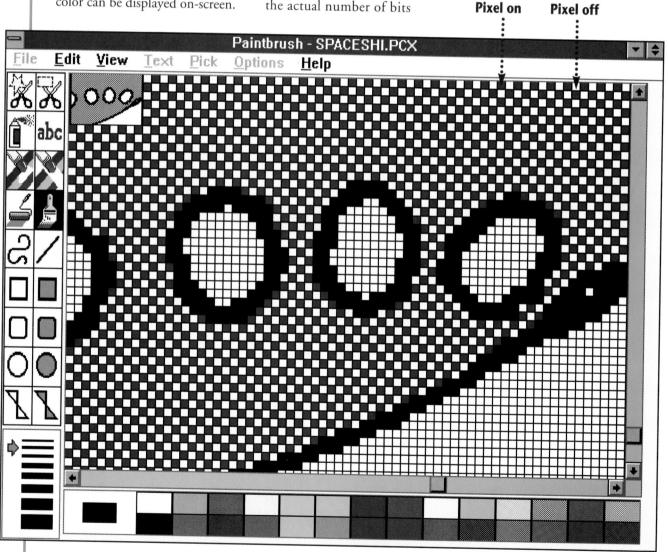

Bit-mapped fonts and bit-mapped graphics use pixels to form pictures or letters. However, because of the number of bits required to encode a single pixel, bit-mapped fonts and graphics consume a great deal of memory. In comparison, trying to create a perfect circle by coloring the squares on a piece of graph paper demonstrates the problems inherent with this method of displaying text and graphics. Because a computer screen is layed out in a grid of dots (pixels) like graph paper, a distortion will show up along the angled and curved lines in an image. This distortion is called "jaggies" or "aliasing." Also see Bit, Font, Graphics, and Monitor.

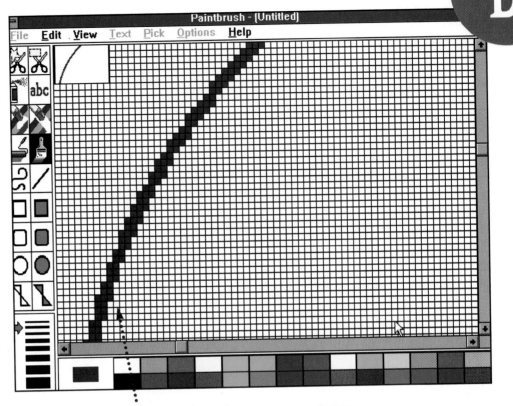

Close up view of the circle reveals jaggies.

BIT

A binary digit representing an on or off state. A 1 is on, and an 0 is off.

PAINT PROGRAM

A program for creating graphics on the computer. A paint program stores the graphic as a bit map, allowing the user to change individual pixels in an image.

PIXEL

Short for picture element. A computer screen is made up of thousands of dots of light called pixels.

JAGGIES AND ALIASING

The jagged edges that appear around angled and curved lines on a computer (also called aliasing). This results from the fact that the computer display is made up of tiny squares of light called pixels. The higher the number of pixels per inch on the screen, the smoother the curve or angle of a drawn line.

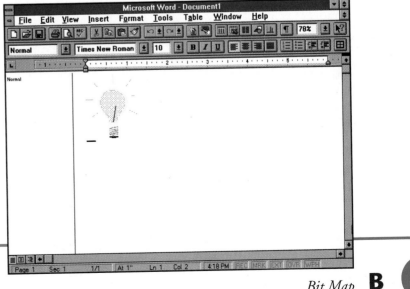

Boot

From the saying "pull your self up by your bootstraps," the term boot refers to a computer's startup procedure. When the computer is first turned on or restarted, it reads the startup instructions found in the ROM BIOS chips. These instructions tell the computer to check the system over (a series of tests called the POST). Certain information (such as the amount of memory and the number and type of disk drives) about the PC is stored in a special chip called CMOS, and that information is also verified during boot. The last thing that happens during boot is the loading of the operating system, which is found on the hard disk drive or on a floppy disk in drive A. The computer cannot do anything without first loading an operating system into memory, because it's the operating system that manages all of the computer's basic functions.

Information in the operating system files continues the booting process. During a PC boot, the CONFIG.SYS file is located, and its instructions are executed. The CONFIG.SYS is a special file that fine-tunes the PC, customizing it so it can access optional peripherals (such as the mouse or the modem) and unused areas in

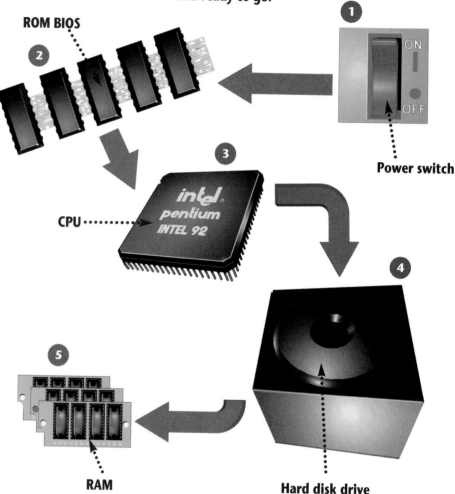

When a PC is powered on, ROM BIOS starts the boot process. This copies the operating system from the hard disk into memory. The PC is "booted" and ready to go.

ROM BIOS

Power switch

CPU

RAM

Hard disk drive

memory. Next, the AUTOEXEC.BAT file is located, and its instructions are executed. The AUTOEXEC.BAT file contains commands (such as those to start a particular program or change the prompt) that the user wants run at boot. Once the

startup files have been found and executed, the computer is fully booted and ready to go. Also see AUTOEXEC.BAT, BIOS, CONFIG.SYS, and Memory.

How Does It Work?

DOS is made up of three parts: IO.SYS, MSDOS.SYS, and COMMAND.COM. IO.SYS works with ROM BIOS to control the computer's input/output functions; MSDOS.SYS (sometimes called the kernel) manages files, runs programs, and performs basic system functions; COMMAND.COM performs all the DOS commands. In addition, COMMAND.COM functions as the overall "manager" for the computer.

During the boot process, the three parts of the operating system are loaded into memory one at a time. After IO.SYS is loaded, it checks to see if all the system components are responding properly. MSDOS.SYS is loaded next so it can perform the commands in the CONFIG.SYS (a special configuration file). COMMAND.COM is loaded last and is kept in memory so that DOS commands (such as COPY) can be executed when needed. COMMAND.COM then executes the commands in AUTOEXEC.BAT, which completes the boot process.

POST

A series of tests performed at boot. POST determines whether each component (memory, disk drives, keyboard, monitor, etc.) is connected properly and responding to a signal sent to it. POST does not determine whether a component is malfunctioning (for example, whether or not the hard disk can read and write data).

AUTOEXEC. BAT

A file which contains commands which are performed automatically at system startup..

COLD BOOT

Also known as boot. To start a computer by physically turning the power on.

WARM BOOT

Also known as a reboot. To reload the computer's operating system while the computer is still turned on. This is accomplished by pressing a Reset button on the front of the computer, or pressing the Ctrl, Alt, and Del keys on the keyboard all at the same time.

CMOS

CMOS is short for Complimentary Metal Oxide Semiconductor. The CMOS chip stores information about the system, such as the amount of memory, the size of the hard disk, the size and type of disk drives, etc. This information is maintained in CMOS more or less permanently, through a tiny battery. CMOS must be adjusted whenever the system is changed, such as when additional memory is added, because the information it contains is checked against what is really found when the system is booted.

Borland

Chairman, president, and CEO of Borland, Philippe Kahn

Specializing in programming languages for PCs, Borland International, Inc. was founded in 1983 by Philippe Kahn. Borland's first product, Turbo Pascal, remains the most popular version of the Pascal programming language. Two other Borland products, Turbo C++ and Borland C++, are the most popular versions of the C++ programming language.

The success of Borland's C++ products has helped popularize object-oriented programming (OOP), a method of writing programs by using objects. With OOP, parts of a program are divided into self-contained sections called objects. Each object (each section of programming instructions) is responsible for understanding its own function and for handling its own data. That means that with OOP programs, adding new features is easy because each feature's function is independent of the other features. C++ is an ideal language for creating Windows programs that are object-based, full of dialog boxes, windows, and special icons. In fact, many industry leaders, such as Novell, Intel, IBM, Claris, Aldus, and WordPerfect, use Borland C++ to write their programs.

In 1984, Borland released the first DOS utility program, called SideKick. It contained a notepad, appointment calendar, calculator, and address book all in one simple-to-use program. SideKick is a TSR, which is a special program that runs in the "background" behind other programs, such as word processors and spreadsheet programs. When activated, SideKick comes to the "front" allowing the user to enter appointments and make changes without leaving the word processor or other currently running program. Because DOS is limited to running only one program at a time, TSRs were considered to be a great advantage: they allowed the user to "cheat" and run two programs—the TSR and another program. Today, TSRs like SideKick are losing favor because of the popularity of

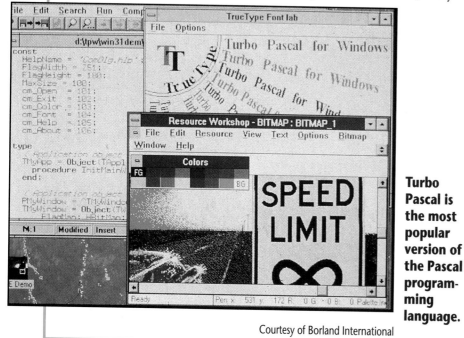

Turbo Pascal is the most popular version of the Pascal programming language.

Windows, which allows a user to run multiple programs at once, and switch between them at will.

With the purchases of Ansa's Paradox and Ashton-Tate's dBASE products, Borland is also becoming well known for producing database management programs. A database management program is used to organize large amounts of related information, such as lists of addresses, merchandise inventories, library books, patient records, bank accounts, personnel records, and more. However, dBASE IV for DOS is much more than just a database management program: it's a database programming tool. With dBASE, a programmer can create his own applications to customize the way his workers enter, sort, and print information in the database. That way, a user doesn't need to learn how to use the dBASE program, and can continue to work using familiar screens and commands that were created with the dBASE programming language. The dBASE programming language, by the way, is supported by every other database management program, such as FoxPro, Paradox, Access, and Approach.

Until 1994, Borland was also known for its popular spreadsheet program, Quattro Pro. In 1994, Borland sold the rights to Quatro Pro to Novell, Inc. A spreadsheet program can manipulate numbers, perform calculations, handle mathematical formulas, and organize data. Quattro Pro is extremely easy to use, yet is sophisticated in features. Also see C/C++, Database, dBase, Object-Oriented Programming, Paradox, Pascal, Spreadsheet, and Terminate and Stay Resident Programs.

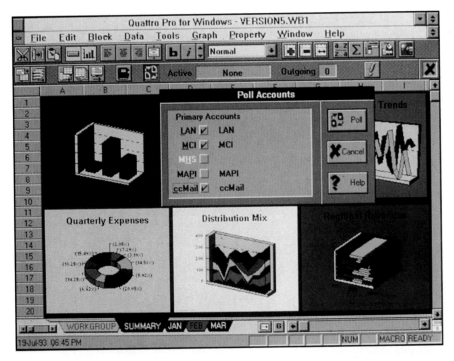

Courtesy of Borland International

Quattro Pro for Windows

DATABASE PROGRAM

An application used to organize large quantities of data. Database programs are commonly used to compile address lists, inventory and pricing lists, and patient records. Borland's dBASE IV and Paradox are database programs.

OBJECT-ORIENTED PROGRAMMING

A method of programming using "objects." An object is a section of a program that knows what its function is, and how to handle its own data. For example, in a chess program, a Pawn object is a section of program instructions that describes how a pawn chess piece moves. When the user wants to move a pawn, the program instructs the Pawn object to move itself, and the object knows what instructions to issue to the computer to make that happen.

TSR (TERMINATE AND STAY RESIDENT) PROGRAM

Also known as a memory resident program, this type of utility stays in memory, waiting until it is activated by the user. TSRs are designed to be used with some other program already running. Borland's SideKick is a TSR program.

Bus

A bus is the internal electronic pathway that carries signals from one part of the computer to another. Located on the motherboard inside the system unit, the bus helps the various parts of the PC communicate. There are a variety of buses found inside the computer. The data bus allows data to travel back and forth between the microprocessor (CPU) and memory (RAM). The address bus carries information about the location of data in memory. The control bus carries the control signals that make sure everything is flowing smoothly from place to place. Although this is a bit confusing, these three different buses are sometimes together called simply "the bus." A user can think of the computer's "bus" as one unit made up of three parts: data, address, and control, even though the three electrical pathways do not run along each other (and therefore don't really form a single "unit") within the computer.

There are different sizes, or widths of data buses found in computers today. A data bus' width is measured by the number of bits that can travel on it at once. An 8-bit bus carries data along 8 parallel lines. A 16-bit bus, also called ISA (Industry Standard Architecture), carries data along 16 lines. A 32-bit bus, classified as EISA (Enhanced Industry Standard Architecture) or MCA (Micro Channel Architecture), can carry data along 32 lines.

The speed at which buses conduct signals is measured in megahertz (Mhz). Typical PCs today run at speeds between 20 and 65Mhz. Also see CPU, Expansion Card, Memory, Motherboard, RAM, ROM, and System Unit.

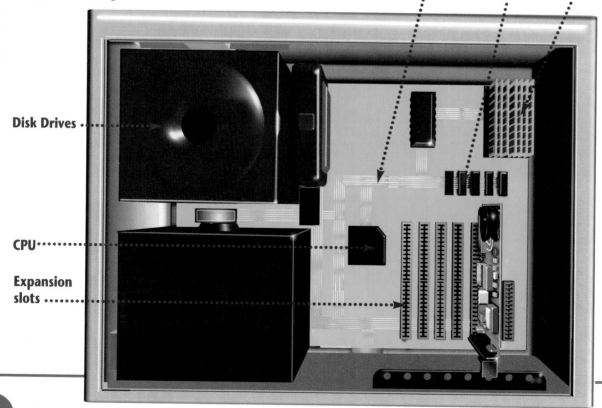

Bus   ROM BIOS   RAM

Disk Drives

CPU

Expansion slots

How Does It Work?

A bus transfers electrical signals from one place to another. An actual bus appears as an endless amount of etched copper circuits on the motherboard's surface. The bus is connected to the CPU through the Bus Interface Unit.

Data travels between the CPU and memory along the data bus. The location (address) of that data is carried along the address bus. A clock signal which keeps everything in synch travels along the control bus.

The clock acts like a traffic light for all the PC's components; the "green light" goes on with each clock tick. A PC's clock can "tick" anywhere from 20 to 65 million times per second, which makes it seem like a computer is really fast. But since each task (such as saving a file) is made up of several programmed instructions, and each of those instructions takes several clock cycles to carry out, a person sometimes has to sit and wait for the computer to catch up.

Control lines

Address lines

Data lines

BUS ARCHITECTURE

The layout and design of the bus pathways and structure, including its size and speed.

ISA

Industry Standard Architecture. The most common of PC buses, this bus architecture carries data at speeds up to 16 megahertz per second.

LOCAL BUS

Separate from the regular bus discussed here, a local bus (if present) is a special bus that connects the CPU directly to a peripheral, such as a monitor. A local bus increases a computer's performance because it carries data at the speed of the computer's CPU chip, instead of the speed of the regular bus, which is slowed down to match the processing speed of the different peripherals attached to the computer.

EISA

Enhanced Industry Standard Architecture. A bus architecture that can transfer data at 32 megahertz per second.

BUS INTERFACE UNIT

The part of the CPU which connects it to the bus.

MCA

Micro Channel Architecture. Created by IBM and found on IBM computers, the MCA bus can carry data at 40 megahertz per second.

Byte

A byte is a group of eight bits. Bit, short for Binary digIT, is the basic unit of information within a computer, equal to a 1 or a 0. Bits are stored within the computer's microchips and are led by control the flow of electrical currents; a 1 is represented by an "on" or high voltage electrical current, and a 0 is represented by an "off" or low current. A byte is formed by combining eight bits together to store the equivalent of one character. For example, the letter A (a single byte) is made up of the eight bits 01000001.

The sequence of eight bits which make up a particular byte is detemined by an internal table called the ASCII (American Standard Code for Information Interchange) table. The ASCII table contains the byte codes for all letters, numbers, and special symbols such as $, * or ^. However, to represent a number greater than 9, two bytes are needed. For example, The number 15 is equal to the two bytes 00110001 (1) and 00110101 (5).

The size of a file, the storage capacity of a disk, or the amount of computer memory can all be measured in bits and bytes. A kilobyte is roughly a thousand bytes; a megabyte is roughly one million bytes. A gigabyte, equal to 1,073,741,824 bytes, is roughly one thousand megabytes. Also see ASCII, Binary, Bit, Data Storage, and Memory.

ANSI TABLE

A built-in table which contains many of the same byte sequences as the ASCII table. The ANSI table was adopted by the American National Standards Institute as the "official" PC table.

ASCII TABLE

A built-in table which contains the byte sequences for all upper and lower case letters, single-digit numbers, and special symbols.

BIT

A single unit of measurement based on a binary digit, 1 or 0. A group of eight bits, equivalent to a single alphanumeric character, make up one byte.

KILOBYTE

Roughly one thousand bytes, a kilobyte is equal to 1,024 bytes.

MEGABYTE

Roughly one million bytes (1,048,576 bytes). A megabyte is equivalent to 500 double-spaced pages of text.

GIGABYTE

Roughly one thousand megabytes (1,073,741,824 bytes). A gigabyte is equivalent to a half-million double-spaced pages of text.

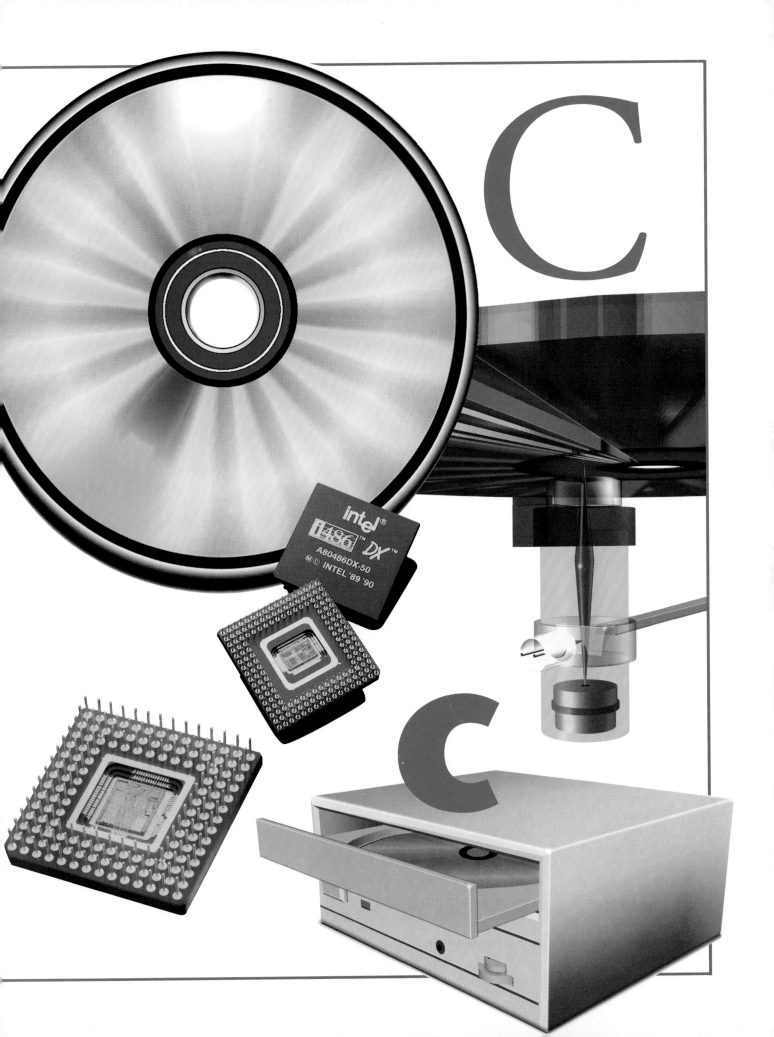

C/C++

C is the name of a programming language first developed by Dennis Ritchie at Bell Laboratories in 1972. C is actually the descendent of an earlier programming language called B. A powerful computer language, C is taught widely in schools and is especially popular for writing commercial applications.

One of the benefits of using C is that a C program can run on almost any type of computer, such as a PC, a Macintosh, or a UNIX based computer. C is a high-level programming language because it is written in an almost English code which is very easy for the programmer to learn. However, C is similar to a low-level programming language because it can be broken down into machine language fairly easily.

C++ is an object-oriented programming language based on C. C++ was created by Bjarne Stroustrup (again of Bell Laboratories) in 1985. C++ combines basic C programming and object-oriented programming. Before the advent of object-oriented programming (OOP), if a programmer changed one part of a program, it often caused unexpected changes to other parts. That's because non-OOP programs are written in sections that are very interdependent. Instructions in one part of the program reference other instructions, and when something is changed, it just doesn't always work.

With OOP, parts of a program are divided into self-sustaining sections called objects. Each object (each section of programming instructions) is responsible for understanding its own function and for handling its own data. That means that with OOP programs, adding new features is easy because each feature's function is independent of the other features.

Borland's Turbo C++

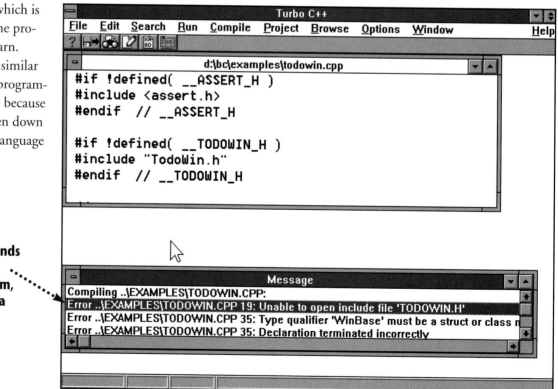

When the compiler finds an error in the program, it displays a message.

C++ is an ideal programming language for creating Windows programs, which are usually object based. Windows programs are chock full of objects, such as dialog boxes (boxes that request information from the user), icons (pictures that represent a command, such as saving a file), and windows themselves (boxes that contain files, such as a letter or a memo). However, the objects in a C++ program do not have to be something that is seen on-screen (although that's the easiest way to think of them); instead, objects are sections of a program that are independent from the main program. Also see BASIC, Binary, Borland, Object-Oriented Programming, Pascal and Programming.

VISUAL C++

Microsoft's version of C++. Visual C++ allows a programmer to draw certain types of objects rather than writing the commands to describe how they look.

INTERPRETER/COMPILER

Each time an interpreted program is run, it is converted into machine language by an interpreter. This is unlike a compiled program, which is converted into machine language only once. A compiled program written with C is converted into machine language and stored permanently in a file, which is then reused anytime

HIGH-LEVEL PROGRAMMING LANGUAGE

A programming language that is easier for programmers to understand because it is written more closely to English than to the rudimentary 1s and 0s of machine language. High-level languages require a compiler or an interpreter to translate the program instructions into 1s and 0s that the computer can understand. BASIC, C, C++, and Pascal are all high-level programming languages.

OBJECT-ORIENTED PROGRAMMING

A method of programming using "objects." An object is a section of a program that knows what its function is, and how to handle its own data.

```
                    Turbo C++ - [d:\bc\examples\todowin.cpp]
  File   Edit   Search   Run   Compile   Project   Browse   Options   Window        Help

int WinBase::show = _cmdShow;

//------------------------------------------------------------
//
//   members and data for class ModalDialog
//
//------------------------------------------------------------

ModalDialog *ModalDialog::curDlg = 0;

WORD ModalDialog::run()
{
    FARPROC dlgProc =
        MakeProcInstance( (FARPROC)ModalDialog::dlgProc, hInst
    DialogBox( hInst, getDialogName(), hWnd(), dlgProc );
    FreeProcInstance( dlgProc );
    return result;                                        I
}
  1:1              Insert
```

Part of a C++ program

LOW LEVEL LANGUAGE

A programming language that is similar to machine language, just one level removed from the binary language of 1s and 0s. Assembler is a low level programming language.

Cache

Cache, pronounced "cash," is a reserved portion of the computer's memory used to store frequently used data. Having data held in a cache can increase the speed in which the CPU (the computer's central processor or "brain") retrieves information. That's because it takes less time for the CPU to retrieve data that's already in RAM than it does to copy data from a hard disk and then retrieve it.

This type of cache is called a disk cache, because it contains frequently used data from a disk. A disk cache might also be located in separate RAM chips on the disk controller, instead of in regular RAM. The disk controller connects the disk

drive to the computer and manages the data coming to and from the drive, which makes it an ideal place to locate a disk cache.

A different kind of cache is called a memory cache. A memory cache contains frequently used data from memory (RAM). A memory cache is created with super fast RAM chips called SRAMs. These RAM chips are faster than regular RAM chips (DRAMs) because they operate at

about the same speed as the CPU (central processing unit, the "brains" of the computer). A memory cache, which is set up in super fast RAM, contains the most recently used data from ordinary RAM. This is different from a disk cache, which is set up in ordinary RAM, and contains the most recently used data from the disk drives. Also see Data Storage, Memory, and RAM.

When the CPU needs data, it first looks in the disk cache. If it finds the data there, it doesn't have to look for the data on the disk. which saves time.

These RAM chips store recent data from the disk.

Disk drive

DISK CACHE

Located either in ordinary RAM (DRAMs) or on the disk controller board, this contains the most recently used data from disk. The disk cache is checked before the computer's random access memory (RAM) reads data from the disk.

How Does It Work?

Large blocks of data are copied into the disk cache (RAM) whenever the disk drive is read. As the cache gets full, the block of data that's been in the cache the longest without being used is overwritten. Therefore, only frequently used data is kept in the disk cache.

By keeping recently used data in the cache, the CPU

CACHE

Last Used: 11:59

Last used: 11:50

Last Used: 11:58

Last Used: 11:56

can read it quickly—rather than going through a search and retrieval process to locate it on the disk.

DISK CONTROLLER

A circuit board that controls the operation of a disk drive, either the floppy drive or hard drive. The disk controller plays an important part in relaying information back and forth between the CPU and the disk drive.

MEMORY CACHE

Composed of super fast RAM chips called SRAMs. A memory cache holds the most recently used data in RAM, for quick access.

New Data: 12:10

DRAM

Stands for Dynamic Random Access Memory. DRAMs make up most of the standard RAM chips found in computers today. A pulse of electricity must be sent through DRAMs regularly or they will lose their data. So the data stored in DRAMs is said to be "dynamic," which is just a fancy word for "easily changed."

SRAM

Stands for Static Random Access Memory. SRAMs are super-fast RAM chips usually used in caches. SRAMs do not need to have a pulse of electricity sent through them as frequently as DRAM chips do; therefore, they are much faster and easier for a computer to use. However, SRAMs are considerably more expensive than DRAM (regular RAM) chips.

RAM

. Random Access Memory. RAM is the computer's electronic memory. Data stored in RAM is maintained only while the computer is turned on. When the computer is turned off, all information in RAM is cleared. This could result in the loss of data, unless the data is stored on disk.

CD-ROM

CD-ROM stands for Compact Disc Read-Only Memory. CD-ROM technology, which began in 1985, utilizes the same type of discs used in audio CD players. CD-ROMs measure about 4 1/2-inches in diameter, and can store vast amounts of computer information, including software programs, entire sets of encyclopedias, sounds, pictures, and movie or video clips. A single CD-ROM can store over 650 megabytes of information,

compared to a 3.5-inch high-density disk that can only hold 1.44 megabytes. This means that it would take about 452 3.5 high-density disks to hold all the information contained on a single CD-ROM disc.

The data on the disc is stored in the form of pits (indents) and lands (bumps) on a reflective surface within the disc. The data is placed

on the CD-ROM by special equipment where the CD-ROM is made. This data cannot be changed by the CD-ROM drive found in a PC, but it can be retrieved (read). The CD-ROM drive uses lasers to read the data. The small laser in the CD-ROM drive bounces light off of the pits and lands to read the data. A pit reflects less light and is read as a 0; a land reflects more light and is read as a 1. These 1's and 0's form the binary data that's universal to all computers.

Floppy disks store data in circles called tracks. There are several of these tracks, placed one inside each other like the age rings of a tree. But the data on a CD-ROM is stored on one single track that spirals from the outer edge of the disk to the center, like the track of music on an LP record. This long track is divided into equal parts called sectors. Files are stored in consecutive sectors on this track. A CD-ROM drive is used to read compact discs, or CD-ROMs. To insert a CD into the drive, the disc is placed in a caddy (a plastic cassette which encases the disc). The caddy is then inserted into a slot in the front of

Land **Pit**

BINARY

Binary numbers are the foundation for computer storage. A binary numbering system uses only 1's and 0's. Letters, numbers, and characters (such as a question mark) are assigned an eight digit binary number so that they can be stored within the computer. The 1's and 0's of a computer's binary system are represented by two electronic states: on (high current) or off (low current). Quite simply, the 1's and 0's are like little on/off switches inside the computer.

the CD-ROM drive. Some CD-ROMs do not use a caddy; instead, a drawer opens from the front of the CD-ROM drive, the disc is placed in the drawer, and the drawer closes. A CD-ROM drive contains a stereo headphone jack, into which the user can plug a standard set of headphones for listening privacy—that is, if there are any sounds recorded on that particular CD-ROM.

A CD-ROM drive can only read the data on a disc. It cannot write

new data to a disc, although this technology is changing rapidly. CD-ROM drives in the future might very well be able to both read and write data to disks. However, because of their high storage capacity, CDs are already perfect for storing the large files required for a multimedia program. CDs are also useful in electronic publishing. Also see **Binary, Computer Based Training, Data Storage,** and **Multimedia.**

MEGABYTES

A megabyte is 1,048,576 bytes, equivalent to 500 double-spaced pages of text.

MULTIMEDIA

The combination of text, sound, graphics, and video for use in presentations.

The caddy is a plastic case into which the CD-ROM disc is inserted.

CD-ROM disc ·····················

JEWEL CASE

The plastic case that the CD-ROM disc comes in. The disc is removed from this case, placed in a caddy or a tray, and inserted into the CD-ROM drive.

CD-ROM drive

A headphone jack allows the user to plug in headphones and listen to recorded sounds.

continues

CD-ROM continued

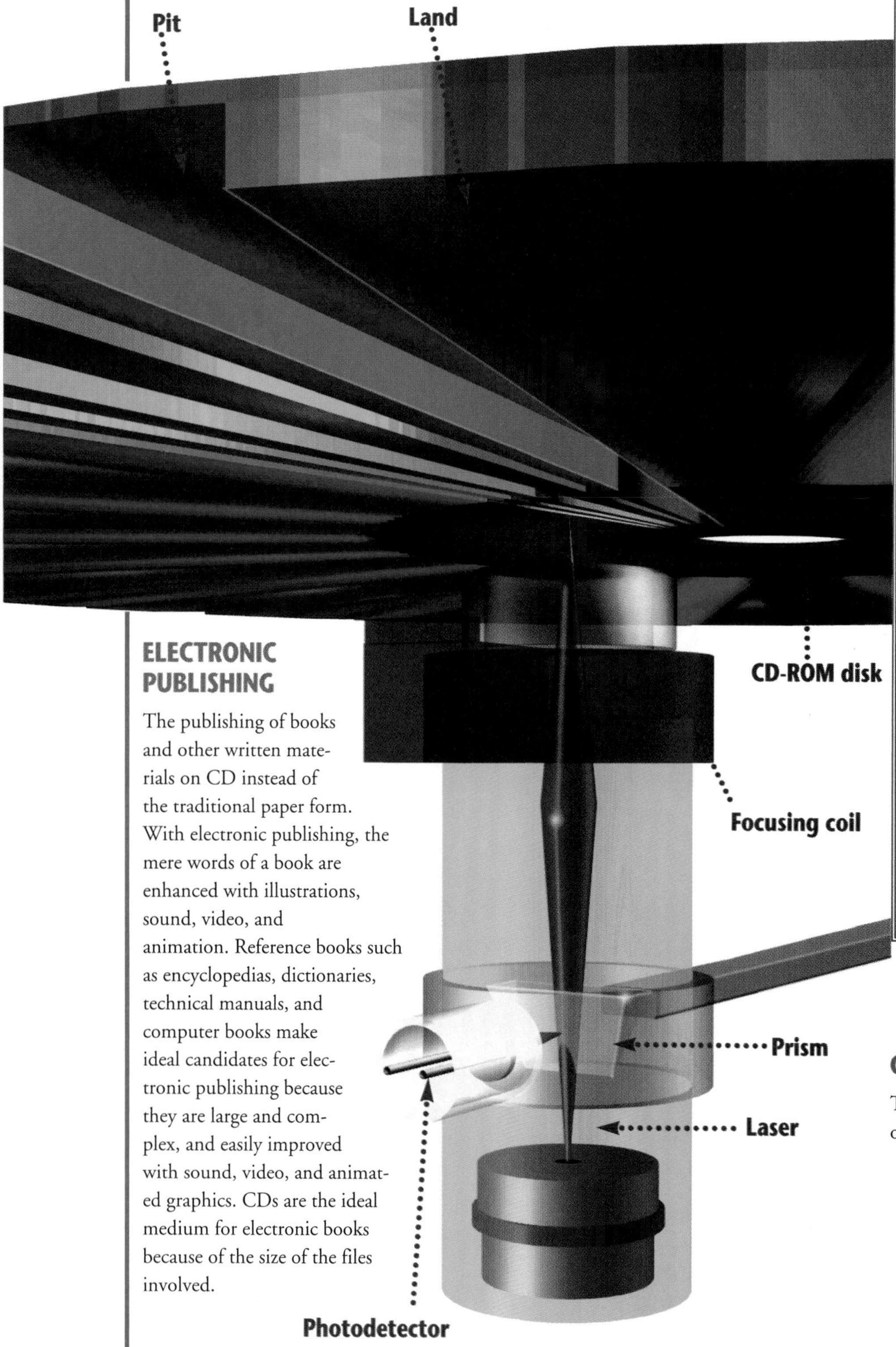

Pit **Land**

How Does It Work?

How Does It Work?

A CD disc inserted into a CD-ROM drive is spun by a motor at a varying rate. This allows the data to be read at a constant speed, regardless of whether that data is located way out on the edge of the disk, or towards the center.

A tiny laser inside the drive focuses on the spinning disc. The laser beam strikes a reflective aluminum inner surface covered with indentations (called pits) and bumps (called lands). Light is reflected back to an optical reading head. Light striking a pit reflects less light than does light striking a land. A prism bends the reflected light to a photodetector, which in turn measures the intensity of the reflected light and converts it into electrical pulses that are sent back to the CPU for processing.

CD-ROM disk

Focusing coil

ELECTRONIC PUBLISHING

The publishing of books and other written materials on CD instead of the traditional paper form. With electronic publishing, the mere words of a book are enhanced with illustrations, sound, video, and animation. Reference books such as encyclopedias, dictionaries, technical manuals, and computer books make ideal candidates for electronic publishing because they are large and complex, and easily improved with sound, video, and animated graphics. CDs are the ideal medium for electronic books because of the size of the files involved.

Prism

Laser

CADDY

The tray that holds the compact disc on a compact disc drive.

Photodetector

Central Processing Unit

The CPU, or central pro cessing unit, is the "thinking" part of the computer. Also known as the microprocessor, the CPU acts as the computer's "brain," carrying out software commands, performing calculations, and conversing with the different hardware components needed to operate the computer. Made of silicon, the CPU is a microchip about the size of a thumbnail. Enclosed in a black casing, the CPU is connected to the motherboard through tiny pins. This tiny integrated circuit is packed with transistors (miniscule on/off switches), resistors (which control the flow of electricity), and capacitors (which store electricity).

Intel 80486 chips

CPU chip

Plastic casing

Connector pins

Courtesy of Intel Corporation

Courtesy of Intel Corporation

The first true CPU chip, the Intel 4004 chip, was introduced in 1971. Intel corporation was founded in 1968 as a producer of memory chips. After its microprocessor chip, the 8088, was chosen for the IBM-PC, Intel sales took off. CPU chips are usually identified with numbers—the higher the number, the newer and more powerful the chip. In 1978, Intel introduced the 8086 chip, used with the IBM PC/XT. This innovative microprocessor included 29,000 transistors and a 16-bit data bus (the connector that moves data to and from the CPU), and ran at a speed of 10 megahertz. A transistor is where a microchip stores data and makes decisions; so the more transistors it has, the more powerful a CPU is.

Intel continue to introduce a new, more powerful CPU chips about every four years. After introducing the 80486 chip in 1989, Intel decided not to number the next CPU chip, but to give it a name. The name they chose was the Pentium™ chip.

In 1993, Intel introduced the Pentium chip, featuring 3,000,000 transistors and a 64-bit data bus. Like the 80486 ™chip before it, the Pentium also has cache memory (a place in the CPU where data is stored until it is processed), and a built-in math coprocessor. The math coprocessor processed all the instructions having to do with math, such as adding two numbers together. This freed the CPU to process other instructions, such as those for copying a file.

continues

Central Processing Unit

In addition, the Pentium chip contains two instruction paths, allowing it to process two program instructions in the time it would normally take to process only one. Some programs (especially those with video and graphics) process more than two times faster on computers with a Pentium chip than on those using the 80486. Year after year, the Intel CPU has grown in power and speed, but there are new competitors in the CPU market making the future of CPU technology exciting.

The Apple Macintosh uses a different kind of CPU chip, the 68000-series manufactured by Motorola Corporation. Motorola chips are just as fast as Intel chips, and when dealing with video and graphics, they are sometimes faster. However, computer manufacturers can purchase Intel chips in quantity at a much lower price than they can purchase Motorola chips. So comparable Mac and IBM-PC compatible computers differ a lot in price—making Macs much more expensive.

CPU chips differ in speed, which is measured in megahertz. For example, a 486-33 megahertz CPU is faster than a 486-25 megahertz CPU. A megahertz is equal to one million cycles per second.

Think of a cycle as a tick of the clock; anything that happens within the computer, happens during that tick. The next event must wait until the next tick. So the more megahertz (or processing cycles) per second, the faster the computer can process data and perform tasks.

CPU chips also differ in the amount of data they can send and receive at one time. The width of the chip's connecting "highway," or data bus, is measured by how many bits of information can travel along the electrical highway at a time. The wider the data bus, the more data can be sent to and from the CPU during a single clock cycle. A 486-25 megahertz CPU has the same data bus width as a 486-33 megahertz CPU; however, it processes the data slower because it has less clock cycles per second. A 386 CPU has a smaller data bus than a 486 CPU, so not only is it slower, it's less efficient since not as much data can come to or from the CPU during a clock cycle.

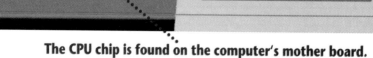

The CPU chip is found on the computer's mother board.

How Does It Work?

The CPU contains many components that perform particular tasks. For example, the Bus Interface Unit is the part of the CPU that connects it to the data bus. The CPU cache (when present) receives data from the Bus Interface Unit and holds it until it is processed. The math coprocessor (which was included as part of the CPU beginning with the 80486 chip), processes instructions having to do with math, such as subtracting two numbers.

An internal clock acts as a metronome, sending a clock signal periodically from the CPU, keeping each PC component in synch.

The Decode Unit prepares each instruction for processing. The most important component, however, is the Execution Unit, which actually performs each CPU instruction.

Microprocessor chips come in many different types, or versions, depending upon how they are going to be used. Intel differentiates its chips with letters that describe how the chips can be used. Chip numbers ending with the letters DX are faster, and use a 32-wire bus—for example, the 80486-DX CPU. DX chips, and variations of the DX chips (DX2), are best for business purposes such as spreadsheet work because they are fast. Chip numbers ending with the letters SX such as the 80486-SX chip are slower and less expensive, using a 16-wire bus. SX chips are more suitable for home computers, where speed might not be as big a consideration as expense. Also see Intel, Motherboard, Motorola, and System Unit.

MEGAHERTZ

A unit of measurement equal to one million pulses or electrical cycles per second. Anything that happens within a computer must happen within a clock cycle. Most tasks, such as the display of data or the processing of a single instruction, take more than one clock cycle. The more cycles or megahertz that a CPU has, the faster it works.

CLOCK SPEED

The speed at which the computer can perform calculations and carry out tasks, usually measured in megahertz. Located inside the microprocessor, the internal clock acts as a metronome, counting out each cycle.

TRANSISTOR

The equivalent of an on/off switch inside a microchip. When this switch is "on," it represents a 1; when it is "off," it represents a 0. These 1's and 0's make up the computer's data and instructions.

MATH COPROCESSOR

Processes the CPU's instructions involving math, such as adding or subtracting two numbers. Once a separate microchip, the math coprocessor is now included within the CPU's own circuitry.

DATA BUS

The electrical pathway connecting the CPU to the PC's different components. Data travels along this bus.

Courtesy of Intel Corporation

Commands

In order to tell a computer to carry out a particular task, the user must issue a command. Computer commands are orders that tell the computer what to do. There are several types of commands that computers use. Command-driven programs require the user to memorize commands and type them on the key-board before the computer can act upon them. DOS is an example of a command-driven program.

A more graphical and easier way to issue commands is found with menu-driven programs. Instead of requiring the user to memorize keystrokes to give commands, menu-driven programs offer lists of commands that can be selected from menus. Microsoft Windows is an example of a menu-driven program. Typically, menu-driven programs are used with a mouse, an input device used as a selecting tool on the computer screen. Also see Input Devices, Keyboard, and Motherboard.

A typed DOS command

```
C:\>dir

 Volume in drive C is SAMS-JF
 Volume Serial Number is 1B7D-5AA6
 Directory of C:\

DOS          <DIR>         10-20-92  12:28p
BIN          <DIR>         10-20-92  12:47p
WINDOWS      <DIR>         10-20-92   4:07p
CHKLIST  MS         189    02-14-94   4:43p
SYSTEM       <DIR>         11-16-92   3:54p
SIERRA       <DIR>         01-12-93  10:47a
SCANDISK LOG        465    11-03-93   1:49p
CONFIG   SYS        254    11-29-93  11:21a
AUTOEXEC BAT        258    01-04-94   4:22p
TEMP         <DIR>         02-18-94   9:17a
COMMAND  COM     54,619    09-30-93   6:20a
DSVXD    386      5,741    12-23-92   6:00a
WINA20   386      9,349    09-30-93   6:20a
UNDELETE INI        230    01-14-93  11:43a
MSAV     INI        248    12-14-92  12:59p
        15 file(s)         71,353 bytes
                      11,616,256 bytes free

C:\>
```

How Does It Work?

Commands entered through the keyboard are first checked to determine exactly which keys were pressed—each key has a unique scan code assigned to it to help identify that key. The scan codes for the pressed keys are then stored temporarily in a keyboard buffer chip located inside the keyboard. A buffer is a temporary storage area.

Next, the keyboard sends a signal to the CPU via controller chips. The CPU in turn instructs ROM-BIOS to retrieve the scan codes and translate them into binary (the binary number assigned to them on the ASCII chart). They are then stored in RAM until some program asks to read and respond to them. For example, if a program wanted to display them on the monitor, it would ask the CPU to pass the codes on to the monitor to display the characters.

COMMAND-DRIVEN PROGRAM

A program that relies on typed-in commands in order to carry out tasks; the commands are entered into the computer using the keyboard. DOS is an example of a command-driven program.

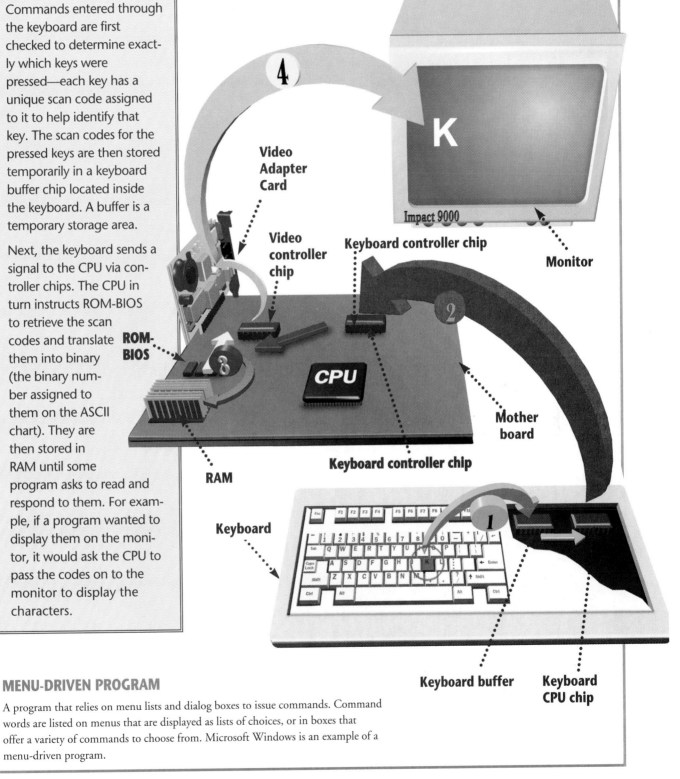

Video Adapter Card

Video controller chip

Keyboard controller chip

Monitor

Impact 9000

ROM-BIOS

CPU

Mother board

RAM

Keyboard controller chip

Keyboard

Keyboard buffer

Keyboard CPU chip

MENU-DRIVEN PROGRAM

A program that relies on menu lists and dialog boxes to issue commands. Command words are listed on menus that are displayed as lists of choices, or in boxes that offer a variety of commands to choose from. Microsoft Windows is an example of a menu-driven program.

Communications

From the early 1900s until now, long distance communication has primarily been in the form of the telephone line. Now telephone lines are being used for more than the transmission of voice; they are also used for the transmission of computer data. There are many reasons why someone might want to transfer data between one PC and another using phone lines. For example, communications software makes it possible to share data with a PC that is some distance away (maybe even around the world), to connect to a BBS (bulletin board service) in order to get help with a PC problem, or to connect to a pay for use on-line service (such as CompuServe or Prodigy) in order to leave messages for other users, buy and sell stocks, download programs, read articles, and more.

The telephone system transmits sounds and tones known as analog communications with a continuous electronic current that varies in frequency and amplitude (volume). The PC can't understand the tones and pulses transmitted over a phone line directly, so a device called a modem is used. The purpose of a modem is to change the tones and pulses heard through a telephone line into data

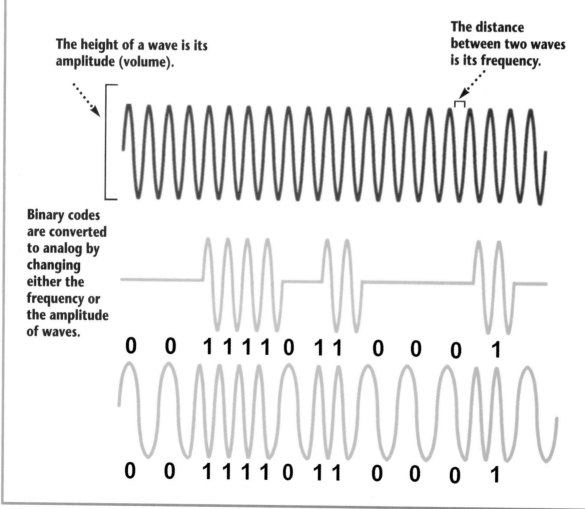

The height of a wave is its amplitude (volume).

The distance between two waves is its frequency.

Binary codes are converted to analog by changing either the frequency or the amplitude of waves.

0   0   1 1 1 1 0   1 1   0   0   0   1

0   0   1 1 1 1 0   1 1   0   0   0   1

that the computer can understand. So it's the modem that receives the transmission and changes the tones into binary codes that the computer can understand. Likewise, before computer data can be transmitted over telephone lines, it must first be changed from binary codes (data) into analog signals (tones and pulses) by the modem. Binary codes involve only two signals, 1's (on) or 0's (off). By changing either the frequency or the amplitude (volume) of an analog signal, the 1's and 0's of computer data can be sent through telephone lines.

There is another way that computers can communicate: through a local area network. A local area network is a collection of computers (usually located within a single building) connected to each other through a series of cables or wires.

LANs (local area networks) are popular in educational settings, such as universities, and in large corporations. Small businesses usually can't afford to connect everyone to a LAN, so when they do invest in a network, it's usually limited to only certain departments such as payroll and personnel.

LANs are made up of several components. A file server is a centrally located PC with a large storage capacity that holds data and programs shared by all the users on the network. Workstations are user PCs connected through a cable (or telephone wires) to the network. The network operating system handles the transmitting of data throughout the network. In addition to sharing data and programs, LANs can be used to share printers. A printer server is a printer connected to the network so it can be shared by all the users on the LAN. Through modems, two or more LANs can be connected into larger groups called WANs (Wide Area Networks). See LAN and Modem.

Workstation

Workstation

Print server

File server

A typical LAN.

continues

Communications

continued

BINARY

The two-digit numbering system on which all digital computers are based. Binary digits are represented within a PC's microchips by controlling the flow of an electrical current; 1's are on and 0's are off.

LAN

Stands for Local Area Network, a group of local computers connected with high-performance cables or wires. Networks share data, programs, and peripherals.

UPLOADING

When a user sends computer files through a modem from his PC to another computer, the process is called uploading.

BBS

Stands for Bulletin Board Service. A BBS is an electronic bulletin board established for computer users. A BBS can be accessed through the use of a modem and communications software. A BBS offers users a chance to communicate with others through the computer, exchange information, upload and download files, and get help with computer problems. There are thousands of BBSs across the globe offering a variety of topics and interests ranging from software support to dating services.

How Does It Work?

Data is exchanged between two distant personal computers through the use of a modem, a telephone line, and communications software.

The communications software handles the method of data transmission, using a particular protocol. The protocol is a set of rules that helps determine whether the correct character was received. If not, that character is retransmitted. Retransmitting a character takes longer than one might expect, since modems transmit only one bit (one part of a character) at a time. In order to transmit data between them, the two PCs involved must use the same protocol. There are many standard protocols included in the communications software available today.

Modem stands for MOdulator/ DEModulator. It changes the computer's digital signal into an analog signal that is sent over the telephone lines.

Modem

DOWNLOADING

When a user receives computer files through a modem from someone else's computer, the process is called downloading.

PROTOCOL

A set of standards that govern how computers communicate with each other. In order for two computers to talk, they must use the same protocol. The protocol determines how each bit (a 1 or a 0) is sent, and how to detect errors in transmission.

BPS

Short for bits per second, a measure of the amount of data a modem can transmit. Common rates range from 2,400 bps to 14,000 bps depending on the modem being used.

FAX MODEM

A special modem designed to send and receive faxes.

PARITY

The procedure for identifying whether the correct character was received. With even parity, an extra bit is added to the eight bits that make up a character (such as the letter D, which is represented by the eight bits 01000100). This ninth bit makes the total of all the bits an even number. So in the case of the letter D, the ninth bit would be 0, as in 010001000. With odd parity, the ninth bit makes the total come out odd, as in 010001001. After the modem receives the ninth bit for a character, it adds them up and determines whether one of the bits was scrambled. If so, that character is retransmitted.

HAYES

A major manufacturer of modems. Hayes modems are the most popular modems purchased today. Hayes has set many industry standards in the area of computer communications.

MODEM

Short for MOdulator/DEModulator, a modem is an electronic device used for communications between computers via telephone lines. Modems convert digital signals into analog signals and back again.

ONLINE SERVICE

Fee-based services that allow computer users to access information, buy and sell stocks, download programs, read articles, and more. Through the use of a modem, subscribers can connect to such services as Prodigy, CompuServe, GEnie, Delphi, Internet, and America OnLine.

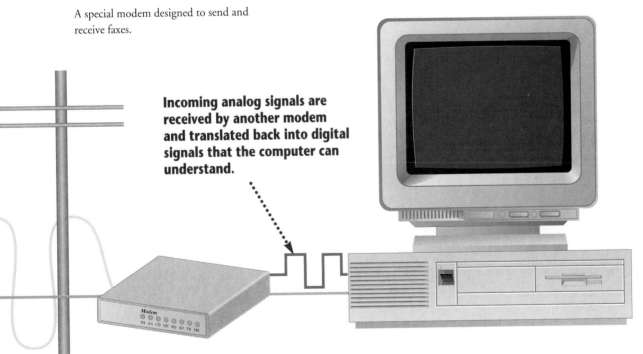

Incoming analog signals are received by another modem and translated back into digital signals that the computer can understand.

Computer Based Training (CBT)

Computer Based Training (CBTs) are training programs designed to be used on a computer. In the workplace, CBTs train employees to perform tasks related to their jobs—from learning to use the computer to handling a punch press. A typical CBT might take a user through the step-by-step process for completing some task, such as fitting a part to an automobile chassis. In such a CBT, the user typically "follows along" with pictures on the screen or text that describes what to do. A CBT can incorporate text, animation, pictures, video, and voice during the training session. Some CBTs require that the user participate in the session by indicating when he is ready to proceed to the next screen, or by answering review questions. CBTs are more cost effective than an entire training staff, because once they are designed, CBTs provide the same training course over and over at no additional cost.

However, CBTs are not restricted to customized training courses found in the workplace. Small computer based training programs are often included in popular applications such as Word for Windows, Excel, Ami Pro, Lotus 1-2-3 for Windows, and so on. Some CBTs can be purchased separately. For example, Individual

Math story problems become effective teaching for children using Super Solvers Outnumbered!, a math program by The Learning company.

Software has a nice series of CBTs on DOS, Windows, and various applications.

Adults are not the only ones to benefit from computer based training. A broad range of CBTs developed for children (also known as education software or "edutainment") provide a fun way to learn. Education software is currently available for teaching such simple skills as identifying colors, numbers, and shapes, and more complex skills such as math, reading, algebra, geometry, history, geography, language, and science.

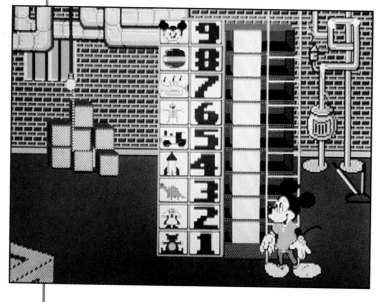

Mickey's 1,2,3's is a popular children's CBT program from Walt Disney Computer Software.

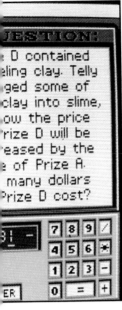

Many popular applications, such as Word for Windows, include CBTs.

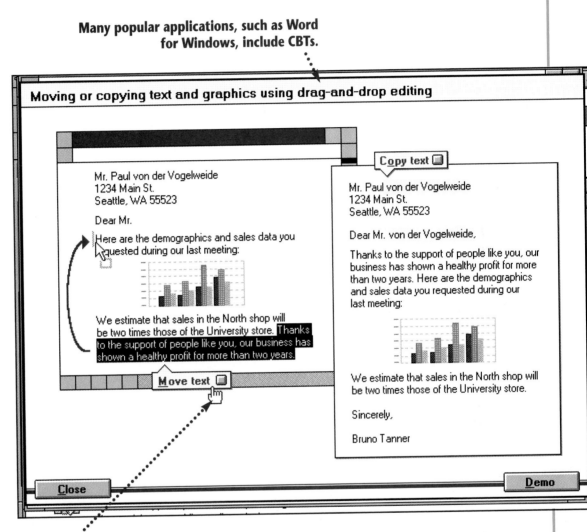

Clicking on this hypertext link jumps the user to that topic.

A major advantage of using CBTs is that the students can proceed at their own pace. If a concept is unclear, they can return to a previous spot within the program and review it. Also, a CBT can keep track of a student's progress and even provide quizzes and reviews of difficult material.

Some CBTs take full advantage of the computer, incorporating text, voice, video, animation, and graphics. This is why a lot of CBTs are found on CD-ROMs (special disks with a large storage capacity), on mainframes (large computers which fill entire rooms), or on a network server (a central PC to which many users are connected).

continues

Computer Based Training (CBT) continued

Pierre
Thursday, 10 a.m.

Welcome to South Dakota, the Coyote State.

South Dakota is the site of Mt. Rushmore. Carved into the granite are the faces of Washington, Jefferson, Lincoln, and Theodore Roosevelt.

DEPART   SHOW   ?   CRIME

Where in the U.S.A. is Carmen Sandiego? is a popular edutainment program made by Broderbund Software.

A typical CBT program is divided into manageable sections with a main menu offering different topics. After choosing a topic, the student may not have to do anything at all; in a lot of CBTs, the computer displays one screen of information after another without any additional input. If the student needs to pause the program in the middle of a session, there's usually a way to do that, such as by pressing the Esc (escape) key. Otherwise, the student just sits back and watches the screen.

More sophisticated CBTs offer ways for a student to jump around within the program, learning not only at his own pace, but in his own way. This is done using hypertext, which is a special link that connects different parts of a CBT program. Hypertext usually consists of one or two words displayed on-screen in a bold or contrasting color. Hypertext allows a student to progress more naturally from topic to topic, instead of in a fixed order. For example, a student learning about World War II might select the hypertext word "Pearl Harbor" to jump to the section that covers that particular event.

These hyperlinks do not have to be displayed as text, although that's the most common form. A hyperlink could connect a picture (such as a dinosaur) or an icon to the text that explains more about it. A hyperlink could also connect these same items to a recording or a video that explains more about them. The possibilities of hyperlinks are endless.

CBTs are not always meant to teach a specific skill. These CBTs (edutainment CBTs) are perhaps closer to entertainment than education, providing an interesting way to learn more about a favorite hobby or pastime. Microsoft has a nice series of such CBTs, which specialize on a vast array of topics from music to dinosaurs. Another popular program, BodyWorks, explains in detail the workings of the human body. Also see Application, Programming, and Software.

EDUTAINMENT

A nickname given to educational software (CBTs) that also entertain. Children's education software is one example.

HYPERLINKS

Similar to hypertext, but in a different form, such as a picture or an icon (symbol). Hyperlinks connect different sections of a CBT, allowing the user to jump from place to place. It's like jumping back and forth in a book.

ComputerWorks

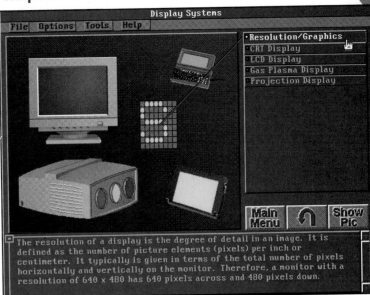

BodyWorks includes both movies and pictures.

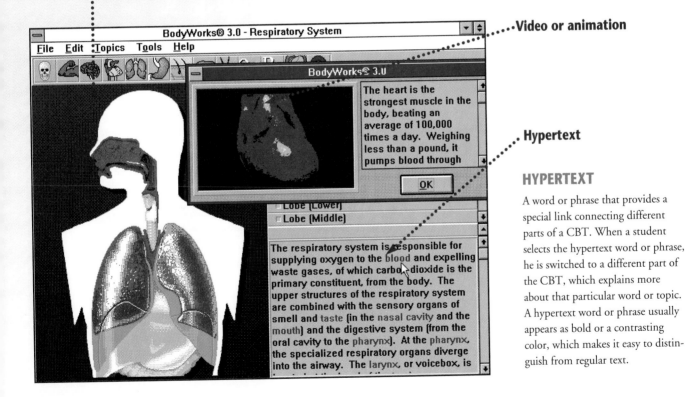

Video or animation

Hypertext

HYPERTEXT

A word or phrase that provides a special link connecting different parts of a CBT. When a student selects the hypertext word or phrase, he is switched to a different part of the CBT, which explains more about that particular word or topic. A hypertext word or phrase usually appears as bold or a contrasting color, which makes it easy to distinguish from regular text.

CompuServe

CompuServe is a popular pay-for-use information service founded in 1977. Started in Columbus, Ohio, CompuServe was originally created as an information service for a local newspaper. CompuServe is more than just a bulletin board service (BBS): with a modem, a user can connect to CompuServe and (for a fee) catch up on the latest breaking news, make travel arrangements, participate in conferences with other users, and download files.

E-mail, or electronic mail, is one reason a lot of people use CompuServe. Through its service, a user can leave a message or send a file (upload) to any other member. He can also receive a message or file (download) from any other member, regardless of where that user lives. Because CompuServe charges for the amount of time a person is connected to its service, most people prepare their electronic message ahead of time, and simply transmit the file.

CompuServe is very large, offering forums (areas of interest) on just about any topic—not all of them related to computers. Because of its size, it is very difficult to find your way around. Most members use a specialized software program that provides easy-to-use menus

Menus within CompuServe Information Manager offer additional options, such as locating a topic.

CompuServe's many services are easy to access using simple icons.

DOWNLOADING

When a user receives computer files through a modem from someone else's computer, the process is called downloading.

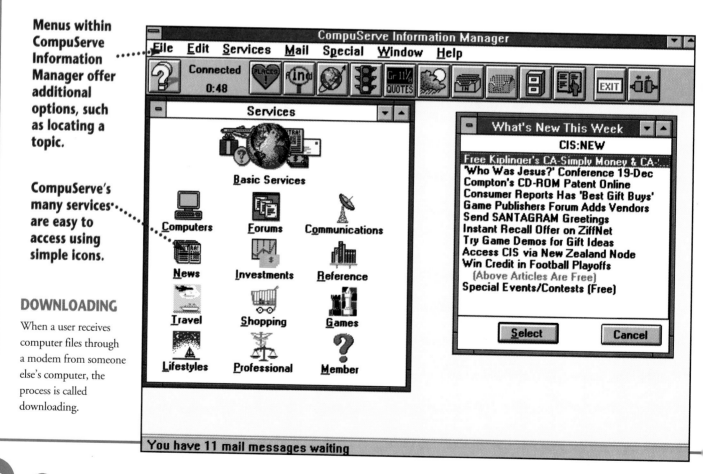

```
WinZip (Unregistered) - H:ENCYCL.ZIP
File   Actions   Options   Help

New   Open   Add   Extract   View   CheckOut

Name          Date      Time    Size   Ratio   Packed   Path
c.doc         01/10/94  16:32   48,128  65%    17,071
clipart1.pcx  01/03/94  17:55   56,661  80%    11,810
command1.pcx  12/21/93  14:39    6,403  96%       278
compusv1.pcx  12/20/93  12:48   67,723  75%    17,417
coreldr1.pcx  12/21/93  13:40   71,534  74%    19,204
coreldr2.pcx  01/10/94  15:45   65,393  77%    15,465

Selected 1 file, 64KB              Total 6 files, 309KB
```

WinZIP is a popular shareware program that allows the user to use PKZIP and other file compression programs with Windows.

and icons for accessing forums, finding information about a specific topic, downloading multiple files unassisted, and so on. One such program is called CompuServe's Information Manager, or CIM.

Downloading files is popular because it provides a great way to try out new programs before purchasing them. CompuServe is filled with shareware programs, which are initially free. If a person decides to keep and use a shareware program, he must pay a fee, but it is usually minimal (around $15). Shareware programs are often written by professional programmers in their spare time, and they are usually just the thing the user needs to solve some computer problem. For example, PKZIP is a shareware program that allows the user to compress files (make them smaller). Smaller files take less time to transmit and take up less storage room on disk—which is a big advantage of compressing files that aren't used every day. WinZip, another shareware program, acts as a Windows interface for PKZIP

and other compression programs. The latest versions of PKZIP and WinZip, like most shareware programs, can be found on CompuServe; however, there is a small one-time fee for using it.

CompuServe includes a number of forums (meeting places where members can find answers to problems, exchange ideas, and download files on specific topics). For example, WordPerfect, a popular word processing program, has its own forum, offering assistance and ideas on using it. Prentice Hall Computer Publishing (of which Alpha Books is a part), has its own forum too! Just type GO PHCP at the CompuServe prompt to find out more about exciting books like this one. There are many other on-line services like CompuServe, such as Prodigy, America OnLine, Delphi, and GEnie. See BBS, Communications, Modem, and Prodigy.

FORUM

A section of CompuServe devoted to a specific topic such as Photography, Games and Entertainment, Science Fiction, etc. Software manufacturers (like Microsoft and Lotus) offer forums so users can find help for their products quickly. Computer manufacturers, such as IBM, Hewlett Packard, and Intel, also offer their own forums. Prentice Hall Computer Publishing has its own forum on CompuServe called PHCP.

MODEM

Short for MOdulator/DEModulator, a modem is an electronic device used for communications between computers via telephone lines. Modems convert digital signals into analog signals and back again.

Modem

UPLOADING

When a user sends computer files through a modem from his PC to another computer, the process is called uploading.

CONFIG.SYS

CONFIG.SYS is a special file, so called because it enables a user to customize (CONFIGure) his computer (SYStem). A CONFIG.SYS file might contain commands to change the type of available memory (RAM), or to load drivers. Drivers are special files that help the computer send data to an optional device such as a mouse, a printer, or a CD-ROM drive. A CONFIG.SYS file might also contain commands that change the operating system defaults. (The system defaults are preset values that the computer uses unless the user specifies something different.)

The CONFIG.SYS (when present) is located in the main directory (root directory) of the PC's hard disk. Although a CONFIG.SYS file is not required, there are not many PC's today that don't have one. For example, a CONFIG.SYS is necessary if the PC has more than 1MB of RAM, a mouse, a CD-ROM drive, or any other special device. When DOS is first installed on the computer, a CONFIG.SYS is automatically created with "suggested commands." The user can edit this starter version to further customize the commands in the CONFIG.SYS to fit his exact needs.

When a computer is turned on or restarted (booted), DOS reads the commands in the CONFIG.SYS file. If a command tells DOS to load a driver file into RAM, it does. DOS also changes the system defaults to match the ones specified in the CONFIG.SYS file. A configuration file similar to

the CONFIG.SYS is the AUTOEXEC.BAT. Like CONFIG.SYS, the commands in the AUTOEXEC.BAT are automatically performed when the system is booted. The CONFIG.SYS contains commands which change the system defaults, whereas the AUTOEXEC.BAT contains

An example of a CONFIG.SYS file

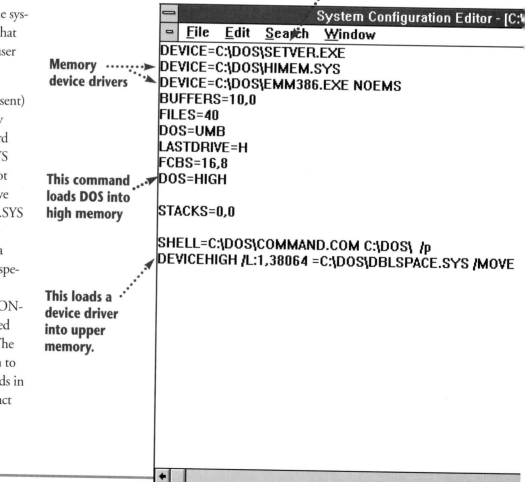

Memory device drivers

This command loads DOS into high memory

This loads a device driver into upper memory.

BOOT

The process of starting or restarting a computer. Booting is the process that the computer goes through to get ready to receive input. During this boot process, certain configuration files, such as the CONFIG.SYS, are used. For example, at startup, the commands in CONFIG.SYS change the system defaults.

regular DOS commands, such as a command to start a program, change the way the DOS prompt looks, or display the current date or time. The AUTOEXEC.BAT, like the CONFIG.SYS, is created with "suggested commands" when DOS is installed on the computer.

Some of the more important commands found in CONFIG.SYS are those which manage memory. Memory device drivers such as HIMEM.SYS and EMM386.EXE allow DOS to use areas of memory it can't access on its own. Another thing the CONFIG.SYS can do is to load device drivers into upper memory. Upper memory is an area

in RAM which DOS uses for its own purposes, not for running programs. High memory is similar; it is usually not used unless DOS itself is loaded there, to get it out of the way. By loading device drivers (and DOS itself) and into upper and high memory, more conventional (regular) memory is left for running programs. Also see AUTOEXEC.BAT, Boot, and DOS.

CONFIGURATION FILES

Special files, such as the AUTOEXEC.BAT and the CONFIG.SYS, that help to define the current operating environment of the computer. For example, configuration files tell the PC what the DOS prompt should look like, what peripheral devices are currently attached, and what parts of memory (RAM) are available.

DOS

Disk Operating System. A software program that tells the computer how to execute its basic tasks (such as displaying a prompt, keeping track of files, and performing commands). DOS acts as the computer's manager, directing tasks and overseeing the different activities requested of the computer.

AUTOEXEC.BAT

Special configuration file containing DOS commands which are automatically performed whenever the system is booted.

DEVICE DRIVER

Program which enables DOS to communicate with some optional device, such as a mouse or a printer, or with areas in memory that DOS can't access by itself.

DEFAULTS

Preset values that DOS uses unless the user overrides them with commands placed in the CONFIG.SYS file.

CorelDRAW!

First introduced in 1989 by Corel Systems Corporation, CorelDRAW! is a drawing program used by professionals to create beautiful artwork. The program includes page layout, charting, and animation capabilities, along with the standard drawing options. CorelDRAW! is available for Windows-based PCs and Macintosh computers.

With a drawing program, a user creates an image by combining such objects as rectangles, circles, and squares to complete a picture. With a professional drawing program like CorelDRAW!, a person can bend and twist the shape of each of these objects until he has the desired effect. Objects can be connected to each other to form a single group, which can then be copied, moved or otherwise manipulated. In addition, an object can be placed in front or in back of another object to partially obscure its outline.

CorelDRAW! includes a toolbar, which is a collection of icons representing various drawing tools such as a pencil or a pen. These tools allow the user to easily copy, move, or change the color or shape of any object. With the Zoom tool, the user can enlarge a specific area of the drawing for detail work.

CorelDRAW! allows users to manipulate text by rotating, curving, and stretching. In addition, CorelDRAW! includes hundreds of unique fonts to create exactly the right mood. A font is any set of characters that share the same typeface (style or design).

Textures can be applied to objects as well. For example, the texture of wood, marble, or a thick carpet can be added to a rectangle to simulate a floor. These textures can be changed to create a custom effect. Other special effects, such as gradients (the gradual fading of one color into another), can also be added to objects in order to make them look more realistic.

CorelDraw! is a full-featured package that includes other programs, such as CorelPHOTO-PAINT, which enables a user to manipulate scanned photos and CorelMOVE, which helps a user create simple animations. In addition, CorelMOSAIC helps the user organize his drawings,

CorelTRACE enables the user to convert bitmapped images into Corel files, and CorelSHOW helps the user to create slide show presentations with his artwork and animations. Also see Desktop Publishing, Drawing Programs, and Graphics.

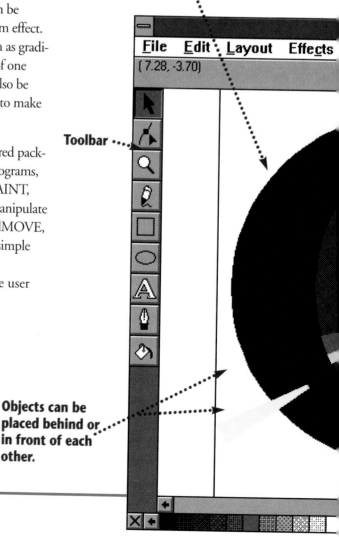

When placed together, these objects form the picture of a CD-ROM.

Toolbar

Objects can be placed behind or in front of each other.

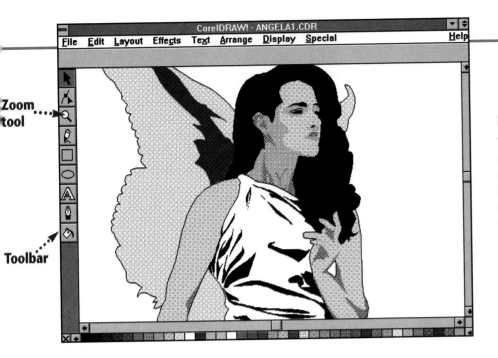

Zoom tool

Toolbar

HANDLES

When an object is selected (clicked on), tiny black boxes mark its edges. These black boxes are called handles, which can be used to resize or move the object.

OBJECT

An item that is considered separate from the drawing as a whole. For example, a rectangle could be one part of the more complex drawing of a PC. Common objects include rectangles, circles, ellipses, and squares. Objects can be combined into larger groups and changed in one step, and they can be stretched

CHARTING PROGRAM

Software that can create various types of charts (graphs) from columns of related numbers. For example, if one sales figure was larger than another, the column (or bar) representing it on a chart would also be larger. The larger sales figure could also be represented by a larger portion of a pie, or a higher line.

FONT

A collection of characters which share the same type style.

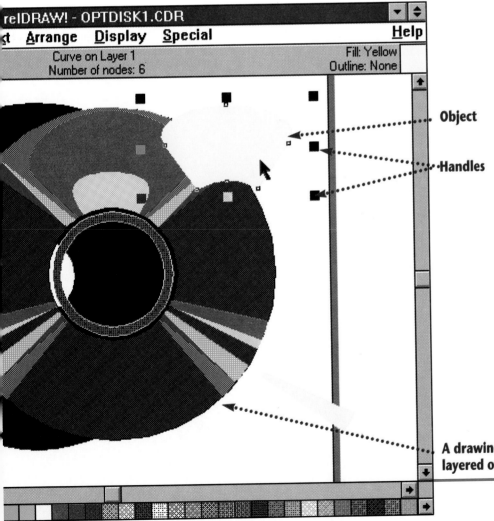

Object

Handles

A drawing is a series of layered objects.

Data

F acts and figures entered and stored in the computer are considered data. Data can be words typed into a word processing document, numbers entered in a spreadsheet file, or art created with a drawing program. The words "data" and "information" are often used interchangeably; however data is actually what is entered into the computer, and information is what the computer outputs.

Data entered into the computer is converted into binary numbers that the computer can understand. A binary numbering system uses only 1's and 0's. The 1's and 0's are represented inside the computer by two electronic states: 1's are ON (high voltage electrical current), and 0's are OFF (low current). Each binary value is equal to one bit. Eight bits make up a byte, which is equivalent to one character (such as the letter D or the number 7).

When a user inputs data, he usually wants to save it so that he can work on it again. Data can be saved in a number of ways. It can be stored on the computer's hard disk drive, located inside the computer's system unit. The hard disk

drive uses non-removable magnetic disks to save information. Data can also be stored on removable magnetic storage devices, such as floppy disks or tape backup units. Data can be retrieved from CD-ROMs, but can not be stored on them by the user. CD-ROMs look similar to audio CDs. Data is stored on a

CD-ROM as microscopic bumps, which are read by a laser in the CD-ROM drive.

The ability to manipulate and store data is what makes the computer such an invaluable tool. Also see Binary, Bit, Byte, Data Storage, and Memory.

BINARY

All computers use a binary system of 1's and 0's that the computer interprets as data and instructions.

01100100

00110111

DRAWING PROGRAMS

Programs created for designing and drawing on the computer. Drawing programs can create art for a myriad of uses, including brochures, letterheads, and other promotional materials.

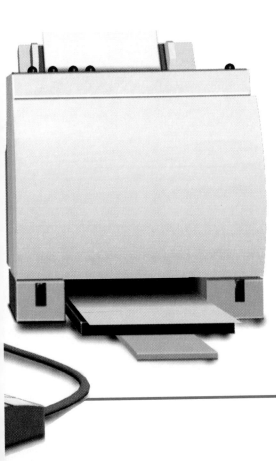

Data is converted into binary numbers before it is stored.

BIT

A binary digit, which represents an on or off state: 1's are ON, and 0's are OFF.

BYTE

A group of eight bits; equivalent to a single alphanumeric character.

WORD PROCESSING

An application that allows a user to manipulate text to create letters, memos, résumés, manuscripts, and other written documents.

SPREADSHEET PROGRAMS

Special applications designed for accounting purposes. Spreadsheet programs can organize numerical data, perform calculations, handle mathematical formulas, and organize data. Spreadsheets enable the user to perform various business analyses and forecasts on complex data.

Data Storage

Hard Drive

Platters

Read/write head

When a computer is processing data, such as making changes to a letter created with a word processing program, that data is stored in electronic form in RAM. RAM (random access memory) is the computer's working area; as such, it's meant only for temporary storage. RAM chips need electricity to store data, even if only temporarily. As soon as the computer is turned off and the flow of electricity stops, anything that is in RAM is lost. If the changes to that letter document were not saved in some type of permanent form (such as on a hard disk drive), the changes would be lost. Because of the temporary nature of RAM, there has to be a permanent way to save data so that a user can work on it again. There are several types of permanent data storage devices available today.

The most common place to store data is on the computer's hard disk drive. The hard disk drive contains a stack of platters covered in a magnetic coating. Data is stored by magnetizing the particles in this coating. Tiny read/write heads float just above the surface of each platter, ready to retrieve (read) or save (write) data. The storage capacity of a hard disk is measured in bytes, ranging from 20 megabytes to 600 megabytes and beyond. Most PCs come with a hard disk that stores at least 80 megabytes (MB) of data.

Another form of data storage is the floppy disk, also called a diskette. A floppy disk is a portable magnetic storage device that is inserted into a floppy disk drive to be used by the computer. Because they do not store a lot of data, floppy disks are typically used in storing copies (backups) of data already on the hard disk. Floppy disks are also convenient for transporting data between PCs. In addition, programs that are installed on the PC usually come on floppy disks. There are two sizes of floppy disks commonly used today: 3.5-inch and 5.25-inch. (Macintosh computers use only the 3.5-inch floppy disks.)

Inside a floppy disk is a thin piece of plastic coated with magnetic material that records data. A 3.5-inch floppy disk holds from 720 kilobytes to 2.88 megabytes of data, depending on its density. A 5.25-inch floppy disk holds from 360 kilobytes to 1.2 megabytes of data, again depending on its density. Floppy disks commonly used today come in two densities: double-density and high-density. A disk's density determines the amount of data it is capable of storing—the higher the density, the greater the storage capacity.

Yet another form of magnetic data storage is the tape drive. Tape drives store data onto tape cartridges similar

Tape Drive

to audio cassettes (but slightly different). Tape drives are mainly used to back up information from the hard disk drive in case the drive fails, which they all inevitably do. Storage tapes come in different sizes: .25-inch (also called quarter inch cartridge or QIC), 8 millimeter, and 4 millimeter (also called digital audio tape or DAT). These tapes can store anywhere from 20 megabytes to 10 gigabytes of data.

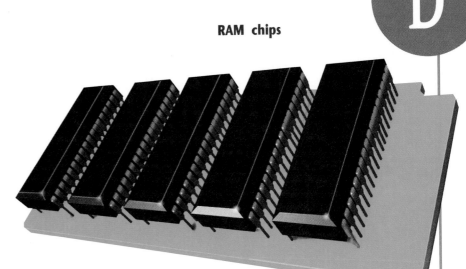

RAM chips

MEGABYTE

Made up of 1,048,576 bytes, this is equivalent to 500 double-spaced pages of text.

BYTE

A group of eight bits; equivalent to a single alphanumeric character.

GIGABYTE

Made up of 1,073,741,824 bytes, this is equivalent to a half-million double-spaced pages of text.

DATA COMPRESSION

A process that makes it possible to store a file in a smaller amount of space than it is normally stored in. The compression process analyzes the order of characters within a file and encodes them so that the original order can be remembered. For example, the phrase, "The Man and the Woman" might be compressed to "The Man and 1 Wo2," which takes less space to store. Data compression is most often used for files that are rarely used, files sent over a phone line with modems, or large files exchanged by users on floppy disks.

Floppy disk drives

5.25-inch floppy disk
5.25-inch drive
3.5-inch drive
3.5-inch floppy disk

continues

Data Storage continued

CD ....

A tape drive writes a copy of the hard disk data onto the tape cartridges for backup. Tape backups are easy to perform since they can be set up to run at a specific time, like an alarm that periodically "goes off" without the user doing anything. Because of this capability, tape backups are often performed late at night so that they don't inconvenience users; yet they are done often enough that they could provide a backup copy of recent data if needed. Tape drives are always found on network servers (PCs with a large storage capacity). But as the storage capacity of the hard disks in individual PCs continues to grow, tape drives are becoming more popular as a regular storage option.

Optical storage devices are another option for saving computer data. Instead of storing data magnetically, optical storage media use lasers to record and store data. One such storage device is the CD-ROM (Compact Disk Read-Only Memory). CD-ROM discs look just like audio CDs. They can hold more than 600 megabytes of information, which makes them ideal for storing books, art, games, and software programs. Data stored on a traditional CD-ROM cannot be changed; however, writable CD-ROM drives (called CD-R) are beginning to appear. These discs allow users to write data onto a CD one time only.

Similar to CD-ROMs is an optical storage technology called WORM, write once read many. As with a CD-ROM, data is written to the WORM optical disk once and then cannot be changed—yet it can be accessed numerous times. Having a WORM drive is like having a CD-ROM factory, because a user can write the non-changeable data to the disc. WORM technology is useful for businesses or organizations that keep large databases and enormous catalogs of information.

Magneto-optical disks are combinations of both magnetic and optical data storage technologies. Magneto-optical disks are rewritable optical disks that look like floppy disks but are thicker. Inside the plastic cover is an optical disk that can store 88 times the amount of data of a regular 3.5-inch floppy disk (approximately 128 megabytes). A 5.25-inch mag-

neto-optical disk can store up to 650 megabytes of data. Data on a magneto-optical disk is changed by a fine laser beam that heats the magnetic particles trapped in the plastic.

Floptical disks combine magnetic and optical technologies, but in a very different manner. Floptical technology, created by Insite Peripherals, Inc., records data magnetically just like a regular floppy disk. The greater storage capacity is a result of a laser that tunes the read/write heads so finely that data can be placed closer together. Because flopticals are basically better-designed floppy disks, most hard disk drives can take either 3.5-inch floptical disks or 3.5-inch standard floppy disks. A floptical disk can store 21 megabytes of data—14 times the capacity of a standard 3.5-inch disk. Also see CD-ROM, Floppy Disk, Floppy Disk Drive, Hard Disk Drive, Laptop Computer, Memory, Optical Disk, RAM, System Unit, and Tape Backup Unit.

Magneto-optical disk

How Does It Work? D

Currently, the most common method of data storage is magnetic storage. Before any data can be stored on a magnetic disk, the disk must be formatted. Formatting a disk erases any data on the disk, then divides it into sections. Tiny magnetic codes on the surface of the disk mark each section. These codes divide the disk into sectors (pie-like slices) and tracks (concentric circles around the disk). Sectors and tracks help to organize the placement of data and make it easy to relocate again when needed.

After a disk is formatted, data can be written to it. The read-write head places data on the disk by changing the alignment of iron particles that are scattered over the magnetic surface. Electricity pulses through the read-write head turning it into a magnet. As it passes over the disk, the read-write head changes the position of the iron particles in the magnetic coating to represent bits of data. Each bit is equal to a binary digit, 1 or 0, that the computer reads as data.

Database

A database is a collection of related information, such as a list of addresses, merchandise inventories, library books, patient records, bank accounts, or personnel records. Before computers, common databases included information kept on index cards in rolodexes, library card catalogs, and address books. Keeping track of such information is time consuming, and those items are prone to error or damage. With today's computers, large amounts of information can easily be placed in databases, sorted electronically, retrieved with the touch of a button, and printed in reports. Popular database programs include dBASE, Paradox, FoxPro, Microsoft Access, and Lotus Approach.

A database is composed of fields and records. The structure of a database may vary from program to program, but generally the data is organized into columns and rows. A record, which might comprise a row in the database, is a set of all the information about a single person, place, or thing. For example, the name, address, city, state, and ZIP code of a single customer would comprise a record. A field, which might form a column in the database, is a space for a specified piece of information

that the user would fill in for most (if not all) records. For example, a database could have a ZIP code field that would be filled with the ZIP codes of the customers in the database. Filling in several fields of information for one record makes a complete entry in the database. Some database programs allow the user to customize the way in which fields and records are entered, eliminating the formal columns and rows that are seen here. For example, a user could set up his database so that one record is entered into a

single screen, is saved, and is then cleared in order to enter the next record.

There are two types of databases available: relational and flat-file. Relational databases allow the user to inter-relate data from more than one database file. For example, a database file containing client information can be combined with a database file containing inventory pricing information to create an invoice detailing a client's purchase. In

te	PostalCode	Hc
	46290	000-0
	46038	000-0
	46032	000-0
	46033	000-0
	46287	000-0
	46038	000-0
	46032	000-0
	69594	000-0
	68950	000-0
	65849	000-0
	58949	000-0
	61701	000-0
	46293	000-0
	46038	000-0
	89706	000-0
	23019	000-0
	98765	000-0
	98066	000-0
	21938	000-0
	10029	000-0
	46389	000-0
	46389	000-0
	65948	000-0
	69850	000-0
	46859	000-0
	46980	000-0

NUM

addition, relational databases allow the user to easily add, delete, or rearrange the fields within each record of the database. In a flat-file database, files cannot be combined and related. In addition, flat-file databases do not allow fields to be added or deleted once the records contain data. However, flat-file databases are simpler than relational databases and are easier to learn how to use. A flat-file database is ideal for single-purpose use, such as an address book or client list.

Databases are commonly used by large and small businesses, universities, and home computer users. Databases are an exceptional tool for keeping track of large amounts of information. Also see Access, Application, Approach, Data, dBASE, and Paradox.

Relational databases allow a person to use separate database files to exchange data and create new files. The way this works is that the user identifies a key field that is the same in both databases. For example, consider a file that contains a list of client names and their purchases, and another file that contains inventory prices. A key field, such as a product ID number, can be used to relate a particular customer's name (from the first file) to a particular item and its price (from the second file) in order to create an invoice.

FIELD

In most databases, a field is stored in a column. Each field contains a specified piece of information that a user would fill in for most (if not all) records. For example, a database could have a ZIP code field that would be filled with the ZIP codes of the customers in the database.

INVOICE

GREAT LAKES FOOD MARKET
HOWARD SNYDER

	TOFU		
1	UNCLE BOB'S		TOTAL
		$50.00	100.00
		20.00	20.00
	SUBTOTAL		$120.00
	TAX		$12.00
	TOTAL		$132.00

RECORD

In most databases, a record is stored in a row. Each record contains pieces of information about a person, a thing, or an event. For example, all of the information about one person (such as his name, title, address, and phone number) would be contained in a single record.

dBASE

dBASE is a popular relational database management system currently owned by Borland. Database programs are designed to organize large quantities of data, such as address lists, merchandise records, payroll information, and more. Data can quickly be sorted and retrieved, as well as presented in reports and analyzed. Introduced in 1981, dBASE is noted for being the first comprehensive database management system designed for the personal computer. Until that time, databases were used exclusively with large mainframe computers.

dBASE owes it's origins to C. Wayne Ratliffe, who designed the program to handle a company football pool. It was originally named Vulcan, and was modeled after another database management system used by Jet Propulsion Laboratories in Los Angeles. dBASE II, marketed by Ashton-Tate Corporation, was released for personal computers in 1981 and became a big success because it was the first database management system for PCs. However, dBASE was difficult to learn back then, since all the user saw was the now famous "dot prompt," a single dot on-screen, which showed that dBASE was waiting for the user's command. Since that time, dBASE has come a long way. In 1984, dBASE III was introduced for the IBM PC. It was more powerful and could handle larger databases, but it still contained the unfriendly dot prompt. Then in 1986, dBASE III

Plus was released, offering a friendly menu-driven interface that dominated the database market.

Unfortunately, dBASE IV (released in 1988) contained many errors that were not corrected for over a year. Later, dBASE Mac was introduced, but to much criticism; regrettably the program was incompatible with dBASE for the PC.

In 1991, Ashton-Tate and dBASE were acquired by Borland International. dBASE remains one of the most widely used database system for the PC, although it is losing ground because a Windows version of dBASE does not currently exist. Also see Access, Application, Approach, Borland, Data, Database, and Paradox.

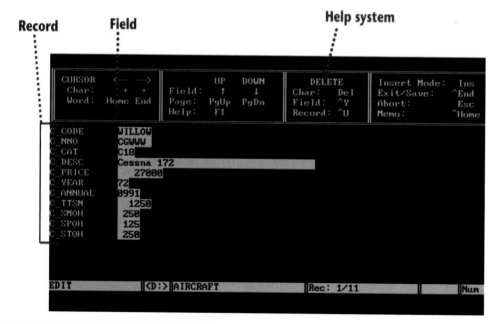

Record   **Field**

Help system

DBMS

DataBase Management System. A software program that controls the organization, storage, and retrieval of information found in a database. Additionally, a DBMS can provide security to prevent unauthorized usage.

RELATIONAL DATABASE

A database that allows the user to inter-relate data between two or more files.

Defragmentation

To understand what defragmentation is, a person must first understand how data files are saved onto magnetic storage disks. Whether on a floppy disk or a hard disk, data is stored in a certain format. Formatting consists of dividing a disk into organized sections so that data can be located by the computer. Formatting organizes disks into concentric rings called tracks. Tracks are divided into sectors (pie shaped wedges) in which files and parts of files are stored.

Some files are larger than others and require more storage space. Such files are often stored in several neighboring sectors on the disk, called a cluster. As files are deleted from a disk, various sectors become available. The next time a file is saved, the computer tries to use the newly available sectors. If those sectors aren't large enough to hold the complete file, the remaining parts of the file are stored in one or more other sectors.

Obviously this results in a file being broken into pieces and scattered over the disk. This doesn't present a huge problem, since the operating system keeps track of the location of the different parts. However, when a file is fragmented, it takes a longer period of time for the computer to locate all of the pieces of information that make up the complete file. As more and more files are fragmented over the disk, the computer slows down noticeably.

Defragmentation alleviates this problem by rewriting the files so that they are again stored on neighboring clusters. This procedure results in a significant improvement in file retrieval time.

DOS version 6.x includes a defragmentor for taking care of this problem. In addition to DOS 6, there are

A fragmented disk stores parts of a file in different areas on the disk.

special programs (such as DiskExpress and PowerUp for the Macintosh, and DOS Rx for the PC) that can be purchased for defragmenting files. Utility packages, such as PC Tools and Norton Utilities, also include a defragmentor. Also see Data Storage, File, Floppy Disk, Format, Hard Disk Drive, Norton Utilities, and PC Tools.

FILE

A document, spreadsheet, graphic, or other item created with a computer program and saved with a unique name.

MAGNETIC STORAGE

A type of computer storage that relies on magnetically coated disks or tape cartridges to store bits of data.

A defragmented disk stores files in adjacent sectors.

Density

Density reflects the closeness of data on a disk: the closer the data is, the more dense a disk is said to be. Of course, when data is placed closer together (more densely), a disk can store more data. Floppy disks, which are magnetic data storage devices, come in two commonly used sizes: 3.5-inch and 5.25-inch. Both sizes are available in two densities: double-density and high-density.

Inside a floppy disk is a thin piece of film with a magnetic coating. The magnetic coating is where data is stored. Density refers to the amount of magnetic particles in the coating. Regardless of the size of the particle, it can only store one piece of

data. A high-density disk has smaller magnetic particles, which allows more particles to fit on a disk, and makes it possible for the disk to store more data. A double-density disk has larger particles that are not so tightly packed; therefore, it holds less data. (A hard disk, by the way, uses a different type of magnetic material that is much more dense than the magnetic material used on any floppy disk. This allows a hard disk to hold a lot more data.)

A 3.5-inch double-density disk can hold 720 kilobytes of data. A 3.5-inch high-density disk can hold 1.44 megabytes of data. A 3.5-inch disk can only be used in a 3.5-inch floppy disk drive. A 5.25-inch double-density disk can hold 360 kilobytes of data, and a 5.25-inch high-density disk can hold 1.2 megabytes. A 5.25-inch disk can only be used

in a 5.25-inch floppy drive. It is also important to know what type of density the floppy drive is made to handle. Most new disk drives are high-capacity drives, and can handle both high-density and double-density disks. However, older drives were low-capacity and can only handle double-density disks. Also see Data Storage, Floppy Disk, Floppy Disk Drive, and Format.

KILOBYTE

A standard unit used to measure storage, memory, or the size of a file. A kilobyte is equal to 1,024 bytes.

FLOPPY DISK DRIVE

A device used to read and write data to and from floppy disks. Drives are available in different sizes and densities.

MEGABYTE

Made up of 1,048,576 bytes, this is equivalent to 500 double-spaced pages of text.

BYTE

A group of eight bits; equivalent to a single alphanumeric character.

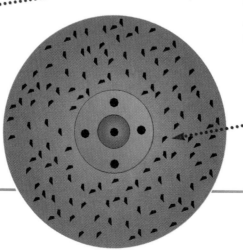

Double-density

High-density

Desktop Publishing

Computer programs that incorporate text, graphics, and page layout are referred to as desktop publishing programs (DTP). Desktop publishing programs are used to create newsletters, brochures, manuals, and other types of printed materials.

Traditional printing methods are very costly, requiring the services of many production personnel to create a professionally printed piece. The methods are also time consuming, and last-minute changes escalate the costs even further. The advent of desktop publishing (publishing with a computer) has considerably reduced publication costs, improved timeliness, and made last-minute changes relatively painless. Popular desktop publishing programs include sophisticated programs such as PageMaker, Quark Xpress, and Ventura Publisher. Less complex desktop publishing programs

A newsletter created with PageMaker by Aldus

include Microsoft Publisher, Publish It!, and Express Publisher.

Desktop publishing programs owe their origins to word processing software. Early word processing programs not only allowed the user to work with words, but also included features that controlled how text fit on a page, and options such as changing the styling and size of text. With the introduction of WYSIWYG (What-You-See-Is-What-You-Get) software, the user could also see on-screen how the text would look when printed. Additionally, high-quality laser printers threw open the door to do-it-yourself publishing, making desktop publishing on the computer a mainstay of the computer industry. This book was designed and laid out using desktop publishing software for the Macintosh.

continues

Desktop Publishing
continued

With desktop publishing programs (such as PageMaker by Aldus, and Ventura Publisher by Ventura Software), users can merge text and graphics with a variety of special features (for example, borders or magazine-style columns) to create printed materials for business, educational, and home use. Simpler desktop publishing programs exist, such as Publish It!, Express Publisher, and Microsoft

Publisher for Windows, that are a little less complicated. In addition, all of today's leading word processors (Word for Windows, Ami Pro, etc.) include some desktop publishing features. Also see Graphics Programs, PageMaker, and Word Processing.

In a high-end desktop publishing program such as PageMaker, the text and graphics for the finished piece are traditionally created elsewhere. For example, a newsletter article is often created in a word processor, edited, spell checked, and then saved. Likewise, the art is drawn in a drawing program and saved. These separate pieces are then imported or brought into PageMaker and laid out on the page.

Desktop publishing programs give the user total control over each piece of a newsletter, brochure, or pamphlet. But they do not offer the same capabilities that word processors do for editing text, or the capabilities that graphics programs do for manipulating images. More and more, however, the lines between these separate programs are fading as applications add more features.

WYSIWYG

What-You-See-Is-What-You-Get. WYSIWYG software displays a file on-screen just as it would appear when printed.

WORD PROCESSING PROGRAM

Software designed specifically to work with text. Documents created with word processing programs include memos, letters, and manuscripts.

Device Driver

A device driver is a special program that handles communication between the computer and a peripheral device, such as a printer or mouse. For example, many computers do not initially come with a mouse. To add the use of a mouse, a mouse driver must be installed so the computer will know how to understand the mouse's signals and can tell the mouse how to work.

When a device driver is installed, the program is copied onto the PC's hard disk. From then on, the device driver must be loaded onto the computer's memory whenever the computer is powered on or restarted. From memory, the device driver can help the operating system communicate with the device (such as a mouse). In DOS, the device driver is loaded into memory with a command placed in a special file called the CONFIG.SYS. This file is called CONFIG.SYS because it enables the user to customize (CONFIGure) their computer (SYStem).

A device driver can also be used to help the operating system communicate with an area of memory it ordinarily does not use. DOS, for example, was designed to use only a small amount of memory—which seemed like a lot at the time PCs were invented. Today, computers use a lot of memory, and in order to get DOS to communicate with these larger amounts of memory, special memory drivers are used. They work the same way as other device drivers do: the memory driver is copied onto the hard disk and activated with a command in the CONFIG.SYS. Also see CONFIG.SYS, DOS, Memory, and Peripherals.

CONFIG.SYS FILE

The CONFIG.SYS is a special DOS file that enables the user to customize their computer. A CONFIG.SYS file might contain commands to change the type of available memory (RAM), or to load device drivers

DEFAULTS

Preset values that DOS uses unless the user overrides them by placing commands in the CONFIG.SYS file.

Impact 9000

Impact 9000

3 The arrow is moved on-screen.

Device Driver

2 The device driver detects the mouse movement.

PERIPHERALS

Additional hardware components that are attached to the computer, such as printers, modems, and scanners.

1 The user moves the mouse.

DIP Switch

S hort for Dual In-line Package, a DIP switch is a set of tiny toggles or switches that are encased in plastic and attached to a circuit board. Think of a DIP switch as a light switch with only two settings: ON or OFF. By changing the switches to either ON or OFF, the user can set defaults for his computer (the values that a computer uses when it is started up). The computer checks the DIP switches every time it is turned on to see what special settings or information should be used when working with a particular component. DIP switches are commonly found in printers, modems, and on some expansion cards (such as network cards).

DIP switches look like tiny ON/OFF switches lined up in a single row. They turn a circuit on or off, activating options on a computer component. The more complex the option is, the more switches that might be used to represent it. Because of their tiny size, the switches can be changed by using the point of a pencil to slide them into the on or off positions. Most DIP switches come in groups of four or eight.

The DIP switches are checked by the computer every time it is turned on. Although the switches may be changed, the new settings will not take effect until the computer is shut off and restarted again. DIP switches are quite common in older machines, but are now being replaced by software-based selections (selections made through a special program) in newer computers. Also see Expansion Card, Motherboard, and System Unit.

For an example of DIP switches, consider the common printer, a peripheral device that usually uses DIP switches. A printer may have four fonts (type styles) available for use, each one of which is represented by a particular setting of the DIP switches. For example, the first font may be represented by two DIP switches turned to the off position. The next font may be represented by one switch set to the off position and another set to the on position. Anytime the user wishes to reset the printer's font, the DIP switches must be changed to the setting that represents that font.

Even printers are becoming more modern, however. Today, it is not unusual to be able to change these same font options through a computerized display area on the front of the printer. Using a display is much more convenient and friendly than using DIP switches, which are often difficult to get to and to understand.

DIP switches

DEFAULTS
The values that the computer uses unless the user overrides them by inputting different values.

TOGGLE
Device that can be set to either ON or OFF, like a light switch.

Directories

Directories are like electronic filing cabinet drawers that the computer uses to organize the files on hard disks and floppy disks. Directories are used to store similar files in the same logical area on the disk, making it much easier to locate them again when needed. For example, all the files associated with Excel (a popular spreadsheet program) could be stored in one directory, making them easy to locate. In the analogy of a filing cabinet, the Excel directory would be like a drawer in the cabinet, holding lots of files ("file folders" that contain information). Some directories are automatically created during the installation procedure of a program, while other directories are created by the user.

Directories can also contain other directories called subdirectories. For example, Word for Windows (a word processing program) comes with clip art (pictures that can be used in letters, memos, etc.) that are stored in a subdirectory off of the main Word for Windows directory. To visualize what a subdirectory is, picture a hallway instead of a filing cabinet. Off the hallway, there are many rooms (directories), each with its own special purpose. The Word for Windows directory would be one of these "rooms." Inside the Word for Windows "room," one might find several closets, with labels identifying their contents. The clip art subdirectory would be one of these "closets." Files are placed in directories and subdirectories; so some files would be stored within the Word for Windows "room," and other files would be stored within the clip art "closet."

Directories are structured with one main directory, called the root directory, and additional directories that branch off of it. Using the room/closet analogy, think of the root directory as being the hallway. All directories branch

Files

Directories

off of this hallway. Because the whole structure is hierarchical, with many directories branching out from the root directory, it is referred to as a directory tree. Also see Data Storage, Files.

WORDPERFECT

DOS

EXCEL

WINDOWS

continues

Directories
continued

SUBDIRECTORY

A directory within any main directory.

FILE

A document, spreadsheet, graphic, or other item created with a computer program and saved with a unique name.

PATH

The part of a DOS command that tells the operating system where to locate a file.

A DOS directory tree

ROOT DIRECTORY

The main directory in a directory tree from which all other directories spring.

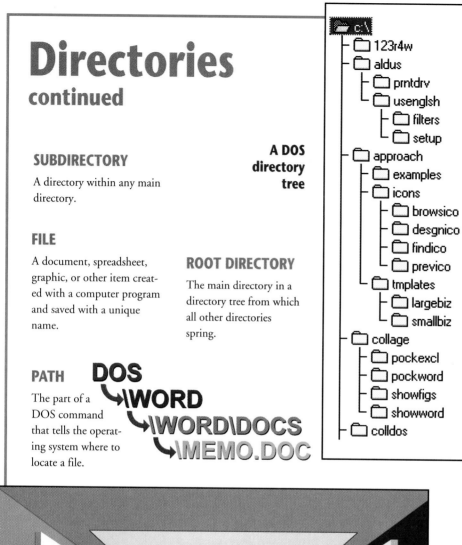

DOS
↳ **\WORD**
↳ **\WORD\DOCS**
↳ **\MEMO.DOC**

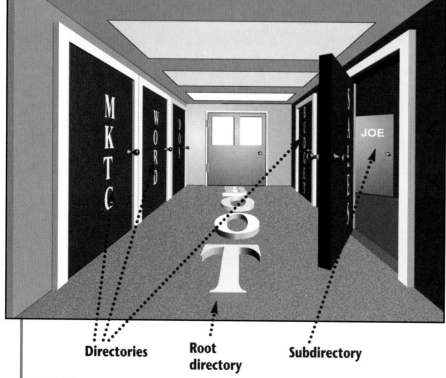

Directories   Root directory   Subdirectory

Most applications include a graphical representation of this directory tree to help a user locate his files. Therefore, all the user has to do is move from branch to branch on the tree until the correct files are displayed. Then he simply selects the file he wants to use.

In an operating system like DOS, it might be necessary to type out the path that DOS must follow to find the file. (It's kind of like telling a friend how to find the post office; DOS is very slow and must be told everything exactly. The DOS path consists of three parts. The first part is the drive the file is located on, followed by a colon, as in C: (the hard disk is usually named C). A backslash (\) is added, followed by the name of the directory in which the file is located. For example, to locate the file SMITH.DOC created with the WordPerfect program, the user might type this path: C:\WP\SMITH.DOC. Subdirectories are separated with another backslash.

DOS

DOS, short for Disk Operating System, is a standard operating system introduced by Microsoft Corporation in 1981. DOS provides the most basic instructions the computer needs to operate. DOS tells the computer how to process information, how to manage files and directories, and how to interpret commands.

DOS owes it's origins to CP/M, an early operating system for PCs that never really caught on. DOS was first developed by a small company in Seattle, Washington, but was purchased by Microsoft who refined it and sold it to IBM as the operating system for their IBM-PC. DOS was shipped with all IBM PCs and marketed as PC-DOS. Microsoft also supplied the operating system to companies manufacturing IBM-PC compatible computers, calling the version MS-DOS. Both MS-DOS and PC-DOS are virtually the same, although PC-DOS is designed to run on IBM PCs, and not compatibles. The widespread popularity of the IBM-PC and its clones made DOS the standard operating system for the personal computer.

It has gone through many improvements, and is now available as MS-DOS version 6.2.

Operating systems like DOS are essential for a computer to function. They oversee the many tasks and behind-the-scenes activities that make the computer an invaluable tool. DOS manages the computer's storage devices, data files, and peripherals (such as a printer or a mouse). DOS also manages the requests of software programs running on the computer, and provides the user with an interface for communicating with the computer itself. (DOS is the operating system found on IBM PCs and compatibles. Macintosh computers use an operating system called System. OS/2 is an alternative operating system for IBM PCs and compatibles, which features multitasking—the ability to run two programs at the same time. DR DOS is an operating system similar to MS-DOS but with a few more features.).

DOS is a command-driven program, meaning that commands given to the operating system are

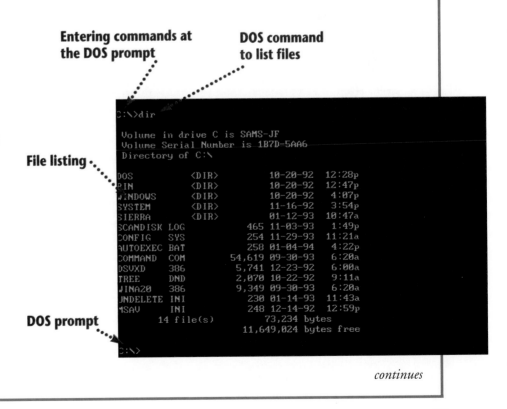

Entering commands at the DOS prompt

DOS command to list files

File listing

DOS prompt

continues

DOS continued

typed in. Command-driven programs require users to type commands in an exact way in order to be understood. This makes DOS a bit difficult to work with. However, with MS-DOS version 5.0, a menu-driven interface was added as an optional feature, called the DOS Shell. With the DOS Shell, the mouse is used to select commands that are represented by graphical pictures so

the user doesn't have to memorize and type in commands. With MS-DOS 6.2, the Shell was dropped as a feature because most people use Windows and don't actually type commands anymore anyway. Also see AUTOEXEC.BAT, BIOS, Boot, Commands, CONFIG.SYS, Microsoft, and Operating System.

PC-DOS

IBM's version of Microsoft DOS (MS-DOS).

DR DOS

A competitive disk operating system created by Digital Research that is comparable to MS-DOS.

DOS PROMPT

An on-screen prompt where DOS commands are entered. The DOS prompt typically looks like C:\>.

How Does It Work?

The disk operating system (DOS) is made up of three parts: IO.SYS, MSDOS.SYS, and COMMAND.COM. IO.SYS works with ROM BIOS to control the computer's input/output functions; MSDOS.SYS (sometimes called the kernel) manages files, runs programs, and performs basicsystemfunctions; COMMAND.COM performs all the DOS commands. In addition, COMMAND.COM functions as the overall "manager" for the computer.

COMMAND.COM is kept in memory at all times so that DOS commands (such as COPY) can be executed when needed. If a program needs that memory for processing, COMMAND.COM is over-written. If it's needed later on, COMMAND.COM is copied back into memory.

Drive icons

Directory tree

File listing

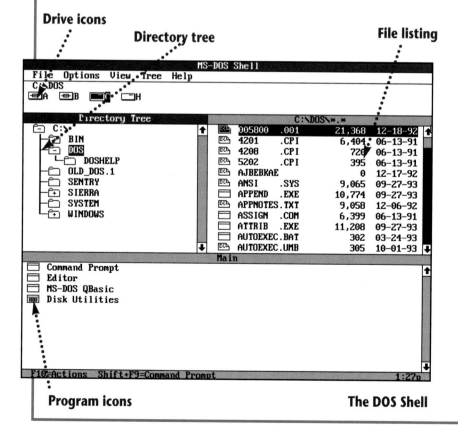

Program icons

The DOS Shell

KERNEL

The core portions of an operating system that control the most essential tasks, such as how input, output, and memory is managed.

Drawing Programs

A drawing program is a special application that allows the user to create illustrations on the computer. A drawing program uses objects, such as squares, circles, rectangles, and lines to create a picture. Objects can be connected to each other to form a single group that can be copied, moved, or otherwise manipulated.

Drawing programs are different than painting programs in that painting programs keep track of every dot that makes up an image. Drawing programs treat each graphic object as a mathematical formula, rather than a pattern of dots. The formula contains specific codes that tell the program how to display and print the object as a series of smooth lines.

The user never sees the formula or works directly with it; however, it is the use of the formula that makes the graphic objects so easy to work with. For example, because a circle object is seen as a formula and not a series of dots, a user could twist and enlarge the circle without any distortion—the drawing program would simply adjust the formula and redraw the image.

Drawing programs include a toolbar, which is a collection of icons representing various drawing tools, such as a pencil or a pen. These tools allow the user to easily copy, move, or change the color or shape of any object. With a magnification tool, the user can enlarge a specific area of the drawing for detail work.

Drawing programs usually include a feature that allows the artist to manipulate text by rotating, curving, and stretching. In addition, they often include a feature that allows the artist to create the right "texture" for an object, adding realism. For example, the texture of water could be added to a flattened circle, creating a realistic lake or pond. Other special effects such as gradients (the gradual fading of one color into another) can also be added to objects in order to make them appear more realistic.

Drawing programs include such popular software as Adobe's Illustrator, CorelDRAW!, and SuperPaint. These programs are used to illustrate and design books, brochures, presentations, and more. Also see CorelDRAW!, Desktop Publishing, Graphics Programs, and Paint Programs.

OBJECT

An item that is considered separate from the drawing as a whole. Common objects include rectangles, circles, ellipses, and squares. Objects can be stretched and shaped to create any form.

CLIP ART

A collection of graphics that are stored on disk and used in various software programs.

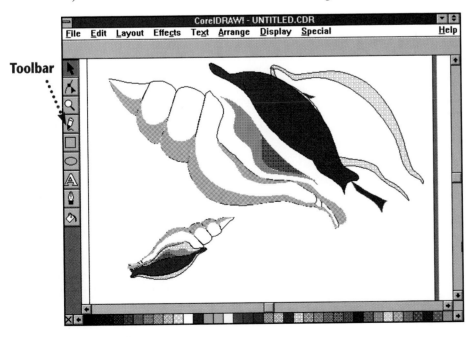

Toolbar

The CorelDRAW! drawing program

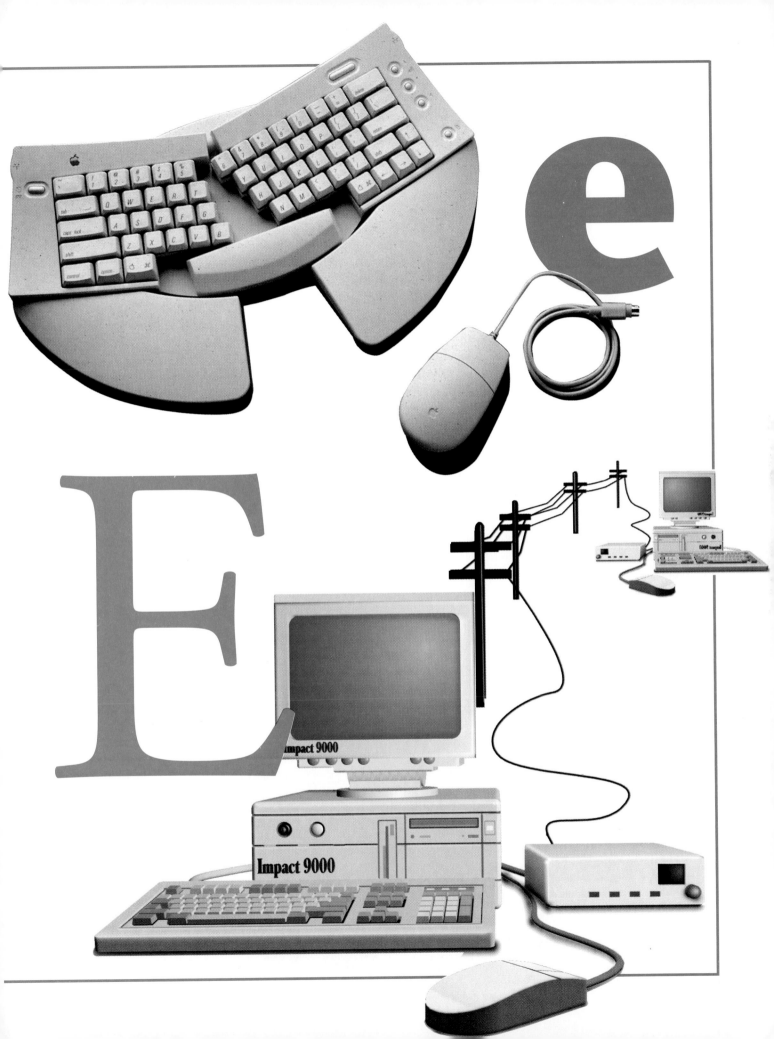

Electronic Mail

Electronic mail (e-mail) provides a method of sending messages and memos across a network or by modem. It works much like the postal service does, in that a message is sent to a person with a specific address. The "address" in this case is the user's name (usually some abbreviated form of the person's name), followed by the name of the "post office" (network server) to which that person is attached. E-mail can be sent to an individual, or it can be sent to many addresses at once.

E-mail is often used within corporations because it's convenient and fast, and it saves paper. E-mail can also be sent by modem to an on-line information service, such as CompuServe or America OnLine. To send the e-mail message via an on-line service (such as CompuServe, Prodigy, or MCI

Mail), a user simply connects to that service using his modem, and then sends the message file to the intended recipient. The recipient is notified that he has a message the next time he uses the service. The process for sending and retrieving e-mail is the same whether it's done through an inter-office network or by modem (the latter just requires different software and a modem). There are also services like MCI Mail that are

specifically set up for electronic mail and that can be accessed with a modem (for a fee). Popular e-mail programs include cc:Mail by Lotus Corporation and Microsoft Mail. Also see Communication, CompuServe, Modem, Network, and Prodigy.

Impact 9000

Impact 9000

How Does It Work?

To send an electronic mail message with an inter-office network, a user runs the e-mail software, types the message, and then "sends" it to the recipient. The e-mail software then "attaches" the network address for this user to the message, to identify the person for whom the message is intended.

The message itself is not actually "sent" anywhere; it is simply stored in a special directory on the network server (the central computer to which all the network users are connected). So "sending" a message simply makes that message accessible to the recipient. In addition, most e-mail systems allow the sender to "attach" additional information to the message, such as a database, spreadsheet, word processing, or chart file.

When the recipient logs on (connects) to the network, he will be notified that he has new mail. The recipient can read the message, delete it, forward it, print it out, and so on (depending upon the particular e-mail system).

ON-LINE INFORMATION SERVICE

An electronic service that allows a user to send and receive mail, shop, talk to other users in a forum, and so on. The services charge a monthly fee, which usually covers a specific amount of on-line time and allows the subscriber to send a certain number of mail messages.

NETWORK

Two or more computers connected to each other (or to a network server) by cables. The users of the computers are able to share data files and printers and to communicate with each other with e-mail messages (if they have the software).

MODEM

A device used to communicate with other computers across telephone lines.

Recipients

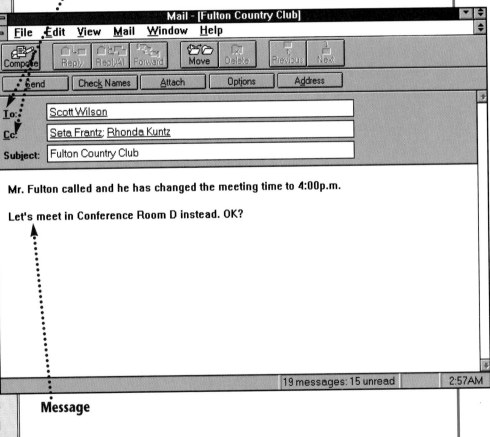

Message

NETWORK SERVER

The main computer that manages the network. It normally has a huge hard drive and runs the software that maintains the network. This large hard drive also houses the programs and files that network users share. Each computer that is connected to the server is called a workstation.

Ergonomics

Ergonomics is the science that studies how to best create a comfortable and safe working environment in which people can be productive without pain. For example, there are certain ways a person should sit in a chair if he wants to be comfortable and reduce pain and pressure to the lower back (especially if he will be sitting for long periods of time). Most computer furniture and peripheral manufacturers are now taking ergonomic considerations into account when designing their merchandise because workers' pain and discomfort not only lowers productivity, it also increases medical costs.

Ergonomics has become a real concern recently, mainly because the number of workers who regularly use computers has increased in the last decade. The problem arose when companies incorporated technological advancements (such as using word processing programs on the PC instead of using a typewriter) without adjusting work environments. People who were used to springy typewriter keys and manual carriage returns started to experience wrist and hand pain when using their computers.

The cause of the pain eventually became apparent: the workers were holding their wrists at unnatural angles for extended periods of time with no breaks. The actual pain is caused by pressure on the median nerve, a nerve that runs through the carpal tunnel of the wrist. (The carpal tunnel is a circle of eight bones in the wrist through which nerves and tendons run to the hand.) When the nerve is pinched or compressed, it causes numbness, tingling, and pain in the fingers. The condition is called Carpal Tunnel Syndrome (CTS), and it is becoming increasingly common in workers who spend long hours typing on keyboards. The syndrome used to be considered an excuse for lazy workers to stop working, but as more cases were reported, it was soon evident that the most diligent workers were affected because they were more likely to type longer without breaks.

Carpel tunnel

Median nerve

Courtesy of Apple Computer, Inc.

An ergonomic adjustable keyboard by Apple Computers.

Carpal Tunnel Syndrome has recently been compared to other repetitive stress injuries (RSIs), which until now have mainly been associated with factory workers and people whose jobs require them to perform the same action repeatedly. RSI is not a new phenomenon; it already costs about $7 billion a year from lost worker productivity combined with medical costs. With more and more workers developing Carpal Tunnel Syndrome, that number will probably skyrocket—unless employers can improve their workers' environments.

Simple equipment improvements that can be made to a computing area include:

■ **Wrist rests** A small foam-covered, shelf-like unit placed in front of a keyboard on which the typist can rest his wrists. A wrist rest helps to ensure that the wrists are flat (parallel to the floor), which reduces the risk of CTS.

■ **Adjustable keyboards** Many keyboard manufacturers have developed more ergonomically correct keyboards. Some of these keyboards are separated into adjustable sections so the worker can position the keys at a more comfortable level. Other "keyboards" have eliminated keys altogether: they rely on finger pressure instead of hand movement. One new keyboard is split into two sections that are more vertical than horizontal, which means the user's palms face each other while he is typing. This position is desirable because wrists are more comfortable in a vertical position than they are in a horizontal position (as most traditional keyboards force them to be).

■ **Adjustable keyboard drawers** A tabletop is very rarely the ideal position for a keyboard. The keyboard should be on a special shelf or drawer that can be adjusted for each individual user. The keyboard should then be positioned so that the user does not have to bend his wrists to type on it when the elbow is bent at a 45-degree angle. The wrists should be flat at all times in order to avoid CTS. In addition, the knees should not bump the keyboard drawer.

■ **Monitor stands and glare guards.** To avoid unnecessary eye strain, the monitor should be at eye level or slightly lower. If it is lower than eye level, it

Maintain good posture and keep feet on the floor to reduce strain on neck, shoulders, and back.

Attach a glare guard and adjust monitor height to reduce eye strain.

Use wrist rests and adjustable keyboards to support the wrists at the correct angle for typing.

Place feet flat on floor.

should be tilted upward a bit. The monitor should be roughly two feet away from the eyes. If glare is a problem, there are several glare guards on the market that help reduce eyestrain. Glare guards are basically screens that prevent reflections on the monitor from the many light sources in a room.

■ **Adjustable chairs** A good chair allows a person to adjust not only the height, but also the backrest and armrests. The seat of the chair should be positioned so the user can sit in it with his feet flat on the floor; the backrest should give support to the person's lower back; and the armrests should support the elbows and forearms when the elbows are bent at a 45-degree angle. Ideally, the seat should be tilted slightly forward. All of these conditions reduce stress on the lower vertebrae and promote good posture.

■ **Foot rests** To avoid back,

shoulder, and lower neck pain, good posture should be maintained at all times. If the chair cannot be adjusted so that the feet are flat on the floor, a foot rest should be used. If all else fails, a sturdy book or something comparable should be placed under the feet for support. Foot rests are good for shorter people, but are not necessary. Feet should not dangle, but they should not be elevated so the knees are too high, either. The knees should be slightly lower than the hips and should not bump into the keyboard drawer.

In addition to ergonomic changes in furniture and posture, workers should also take frequent breaks to avoid RSI. Experts recommend a ten minute break every hour. That doesn't mean that the worker has to stop working ten minutes out of every hour, it just means that he should stop using the computer for ten minutes and focus his attention on other tasks. It is also important to move around often. A worker should not sit in the same position for a long time.

Since using the computer can often cause eyestrain, it is important to exercise the eyes every once and awhile. Try this simple trick: focus on something far away (look out a window, or look up at the ceiling), and then focus on something close (like your hand). Repeat this ten times. This exercise uses all the muscles in the eye, and allows them to easily refocus on the computer screen once a person begins working again. There are also software and shareware programs on the market that will help exercise the eyes to reduce eye strain.

Another concern about frequent computer use that has recently come to light is that computer monitors (except the LED screens used in portable computers) emit extremely low frequency magnetic fields (ELFs). Exposure to such fields over time has not yet proven to cause harm, but scientists are warning users to be careful. These fields are the most powerful along the sides of the monitor, so users should be careful when sitting too near other computers. Be sure to remain at arm's length from the front of the monitor as well; the electron beams that light up the display flow out of the front of the monitor and may also cause harm. (This is similar to the warning about sitting too close to a television set.) Also see Keyboard and Monitor.

CARPAL TUNNEL SYNDROME

A painful condition of the wrist and hand resulting in tingling and numbness of the fingers. Carpal Tunnel Syndrome is caused when the median nerve is pinched or compressed, usually resulting from long periods of time spent typing at a keyboard with the wrists held at unnatural angles.

RSI

Stands for repetitive stress injuries. RSIs are caused by jobs requiring repetitive actions, such as those found in factories. RSIs are common among today's computer users who type at the computer for long periods of time without the proper equipment or setup. Carpal Tunnel Syndrome is a repetitive stress injury.

ELF

ELFs are extremely low frequency fields emitted by computer monitors that are suspect in causing harm if the user is sitting too close to the monitor. Although there is no scientific data proving such suspicions, users are warned not to sit too close to the sides of the monitor where the ELFs are the strongest.

Excel

Excel is a powerful spreadsheet program by Microsoft. In addition to being sold individually, it is now included in Microsoft Office, a bundle of six Microsoft programs aimed at the corporate market. Excel was originally designed to be a DOS-based program (at the time, Windows had only been recently introduced), but as the popularity of Windows increased, the format was changed to Windows-based instead. Excel was one of the first big Windows applications, and it is arguably the most popular spreadsheet program on the market today.

A spreadsheet program is an application designed for accounting purposes. Spreadsheet programs can organize numerical data, perform calculations, and handle mathematical formulas. A spreadsheet (also known as a worksheet) can be used for more than just number crunching; a worksheet is often used as a simple database tool to organize data, such as names and addresses. In addition, a user can perform forecasts on complex data and can create charts (graphs) of numerical data for easier analysis.

Excel has many standard features that are common among Microsoft programs made to run in the Windows environment. For example, there is a Standard Toolbar across the top of the screen that allows the user to issue one of many

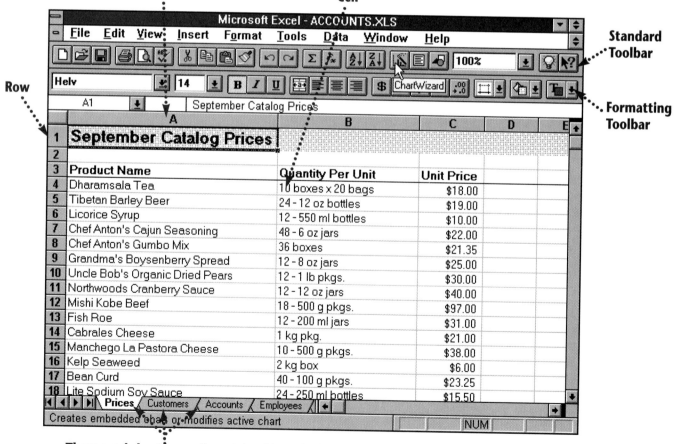

These worksheets are all contained in a single workbook.

How Does It Work?

An Excel spreadsheet is filled with columns and rows. The intersection of a column and a row creates a cell. Each cell's address consists of the row number and the column letter: for example, cell C5 is the third cell in the fifth row. The row numbers and column letters appear at the beginning of each row or column.

To use Excel, the user types data into cells. A user can then enter formulas into other cells which calculate results based on this data. When typing a formula, the user specifies cell addresses, which tell Excel where to find the numbers he wants to use in the calculation. For example, to add the contents of the cells A2 and A3, the user types the formula: =A2+A3. (All Excel formulas begin with an equals sign.)

Cell address

Formula

The result, not the formula itself, appears in cell D12.

	Salesperson	Items Sold	Price per Item	Total Amt. Sold
3	Sharyn Cooksey	734	$22.95	$16,845.30
4	Jennifer Fulton	689	$22.95	$15,812.55
5	Jason Galloway	793	$22.95	$18,199.35
6	Sherry Kinkoph	785	$22.95	$18,015.75
7	Joe Kraynak	264	$22.95	$6,058.80
8	Kirk Mattingly	574	$22.95	$13,173.30
9	Richard Miller	845	$22.95	$19,392.75
10	San Dee Phillips	596	$22.95	$13,678.20
12	Total Sales			$121,176.00

=SUM(D3:D10)

common commands with the click of a button instead of having to access a menu. Additional toolbars, which contain tools for a specific task such as charting or drawing, can also be displayed. The latest release, Excel 5, includes such new features as ToolTips (which help the user understand what each tool is for), TipWizard (which gives the user information on how to accomplish Excel tasks), and ChartWizard (which guides the user step by step through the charting process). Excel also comes with drawing tools for enhancing charts with arrows, lines, and text.

A cell is the intersection of a column and a row within the worksheet. The user enters data into cells or enters formulas (which use the data found in other cells). Cells are grouped into worksheets, which are in turn grouped into workbooks (the workbook concept was introduced in version 5 of Excel).

To make the numbers in a worksheet more visually pleasing, a user can add borders, shading, and lines to cells. The font (typeface) and character formatting (appearance) of a cell's contents can also

continues

Excel continued

be changed. In addition, each cell has a format that tells Excel how to display the data in it. For example, if a cell has the default General number format, values (numbers) will be right-aligned, and labels (text) will be left-aligned. Excel users can set the Date/Time format, change the alignment, create a border, or add a pattern or shade to the cell.

To illustrate the relationship between numbers, a user can create a chart and add it to the worksheet. If the worksheet is used as a database, there are special sorting and searching commands that can be used to manage the database information. Also see Application, Database, and Spreadsheet.

FUNCTION

A special type of mathematical operation that has already been written; all the user has to do to use the function is type its name into a formula. For example, in the formula =SUM(A1,A2,A3), the SUM function adds the values in cells A1, A2, and A3.

Excel used as a database (which can be searched and sorted any number of ways)

	A	B	C	D	E	F	G	H
1	Last Name	First Name	Address	City	State	ZIP	Phone#	
2	Cantrell	Amy	2859 Eileen St.	Phoenix	AZ	73829	555-9372	
3	Cooksey	Sharyn	6544 Hidden Lake Dr.	Harmony	IN	46250	555-8492	
4	Dali	Sal	1904 Gala Lane	St. Petersburg	FL	35297	555-4795	
5	Dine	Jim	8464 Bathrobe Ave.	Bangor	ME	12363	555-8474	
6	Edmondson	Adrian	35 S.P.G. #23A	Syracuse	NY	23937	555-7653	
7	Fulton	Jennifer	3433 Kessler Blvd.	Portland	OR	97574	555-7893	
8	Galloway	Jason	832 Chaplin Lane	Compton	CA	94571	555-6781	
9	Kinkoph	Sherry	475 St. Charles Lane	Mansfield	OH	46290	555-4894	
10	Kraynak	Joe	4789 Burroughs St.	Chicago	IL	65068	555-8638	
11	Lyon	Jack	517 Main St.	Danville	CA	94523	555-8378	
12	Mayall	Rik	15 Credibility St.	Boulder	CO	72983	555-1983	
13	Miller	Richard	242 E. 63rd St.	Seattle	WA	98732	555-9842	
14	Miro	Joan	722 Small St.	New Orleans	LA	73645	555-8383	
15	Nordgulen	Eric	1994 Fresnel Pkwy.	St. Louis	MO	67393	555-7394	
16	Oliver	Marilyn	635 Joesph Rd.	Atlanta	GA	35738	555-0982	
17	Planer	Nigel	4983 Lentil Ave.	Lincoln	NE	63898	555-3259	
18	Rogers	Rhonda	223 E. Jefferson St.	Muncie	IN	47333	555-9862	

Microsoft Excel - DATABASE.XLS

File Edit View Insert Format Tools Data Window Help

Arial   10   B I U $ % ,   100%

A2   Cantrell

Sheet1 Sheet2 Sheet3 Sheet4 Sheet5 Sheet6

Ready NUM

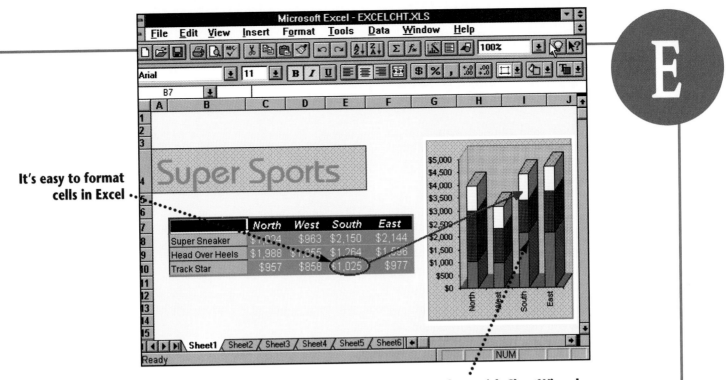

It's easy to format cells in Excel

Create an instant chart with ChartWizard

RANGE

A group of adjacent cells that form a rectangle. If a user names a range, that name can be used in a formula to refer to the range of cells.

WORKSHEET

A page of an Excel workbook. There are 16 worksheets in each workbook, but worksheets can be deleted and inserted as needed.

FORMULA

The sequence of numbers and symbols that tells Excel how and what to calculate. Excel formulas always begin with an equals sign (=), and may include a function.

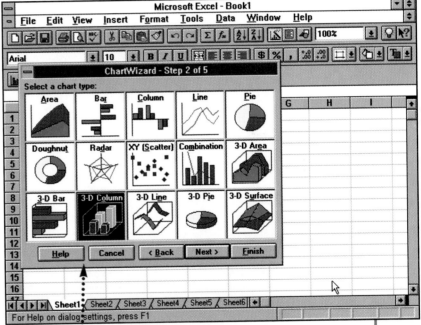

Excel's Chart Wizard dialog box has many chart options to choose from.

CELL

The rectangular space that is formed where a row and a column meet. Each cell has its own address: the row number followed by the column letter (for example, cell B4 is the second cell in the fourth row).

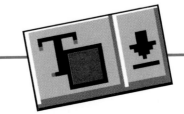

Expansion Cards

An expansion card is a circuit board that expands the normal capability of the computer in some way. An expansion card can control a peripheral (like the video adapter card, which controls the monitor), add memory, or connect the PC to a network. The expansion card fits into an expansion slot, which connects it to the expansion bus; the expansion slots and the expansion bus are located inside the PC's system unit. When an expansion card is inserted into a slot, it is connected (through the expansion bus) to the rest of the PC's components. The expansion bus is the electronic pathway connecting all the expansion slots to the CPU and to the other components. The expandability of a computer depends upon the

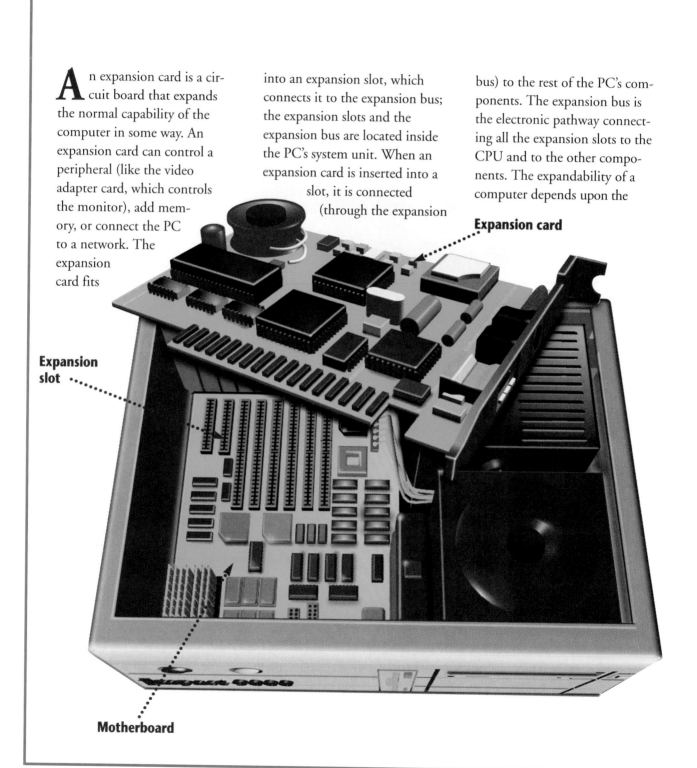

Expansion card

Expansion slot

Motherboard

number of expansion slots it has; all computers come with at least a few expansion slots.

Some expansion slots may already be filled when the computer is purchased. For example, most computers have one expansion card that controls the disk drives, and another that controls the monitor. But a user can add more cards if he wants to and if space allows. For example, if a user needs to add more memory to his computer but the motherboard does not have any more room, he could buy a memory expansion card and fit it into an empty expansion slot inside the computer. Other types of expansion cards include modem cards, sound boards, network interface cards, and fax cards.

There are several types of expansion slots available, and some computers contain more than one type. One type, ISA (Industry Standard Architecture), allows the user to connect either 8-bit or 16-bit expansion cards. The number of

bits refers to the amount of data a card can send or receive at one time; obviously, a 16-bit card is faster and more efficient than an 8-bit card. EISA (Expanded Industry Standard Architecture) expansion slots allow the users to connect 8-bit, 16-bit, and 32-bit expansion cards. Microchannel slots are found in IBM PCs and

support 16-bit and 32-bit expansion cards. Also see Motherboard, Peripheral, Sound Board, and Video Card.

MOTHERBOARD

The main circuit board in the system unit. Expansion cards connect to the motherboard through the expansion slots.

Expansion Card

EXPANDABILITY

The amount of room in a computer's system unit for additions. A computer's expandability depends on how many expansion slots, memory slots, and ports it has.

EXPANSION BUS

The expansion bus connects the expansion slots to the various parts of the computer. The CPU sends data over wires in the bus to the cards that are in the slots. Sometimes the expansion slots themselves are referred to as "expansion buses."

File

A file is a collection of related information. For example, when a user creates something, such as a letter, and then saves that letter to disk, he is creating a file. There are many different types of computer files: for example, program files contain the instructions to run a program, such as a word processor or a spreadsheet program. These files are easy to identify: they generally end with the letters .EXE or .COM. For example, the file WINWORD.EXE runs the Word for Windows program. System files are similar to program files, but they are used to run the operating system. For example, DOS uses a system file called COM-MAND.COM, located in the main (root) directory of the hard disk. System files also end with the letters .EXE or .COM.

Data files are files that the user creates. To create a data file, the user enters information into the computer and then saves it. Data files can contain anything, such as a spreadsheet made with a spreadsheet program, a doc-ument written with a word processing program, or a graphic designed with a drawing program. For example, if the user created a drawing and then saved it, he would be saving the drawing in a data file.

When saving a file, the user assigns it a unique name that will distinguish it from other files. For example, a memo created with a word processing program could be named MEMO1. A spreadsheet created with a spreadsheet program might be named SALESJUN. In the DOS and OS/2 operating systems, the file name can include an extension, three extra letters preceded by a dot that specify what type of file it is. For example, the file named SALESJUN might have an extension of .RPT (SALESJUN.RPT) to help the user remember that the file is a report. Some programs automatically add their own extensions to files. For example, this same file might have an extension of .WP (SALESJUN.WP) to identify it as a WordPerfect file.

In the Macintosh operating system, a file name can contain 32

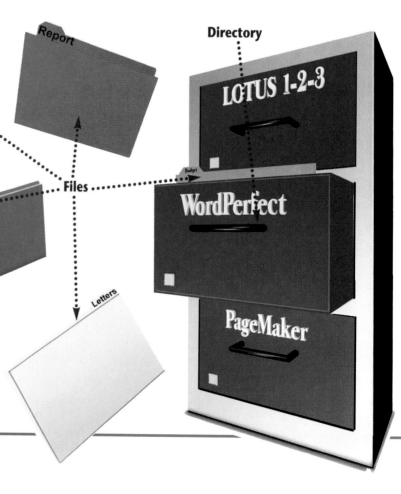

How Does It Work?

Data is stored on a disk in a certain format. Formatting is a process which divides a disk into sections called sectors. Files are saved within these sectors. Adjacent sectors make up a "cluster." The smallest space that a file can occupy is one of these clusters. If a file is large, it may occupy several adjacent clusters. Sometimes, adjacent clusters are occupied, so a file must be "split up" and stored in clusters located in different parts of the disk. On each formatted disk is a special table, called the file allocation table (FAT) that keeps track of where files are located on the disk. For example, when a program needs to locate a file, and operating system such as DOS looks up the file's location in the FAT and retrieves the file. When a file is deleted from disk, it is not actually erased; instead, its location is simply deleted from the file allocation table. The file itself is still there, but the space that it occupies is marked "available." The next time a file is copied to disk, the space that the deleted file was occupying can be used by another file.

characters, and there is no extension. Instead, file names look more like a real description of the file's contents: for example, Sales Report for 2nd Quarter. With any operating system, there are certain file naming restrictions that prohibit the use of some characters. For example, in DOS a file name cannot contain a space, or punctuation symbols as @ or #.

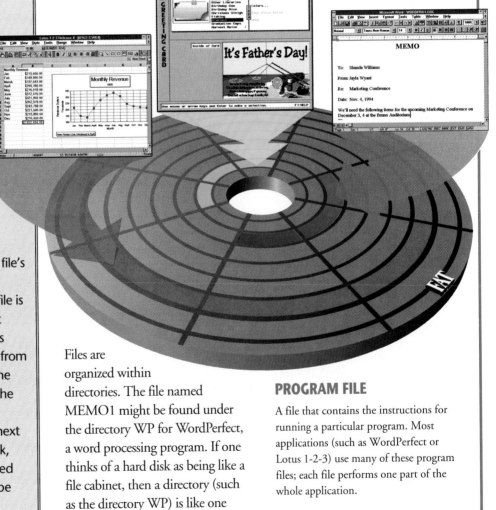

Files are organized within directories. The file named MEMO1 might be found under the directory WP for WordPerfect, a word processing program. If one thinks of a hard disk as being like a file cabinet, then a directory (such as the directory WP) is like one

drawer in the file cabinet. Inside this file drawer (directory) are many file folders—each one a program or a data file. Also see Application, Binary, Bit, Byte, Data Storage, and Directory.

DATA FILE

A file created by the user with some type of program, such as Excel, WordPerfect, etc. A data file can be any type of data: a drawing, a letter, or a complex spreadsheet.

PROGRAM FILE

A file that contains the instructions for running a particular program. Most applications (such as WordPerfect or Lotus 1-2-3) use many of these program files; each file performs one part of the whole application.

Floppy Disk

5.25-inch floppy disk

Write-protect

Write-protect notch

3.5-inch floppy disk

A floppy disk, also called a disk or diskette, is a removable storage disk used to save computer data. A floppy disk is inserted into a special drive when its data is needed, and then is later removed. Floppy disks are great for transporting data between PCs, such as a PC at work and a PC at home. Floppy disks, like hard disks, store their data magnetically on a specially coated film. They are called "floppy disks" because the film found inside the disk's plastic shell is flexible (floppy).

Floppy disks come in two sizes: 3.5-inch, and 5.25-inch. They also come in two densities: double-density and high-density. A disk's density determines the amount of data it is capable of storing—the higher the density, the greater the storage capacity. A high-density disk has smaller magnetic particles embedded in its magnetically coated inner film, which allow the disk to

store more data in less space. A double-density disk has larger magnetic particles; therefore, it cannot store as much data.

The amount of data that a floppy disk can hold depends on its size and density. A 3.5-inch double-density disk holds 720 kilobytes of data, while its high-density cousin holds 1.44 megabytes. A 5.25-inch disk holds 360 kilobytes (double-density) to 1.2 megabytes (high-density) of data. IBM PCs and IBM-compatible computers use 3.5-inch or 5.25-inch floppy disks, depending upon what kind of floppy disk drives the computer has. Macintosh computers also use 3.5-inch disks, however they are formatted differently than those used in IBM-compatible PCs. Interestingly enough, most Macintosh computers today come with a high-density 3.5-inch disk drive that is capable of reading data that came from an IBM-PC compatible drive. However, IBM-PC compatible

drives cannot read information on a Macintosh disk.

Before data can be written to a disk, the floppy disk must be formatted. Formatting a disk establishes sections in which files can later be stored. A formatted disk is divided into concentric circles, called tracks. The tracks are further divided into sectors. Adjacent sectors are known as clusters. The smallest space that a file can occupy is a cluster. Some files take up more than one cluster, and are subsequently stored in multiple clusters on the disk. A file allocation table (FAT), created when the disk is formatted, helps keep track of where data is stored on the disk.

Floppy disks are inserted into the floppy disk drive located on the front of the computer's system unit. A 3.5-inch disk fits into the

Double Density

High Density

How Does It Work?

Data is stored on a disk magnetically. The mylar film inside a disk has a magnetic coating that contains tiny particles. In order to write data onto the disk, each particle is magnetized a particular way by the read/write head of the floppy disk drive. Depending on how a particle is magnetized, it is read by the computer as a 1 or a 0. These 1's and 0's form the binary language of the computer, which is eventually translated into characters like "A" or "?" or other types of computer data.

When a file is saved on disk, its location is written to a special area called the FAT (file allocation table). Later, when the file is needed, its location is found in the FAT. A signal tells the read/write heads to move to the first sector that contains a piece of the file. That sector is read, and the head moves to the next sector that contains a piece of the file. This continues until the entire file has been read.

3.5-inch drive; a 5.25-inch disk fits into the 5.25-inch drive. Each floppy disk has a write-protect notch or tab that is used to prevent accidental erasure of data. To write-protect a 5.25-inch disk, cover the notch on the side of the disk with a small piece of adhesive tape. To write-protect a 3.5-inch disk, push the tab up to reveal an open hole.

Other safety measures for protecting data on disk include keeping the disk out of extreme heat, keeping it away from dust and

moisture, and making sure it is never bent or placed near magnets. It is important to never touch the exposed areas (the film) of a disk. In addition, smoking around a computer is not advised, because smoke particles can wedge themselves between the film and the read/write head of the disk drive, causing damage. Also see Data Storage, Density, File, Floppy Disk Drive, and Hard Disk Drive.

Filename	Track	Sector
Letterz.WP	2	3
Sales.WKS	14	2
Memo.DOC	10	6
DPT.CHT	Deleted	
LOGO.ART	18	2
Forecast.WKS	13	6
Agenda.DOC	21	4

The FAT Table

continues

Floppy Disk continued

FORMAT

Formatting prepares a disk for use by dividing it into special sections, called tracks (concentric rings) and sectors (sections of a track). A disk needs to be formatted only once.

DENSITY

The capacity of a disk. A high-density disk holds at least twice as much data as a double-density disk of the same size.

FAT

File Allocation Table. A table that keeps track of where files are located on a disk.

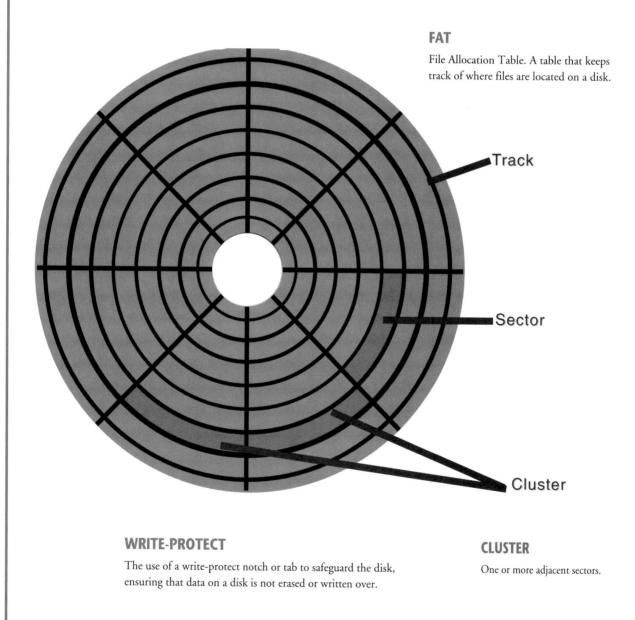

Track

Sector

Cluster

WRITE-PROTECT

The use of a write-protect notch or tab to safeguard the disk, ensuring that data on a disk is not erased or written over.

CLUSTER

One or more adjacent sectors.

Floppy Disk Drive

A floppy disk drive is a device used to retrieve (read) and save (write) information to floppy disks. Floppy disks are portable disks used to save data magnetically. Before the invention of hard disk drives, floppy disks and floppy disk drives were the only method of saving and retrieving data and programs. (Even before the invention of floppy disk drives, some early PCs stored data on tape cassettes.)

Most IBM-compatible PCs have two sizes of floppy drives: 3.5-inch and 5.25-inch. The 3.5-inch drive reads 3.5-inch disks; the 5.25-inch drive reads 5.25-inch disks. Macintosh computers use only 3.5-inch disk drives. The top or left-most floppy drive is usually referred to as drive A. (On newer systems where dual floppy drives occupy a single slot, drive A is usually the top one.) If a computer has a second floppy drive, it is referred to as drive B. There are two types of drive densities: double-density and high-density. A drive's density determines the amount of data it is capable of storing. The proper type (density) disk must be used with the floppy disk drive. For example, a double-density disk must be used with a double-density drive. Most floppy drives today are high-density. However, users should consult the PC's manual to be sure before purchasing any disks.

Floppy disk drives work in a way that's very similar to hard disk drives. Information is stored on a floppy disk in concentric circles, called tracks. Each track is divided into equal parts, called sectors. Adjacent sectors are called a cluster, which is the smallest space that a file can occupy on the disk. If a file is too large, it is divided into pieces and saved in several clusters. In order for the computer to retrieve a file, a tiny motor spins the disk, allowing the read/write head to access a particular track and sector and read the first section of a file. The read/write head then moves to the next sector containing a piece of the file

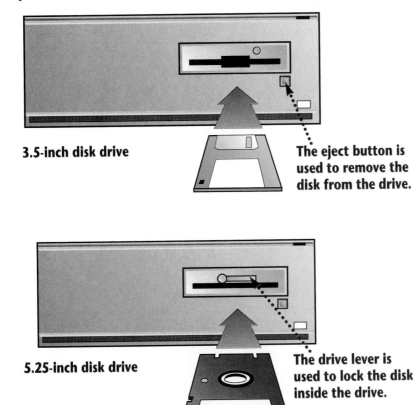

3.5-inch disk drive

The eject button is used to remove the disk from the drive.

5.25-inch disk drive

The drive lever is used to lock the disk inside the drive.

continues

Floppy Disk Drive
continued

A tower system unit stacks the drives vertically.

IMPACT 9000

LOCK   RESET

TURBO

and continues reading the data. This process continues until the entire file has been read. Writing a file to the disk is a similar process, which involves moving the read/write head over the disk to various sectors, until the entire file has been stored. Also see Data Storage, Density, Floppy Disk, and Hard Disk Drive.

DENSITY

The capacity of a disk. A high-density disk holds at least twice as much data as a double-density disk of the same size. Density refers to how closely the magnetic particles (used to store data) are packed onto the disk surface.

FORMAT

Data must be stored on a disk in a logical order so that it can easily be retrieved again. Because of this, all disks must be formatted into sections where data can be stored. Once formatted, the computer keeps track of where data is located and where there is space for more data.

READ DATA

To retrieve information (data) from a disk.

WRITE DATA

To save information (data) onto a disk.

How Does It Work?

A floppy disk is inserted into the floppy disk drive with the label side towards the top of the drive. Once loaded, a spindle motor spins the disk so that the FAT (file allocation table) is under the read/write head. The read-write head first finds the location of the file in the FAT. Then a stepper motor moves the read-write head to the correct track and sector on the disk to retrieve the file.

To read the disk, the read-write head checks the magnetic particles on the surface of the disk. Depending on how a particle is magnetized, it is read as a 1 or a 0. (These 1's and 0's form the basis of all computer data. For example, the pattern 01100100 is equal to the letter d.) As they are read, the 1's and 0's are sent to the disk drive controller as electrical pulses. The disk drive controller, which connects the disk drive to the computer, manages data as it goes to and from the disk drive.

To write to the disk, the read-write head uses a magnetic pulse to align the particles on the magnetic surface in a pattern that represents the data.

FAT

Stands for file allocation table. Each formatted disk has a FAT area on the disk that keeps track of where data is stored.

WRITE-PROTECT TAB OR NOTCH

A tab or a notch that is used to indicate whether data can be written to a disk. To write-protect a 5.25-inch floppy, cover the notch on the side of the disk with a small piece of adhesive tape. To write-protect a 3.5-inch disk, push the tab up to reveal an open hole.

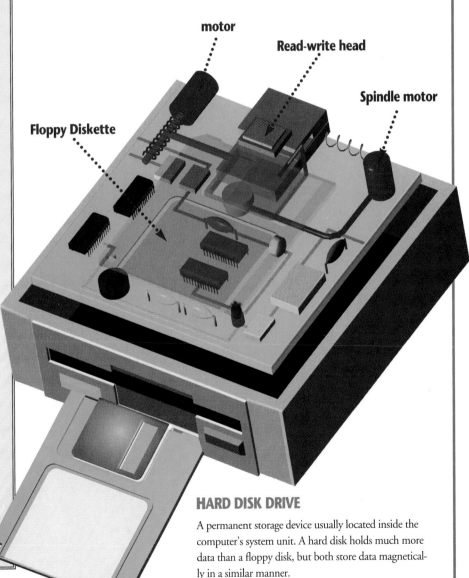

motor

Read-write head

Spindle motor

Floppy Diskette

HARD DISK DRIVE

A permanent storage device usually located inside the computer's system unit. A hard disk holds much more data than a floppy disk, but both store data magnetically in a similar manner.

Font

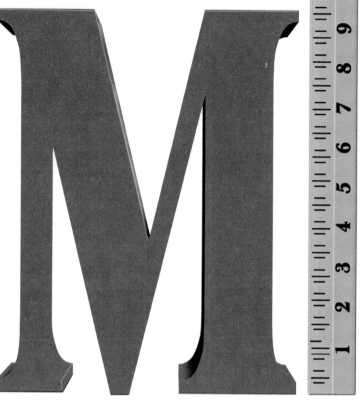

A font is a set of characters of the same size and typeface. Fonts are often referred to as type styles or typefaces because they describe how text looks. But actually, a typeface is the design of a set of characters—a special structure and look. For example, the Times New Roman typeface is the style of characters usually used in a newspaper. This typeface has a flat, unrounded, crisp look that's easy to read in any size. In addition, Times New Roman uses serifs, tiny extensions on various letters. For example, the letter "N" has tiny serifs (extensions) at the bottom left and top right of the letter.

But in the truest sense of the word, a font is a set of characters all in the same typeface and size. For example, the font Times New Roman 20-point describes a set of characters 20 points in size, of the Times New Roman typestyle. (There are 72 points in an inch.) Because the terms font and typestyle are often used interchangeably, the differences are usually lost to the average computer user. Although it's not technically correct, it is more common to refer to a font using the name of a typeface, as in the Times New Roman font.

A font includes alphabet letters, punctuation, numbers, and any special characters (such as @ or #), all with the same style (typeface).

Each character in a font has a consistent look or style that matches the characters in the rest of the font set. Font sets include different sizes and different weights or thicknesses for each character.

Typefaces can be separated into two categories: serif and sans serif. Serif fonts have extensions on the ends of the characters that look like little lines or balls, and are sometimes called feet. Sans serif fonts do not have these embellishes, and are more block-like in structure. Fonts are given specific names, such as Helvetica or Times Roman. Within each font there are different line weights or thicknesses of characters. The

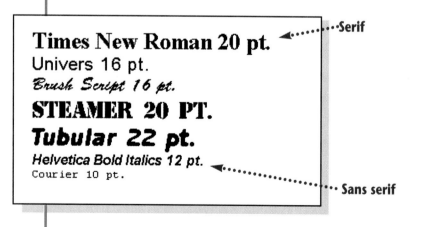

Times New Roman 20 pt. ← **Serif**
Univers 16 pt.
Brush Script 16 pt.
STEAMER 20 PT.
Tubular 22 pt.
Helvetica Bold Italics 12 pt. ←
Courier 10 pt. ← **Sans serif**

How Does It Work?

Some printers come with one or two built-in fonts, which is all they can print without additional help from a program. Laser printers allow the user to increase the number of built-in fonts by plugging in a font cartridge. DOS programs can only print the fonts that come with the printer, while Windows programs can print an almost endless array of fonts. When one of the Windows fonts (known as TrueType fonts) is used, additional instructions are sent to the printer so it can print the new font. Some fonts print out exactly the same as they appear on the monitor. These fonts are called WYSIWYG (What-You-See-Is-What-You-Get) fonts. TrueType fonts are WYSIWYG.

Whether built-in or supplied by a program, computer fonts fall into two groups: bitmapped and outline. Bitmapped fonts are stored in the computer as patterns of dots. For each point size of a bitmapped font, the computer must store a separate set of font characters. This consumes a great deal of disk space. Outlined fonts are stored as sets of lines, curves, and points, using a mathematical formula instead of a pattern of dots.

Bitmapped font

Outline font

characters that make up Helvetica Bold look darker and thicker than those of regular Helvetica.

Fonts are measured in units called points. There are 72 points to an inch, and twelve points make a pica. While points are used to describe the height of a character, picas are used to measure the distance between lines of text. Most software programs allow the user a choice of typefaces and sizes. Also see Bitmap, Desktop Publishing, and Word Processing.

JAGGIES OR ALIASING

The jagged edges that appear around angled and curved lines on a computer, most notably in bitmapped fonts and graphics. This results from the fact that the computer display is made up of tiny squares of light called pixels. The higher the number of pixels per inch on the screen, the smoother the curve or angle of a drawn line.

TRUETYPE

An outline font format first created by Apple. TrueType fonts are used with Windows 3.1, Macintosh System 7, and OS/2 operating systems to produce fonts that look the same on-screen as they do when printed.

FONT CARTRIDGE

A font cartridge can contain several fonts held in ROM (read only memory) chips. When plugged into a laser printer, it provides the user with additional font choices.

KERNING

The spacing between characters on a line. When printed together, some letters (such as A Y) look farther apart than other letters. Kerning allows the user to bring such letter pairs closer together. Kerning is necessary in large headlines, where this "visual space discrepancy" really shows up.

Fractals

Courtesy of Dick Oliver, Cedar Software, RR 1 Box 4496, Wolcott, VT 05680

Fractals are complex mathematical formulas that can be used to create natural shapes, such as fern leaves, coastlines, and entire simulated worlds. A fractal formula takes advantage of the fact that many natural shapes contain repetitious patterns (fractional iterations or fractals). For example, the edge of a fern leaf contains many jagged indentations, which themselves contain smaller versions of these same indentations. By creating a formula that describes one indentation pattern and then repeating it in larger and larger sizes, a fern leaf with realistic contours is created.

In 1975, mathematician Benoit Mandlebrot noticed this "self similarity" of natural shapes, and began to study them in detail. To Mandelbrot, many shapes (such as a fern leaf or a mountain) could be broken down into smaller and smaller segments, each with a similar shape. Mandlebrot used computers to draw such shapes because the shapes were so infinitely complex that they would be impossible to render by hand.

What makes fractals so fascinating to mathematicians and the like is that they can define shapes that were once "undefineable."

For example, a mountain may contain the general shape of a cone (something that can be defined using geometry), but it isn't really cone-shaped. Using fractals, a mountain could be described as a repetitious pattern of tiny cones, placed on other cones, placed on other cones, etc.

Scientists use fractals to explain "chaos," or the seemingly randomness of the galaxy, as found in nature, weather, stock prices, seismic activity, and the human body. By dividing such complexities into infinitely smaller and smaller segments (fractionals or fractals), a relatively simple repetitious pattern emerges. By repeating this simple pattern over and over, a more complex—seemingly chaotic—picture arises of things like a lightning bolt, the pattern of stock prices over a century, and the progress of certain diseases.

FRACTALS

Short for fractional iterations, fractals are simple patterns that, if repeated infinitely, resemble complex shapes and patterns found in nature.

CHAOS

A theory which seeks to explain the "unpredictable" randomness of nature. Scientists use fractals as aids in explaining such seemingly random patterns as the spread of a disease, or the pattern of earthquakes in California.

Courtesy of Dick Oliver, Cedar Software, RR 1 Box 4496, Wolcott VT 05680

Games

There is a wide variety of games available for computers today, including educational games, action/adventure games, arcade games, board and card games, sports games, flight simulators, and more. Computer games are actually computer applications written by programmers for entertainment or educational purposes. Behind all of the flashy graphics and sound effects are instructions telling the computer to act like an arcade game or behave like a simulated airplane cockpit. Like in other computer applications, the programming behind games is very complex, requiring the computer to analyze the user's input and to sometimes offer competitive counter-moves.

The very first computer games were variations of traditional chess and checkers. In the late 1960's and early 1970's, computers programmed to play chess were entered to play in tournaments—and even ended up winning a few times, to the surprise of the chess community. The first popular arcade-style game for the computer was Pong, an electronic version of the table-top game of ping pong. Other early computer games were limited to

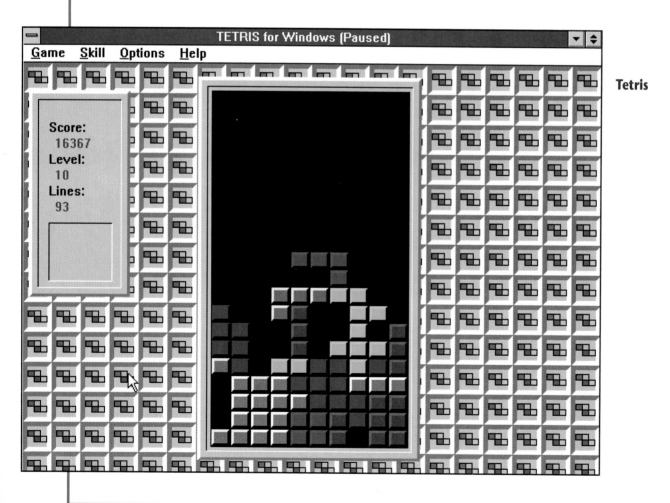

Tetris

SimCity

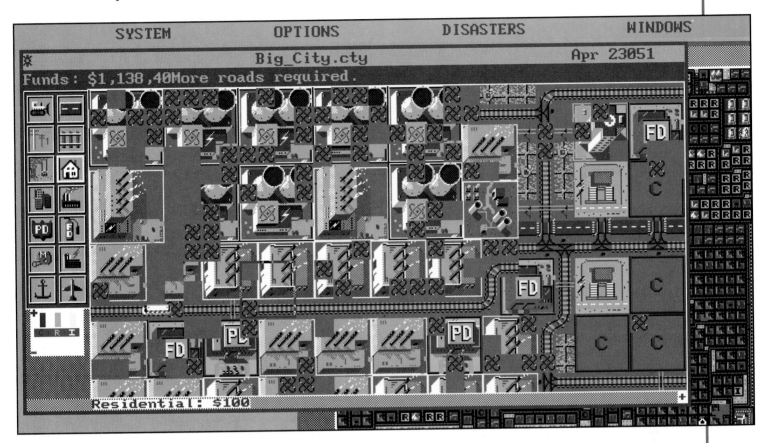

text-based adventure games that walked the user through different worlds and adventures based on his reading paragraphs and making choices to "enter a room" or "follow a path." Today's computer games are much more sophisticated, graphical, life-like, and challenging.

Arcade games, like Tetris, challenge the user in tests of skill, such as controlling blocks that fall from the sky. Most computer arcade games today display the look and feel of electronic games like Nintendo or Sega Genesis.

Action/adventure games have made progress with better graphics and story-telling, becoming interactive fiction. The user takes on the role of a hero who must tackle an adventurous mission that usually involves collecting treasures and valuable tools to help along the way. In programs like Sierra On-Line's King's Quest game, the user does not read and type in complex text (as was required by earlier adventure games). Instead, he makes choices by listening to sounds and clicking the mouse on parts of the screen.

Simulation games are another market in computer entertainment. Maxis' SimCity, SimEarth, SimLife, and SimAnt have the user building complex cities and life forms to study growth rate, evolution, and natural disasters—all of which simulate real experiences. Flight simulators are a type of simulation game that puts the user in the pilot's chair, learning to read an instrument panel, handle take-offs and landings, gauge wind conditions, and more. Computers are still used to play the old standards such as card games, bridge, and chess—electronically, of course.

continues

Games continued

Where in the World Is Carmen Sandiego?

Card games like Windows' Solitaire are quite easy to use, yet are challenging enough for repetitive play.

Children's computer games, such as Where in the World Is Carmen Sandiego?, are used to teach geography, history, math, and spelling. Preschoolers can learn the alphabet and how to count by playing computer "games." The world of computer games, whether educational or just plain entertaining, will be a mainstay of computer usage in the years to come. Also see Application, Programming, and Software.

ACTION/ADVENTURE GAMES

Computer games that place the user in the role of a hero with a mission that usually involves a journey or quest, often through several stages of difficulty.

SIMULATION GAMES

Games that allow the user to pretend to be someone else, and therefore to explore simulated scenarios like flying a plane, running a city, or acting as the creator of the universe.

SPORTS GAMES

Computer games that resemble basic sports activities, such as baseball, golf, and football.

Microsoft Flight Simulator

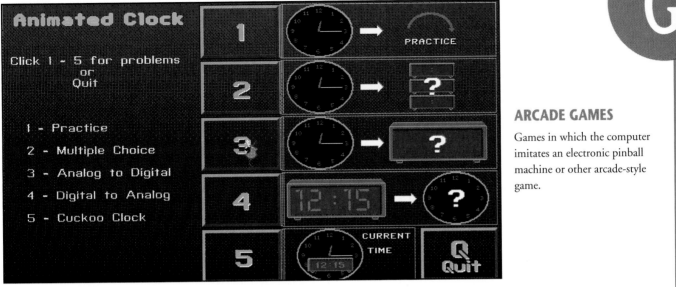

An animated shareware game for children.

ARCADE GAMES

Games in which the computer imitates an electronic pinball machine or other arcade-style game.

Windows Solitaire

EDUTAINMENT

A nickname given to educational software that also entertains. Children's education software is one example.

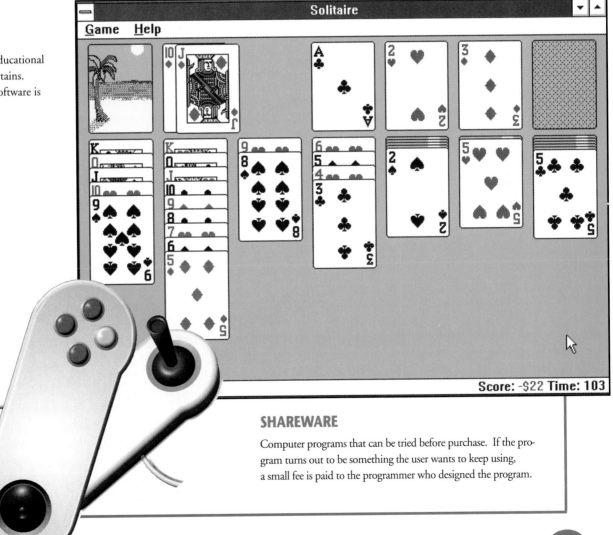

SHAREWARE

Computer programs that can be tried before purchase. If the program turns out to be something the user wants to keep using, a small fee is paid to the programmer who designed the program.

Graphics

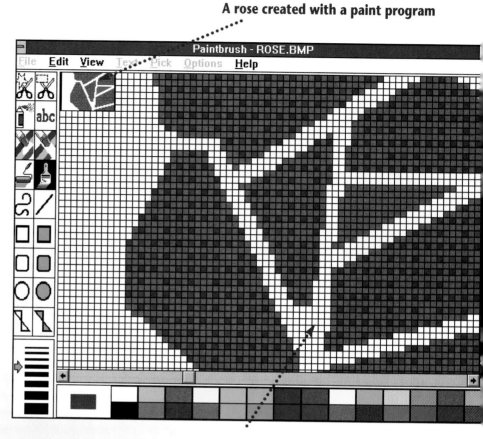

A rose created with a paint program

Paintbrush - ROSE.BMP

The enlarged image reveals the pixels that make up the picture.

Graphics are computer-generated graphic images, such as pictures or illustrations. Graphics can be circles, squares, lines, illustrations, and clip art (pre-drawn art). A drawing or painting program can be used to create a graphic, or pre-drawn art may be scanned into the computer and then manipulated. A drawing may also be "sketched" on a graphics tablet and input into the computer. A graphics tablet is a special device that looks like an ordinary tablet, but which has a touch sensitive surface. When a person draws on it with a special pen, the tablet relays the drawn image to the computer where it can be further manipulated.

A Stylus

There are two basic kinds of graphics: bit-mapped graphics (also called raster graphics) and object-oriented graphics (also called vector graph-

ics). Bit-mapped graphics, common in paint programs such as MacPaint and PC Paintbrush, allow the user to control each pixel or dot pattern to create an image. Object-oriented graphics, created with drawing programs such as CorelDRAW! or CAD programs (computer aided

design), treat the image as a set of separate parts called objects. Each object can be manipulated separately. In addition, the object (such as a rectangle, a line, or a circle) is seen not as a series of dots, but as a mathematical formula. Because object-oriented graphics are based on mathematical formulas, the size of an object-oriented graphic can be changed easily with no loss in detail. Art within a paint program is not resizable. Instead, the individual pixels must be manipulated to enlarge the image. Computer graphics can be put to use in a

How Does It Work?

A computer screen is made up of pixels or tiny dots of light. Each pixel is a blending of up to three different rays of color: red, blue, and green. Each pixel is simply a series of bits (1's and 0's) stored in the computer's memory. Together, the bits tell the computer how much of each color is needed to display that pixel correctly on-screen.

To display a bit-mapped graphic, a large number of bits is needed (one group of bits for each pixel or dot making up the graphic). Consequently, bit-mapped graphics take up a lot of memory.

A vector or object-oriented graphic uses a lot less memory, because the image is simply a series of formulas. With a vectoring system, the object is plotted as a series of dots in a large connect-the-dots map. To draw a vector graphic on-screen, the computer starts at some given point, calculates the ending position, and then draws a line or an arc between these two points. With an object-oriented graphic, each object's outline is seen as a complex formula that describes an exact curve, which is plotted and drawn.

number of very effective ways. For example, adding a graphic to a document can create interest and stress a point made in the text. Graphics are used in a variety of ways with desktop publishing programs to illustrate newsletters, brochures, and flyers. Graphics not designed with a paint or drawing program are entered through such input devices as a scanner, a graphics tablet, or even video images, and can be easily manipulated to enhance work created with the computer.

An important part of working with computer graphics is the ability to display them on-screen as they will look when printed. A monitor's resolution, or sharpness, effects how these images are displayed. The higher a monitor's resolution, the sharper the graphic. Printers also play an important part in producing quality output. Instead of resolution, printed images are measured in dots-per-inch (dpi). The higher a printer's dpi, the sharper the graphic image. Also see Bit Map, Drawing, Monitor, Print Program, and Printer.

A series of bits describes one pixel in a bit-mapped graphic.

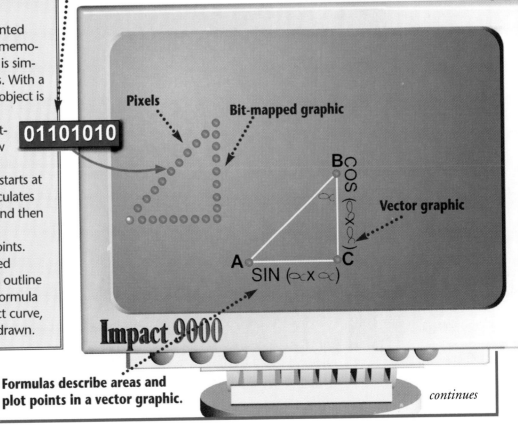

01101010

Pixels

Bit-mapped graphic

Vector graphic

B
COS (∝x∝)

A
SIN (∝x∝)
C

Impact 9000

Formulas describe areas and plot points in a vector graphic.

continues

Graphics continued

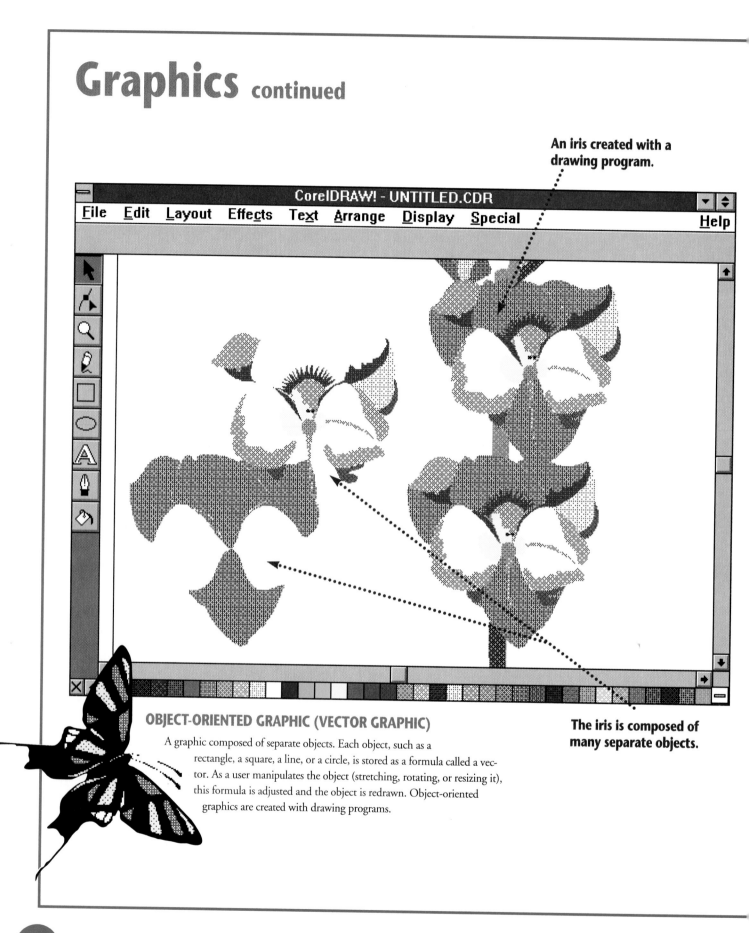

An iris created with a drawing program.

CorelDRAW! - UNTITLED.CDR

File Edit Layout Effects Text Arrange Display Special Help

OBJECT-ORIENTED GRAPHIC (VECTOR GRAPHIC)

A graphic composed of separate objects. Each object, such as a rectangle, a square, a line, or a circle, is stored as a formula called a vector. As a user manipulates the object (stretching, rotating, or resizing it), this formula is adjusted and the object is redrawn. Object-oriented graphics are created with drawing programs.

The iris is composed of many separate objects.

BIT-MAPPED GRAPHIC (RASTER GRAPHIC)

A type of graphic image that is stored as a pattern of dots. With a paint program, the user can control how each dot of light (called a pixel) appears. The color of each pixel on-screen is stored as a series of bits, or 1's and 0's, which is why this type of graphic is called bit-mapped. A raster is one line

RESOLUTION

The sharpness of an image on a monitor screen is controlled by the monitor's resolution. Resolution is measured in pixels, tiny dots on-screen. The higher the number of pixels that can fit on a monitor screen, the higher the resolution and detailing of an image. Printers also use resolution, measured in dots per inch (dpi).

CLIP ART

Pre-drawn art that is stored and ready for use with other computer programs. Clip art is used with desktop publishing programs, word processing programs, and even spreadsheet programs.

JAGGIES OR ALIASING

Jaggies are the ragged edges found on bit-mapped graphics. Because a bit-mapped graphic is comprised of tiny squares or dots, a smooth edge is impossible when creating diagonal or curved lines. However, a sharper resolution makes jaggies less noticeable.

Jaggies

GUI

Gstands for Graphical User
Interface, a method of depicting
information graphically on-screen.
With a GUI, the user performs
tasks by manipulating icons. Icons
are little pictures that represent
programs, files, and commands.
GUI programs run "on top of" a
computer's operating system (the

program that instructs the computer how to operate, how to handle input and output, and how to
work with data). The GUI hides
the details of the operating system,
which runs "beneath" it in another
layer. For example, instead of
memorizing a series of words that
tell the computer to copy a file to a
disk, the user manipulates a picture

(an icon) that represents the file,
placing it on top of another icon
that represents the disk. The GUI
translates this action into the actual commands for the operating system, which then copies the file.
The first graphical user interface
was created by a team of
researchers at Xerox Corporation's
Palo Alto Research Center

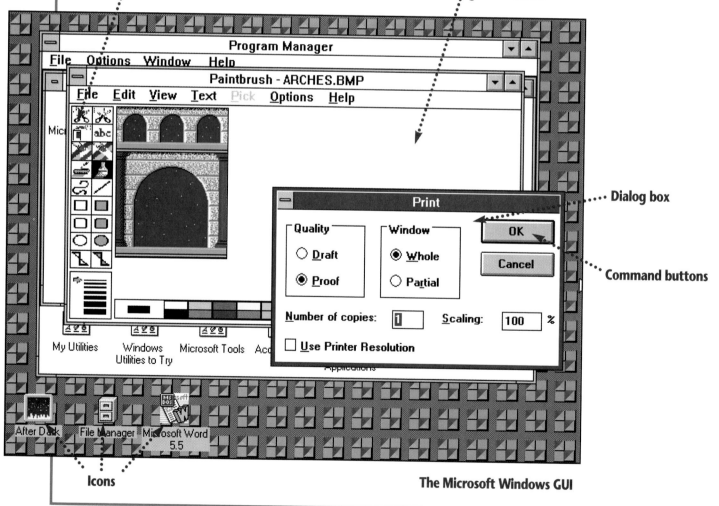

Tool buttons

Program window

Dialog box

Command buttons

Icons

The Microsoft Windows GUI

How Does It Work?

An interface functions as a go-between, allowing two things to communicate. With an operating system such as DOS, the interface is command-driven; the computer displays a prompt, which tells the user that the program is ready for him to type a command. Another kind of interface is a menu-driven interface; instead of typing in a command, the user selects from a list of commands displayed on a menu. By far the easiest way to communicate with the computer is through a graphical user interface, which uses icons or pictures to represent commands.

These windows are easily moved and resized on-screen. All GUIs employ some type of WYSIWYG (What-You-See-Is-What-You-Get) technology to ensure that what appears on-screen is what will be printed out.

(PARC). Developed in 1973, the Alto computer used a new device called a mouse to select things on-screen. The graphical user interface incorporated into the Alto was designed to speed up a user's interaction with the computer, based on research that showed that people more readily understood graphic representations than they did text. But the Alto was never sold commercially because this early GUI technology proved too costly for the computer market. However, in 1979, Steve Jobs (a co-founder of Apple Computers) stumbled across the GUI developments at PARC and used them in

The Macintosh's GUI

Menus drop down from here.

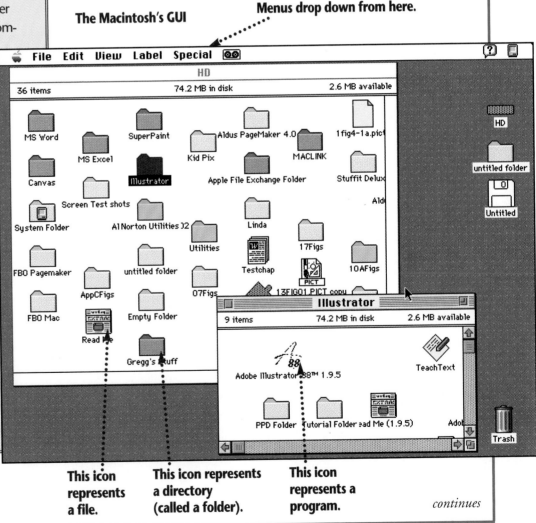

This icon represents a file.

This icon represents a directory (called a folder).

This icon represents a program.

continues

GUI G 133

GUI continued

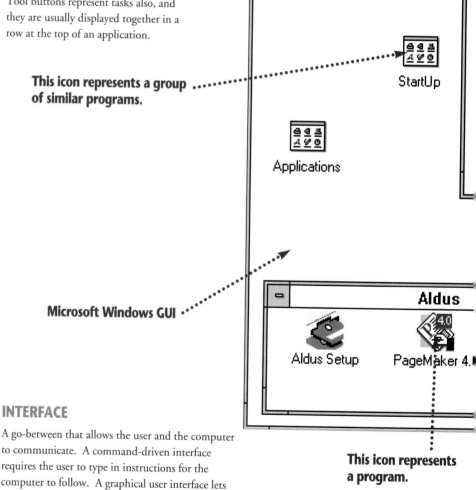

OPERATING SYSTEM

A program that instructs the computer how to operate. An operating system, such as DOS, tells the computer how to handle input and output, and how to work with data.

the development of Apple's Lisa computer. Jobs even went so far as to hire several of the PARC's researchers to work on the development of a GUI for the Lisa computer. Unfortunately, the Lisa computer failed to succeed on the market because it was too expensive. But Apple didn't give up on the idea, and soon after that they released an improved GUI incorporated into a more affordable computer they called the Macintosh. The Macintosh proved a huge success, and it remains the single best-selling brand of computers today. GUIs such as Windows and GeoWorks were created to bring the graphical user interface to IBM-compatible computers. Although GeoWorks did not prove very popular, Windows has become a great success. Today, nearly all IBM-compatible computers that are sold come with Windows installed. Once shunned because the idea of using a GUI seemed like too much fluff, the market has quickly caught on to the ease of use that's possible with GUI programs. The graphical user interface revolutionized the computer screen, making computer technology even more approachable to new users. Also see Apple Computers, Commands, Macintosh, Menu, Microsoft, and Windows.

BUTTON

A small box that looks like it's being depressed when it's selected. Command buttons within a dialog box activate a command or task. OK and Cancel are two buttons found in most dialog boxes. Tool buttons represent tasks also, and they are usually displayed together in a row at the top of an application.

This icon represents a group of similar programs.

Microsoft Windows GUI

This icon represents a program.

INTERFACE

A go-between that allows the user and the computer to communicate. A command-driven interface requires the user to type in instructions for the computer to follow. A graphical user interface lets the user select commands represented by icons, menus, and dialog boxers.

WYSIWYG

Stands for What-You-See-Is-What-You-Get, a computer technology that ensures the user of getting ouput from a printer that looks exactly as the data shown on the monitor screen.

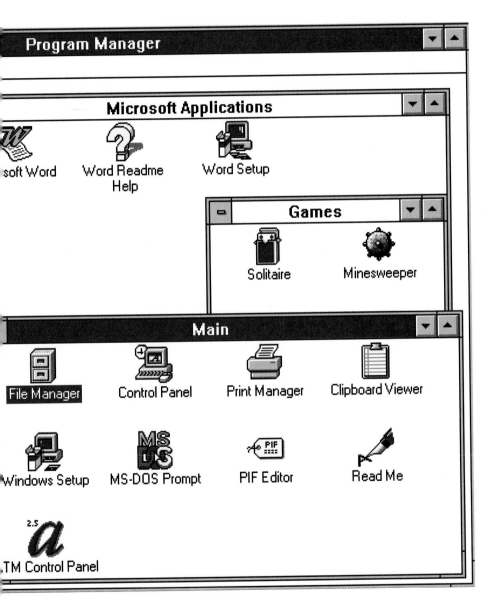

Program Manager

Microsoft Applications

soft Word   Word Readme Help   Word Setup

Games

Solitaire   Minesweeper

Main

File Manager   Control Panel   Print Manager   Clipboard Viewer

Windows Setup   MS-DOS Prompt   PIF Editor   Read Me

TM Control Panel

DIALOG BOX

A special box that appears when the computer needs additional information in order to carry out a task. Dialog boxes often offer additional options for the user to choose from.

ICON

A small picture representing a command, a program, or a file. Icons are found on all graphical user interface programs.

MENU

A box that contains a list of commands from which the user can select. Menus usually drop down like a window shade, allowing the user to scroll through a list to find the correct item.

WINDOW

A rectangular box that appears on-screen and displays a separate file or program. Programs such as Geoworks, Macintosh, and Windows all use this windowing environment.

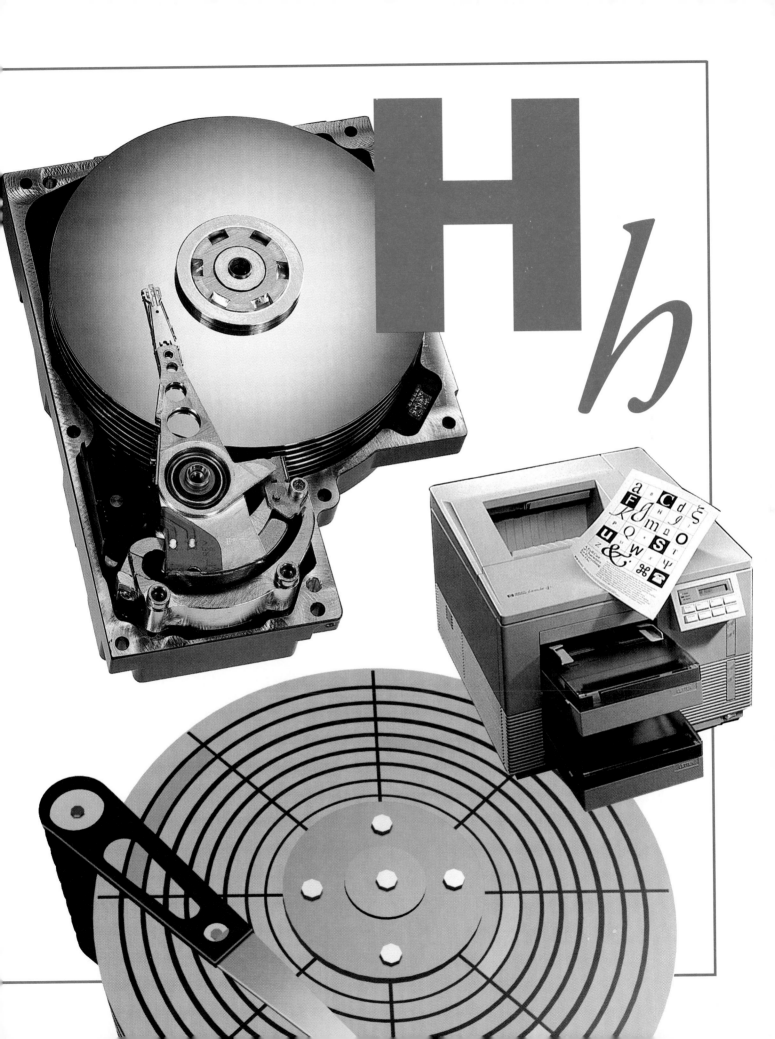

Hard Disk Drive

A hard disk drive, also called a fixed disk drive, is a device used to write and read information stored on metal platters, or disks. Usually located inside the computer's system unit, the nonremovable hard disk is enclosed in an airtight case that prevents damage caused by airborne particles. External hard drives are also encased in airtight boxes, and are connected to the PC by a cable. Removable hard drives are also available. They function like floppy disks in that they too are swapped in and out of a special drive. However, they are like hard drives in that they are encased in a special plastic case. Removable hard drives use a different technology for reading and writing data to the disk, which enables them to prevent damage even though they are not airtight.

A hard disk drive is electromechanical, which means that it is a combination of electrical and mechanical parts. Inside the hard disk drive is a stack of disks called platters that spin on a central hub. In the space above each platter is a read-write head, a device that reads or writes data to the disks. Reading is the process of retrieving a file for use, and

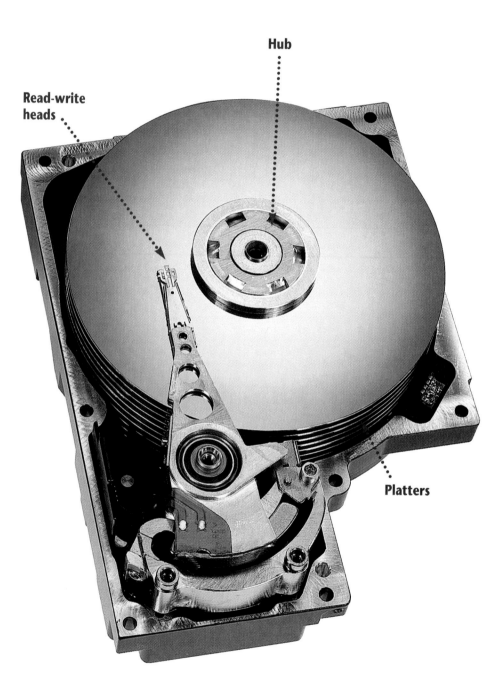

Read-write heads

Hub

Platters

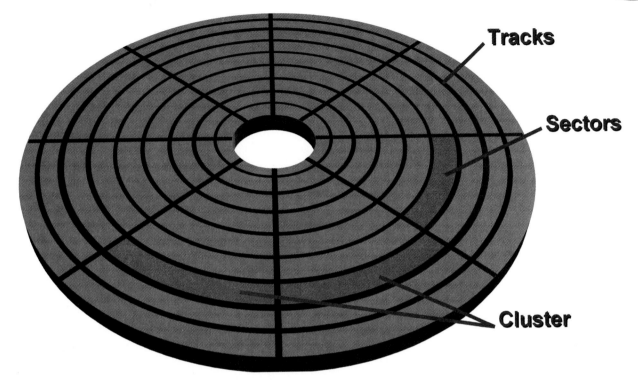

Tracks

Sectors

Cluster

writing is the process of saving a file to disk.

Measured in bytes, the storage capacity of a hard disk drive ranges from 20 megabytes to 2.1 gigabytes and beyond. The speed at which hard disk drives retrieve a piece of data on a disk is measured in milliseconds (1/1000 of a second) and is called average access time. Most hard disk drives have an average access time between 10 and 20 milliseconds. Seek time, another measurement of speed, is the

time it takes for the read-write heads to move to the correct place on the disk to read or write a particular file.

Hard disks first entered the computer scene in 1973. Developed by IBM, early hard disks were known as Winchester drives, because that was IBM's code name for the project. As with many new computer developments, the first hard disks were very expensive. It wasn't until personal computers became commonplace that hard

disks became affordable. Up until the advent of hard disks, floppy disks were the primary storage devices used to store computer data. Compared with floppy disks, hard disks are sturdier, more reliable, and hold a lot of data. Hard disks are also much faster at retrieving and storing data than floppy disk drives are.

The two most prominent interface standards used with hard disks today are IDE (Integrated Drive Electronics, pronounced "I-D-E") and SCSI (Small Computer System Interface,

continues

Hard Disk Drive continued

How Does It Work?

pronounced "skuzzy"). These interface standards determine the way in which the drives are connected to the system unit. Most PCs come with an IDE drive and connector that attaches the drive directly to the motherboard. An IDE drive's controller chip (the chip that controls the flow of data to and from the drive) is integrated into the drive itself, hence the name. SCSI is a special high-speed interface that can be used to connect several SCSI devices (hard disks, floppy drives, and CD-ROM drives, etc.) together on the same expansion bus. SCSI drives are faster and more powerful than IDE drives and, consequently, are more expensive.

Although it contains several disk platters, a hard disk is treated as a single unit and is assigned the drive letter C. (Floppy disk drives are assigned drive letters A and B.) However, hard disk drives can be divided into sections (partitions), which are treated by the operating system as if they were separate disks. These pretend disk drives are called logical drives, and are assigned letters D, E, and so on. Early versions of DOS could not keep track of files on hard disks larger than 32 megabytes, so disk partitioning was sometimes a necessity. Beginning with

DOS version 4.0, this limitation was removed, so disk partitioning is no longer necessary—but with the large hard disks common today, it's sometimes easier for users to partition their hard disks into more manageable chunks.

Before a hard drive can be used, it must be formatted, or divided into sections so that data can be stored in a specific area where it will be easily located. The formatting process is usually done for the user, at the time the computer is purchased. Formatting is a process that only needs to be done once, to prepare the disk for use; therefore, it is unlikely that a user will ever need to format a hard disk himself.

Data is stored on the hard disk in concentric circles, called tracks. Tracks are divided into equal parts, called sectors. Several sectors together form a cluster, which is the smallest storage unit used to save a file. The hard disk's internal map, called the File Allocation Table (FAT), keeps track of where data is stored on the hard disk. Also see Data Storage, Defragmentation, Floppy Disk, Floppy Disk Drive, Motherboard, and System Unit.

When the user enters a command to save a file to the computer's hard drive, a message is sent to the disk drive controller. Using the contents of the file allocation table (FAT), the operating system locates an available cluster of storage space in which to save the file. The controller sends a message to the head actuator to move the read-write heads to the proper spot.

A magnetic pulse realigns the particles on the surface of the magnetic platter to form a pattern representing the file contents. The pattern of magnetic particles on the surface of the disk forms the 1's and 0's used to store data in the computer. When the file is needed again, the read-write heads will scan the platter for the pattern and translate it into pulses the controller can send back to the operating system.

Head actuator

PARTITION

To separate a hard drive into sections, called logical drives, for storage. Each section has a different drive letter, such as C, D, and E. Although the hard disk is one unit, each section is treated by the operating system as if it were its own disk.

FRAGMENTATION

When a file is saved, it is often necessary to break it into parts in order to fill the first available clusters. This fragments data over the disk, making it take longer for the hard drive to locate all the pieces of a file.

File Allocation Table (FAT)

BYTE

A group of eight bits that represents a character, such as the number 10 or the letter F. Hard disk storage is measured in megabytes, roughly 1 million bytes.

DEFRAGMENTATION

Reorganization of the data on a hard disk so that all the pieces of a file are located in adjacent clusters. This makes it easier for the hard drive to locate a file quickly.

FAT

Short for File Allocation Table, the FAT is a map that tells the operating system where files are located on a floppy or hard disk.

BERNOULLI BOX

Essentially a removable hard disk, a Bernoulli box is a series of flexible platters enclosed in a plastic case, which have a storage capacity of between 44MB and 150MB. Bernoulli boxes are not as popular as they once were. A similar technology by SyQuest is gaining popularity.

A file can be stored in several places on the disk

Read-write heads

Hardware

Hardware is the physical equipment that comprises a computer system, including the monitor, printer, keyboard, cables, and more. Hardware works with software to perform tasks on the computer. Software is the program instruction that tells a computer what to do with the hardware and how to process data. Hardware cannot work without software, and vice versa.

Hardware is made up of a number of pieces, each of which has a specific purpose. For example, the computer's system unit is considered the main piece of hardware for the computer. Inside the system unit are dozens of other hardware parts such as the microprocessor (CPU) that acts as the brains of the computer, memory chips that store data as it's being processed, a hard disk that stores data permanently, a power supply unit, and more.

Hardware

also includes other machines hooked up to the computer, known as peripherals. Peripherals include such things as the keyboard, monitor, mouse, modem, printer, joystick, scanner, and tape backup unit. As the uses for computers grow, new hardware is created to serve these new functions. Also see BIOS, Central

Processing Unit, CD-ROM, Data Storage, Expansion Cards, Floppy Disk Drive, Hard Disk Drive, Input Devices, Joystick, Keyboard, Modem, Monitor, Motherboard, Mouse, Output Devices, Peripherals, Power Supply, Printer, Scanner, Sound Board, System Unit, Tape Backup Unit, and Trackball.

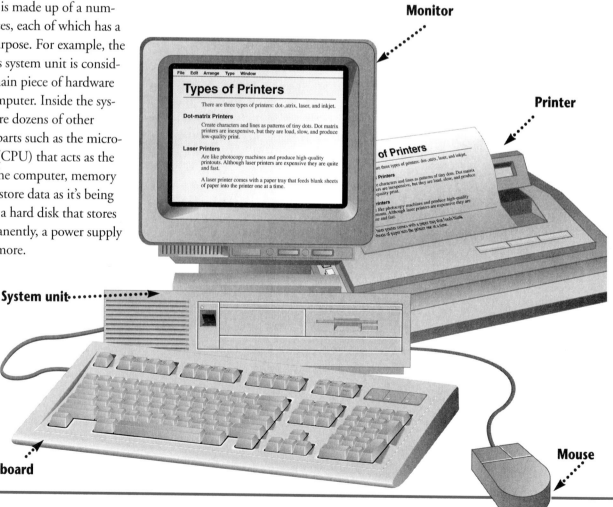

Monitor

Printer

System unit

Keyboard

Mouse

Hayes

Hayes™ Microcomputer Products, Inc. was founded in 1978 by Dennis Hayes. Hayes manufactures computer modems, devices that transmit data from one computer to another through ordinary telephone lines. Hayes makes modems for IBM, IBM-compatible, and Macintosh computers. By far, Hayes modems are the most popular modems on the market today. In fact, they are so widely used and have established so many modem standards, that other manufacturers make their modems Hayes-compatible—which means they support the communication standards set by Hayes.

A modem, which is short for MOdulator/DEModulator, is simply a device that lets computers transmit data through regular telephone lines. A modem converts the digital signals (1's and 0's) that are understood by a computer into analog signals (tones) that can travel through a phone line. The receiving computer's modem converts the analog signals back into digital signals that the computer can understand. Modems are used not only to transmit data back and forth between computers, but also to access electronic bulletin board services and on-line communica-

tions services such as CompuServe, Prodigy, and America OnLine, to name a few.

In 1981, Hayes introduced the Hayes™ Smartmodem™, a product that utilized the Hayes Standard AT Command Set and basically revolutionized the field of computer communications. The Hayes™ AT command set is a standard set of commands that a modem must respond to (for example "dial a number" or "hang up"). Prior to the introduction of the Hayes™ Smartmodem™, a user had to establish communications by

throwing switches and hoping the modem on the other end was set up the same way.

The Hayes™ AT command set soon became an industry standard. This allowed software manufacturers to create communications programs that worked with all modems that supported the Hayes™ AT command set, further automating the process of modem communications. Hayes provides its own communications program, Hayes Smartcom™, with all the modems it sells.

A Hayes pocket-size modem

Reproduced by permission of Hayes Microcomputer Products, Inc.

continues

Hayes continued

Modems from the Hayes family of modems are considered intelligent modems because they can accept instructions as well as handle the transmission, dialing, answering, and receiving of data. Since the introduction of the Hayes Smartmodem, modems have become readily accessible for computer users, and fairly simple to use. Hayes offers a variety of modems, including internal (a modem on a circuit board that is inserted into an expansion slot), external (a modem connected to the PC by a cable), and portable (a miniature modem that can be easily transported; for use with portable computers). In addition, Hayes offers a wide variety of fax modems (modems that can transmit and receive data to/from a fax machine). Also see BBS, Communications, Modem, and Output Devices.

EXTERNAL MODEM

A modem box that sits beside the computer and is connected to it through a serial port (a PC connector that transfers data through a cable, one bit at a time).

INTERNAL MODEM

A modem that plugs into an expansion slot located inside the computer.

Reproduced by permission of Hayes Microcomputer Products, Inc.
The Hayes SmartModem™

BPS

Short for Bits Per Second, bps is the unit of measurement of the speed at which a modem can send bits of data over the telephone line. Modems today transmit data at 2400, 4800, 9600 and 14400 bps.

BAUD RATE

The number of changes per second in the transmission signal is called the baud rate. Baud rate was once used to describe the speed with which a modem transmitted data, but now bps is used.

Hewlett-Packard

Hewlett-Packard was founded in 1939 by William Hewlett and David Packard in Palo Alto, California. The company has a long history of electronic innovations including scientific equipment, midrange computers, calculators, printers, and personal computers. Their first product was an audio oscillator, a device that measures sound. This device was used by Walt Disney Studios during the production of the movie "Fantasia."

In 1966, Hewlett-Packard (also known as HP) produced the first in a series of midrange computers especially for laboratory and manufacturing use. These computers were connected to various HP scientific equipment, and they were used in the collection and analysis of scientific data. In 1972, Hewlett-Packard began developing computers for the business market. This line of computers, called the HP 3000 series, used a command line interface designed with Microsoft's help (the company that would later produce Microsoft DOS). That same year, HP introduced the first pocket calculator. In 1980,

Hewlett-Packard introduced its first personal computer, the HP-85, the first in a long series of personal computers.

In 1984, HP introduced its first printer, the HP Thinkjet, which utilized a new technology called inkjet printing. Inkjet printers spray controlled drops of ink onto paper to form an image, letter, or number. In 1985, HP hit the market with an innovative printer that has gone on to much

fame and fortune, the HP LaserJet. This achievement was no surprise, coming from the company that almost single-handedly developed the plotter (another type of computer printer that uses colored pens and ink).

Hewlett-Packard's laser printers have set standards in the manufacturing of computer printers. The first HP LaserJet offered 300 dots-per-inch resolution that produced sharply detailed output, all

HP Laserjet printer

Courtesy of
Hewlett-Packard
Company

continues

Hewlett-Packard continued

in a convenient desktop printer. The LaserJet's high quality output and relatively low price helped create the demand for desktop publishing applications and capabilities. All HP LaserJet printers use a page description language (called the Hewlett-Packard Printer Control Language, or HPPCL), which enables an application to send detailed information describing an entire page of output to a laser printer. HPPCL has been adopted as a standard description language for most laser printers, although it is not as richly detailed as PostScript, another page description language.

Hewlett-Packard continues to make innovative computers, computer components, electronics, and printers for a variety of functions. Today, Hewlett-Packard products are used around the world. Also see Output Devices and Printer.

The HP Deskjet 1200C printers work in black and color providing superior print quality for text and color using inkjet technology.

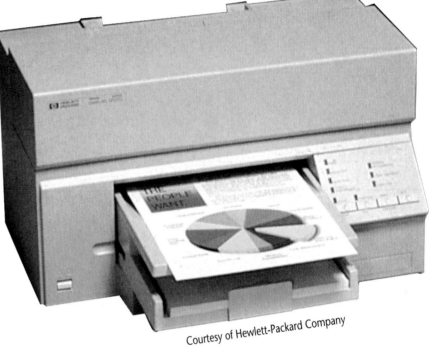

Courtesy of Hewlett-Packard Company

DOT-MATRIX PRINTER

An impact printer that uses an internal printing head to imprint dots on a page by pushing small, blunt-end pins into an inked ribbon.

LASER PRINTER

A non-impact printer that uses lasers to create an image on an electrically charged drum. The image is then transferred to paper. Laser printers produce better quality output than dot-matrix printers do.

INK-JET PRINTER

A printer that creates its image by spraying controlled droplets of ink onto paper through a series of tiny nozzles.

**The HP Vectra 486
personal computer**

Courtesy of Hewlett-Packard Company

POSTSCRIPT

Another page description language, PostScript provides a laser printer with more information, describing the actual fonts (typeface and type size) to be used when printing text. HPPCL, in contrast, assumes that the fonts are already present in the printer.

HPPCL

Hewlett-Packard Printer Control Language, a page description language used with laser printers. A page description language describes how to print a page that contains text and graphic (pictures).

**The HP Palm
computer**

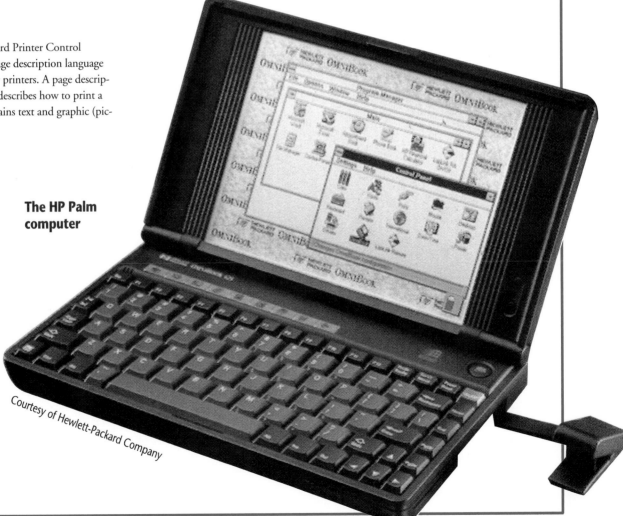

Courtesy of Hewlett-Packard Company

HyperCard

HyperCard, created for Apple Macintosh and Apple IIGS computers by Bill Atkinson, resembles an electronic index card file. HyperCard is similar to a database management program in that it organizes large amounts of related data. As an information management tool, HyperCard is unique. HyperCard is an authoring language that allows a non-programmer to create his own "application." An application created with HyperCard resembles an interconnected stack of cards containing any combination of text, sound, video, graphics, etc. By selecting a particular button, a user can switch to another card in the stack, listen to prerecorded messages, watch an animated demonstration, and more. HyperCard (or a slimmed down version of it) is shipped free with every Macintosh computer. Because the user can move through the stack of cards in his own way, HyperCard is perfect for creating computer based training courses (CBTs). Using the hyperlinks that connect various cards to one another, a user can proceed through a training course at his own pace, detouring to a side card to get additional information on a topic when needed. HyperCard stacks are also useful for creating multimedia presentations, and for creating prototypes for more complex programs, which will eventually be written in a sophisticated programming language. Also see Apple, Computer Based Training, Database, Macintosh, and System 7.

An address card from a HyperCard stack

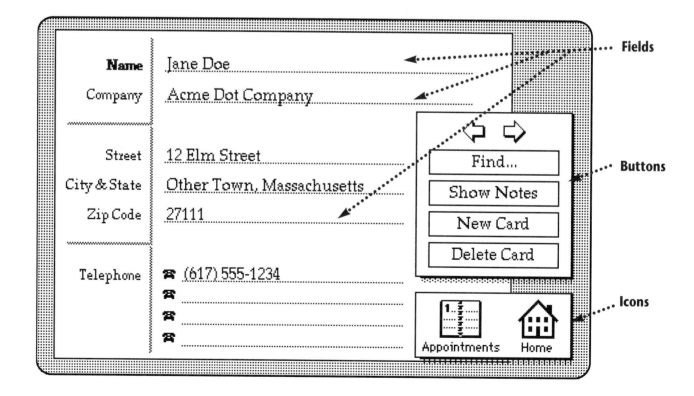

How Does It Work?

There are a variety of uses for cards and stacks. The user can click on a word or picture on one card that immediately takes him to another card with related information. Buttons can be added to a card that will start a series of programmed routines when pressed. These little programs, called scripts, utilize the HyperCard's programming language, HyperTalk. For example, when working with a stack called Address, the user can press a button that opens up another card that functions as an appointment book. HyperCard comes with several pre-formed stacks ready to use. A sample stack called Train can be used to draw a train track and make a little engine run around the track, complete with train noises. This particular stack also demonstrates the programming capabilities of HyperCard.

HYPERTEXT

Words on a HyperCard that, when selected, take the user to related information about the word, show a picture, or even print a definition.

USERLEVEL

To keep HyperCard stacks safe, Apple has programmed several user level settings to keep valuable information from being erased. The word UserLevel is the command for setting this feature.

HYPERTALK

The name of the language used to write instructions on HyperCards.

Click this button to start the train.

Train

Track: Lazy Eight

New Card | Build | Repair | Rotate | Run | Speed

A HyperCard stack called Train

Click this button to change the train's direction.

Clicking on a word or button opens another Hypercard.

WORLDWIDE GROWTH

REVIEW TEST

1.
2.
3.
4.

A1-COMPANY

TEST

We're committed to Worldwide growth and quality products.

REVIEW TEST | COMPANY HISTORY | PRODUCT LINES | OFFICE PRODUCTS

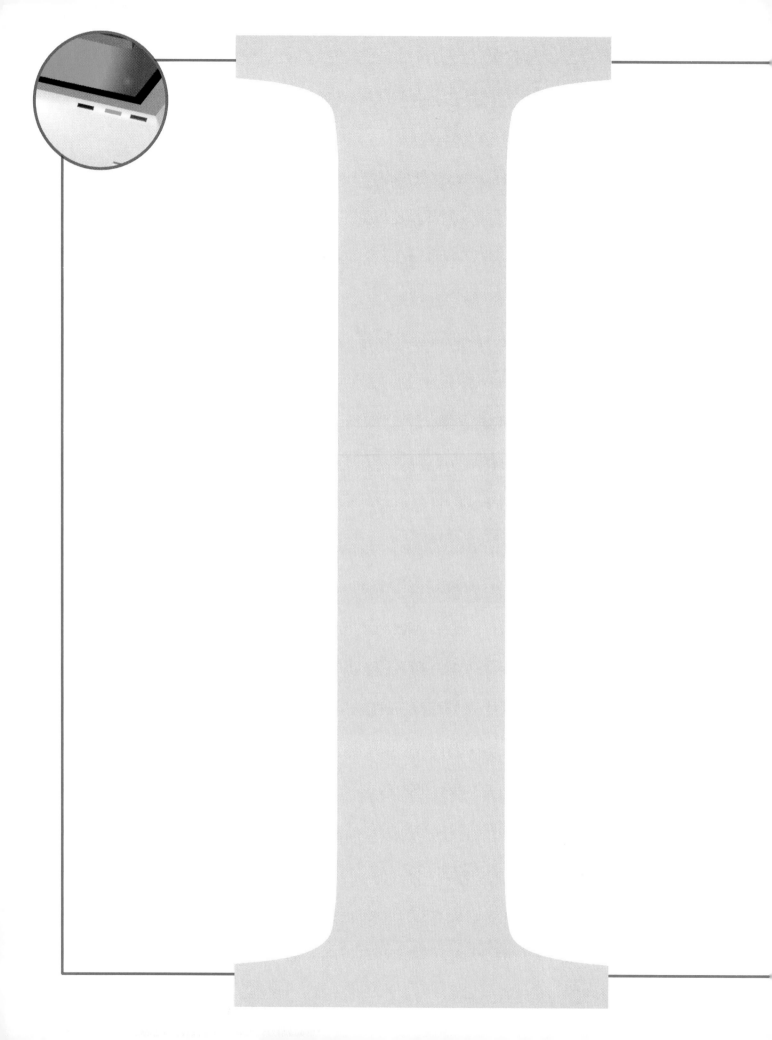

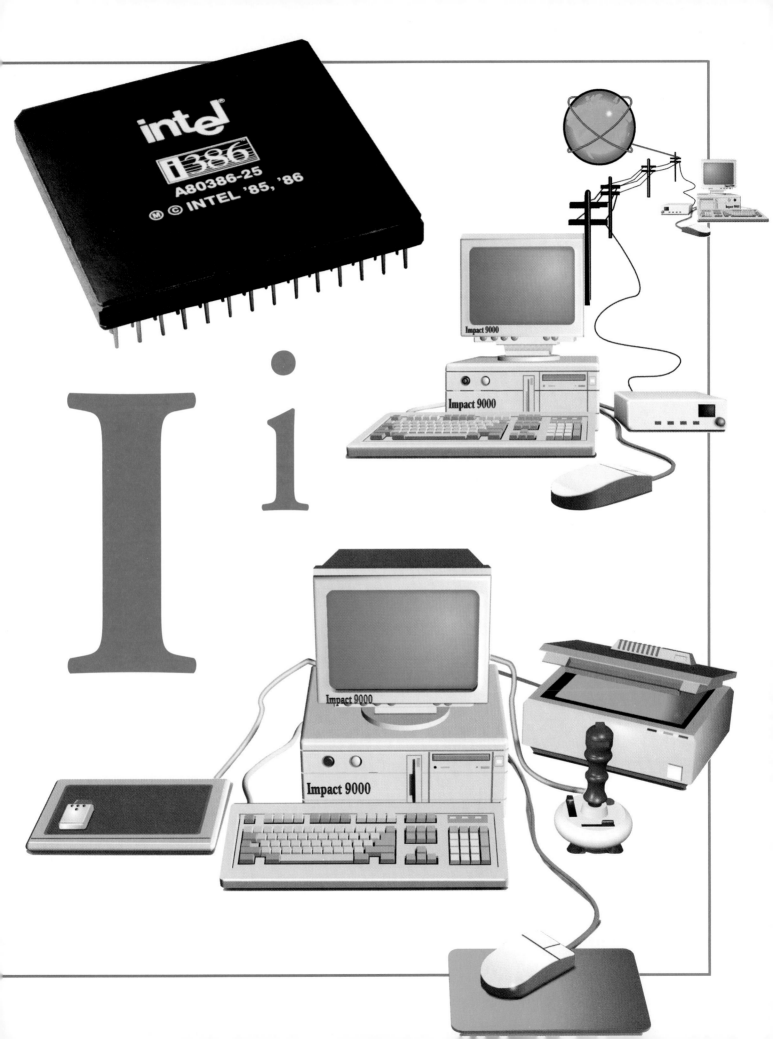

IBM

The world's largest computer company was created in 1924, when the Computing-Tabulating-Recording Co. (CTR) was transformed into International Business Machines (IBM) by Thomas J. Watson, Sr., the general manager of CTR. For several years, IBM manufactured tabulating machines and the punched cards that were associated with them, creating a large customer network. IBM built an empire with high-quality, dependable products and a knowledgeable sales force (many were engineers). For example, although IBM was not the first company to produce electric typewriters, its Selectric line is still considered one of the best and most dependable.

IBM was behind the development of a large partly electrical, partly mechanical calculator called the Mark I. Weighing five tons, the Mark I was capable of performing three calculations per second, and it was used in WWII to calculate trajectories for the guns used in fighter planes. In 1953, IBM introduced its 701 mainframe, several years after Remington Rand had become favored over IBM tabulators at the Census Bureau. IBM quickly followed the 701 series with the 650 in 1954. Using punched cards and magnetic tape, the 650 became the most-used computer in the world by the end of the decade. The 1401 came out in 1959 and was used until the late 1960s. It used punched cards also and had 16 kilobytes of memory.

System/360 was a family of compatible computers that were introduced in 1964 and set the standards for IBM mainframe computers. Two more families of mainframes, System/370 and System/390 were introduced in 1970 and 1990, respectively.

IBM also produced several mini-computers in the 1970s, such as System/3, System/34, System/38, Series/1, and 8100. When each minicomputer was introduced, it practically made the previous model obsolete because the newer one was so much more powerful. In 1988, the AS/400 (Application System) series was introduced and has since been enormously successful, probably because it offers a wide variety of networking connections.

A typical example of a room filled with IBM mainframes.

Tape drives   **Card reader**   **Operator's terminal**   **Printer**

Courtesy of International Business Machines Corporation

Disk drives

IBM introduced its Personal Computer (PC) in 1981, several years after other companies had entered the infant PC market. Instead of designing a computer from scratch, IBM assembled a team of engineers in Boca Raton, Florida to analyze the market. Assembling their computer from the best parts available—and adding innovations of their own—this team produced what was to become a landmark in computing.

The success of the IBM PC was due partly to IBM's reputation for quality and dependability, but mostly to a decision by IBM to make its design available to hardware developers. This led to a sub-industry called "making things for the IBM PC." With so much support available, the IBM PC could be easily expanded with the insertion of additional circuit boards created by outside manufacturers. This idea of expandability had made the Apple a success, and IBM quickly overshadowed all competition. The IBM PC became the standard against which all other PCs were judged. Because of their participation in the development of the IBM PC, two other companies, Microsoft (which supplied the operating system) and Intel (which supplied the microprocessor) have also become extremely successful.

Slowly over the next decade, IBM continued to release new

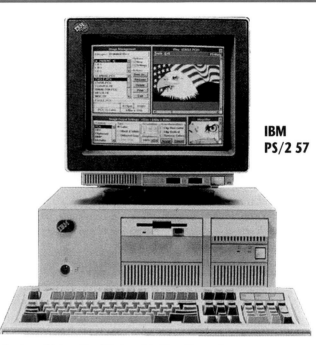

IBM PS/2 57

Courtesy of International Business Machines Corporation

innovations for the IBM PC. In 1983, IBM released the PC XT (Extended Technology), its first computer to include a hard disk. The PC AT (Advanced Technology) followed in 1984, setting many standards that were copied by leading PC manufacturers at the time. The PS/2 (Personal System) family was introduced in 1987, with several versions available. The PS/2 line was designed to be fast, easy to update, and competitive. The IBM PS/1 line, aimed at the home market, was introduced in 1990, but it has enjoyed only marginal success. IBM makes portable computers too. The first one, called the Portable PC, came out in 1983. Since then, IBM has manufactured several other types of portable computers, such as the ThinkPad series, which was introduced in 1993.

IBM is more than just computers. IBM's dot-matrix printers (called Pro Printers) and its LaserPrinters have both been highly successful for the company. IBM printers are now manufactured by a company called Lexmark out of Lexington, Kentucky. Also see IBM-PC Compatible, Mainframe, and PC.

MAINFRAME

A large scale computer that is about the size of a large room. Often used in large corporations and universities, mainframe computers can handle processing chores for a series of PCs or dumb terminals connected to it by cables or modems (a network).

PERSONAL COMPUTER

A line of computers developed for individual home and corporate use.

IBM-PC Compatible

The IBM-PC compatible is a name that refers to all personal computers *not* manufactured by IBM. PC compatibles are made by IBM's competitors and are designed to work the same as IBM's PC. These comparable machines are also called "clones" because they imitate the successful PC so effectively. PC compatibles are usually priced less than IBM's PCs, and they run the same software programs that are available for PCs. PC compatible computers are manufactured by companies such as Gateway, Compaq, Dell, and NEC. In order to understand the importance of PC compatibles in the marketplace, one must first examine the history of the IBM PC itself.

Introduced in 1981, IBM 's Personal Computer included the Intel 8088 microprocessor. Because the IBM team of engineers had just finished creating another computer with an Intel CPU (the IBM DataMaster), they were already familiar with Intel microprocessors. The 8088 had an 8-bit data bus (the electronic highway inside a computer over which data travels), which made it a better choice than the 16-bit 8086 because 16-bit peripherals were expensive at the time and not many people could afford them. The 8088 CPU was also less expensive than the 8086, which made the cost of the IBM PC more affordable.

Microsoft was at the right place at the right time, and landed the most important contract of its life: a contract to design the operating system for the IBM PC. IBM named its operating system PC-DOS. Microsoft retained the rights to DOS, so they came out with MS-DOS, an operating system similar to PC-DOS, which competitors used to create "IBM-compatible" computers. The term "IBM-compatible" has come to include a large group of computers that support these IBM standards: the use of Microsoft DOS, Intel, or clone CPUs, and a host of other standards that include monitor and keyboard design.

Introduced in 1983, the IBM Personal Computer XT (XT stood for Extended Technology) included a hard disk for data storage as one of its main features. In 1984, the IBM Personal Computer AT (Advanced Technology) was introduced. The AT used the Intel 80286 microprocessor, which had advanced memory management capabilities. The AT was also the first PC with a 16-bit data bus. The popularity of the AT spawned an entire breed of "AT compatibles," PCs that included the 80286 CPU and the AT-style keyboard. The PCjr, a less expensive computer meant for home use, was also introduced in 1984 but did not do well on the market and was discontinued in 1985.

DOS

Stands for Disk Operating System. DOS, made by Microsoft Corporation, is an operating system for the personal computer that tells the machine how to run. Without an operating system, the computer is useless and cannot perform any tasks. DOS is famous for being the operating system used by IBM PCs and PC compatible computers.

Courtesy of International Business Machines Corporation

The one that set the trend for PCs to come, the original IBM-PC

IBM

International Business Machines, a leading computer manufacturer responsible for innovative mainframe and personal computers. IBM is famous for inventing the IBM PC, a personal computer that, since its introduction in 1981, has dominated the market and spurred lots of imitations.

INTEL

A leading manufacturer of microprocessor chips, the tiny chips that act as the brains of the personal computer. Intel chips were used in the IBM PC computer as well as its clones made by other manufacturers.

The next major change in the Personal Computer came in April, 1987, when IBM introduced the PS/2 (Personal System/2). The PS/2 had a new design, incorporated a new technology called Micro Channel, and was harder to clone by other companies. The PS/2 was followed by the PS/1 in 1990; the PS/1 was a slightly scaled-down version of the Personal System 2 that was intended for home use.

IBM remains one of the industry's leaders, whose innovations are often copied by competitors.

It is perhaps the single most recognized brand of PCs. The design and idea behind IBM computers has been imitated by many computer manufacturers, whose products are called "IBM-compatible PCs" or simply "clones." Owning an IBM PC may not mean what it once did, since there are several reputable corporations who produce excellent quality machines—which are less expensive than their IBM counterpart. However, IBM's reputation for quality and service (especially for its corporate clients) remains a strong selling point. Also see IBM, Intel, Mainframe, Microsoft, and PC.

IBM-COMPATIBLE OR CLONE

A computer that is compatible with an IBM PC but is not made by IBM. Clones are generally less expensive than IBM computers, but they do not necessarily compromise quality. Popular manufacturers of IBM-compatibles include Compaq, Gateway, Dell, NEC, and Zeos.

Improv

Lotus Corporation (one of the leaders in the development of the electronic spreadsheet) completely revamped the traditional spreadsheet when they created Lotus Improv. A spreadsheet program arranges numbers, performs calculations, handles mathematical formulas, and organizes data. While normal spreadsheet programs (like Microsoft Excel and Lotus 1-2-3) use numbered rows and lettered columns to create the structure of a spreadsheet, Improv uses items and categories. The user can move the items and categories around on the spreadsheet simply by dragging the mouse. This fea-

ture enables the user to change the entire organization and layout of the spreadsheet quickly and painlessly. For example, an Improv spreadsheet that displays quarterly sales by salesperson can be quickly reorganized to display sales per division. With other spreadsheet programs, the user might have to manually rearrange and retype cell data.

The Improv spreadsheet is different from any other spreadsheet in many ways: its spreadsheet can be easily reorganized and the formulas are flexible. For example, the user can define a formula that adds a group of cells to compute a

quarterly total, and no matter where those cells are moved or how they are reorganized, the formula will stay correct. For experienced spreadsheet users, using a dynamic spreadsheet like Improv can seem a bit strange. But for someone who has never used a spreadsheet, Improv's items and categories make designing a spreadsheet easy, and the formula-writing method is easy to understand. Also see Application, Excel, Lotus 1-2-3, and Spreadsheet.

CATEGORY

The largest classification unit in Improv. All items are associated with a category. There can be no more than 12 categories in a worksheet.

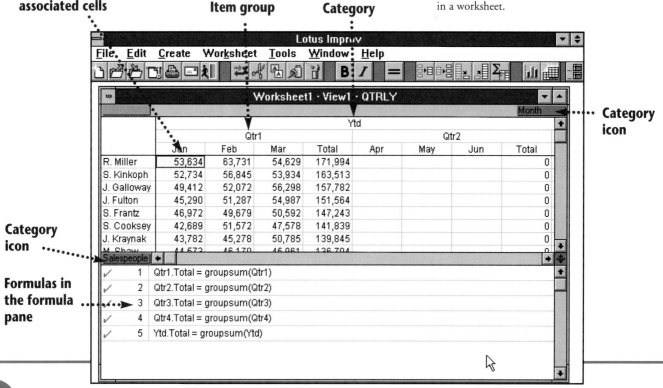

Jan item and its associated cells

Quarter #1 Item group

Category

Category icon

Category icon

Formulas in the formula pane

How Does It Work?

In Improv, an item consists of two things: the item name and the associated cells. Items are separated into item groups and categories. In the figures, the view of the spreadsheet was changed by dragging the category icons. The Total Sales and Year category icons were transposed to give the spreadsheet a totally new look. Another significant difference between Improv and traditional spreadsheet programs is the formula writing method. In a standard spreadsheet, the user writes the formula directly into a cell, using numbers and cell addresses to calculate formulas. Improv formulas are written in a formula pane beneath the spreadsheet, using item names instead of cell addresses. The formulas apply to the whole spreadsheet, making the location of the items irrelevant. No matter where the user moves the items, the formulas still apply.

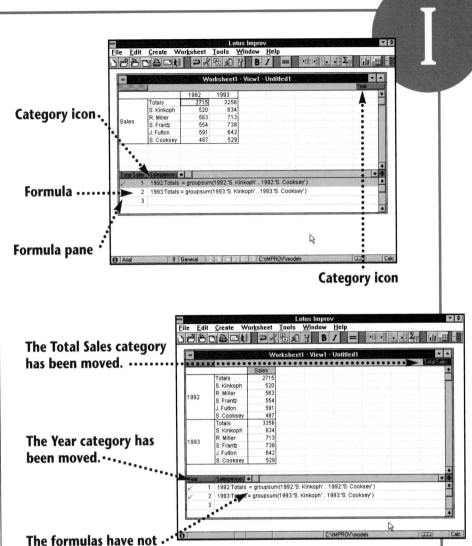

Category icon

Formula

Formula pane

Category icon

The Total Sales category has been moved.

The Year category has been moved.

The formulas have not changed and are still correct.

ITEM GROUP

Several related items that are grouped together. The number of item groups is unlimited. Item groups cannot be rearranged like categories can. For example, the items January, February, and March (and all of their associated cells) form a group called Qtr1.

FORMULAS

Improv formulas consist of words instead of numbers. For example, Total = Income – Expenses is a formula.

ITEM

A collection of cells (the intersection of a row and a column) that contain related information. For example, the item January includes the cell that contains the label "January," as well as all the cells associated with it: the cells containing January sales data. An item is the lowest grouping of cells in an Improv spreadsheet.

FORMULA PANE

The formula pane is the area of the Improv window located below the spreadsheet layout. Any formula in the formula pane can be used throughout the whole worksheet.

Input Devices

Input devices are essential for entering data into the computer. Without them, there is no other means of communicating with the computer. Because of their importance, it is a good idea to keep the input devices in good working condition. Devices such as the keyboard and the mouse should be cleaned regularly to keep them functioning at their greatest potential.

Some might consider computer parts such as a modem or external drive unit to be input devices as well. True, these devices can input data into the computer, but that is not their sole function. A modem assists in the communication between two computers. An external drive unit, such as a hard disk drive or a floppy disk drive, is used to store data. Technically, the only devices that are considered input devices are those that strictly focus on creating an avenue of inputing data

into the computer. The data that the computer receives from a user is called input. In order to calculate, organize, or process information, a computer has to receive input from a source. Thus, any device that a person uses to give a computer information is called an input device. A common input device is a keyboard; another is a mouse. There

TRACKBALL

A device commonly used with laptop computers because of space limitations. A trackball is basically an upside-down mouse. The user rotates the trackball with his fingers instead of pushing a mouse around on a desktop.

are, of course, less common and more sophisticated input devices as well, such as trackballs, voice recognition systems, scanners, touch screens, and graphics tablets. Also see **Device Driver, Expansion Cards, Hardware, Joystick, Keyboard, Mouse, Output Devices, Pen Computing, Peripherals, Scanner, Trackball,** and **Voice Recognition.**

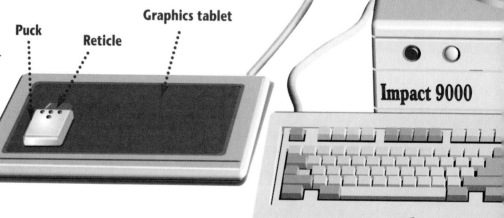

Puck   **Reticle**   **Graphics tablet**

Impact 9000

Impact 9000

Keyboard

GRAPHICS TABLET

Every point on the flat graphics tablet corresponds to a point on the computer's monitor. The graphics tablet is used with a stylus (which is shaped like a pen) or a puck (which is shaped like a mouse). The tip of the stylus sends electrical signals to the graphics tablet, which in turn sends the signals to the computer. The puck has a sighting grid called a reticle attached to it so the user can trace complex drawings.

KEYBOARD

The most common input device. It comes with traditional typewriter keys, function keys, and cursor-movement keys.

VOICE RECOGNITION SOFTWARE

Special software that lets the user select commands by talking. The software converts human speech to a digital code the computer can understand and process. Voice recognition technology is still in its infancy and is currently in development.

PEN COMPUTING

Pen computing is found among users of small, portable computers that require the use of an electronic pen to enter data. The pen itself is considered an input device. Similar to a mouse, a pen allows the user to make on-screen selections, and enter words or pictures. Popular pen-based computers include personal digital assistants (PDAs) that let the user on-the-go record pertinent data to compile address or phone lists, electronic notes, and databases.

Flatbed scanner

SCANNER

There are two types of scanners: flatbed and hand-held. A flatbed scanner works (and looks) like a copy machine. The image (on paper) is inserted in the machine and it is scanned. It is then converted to signals the computer can understand. A hand-held scanner is much smaller, and is good for capturing small images or pictures that are on irregular surfaces. To use it, the user slowly runs the scanner across the image. To view the scanned image on a monitor, the user must have special software. Scanned images can usually (depending upon the software) be edited and printed out.

Joystick

JOYSTICK

A device generally used for moving, jumping, shooting, etc. in computer games. The handle in the center of the joystick is used to move an object on-screen, such as a car, a plane, or a person.

Mouse

MOUSE

A hand-held device that is moved around on a pad or a desktop to control a pointer on-screen.

Integrated Software

Integrated software packages offer simple, scaled-down versions of several different types of applications, all in one unit. For example, most integrated software packages include simple word processing, spreadsheet, and database programs. Most also include extras such as a communications program for use with a modem, a graphics program for creating art, and various personal management utilities. In an integrated software package, the applications are called modules.

There are many advantages to using an integrated package: the user only has to shop for one package instead of several

individual applications, the format of the modules is similar and therefore easy to use once the user is familiar with the format, and the relative cost of the software is cheaper. The main disadvantage is that the modules do not include some of the advanced features of the high-end software programs. For someone who is not interested in creating complex documents but wants to write a few letters, maintain a simple database, or calculate a personal budget, an integrated software package is ideal. Some of the popular integrated software packages include: Microsoft Works for Windows, ClarisWorks (from Claris Corp.), LotusWorks,

and PFS: WindowWorks (from Spinnaker Software Corp.).

For those users who like the idea of having a software package containing multiple programs with a similar format but need the high-end capabilities of a stand-alone application, a suite is probably the answer. Several software companies—including Lotus, Microsoft, and Borland—produce office application suites that combine their most popular programs. For example, Lotus SmartSuite includes Lotus 1-2-3 for Windows, Ami Pro, Approach, Freelance Graphics, and Lotus Organizer. The suite is considerably less expensive than the programs would be individually, but the suite is still much more expensive than a comparable integrated software package. (Suites are generally aimed at the corporate audience.) The most popular suites are Microsoft Office Professional, Lotus SmartSuite for Windows, and Borland Office for Windows. Also see Application, Database, Drawing Programs, Paint Programs, Spreadsheet, and Word Processing.

The Startup screen from Microsoft Works for Windows

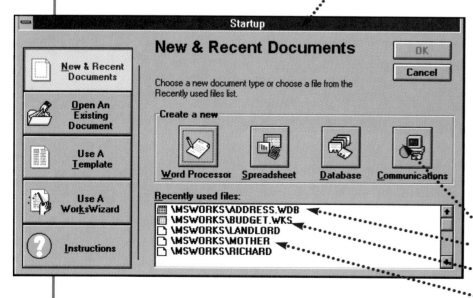

How Does It Work?

From a startup screen, the user selects the module he wants to use. When he is finished with that module, he closes the file and is returned to the startup screen. From there, he can open another module or exit the program.

In addition, a user could conveniently copy a drawing from the graphics module to the Clipboard, and then paste it into a letter in the word processing module. As an example of how the modules work together, a user can create a form letter in the word processing module of Microsoft Works and use entries in a database for addresses in the letter.

Field names from the database

An entry in the Address Book database

MODULE

One of the scaled-down application-like programs in an integrated software package. Most integrated software packages contain word processing, spreadsheet, database, and communications modules.

GRAPHICS PROGRAM

A program created for designing and drawing on the computer.

DATABASE

An application used to organize large quantities of data.

The database and the form letter combine to create a complete letter.

WORD PROCESSING PROGRAM

An application that allows the user to manipulate text to create letters, memos, résumés, manuscripts, and other written documents.

SPREADSHEET

Spreadsheet programs can manipulate numbers, perform calculations, handle mathematical formulas, and organize data.

Intel Corporation

The Intel Corporation was founded in 1968 by Bob Noyce and Gorden Moore in California. They originally manufactured memory chips, but in 1971 they created the first microprocessor, the Intel 4004 chip. The idea and design of this integrated chip has been credited to Ted Hoff, Stan Mazor, and Federico Faggin, who designed it for a Japanese calculator manufacturer called Busicom. Now, Intel is the major manufacturer of personal computer microprocessors.

The history of the microprocessor in PCs (also called the CPU or central processing unit) began in 1973, when Intel introduced the 8-bit, 2MHz 8080 chip that was used with the Altair, the first commer-cially successful personal computer. The chip had 6,000 transistors (compared to 3.1 million transistors in today's Pentium chips). A transistor is a tiny on/off switch that forms part of the decision pathways within the CPU. With 8-bits, not a lot of data could be transferred to and from the CPU at any given time. At a clock speed of only 2 megahertz or MHz (equal to 2 million cycles per second), that small amount of data did not arrive at the CPU very often.

The 8086 microprocessor, which had a 16-bit internal data bus, was introduced in 1978. That chip was not successful because the prices for 16-bit peripherals and support chips were very expensive at the time. As a result, Intel came out with the 8088 chip in 1979, which had an 8-bit external data bus as well as a 16-bit internal bus. (Think of the 8088 chip as being like a highway with sixteen lanes of processing power, funnelling a tunnel with only eight data lanes.) The Intel 8088 chip operated a bit

The Intel 80386 chip

Courtesy of Intel Corporation

faster
than its
cousin, at
4.77MHz, and
could access 1
megabyte of memory. It
was less expensive and could be
used with more affordable
peripherals, so IBM chose the
8088 chip for their IBM
Personal Computer. The
overnight success of the IBM-
PC guaranteed the future of the
Intel CPU.

In 1984, Intel introduced their
80286 microprocessor, which
could address up to 16
megabytes of RAM. The 286
was used in the IBM Personal
Computer AT. The 80286 chip
had two modes: "real mode"
which limited the CPU to 1MB
of memory and allowed it to
emulate the 8088 chip, and
"protected mode" which allowed
it to use up to 16MB of memory. This allowed for compatibility with programs written for the
8088 chip. The 80286 chip led

to
the
80386DX
in 1985. It had
a full 32-bit data
bus structure, could
address 4 gigabytes of RAM,
supported virtual memory, had
more than 275,000 transistors,
and ran at a clock speed of up to
33MHz (some 386 chips were
slower). The 386 chip also has
an SX version (which was a
scaled-down, less-expensive version of the 386DX) and an SL
version (which was a smaller
sized chip used for laptops).

**The Intel
Pentium chip on
a motherboard**

continues

Intel Corporation continued

The basic architecture used in the design of the 386 chip was used for the next two generations of Intel CPUs: the 486 and the Pentium chips. The 486DX chip was introduced in 1989. It has a full 32-bit data bus structure like the 386 chip, but it can address 64 gigabytes of memory. It has over a million transistors and includes an internal math coprocessor. (Up to this time, a math coprocessor was an optional chip that worked in conjunction with the CPU to process mathematical calculations.) It executes instructions faster than a 386 chip, so even the 486 chips operating at 20MHz are faster than 386 25MHz chips. The 486 chip also has an SX counterpart, but (unlike the 386SX chip) it isn't exactly a scaled-down version of the 486 chip: the 486SX chip simply does not include the math coprocessor. Intel also manufactures a 486SL chip for laptops.

In 1993, Intel introduced their newest CPU: the Pentium chip. The Pentium chip operates at speeds up to 66MHz, and is three to five times faster than the 33MHz 486DX chip. Making this chip so much faster and better than the 486DX chip, it uses 3.1 million transistors (compared to 1.2 million in the 486DX chip). In addition, the Pentium chip includes two instruction pathways, so it can literally do two things at once. The Pentium chip is larger than the older chips because of the multitude of transistors, and it also generates quite a bit of heat. Second-generation Pentiums chips are expected to be smaller and cooler than the first chips.

In addition to its famous microprocessors, Intel also manufactures video interface boards, fax/modems, and memory chips. Intel also now markets its own brand of computers. Intel currently faces some competition in the microprocessor market, as other manufacturers (such as AMD, Advanced Micro Devices, and Cyrix) have begun to create Intel clone chips. Also see Central Processing Unit, IBM-PC Compatible, and Motherboard.

MICROPROCESSOR

Also referred to as the CPU (Central Processing Unit), the microprocessor is an integrated chip located on the motherboard inside the system unit. The microprocessor is the "brain" of the computer.

GIGABYTES

A billion bytes, or a thousand megabytes.

MEGABYTES (M OR MB)

Approximately one million bytes.

RAM

An acronym for Random Access Memory, which is a computer's electronic memory. RAM is temporary, which means that any data stored in RAM is lost when the computer is turned off.

DATA BUS

The pathway that data travels between RAM and the CPU.

TRANSISTORS

A semiconductor used open or close an electronic signal. As electricity flows between wires, transistors can act as a gate that lets the signal continue or stops the signal by closing the flow. Microprocessor chips are comprised of millions of transistors.

MATH COPROCESSOR

Also called a numeric coprocessor, this is a support chip that increases the speed at which the CPU can calculate mathematical equations.

MEGAHERTZ (MHZ)

The measure of a chip's clock speed—one MHz is equal to 1 million cycles per second. Most PCs today operate at clock speeds of 20MHz–33MHz. (The Pentium chip clocks in at a zippy 66MHz.)

The CPU processes data and sends it to RAM where a program can retrieve it.

Internet

The Internet is an electronic highway that connects networks around the world. A network is a group of computers connected to a central computer called a server. The networks connected to the Internet belong to universities, government agencies, businesses, libraries, and some public school systems. By connecting to the Internet, a user can send messages (called e-mail), share files, and search a database (a collection of related information). The Internet is a pay-for-use system, similar in concept to information services like CompuServe, Prodigy, America OnLine, and GEnie. But the Internet is entirely different in all other ways.

An information service such as CompuServe is similar to a BBS, only much larger. A BBS consists of a single computer that runs a special program, allowing multiple other computers to dial in and share information. A BBS is usually run by a computer hobbyist, and the number of users connected to the BBS at any given time is usually quite low. An information service is huge in comparison with a BBS, and is composed of several large interconnected computers. A user connects to this centralized system and leaves messages, shares files, chats on-line with other users, plays games, and shares information. All the time, the user is connected to the one set of computers called CompuServe. With the Internet, however, a user connects to a local system (such as a university), and then threads his way to any other systems connected to the Internet.

The Internet began in the '70s as a collection of government networks called ARPAnet (Advanced Research Projects Agency Network). The Defense department was experimenting with networks and ways to keep its system up and running in the case of war. Eventually, other agencies, such as the National Science Foundation, connected to this network of networks in an effort to connect leading scientists and university professors across the country. Such other systems as local libraries, schools, and businesses also connected themselves to the Internet. Even the White House is connected to the Internet.

The Internet consists of over 15,000 networks, with approximately 25 to 30 million users. Some of these networks are located in the United States, and some are overseas, so the Internet is truly an "information superhighway." The Internet as a whole is not owned by any individual; instead it is a collection of diverse networks connected and managed through mutual interest.

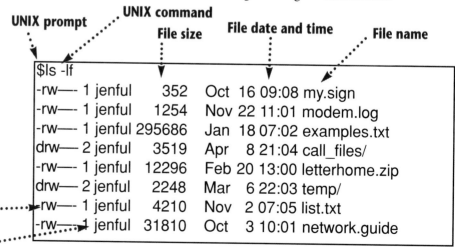

```
$ls -lf
-rw——- 1 jenful      352   Oct  16 09:08 my.sign
-rw——- 1 jenful     1254   Nov  22 11:01 modem.log
-rw——- 1 jenful   295686   Jan  18 07:02 examples.txt
drw—— 2 jenful      3519   Apr   8 21:04 call_files/
-rw——- 1 jenful    12296   Feb  20 13:00 letterhome.zip
drw—— 2 jenful      2248   Mar   6 22:03 temp/
-rw——- 1 jenful     4210   Nov   2 07:05 list.txt
-rw——- 1 jenful    31810   Oct   3 10:01 network.guide
```

UNIX prompt · UNIX command · File size · File date and time · File name · Permissions · Owner of the file

Once connected to a particular network through the Internet, a user can do the same types of things that he might do on a BBS or an information service: send messages, chat on-line (typing what he wants to say and waiting for a response), search databases, receive (download) files, or send (upload) files.

Most computers or terminals (dumb computers) connected to the Internet use an operating system called UNIX instead of DOS, OS/2, or the Macintosh System. UNIX is a command-line interface, which means that the user must type in commands at a prompt instead of selecting them from a menu. This makes UNIX (and the Internet) very difficult to use.

UNIX is different from other operating systems, such as DOS, because the user does not give it commands directly. Instead, the user types commands into a program called a Shell, which then translates the command into UNIX. There are many different UNIX Shells available, but most of them look and act like DOS. There are differences, however. For example, the DOS prompt is a greater than sign >. With most UNIX Shells, the prompt is either $ or %. The user types a command at this prompt, and presses Enter or Return. For example, the user could type ls to see a listing of files. In addition, UNIX is case sensitive, which means that the file name JENNY is not the same as the file name Jenny.

To connect to the Internet, a user needs to contact a local service provider who sets him up with an account. Once that's done, the user dials the service provider's number and connects to the provider's computer using a modem. (A modem is a

The Internet Superhighway

continues

Internet continued

device that allows a computer to transmit data over telephone lines.) The service provider's computer is connected to the Internet, so through it, the user can connect to the other servers on the Internet, such as a local university's main computer. Also see BBS, CompuServe, Modem, Network, Prodigy, and UNIX.

UNIX

An operating system, which is a software program that tells the computer how to execute its basic tasks (such as displaying a prompt, keeping track of files, and performing commands). PCs connected to the Internet usually use UNIX as their operating system. Other operating systems include DOS, OS/2, and the Macintosh System. UNIX was originally created as an operating system for mainframe computers. It allows multitasking (running more than one program at the same time), file sharing by more than one user, and security to protect programs and files from unauthorized use.

TELNET

A program that allows a user to connect to other computers on the Internet.

LOGGING ON

The process of connecting to the Internet. Disconnecting from the Internet is called logging off.

BBS

Bulletin Board Service. An information source and message service (like CompuServe, only much smaller) for computer users. Through the use of a modem, users can dial up BBSs to leave messages and share information. Like on-line services, BBSs typically charge a fee for use. Unlike on-line services, however, BBSs are generally run by a handful of people, sometimes out of a private home. The Internet is like a network of BBSs located around the world.

ON-LINE INFORMATION SERVICES

Fee-based services that allow computer users to access information, buy and sell stocks, download programs, read articles, and more. Using a modem, subscribers can connect to such information services as Prodigy, CompuServe, GEnie, Delphi, and America OnLine.

How Does It Work?

Once a user is connected, he uses a program called telnet to connect to other computers on Internet. To connect to another computer, the user types an address, which is usually just an abbreviated name (called a hostname) for the computer to which he wants to connect. When the connection is established, the user types in commands to get the system to do what he wants it to: list available files, upload a message, download a file, etc. In addition, the user can connect to a newsgroup (a discussion group or forum that focuses on a particular topic or interest).

When the user is through, he logs off (disconnects). How he logs off depends on the shell he is using, but usually the command to log off is something like logoff or exit. Once he's logged off of the Internet, the user terminates the call (hangs up).

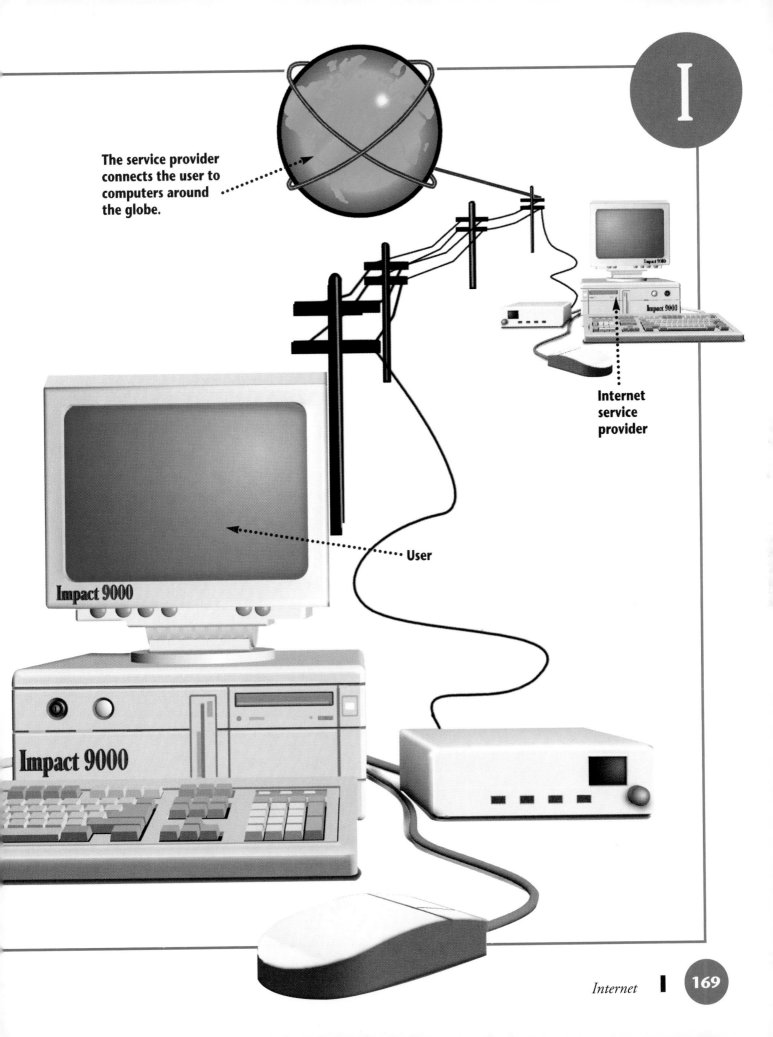

The service provider connects the user to computers around the globe.

Internet service provider

User

Impact 9000

Impact 9000

Joystick

INPUT DEVICE

Any device used to transmit data to the computer. Common input devices include the keyboard and the mouse.

The joystick is an input device that is used to control on-screen movement. Unlike a mouse, which typically controls the movement of a cursor (mouse pointer), a joystick usually controls the movement of some object, such as an animated character in an adventure game, a plane in a flight simulation game, a spaceship in an arcade game, or a car in a racing game. In appearance, the joystick is similar to the joystick found in an airplane's cockpit. Joysticks are popular for use with fast-paced computer games, they allow for greater directional control and manipulation, both important attributes when playing fast-paced electronic games. However, some CAD (Computer Aided Design) programs use joysticks as well. Buttons on the top or sides of the joystick let the user perform selected tasks, such as firing a missile or changing the angle of the view. The joystick was invented in 1977 by Atari for use in their coin-operated video games, and the next year, they adapted it for use with their home video game system.

The Apple II was the first computer to which a joystick could be attached.

Control pads are a variation of the traditional PC joysticks. They are designed to resemble the control pads used in home video game systems, and are preferred by people who have become accustomed to the flat design and button placement. On the control pad, the joystick is separated from the firing buttons located on the other end. Another variation of the joystick is the flight yoke, which is similar to the flight yokes found in an airplane's cockpit. Flight yokes are used with flight simulator games, which are very popular. Also see Games, Input Devices, and Mouse.

Keyboard

The keyboard is the most commonly used input device attached to a computer. With it, a user can type in data or enter commands to the computer. Based on the QWERTY typewriter layout (named for the top row of letters), the PC keyboard looks very much like a regular typewriter, except that it also contains keys that are used with computer programs, such as Escape (which moves the user out of one part of a program into another, Ctrl and Alt (which are used in combination with other keys to enter various commands, such as saving a file), and the arrow keys and cursor movement keys, such as Home and End (which allow the user to move the cursor around the screen). Today, there are many innovative features offered on new keyboards, such as built-in trackballs, adjustable halves, and other ergonomic options. However, the standard typewriter format remains the most popular.

The layout of keys on the first typewriter was deliberately designed to prevent keys from sticking, because that would slow down fast typists. Although that problem was no longer a factor, the same layout was retained for computer keyboards because all typists were familiar with it. In 1932, an alternative keyboard, called the Dvorak keyboard, was introduced, offering easier usage. The idea behind the Dvorak keyboard was to place the most often used letters in the "home" or middle row, making them more accessible. However, by then the Dvorak design, no matter how innovative, could not surpass the acceptability of the QWERTY keyboard design.

The original IBM-PC featured a keyboard with 83 keys that included the typewriter keys, a row of ten function keys on the left-hand side, and a section of keys that served two purposes: a numeric keypad and cursor movement keys. In addition, the IBM-PC keyboard featured additional computer keys such as Escape and Alt. For some reason, IBM decided not to design its PC keyboard like the Selectric's (their line of electric typewriters), which caused some concerns. For example, the Shift and Enter keys were too small, and there were no toggle lights to indicate if the Num Lock, Caps Lock, or Scroll Lock features were on. In response, the keyboard was

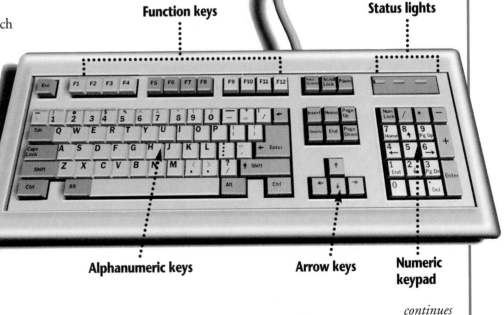

Function keys

Status lights

Alphanumeric keys

Arrow keys

Numeric keypad

continues

Keyboard
continued

changed with the release of the IBM AT. The AT keyboard featured a separate numeric keypad/cursor movement key area, larger Enter and Shift keys, and toggle lights. In addition, the AT keyboard had one extra key, Sys Req, which was used when the PC was simulating a computer terminal.

The main PC keyboard sold today includes 101 keys. Dubbed the "enhanced keyboard," it features 12 function keys arranged at the top of the keyboard, a larger Backspace key, a numeric keypad, a cursor movement keypad, toggle lights, and better placed Ctrl keys.

The first Macintosh keyboard contained only 58 keys —it did not contain a separate numeric keypad or any cursor movement keys, since the Mac was so mouse-intensive. With the introduction of the Mac SE and the Mac II, a new keyboard interface was introduced, and the keyboard changed considerably. Macs today use keyboards that feature either 81 or 105 keys, with a separate numeric keypad, arrow keys, and even some function keys. The layout of the Mac enhanced keyboard is very similar to the PC enhanced keyboard. Also see Ergonomics and Input Devices.

How Does It Work?

There are two categories of keyboards: capacitive or hard-contact membrane. Capacitive keyboards, also called mechanical keyboards, make a soft clicking sound when the keys are pressed. When the user presses a particular key, the key separates two electrically charged plates. This lowers an electrical charge under the key, which makes it easy for an on-board controller chip to identify which key has been pressed.

Hard-contact, or membrane, keyboards are almost silent when the keys are pressed. Inside each key is a foam rubber dome. When pressed, the dome contacts a metal plate, which causes an electrical current to start to flow. The on-board controller chip notices the increase in electricity, and identifies the pressed key.

CAPS LOCK KEY

Locks the uppercase characters in place so that capital letters appear on-screen when the keys are pressed.

TAB KEY

The tab key is used to indent text, set up columns, or move about the screen.

Membrane keyboard

Capacitive keyboard

ALPHANUMERIC KEYS

Letter and number keys on the keyboard that are used to enter data.

ESC KEY

The Esc (Escape) key is used in many programs to exit the task being performed, or to close a menu or dialog box.

ARROW KEYS

Also called cursor movement keys, the arrow keys control on-screen movement of the cursor.

BACKSPACE KEY

This key is used to delete characters to the left of the cursor.

CTRL AND ALT KEYS

The Ctrl (Control) and Alt (Alternative) keys are pressed in combination with other keys when entering commands.

NUMERIC KEYPAD

Most keyboards have a group of number keys, arranged like the keys on an adding machine, located off to the side of the alphanumeric keys. In 84-key models, the numeric keypad doubles as arrow keys.

The Apple adjustable keyboard

SHIFT KEY

As in typewriters of old, the computer Shift key is used to capitalize letters. Pressing the Shift key while typing a character produces an uppercase letter or one of the special characters arranged at the top of the number keys.

STATUS LIGHTS

The Num Lock and Caps Lock lights indicate whether that function is turned on or off.

CAD

Short for Computer Aided Design, this type of program allows the user to create a three-dimensional drawing and view it in different forms and from various angles.

ENTER KEY

The Enter key is used to execute a selected command in most programs. In a word processing application, the Enter key also starts a new paragraph for typing.

Lotus

Lotus was founded in 1981 by Mitch Kapor and a small staff of eight people. In 1982, they released what has become the company's flagship product: Lotus 1-2-3, a spreadsheet program designed for the then newly introduced IBM Personal Computer. More than 200,000 units of Lotus 1-2-3 were sold the first year, and at the end of their first fiscal year Lotus had $53 million in revenue and 300 employees. Today, Lotus 1-2-3 remains one of the most popular spreadsheets of all time. In fact, the popularity of

the first version of Lotus 1-2-3 for business use contributed greatly to the initial success of the PC, because many large corporations bought computers just so they could use the Lotus spreadsheet.

Lotus 1-2-3 was the first program to use expanded memory (extra memory that DOS can use by swapping data in and out of regular memory—the memory under 1 megabyte). Lotus, along with Microsoft and Intel, dubbed this new memory "expanded memory,"

and developed the LIM (Lotus-Intel-Microsoft) standard: a way for a program to use expanded memory. The development of expanded memory greatly increased the capabilities of Lotus 1-2-3 and other programs designed for the early PCs.

Since then, Lotus has built an empire on the success of Lotus 1-2-3 and other products, including a word processor (Ami Pro), a presentation graphics program (Freelance Graphics), an alternative spreadsheet program (Improv), a database

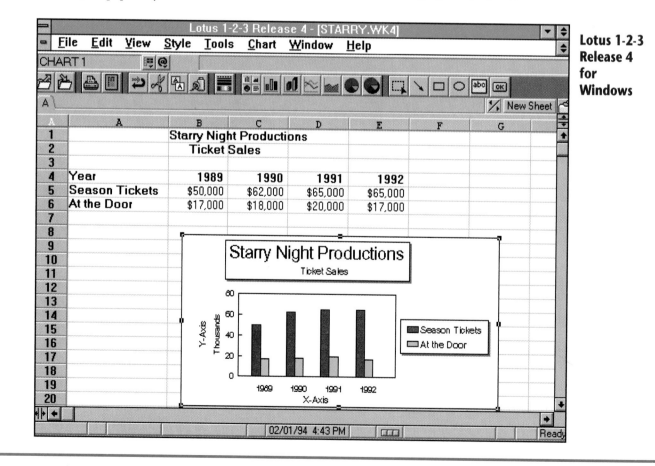

Lotus 1-2-3 Release 4 for Windows

Lotus Notes

[screenshot of Lotus Notes - 3. Activity\ Call Report]

(Approach), and an electronic mail program (cc:Mail). In fact, Lotus offers several of these applications in one package aimed at the corporate audience, called SmartSuite for Windows.

The current Chairman, President, and CEO of Lotus Development Corporation is Jim Manzi. Jim Manzi was one of the people that led the marketing strategy for Lotus 1-2-3 in 1983, and he's been a leader in the company ever since. He was named chief executive officer and appointed chairman of the board of directors in 1986.

Jim Manzi is a strong advocate of the current company strategy of

Jim Manzi; Chairman, President, CEO of Lotus Development Corporation.

Courtesy of Lotus Development Corporation

offering integrated applications—the idea that all the Lotus products should have the same "feel" and "ease of use." To that end, all Lotus products share a similar look, complete with SmartIcons (buttons that allow the user to quickly choose a command) and the capability to share data. For example, a Lotus 1-2-3 spreadsheet can be easily integrated into a report created in Ami Pro, and then combined with graphics created in Freelance Graphics. Lotus is committed to making its products compatible with all major operating systems, including DOS, Windows, OS/2, UNIX, and the Macintosh System.

Lotus Notes, released in 1990, best illustrates the corporate philosophy of integration. Called "groupware," Lotus Notes allows users on a network (a collection of PCs connected with special cables or wires) to share all kinds of data with multiple people at once. Their electronic mail program, cc:Mail, is very popular and is used by nearly 40% of the Fortune 500 companies. Another popular product is Lotus Organizer, a personal information management program that makes scheduling and keeping track of appointments easy and convenient. Also see Ami Pro, Approach, Improv, and Lotus 1-2-3.

Lotus 1-2-3

Lotus 1-2-3 is a spreadsheet program that was created by Mitchell D. Kapor in 1982 for use with the first IBM Personal Computer. Lotus 1-2-3 was meant to replace VisiCalc (which was the original spreadsheet program for personal computers) created by Personal Software. 1-2-3 had the same features as VisiCalc, but it also had database and graphics features and a simpler user interface that made it more desirable and very popular. The name 1-2-3 came from the fact that 1-2-3 combined spreadsheet features with powerful database management and graphics capabilities. It was also said that the program was as easy to use as "1-2-3." Many people bought their first PCs so they could use Lotus 1-2-3. Lotus 1-2-3 remains one of the most popular software programs of all time and has been imitated by many other companies. In fact, the Lotus interface (a menuing system with submenus that are activated by the press of the forward slash key) has been copyrighted by Lotus.

Lotus 1-2-3 works like many other spreadsheet programs: data is stored in cells formed by the intersection of a row and a column. Rows are numbered; columns are assigned a letter. A cell's address is the combination of its column and row—for example, the third cell in the second row is cell C2. Data in the form of the letters of the alphabet is stored as labels and is left-aligned in the cell; data that begins with a number is interpreted as a value and is right-aligned. Calculations are entered into cells as formulas and use cell addresses to refer to ranges of cells. For example, to add the contents of the cells A2 and

An early version of Lotus 1-2-3

The Lotus 1-2-3 menu

Listing of submenus for Worksheet command.

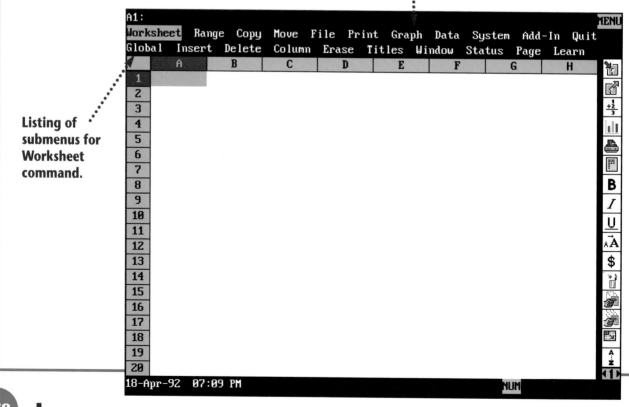

	A	B	C	D	E	F	G	H	I
			Q1 Income						
			Bell Audio						
				Jan	Feb	Mar	Total		
			Net Sales	$12,000	$19,000	$16,000	$47,000		
			Expenses:						
			Salary	$2,000	$2,000	$2,000	$6,000		
			Int	$1,200	$1,400	$1,600	$4,200		
			Rent	$600	$600	$600	$1,800		
			Ad	$900	$2,000	$4,000	$6,900		
			COG	$4,000	$4,200	$5,000	$13,200		
			Total Expense	$8,700	$10,200	$13,200	$32,100		
			Net Income	$3,300	$8,800	$2,800	$14,900		

Lotus 1-2-3 Release 4 for Windows

SmartIcons

Pull-down menus

A3, the user types the formula: +A2+A3. (All Lotus 1-2-3 formulas begin with a plus sign.)

There have been several new releases of 1-2-3 since the original in 1982. Version 2.0 was released in 1986, featuring a macro language (a way to automate 1-2-3) and @functions (preprogrammed calculations like @AVG, which computes the average of a group of numbers). 1-2-3 Version 3.0 was released in 1989, over a year later than expected. Until then, Lotus add-in products (products designed by other software companies to work in conjunction with 1-2-3) helped maintain 1-2-3's popularity. One such product, Allways, allowed the user to enhance a worksheet with bold, italic, underline, special fonts (typefaces), and graphs.

Eventually, Allways was included with the 1-2-3 program. Version 3 featured 3-D spreadsheets (spreadsheets linked to other spreadsheets), additional @functions, and graphing capabilities. But 1-2-3 version 2 lived on for awhile, as users clung to old PCs. Release 3.1 included WYSIWYG, an add-in that helped produce quality printouts, and Solver, an add-in that allowed the user to analyze changing values and pick the best one to solve a particular problem.

In August of 1991, Lotus released a Windows-based version of 1-2-3. But there were already Windows-based spreadsheets on the market by that time that used Windows' features better than 1-2-3 did. The 1993 release, Release 4 for Windows, is much more suited to the

Windows environment and has sold better than its predecessors. Lotus 1-2-3 for Windows allows the user to save several worksheets in a single file, making it easier to enter complex interconnecting formulas and data. New versions of both DOS-based and Windows-based formats of 1-2-3 are expected in 1994. Lotus also has a 1-2-3 version for OS/2 and one for the Mac.

A different type of spreadsheet program, Improv, was released in 1991. Improv allows the user more freedom in manipulating the data in the spreadsheet, combining and re-combining it in various ways. Improv, although popular, has not affected the popularity of Lotus 1-2-3. Also see Applications, Improv, Lotus, and Spreadsheet.

continues

Lotus 1-2-3
continued

RANGE

A group of cells that are somehow related. If a user names a range, he can then use that name in a formula to refer to the cells. (A range name is often easier to remember than the actual cell references.)

FORMULAS

The sequence of numbers and symbols that tells Lotus 1-2-3 how and what to calculate. Lotus formulas begin with a plus sign (+).

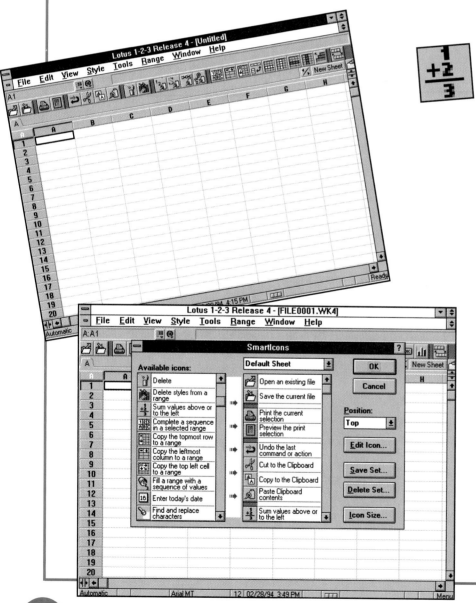

How Does It Work?

How Does It Work?

Perhaps the most interesting detail about the DOS-based version of Lotus 1-2-3, aside from the fact that it has been a best-selling program for over ten years, is its unique menu system. The Lotus menu is different from the pull-down menu that most Windows users are accustomed to in that nothing pops up when the menu is selected; instead, the "menu-line" itself changes. When a menu or option is selected, another line of words (a submenu or a list of commands) replaces the old "menu-line" at the top of the screen, and the user selects the next option from this line. When a menu is highlighted, a list of its commands appears underneath the "menu-line." When a command is highlighted, a description appears instead.

Newer versions of 1-2-3 feature SmartIcons in addtion to the traditional menu system. These icons are grouped in palettes that contain several icons each, and the user can toggle between the palettes. Clicking on a SmartIcon activates its command.

SPREADSHEET

A type of application that is used to organize, calculate, and analyze

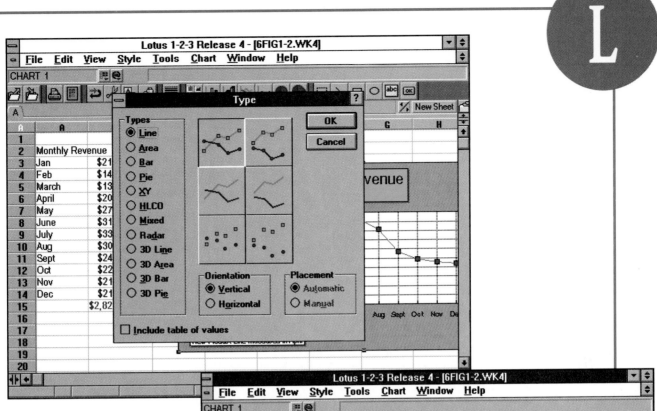

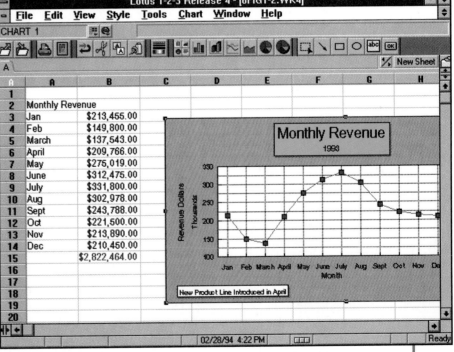

CELL

The rectangular space that is formed where a row and a column meet. Each cell has its own address, consisting of the column letter followed by the row number; for example, cell B4 is the fourth cell over and the second cell down.

LOTUS MENU

Each menu is represented by a name at the top of the screen. To select it, the user clicks on the name or presses the first letter of the name. When the menu is selected, its options appear across the top of the screen. The menu was named for the DOS-version of Lotus 1-2-3, which was the first to use this menu system.

Macintosh

Macintosh computers are a line of personal computers made by Apple Computers, Inc. Macintosh computers are based on a graphical user interface (GUI) that allows the user to select commands, files, and programs that are represented by little pictures called icons. This interface is very visual, friendly looking, and easy to use. At the time of its release, the Macintosh's GUI technology was quite an innovative step in the look and feel of computers. In fact, it wasn't until Windows and OS/2 were released that anything like the Macintosh GUI technology existed for IBM PCs and compatibles.

The Macintosh computer, however, was not the first computer to utilize the GUI technology. In the 1970s, scientists at Xerox's Palo Alto Research Center (PARC) developed an operating system that used icons, pull-down menus, and dialog boxes. One of Apple's founders, Steve Jobs, toured the PARC facility and saw great potential in this new interface technology. He eventually hired several of PARC's scientists, and with a team of Apple developers they came up with the Lisa computer in 1983. The Lisa used many of the features found on today's graphical user interfaces: icons, menus, windows, and dialog boxes. Unfortunately, at $10,000,

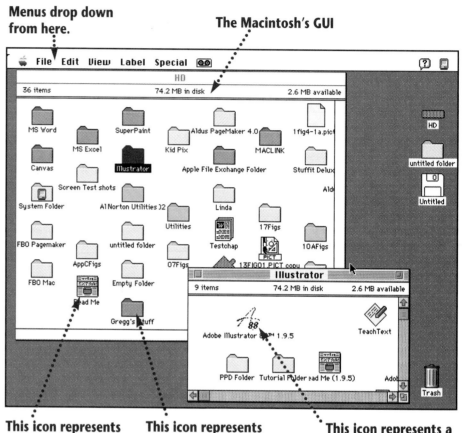

Menus drop down from here.

The Macintosh's GUI

This icon represents a file.

This icon represents a folder (directory).

This icon represents a program.

the Lisa was too costly to succeed in a business market of less expensive IBM and IBM-compatible PCs. Not to be thwarted, Apple turned around and applied the same technology used with the Lisa computer to their next line of computers—the innovative Macintosh.

The Macintosh, introduced in 1984, made quite a splash in the world of personal computers. Not only did it use GUI technology,

but it also used a higher resolution monitor and a 32-bit microprocessor chip (made by Motorola) that could run at 7.8 megahertz. Compared to most other computers, which had low resolution monitors and chips that ran at 4.77 megahertz, the Macintosh looked better and was faster.

Since its introduction, the Macintosh has continued to improve on its performance and

capabilities, making it the leading alternative to the IBM PC and the IBM-compatibles. While the PC still dominates the business market, the Macintosh has made great inroads with educational and home computer users. As the Macintosh has evolved, it has begun to gain some of the business computer market as well. The Macintosh has found great success among the fields of design, printing, and communications, particularly among desktop publishers. In fact, this book was designed and laid out on a Macintosh computer.

Today's Macintosh family of computers offers a variety of models. The LCII is popular because it has an Apple IIe card that lets users run Apple II software. (The Apple II is a widely popular computer that was first released in 1977 and was very successful with schools and educational institutions. Many of these facilities still use the Apple II software in their teaching.) Designed for professionals who work with printing, color, and graphics, the IIvi and IIvx are higher-end versions of the Apple II.

Another line of Macintosh computers is the Performa. The Performa computers are designed to appeal to home users who are looking for a computer that the whole family can enjoy.

The Macintosh Classic, released in 1990 for an incredibly low price (for a Mac) of only $1,000, resembles the earlier Macintosh computers first introduced by Apple, with appropriate improvements, of course. A newer version, the Macintosh Classic II, runs faster and is available at a similarly low price. Another higher-end Macintosh is the Centris, which uses a more powerful microprocessor chip. The most powerful Macintosh, the Quadra, is used in production departments among publishing professionals and graphic designers.

Macintosh went portable with the release of the PowerBook in 1991. Weighing in at 6.8 pounds, the PowerBook proved immensely popular. The latest mini Mac, the Apple Newton, is a personal digital assistant (PDA). Capable of reading handwritten text and commands inscribed with a special stylus, the Newton is popular among business executives who like the

The MAC Classic II

Courtesy of Apple Computer, Inc. Photographed by John Greenleigh.

continues

Macintosh

continued

idea of using a computer, but hate the idea of learning to use it. The Apple Newton can be used to organize appointments, take notes, and manage addresses and phone numbers. The Newton can also run special applications written especially for it. Also see Apple, GUI, Microcomputer, Motorola, PC, Portable Computers, PowerPC, and System 7.

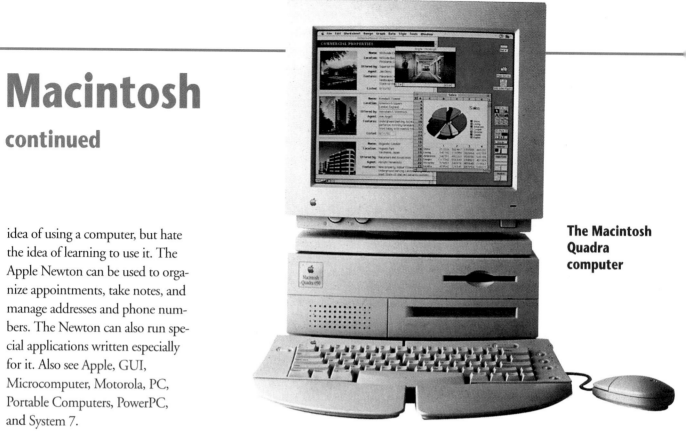

The Macintosh Quadra computer

Courtesy of Apple Computer, Inc. Photographed by John Greenleigh.

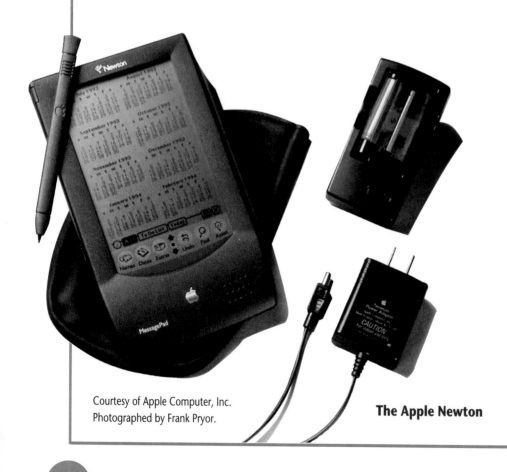

Courtesy of Apple Computer, Inc.
Photographed by Frank Pryor.

The Apple Newton

SYSTEM 7

The operating system used by today's Macintosh computers. System 7 includes both an operating system that tells the computer how to work, and Finder (the graphical user interface).

GUI

Short for Graphical User Interface. A program that provides an easier, friendlier way of communicating with the computer. GUIs use icons, menus, and dialog boxes to display commands and options.

PDA

Stands for Personal Digital Assistant. A PDA like Apples 's Newton, is a portable computer designed to receive data in the form of handwritten text instead of type-in information. PDA's are used to store addresses, notes, and calendar information.

Mainframe

A mainframe computer, also called a maxicomputer, is a large, powerful computer used primarily by government, big corporations and educational facilities. Mainframe computers are the largest computers made today, followed by minicomputers (smaller and slightly less powerful than mainframes) and microcomputers (personal computers and portable computers). It is worthy to note that the distinctions between the different sizes of computers are rapidly breaking down as their processing power and usage change. In fact, today's microcomputers (PCs) and minicomputers are as powerful as early mainframes.

Mainframe computers have a lot of memory, can store vast quantities of data, and process endless amounts of work. Mainframe computers generate a lot of heat, so they are stored in large, temperature-controlled rooms. These rooms contain special removable floors that allow access to the computer and cables when repairs are needed. These floors also increase air flow, cooling the large mainframes. Hooked up to the mainframe computer are smaller computers, called dummy terminals, that allow users to access

information found on the mainframe. Dummy terminals are quite useless on their own, because their processing capability comes entirely from the mainframe itself. Depending upon the organization, a mainframe can have anywhere from a couple of terminals to hundreds of terminals hooked up to the central computer. In addition, personal computers can be hooked up to a mainframe computer to allow desktop users access to centralized information.

In the 1950s and 1960s, companies used mainframes to handle work ranging from accounting tasks to scientific calculations. Today's mainframe computers

accomplish the same kinds of tasks and more. Initially the cost of purchasing a mainframe computer is very high; however, a company can save time and money by centralizing computer memory and processing capabilities. Instead of purchasing separate PCs and "software packages for every employee, a company can connect many inexpensive terminals (dummy terminals) to the mainframe, making the mainframe's applications available to anyone who needs them. In addition, a company can create custom programs and install them on the mainframe, allowing everyone access.

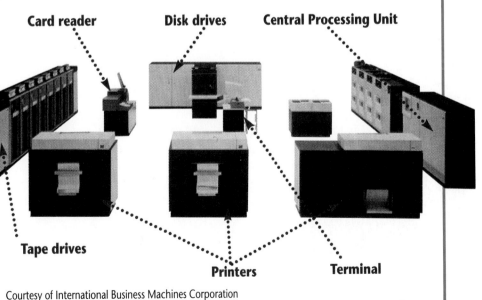

Card reader **Disk drives** **Central Processing Unit**

Tape drives

Printers **Terminal**

Courtesy of International Business Machines Corporation

continues

Mainframe continued

The first mainframe computers were invented in the 1940s. The Mark I and the ENIAC are but two of the famous ones. These early mainframes were incredibly large, often occupying an entire floor of an office building. They were not completely electronic, often times using mechanical switches and relays to control processing. In 1951, the UNIVAC computer

IBM began selling mainframe computers in 1953, starting with the IBM 650. Today, IBM is still one of the largest manufacturers of powerful mainframe computers.

Mainframe computers are also manufactured by Groupe Bull (formerly made by Honeywell), Unisys, and NCR (now part of AT&T). Also see IBM, Microcomputer, and Minicomputer.

Courtesy of International Business Machines Corporation

was invented and sold by the Remington Rand Company (which later merged with Sperry); it is now considered the very first mass-produced computer (they sold over 40 computers from 1951 to 1958). The UNIVAC was huge, mostly because it used large vacuum tubes for memory instead of today's electronic memory.

MINICOMPUTER

Designed as a smaller-scale mainframe computer, the minicomputer is commonly used by several people at once in local area networks or in small organizations or departments within a large corporation.

MICROCOMPUTER

Typically, a microcomputer is a personal computer—one that functions on its own and can fit on a desk or be carried around without a great deal of difficulty. However, today's microcomputers are often as powerful as the minicomputers. Microcomputers use a single microprocessor chip to handle all of the computer's "thinking."

How Does It Work?

A PC's CPU is contained within a single microprocessor. A mainframe's CPU is contained on several interconnected circuit boards. A mainframe can process several instructions simultaneously, making it a perfect choice for large corporations which need computers to process lots of different tasks, such as payroll, invoicing, data management, and inter-office communications.

Large mainframes contain hundreds of megabytes of memory (RAM). Typically, that memory is divided into sections called virtual machines, each acting like a separate computer and running a separate task. Jobs are often batched into the mainframe. These jobs are prioritized by the computer operator to make the best use of a mainframe's processing time. Mainframes often use a front-end processor to connect to the various terminals scattered throughout an office. This front-end processor handles the job of sending and receiving input and output, so the mainframe can concentrate on processing work.

Memory

A computer's memory (RAM or random access memory) is where information is processed—the area where the computer works on data. RAM is located on the motherboard inside the system unit, or on a special memory expansion board located in an expansion slot. Memory is measured in bytes. One character, such as the letter A, is equal to one byte. A byte is broken down into eight bits. A bit represents a 1 or a 0, indicated by an on/off state inside the RAM chips—1's are on and 0's are off. For example, the letter A is represented by the eight bits 01000001. No other character uses this same sequence of 1's and 0's. When the letter A is stored in the computer's memory, it is stored in this binary state. Bytes can be measured in bigger units of storage; a kilobyte is equal to 1,024 bytes; a megabyte is equal to 1,048,576 bytes.

The amount of memory a PC needs depends on what the user is going to process with it. Most PCs today come equipped with 4 to 8 megabytes of RAM, although 2 megabytes might be considered an absolute minimum. If a user is working with large graphics, database, or spreadsheet files, he might need more memory.

To get the best out of the memory a PC has, a memory management program can be used. An operating system such as DOS comes with a program called MemMaker, which analyzes a computer's needs and sets up memory use in the most efficient way. Commercial memory managers for DOS PCs include QEMM 386 and 386MAX. If memory is really a problem, a user can create virtual memory out of available space on the hard disk, and it will pretend that it's RAM. There are two kinds of RAM: dynamic RAM (DRAM) and static RAM (SRAM). In order to maintain their electrical charges, DRAM chips continually refresh themselves. SRAM chips retain their charges of electricity longer than DRAM

RAM chips

chips, and they are faster. However, SRAM chips also take up more power than DRAM chips, and are much more expensive.

The total amount of memory (RAM) that a PC has is divided into three or four types, each serving a specific purpose. The first 640 kilobytes of the computer's memory is called the conventional, or base memory. Data is stored in conventional memory and program instructions are loaded there so they can be quickly accessed when needed. The next 384 kilobytes of memory is known as upper memory. Ordinarily (unless a memory

continues

Memory_{continued}

management program configures this memory for general use) this portion of the computer's memory is not readily usable by most software programs. However, in DOS it is reserved for its own purposes.

The remaining memory, if the computer has more than one megabyte, is called extended memory. Extended memory cannot be used by an operating system such as DOS directly; it is accessed with the help of a special program called a device driver. Once the device driver program is installed, any user application (like WordPerfect or Excel) that wants to can use this section of memory to load additional data. The more data there is in memory, the faster the CPU can access it, and the faster that program will run. A PC may have a fourth type of memory, called expanded memory. Expanded memory is located either on a separate memory board, or within some part of extended memory. Expanded memory is accessed through a special area in upper memory. For example, in DOS data is swapped in and out of upper memory to be accessed at any given time. DOS, a very old operating system, was never designed to use more than 1 megabyte of RAM. This swapping of data between expanded memory and upper memory was the first method ever

developed for getting around this limitation. Extended memory, with its special device driver, is the other method, and it is much more popular than using old-style expanded memory.

Another type of memory chip found on the motherboard is the ROM chip. ROM, or read-only memory, contains the permanent instructions a computer needs in order to operate. ROM contains the instructions for starting up the computer and its basic input-output functions. These instructions are placed into the ROM chips at the factory, and cannot be changed by the user. Even if the computer is turned off, the ROM chips will always hold the instructions stored there. Also see Byte, Cache, Central Processing Unit, Data Storage, Disk Drive, Floppy Disk, Hard Disk Drive, RAM, and ROM.

VIRTUAL MEMORY

Some programs, such as Windows, let the user create more "memory" area by swapping data between RAM and the hard disk drive. Because virtual memory is located on a disk, it takes longer to access it.

Extended

Upper
(384k)

1 Megabyte

Conventional
(640k)

How Does It Work?

Inside these electronic RAM chips are tiny ON/OFF circuits that represent the data that's currently being processed. Power is needed to keep these tiny switches set to ON or OFF, so RAM is only a temporary holding area for data. Once the computer is turned off, any data held in the RAM chips is lost. Data that will be reused (such as a letter or a report) must be saved to disk before turning the computer off. The central processing unit (the brains of the computer) can access data stored in RAM chips very quickly—much more quickly than it can access data stored on a disk.

Memory is one of the most important parts of a computer and how it works. It determines how much information can be processed at a time and what software programs can be run, because programs must also be loaded into RAM before their program instructions can be understood by the CPU. For example, when a program is started, the computer searches the hard drive or disk where the program is stored for instructions detailing how the program works. When those instructions are located, they are transferred to RAM.

SIMM

Single In-line Memory Module. A special strip containing additional memory chips, which can be purchased and inserted onto the computer's motherboard.

DRAM

A dynamic RAM chip that must continually recharge itself electrically in order to retain its contents.

Upper memory

Expanded memory

Data in expanded memory is swapped in and out of upper memory, where DOS can reach it.

TSR

Terminate-and-Stay-Resident (also known as a memory resident program). This is a program that remains in the memory, taking a background position, that can be called into action again with the press of a key. Common TSRs include memory managers, disk doublers, and anti-virus programs.

SRAM

A static RAM chip that maintains its data longer than a DRAM chip does. SRAMs are super fast memory chips, but they are more expensive than DRAM chips—so they are used sparingly if at all.

Microcomputer

Microcomputers are personal computers: computers designed for use by one person; the terms microcomputer and personal computer are interchangeable. In contrast to a PC, mainframe and minicomputers are designed for use by many people at once. Microcomputers (PCs) use just one microprocessor chip (CPU) to handle the computer's "thinking" or processing activities. Microcomputers are stand-alone systems, able to run software programs and manage data without relying on a larger resource, such as a mainframe. Microcomputers can fit onto a desktop and can be carried around without a great deal of difficulty.

Microcomputers did not enter the computer scene until the mid 1970s. When these smaller computers did appear, they were considered toys and were not taken very seriously by the computer industry at large. Most historians name the Altair 8800, built by MITS and introduced in 1975, as the very first microcomputer, or personal computer. This first personal computer did not come with a monitor, a keyboard, or a printer, or any way to store data permanently. To use it, switches were flipped in a particular sequence. The user translated a series of blinking lights from the computer's "machine language" into an intelligible answer. Other microcomputers were available that year, all made from kits and geared towards the home hobbyist. By 1977, computer manufacturers were selling computers that were already put together. Several companies introduced personal computers in 1977: Apple, Processor Technology, North Star, Commodore, and Radio Shack.

The price of the microcomputer was a leading factor in its popularity. Among the companies introducing microcomputers, Radio Shack offered the least expensive and most popular computer, the TRS-80. The Apple II and Commodore Pet computers were also popular and helped start the trend in microcomputers. In 1981, IBM began selling a microcomputer it named the IBM PC, adopting the initials of the term "personal computer" as its brand name. Even though IBM had introduced previous microcomputers, such as the IBM 5100, it was not until the introduction of the IBM PC that serious marketing of the personal computer occurred.

Personal computers have grown increasingly more powerful and more prevalent. They are used in offices, in schools, and in homes to

The Pet computer, by Commodore

Courtesy of International
Business Machines
Corporation

The IBM PC

perform all kinds of applications ranging from accounting to games and education. They have, in effect, revolutionized the computer industry. Today's personal computers are made by a variety of manufacturers. IBM and IBM-compatible PCs (competitors' versions of the IBM PC) are the leading sellers, followed by Apple Macintosh. Popular IBM-compatibles are made by Gateway, Compaq, Zeos, and Dell. Apple produces the family of Macintosh computers. Laptop computers (portable, smaller versions of personal computers) are also making quite an impression in the marketplace. Laptop versions of both IBM compatibles and Macintosh computers exist today, with the trend leaning toward smaller and smaller computers known as notebooks and palmtops. Also see Apple, Central Processing Unit, IBM, IBM-PC Compatible, Macintosh, Mainframe, Minicomputer, PC, and Portable Computers

MAINFRAME

A large, powerful computer used to serve hundreds of users in a company or university setting. Mainframes are capable of storing vast amounts of data and offer centralized processing power.

MINICOMPUTER

Designed as a smaller-scale mainframe computer, the minicomputer is commonly used by several people at once in local area networks or in small organizations and departments within large corporations.

Apple's Mac Microcomputer

IBM-compatible computer

Microsoft

Microsoft Corporation, located in Redmond, Washington, is a leading software publisher. Software tells a computer how to perform some task, such as word processing, database management, graphics manipulation, etc. Microsoft produces a full range of software for both IBM-PC compatibles and Macintosh computers. Microsoft Corporation was founded in 1975 by two enterprising college students, Paul Allen and Bill Gates (the current chairman and chief executive officer). Together, they wrote a version of the programming language, BASIC, for the first personal computer, the Altair 8800.

Microsoft's big break came when it was chosen by IBM to design an operating system for the IBM PC. Microsoft created MS-DOS (Microsoft Disk Operating System), based on QDOS (short for Quick and Dirty Operating System, an existing operating system for personal computers) and TRSDOS (an operating system designed by Microsoft for the TRS-80). DOS provides a method for communicating with the computer. The user types in commands, and DOS carries them out. Because commands must be typed instead of selected from a listing or a group of pictures representing them, DOS is called a command-line interface. DOS shells, special programs

Courtesy of Microsoft Corporation

**Bill Gates, Chairman and
CEO of Microsoft Corporation**

that work on top of DOS, provide the user with easier ways of performing tasks (such as copying or deleting files) without having to type in commands. The IBM PC's version of DOS is called PC-DOS. Microsoft also sold a version, called MS-DOS, to the makers of IBM-compatible computers. DOS is now installed on over 100 million PCs worldwide.

Microsoft has gone on to publish many popular software programs including Microsoft Word and Word for Windows (word processing programs), Excel (a spreadsheet program), Microsoft Works (an integrated program), Access and FoxPro (database management programs), Microsoft Mail (an e-mail program), and PowerPoint (a presentation graphics program). Microsoft sells many "edutainment" programs— programs designed to educate and entertain. These include Microsoft's Encarta, Dinosaurs, Cinemania, and Musical Instruments, among others. Microsoft also sells games including Microsoft Golf, and its popular Entertainment Packs. In addition, Microsoft sells its own version of several programming languages: BASIC, FORTRAN, COBOL, and C. Its visual approach to programming, found in Visual Basic and Visual C++, brings a whole new look and feel to the art of writing software.

Microsoft Windows lets the user work with many programs at one time.

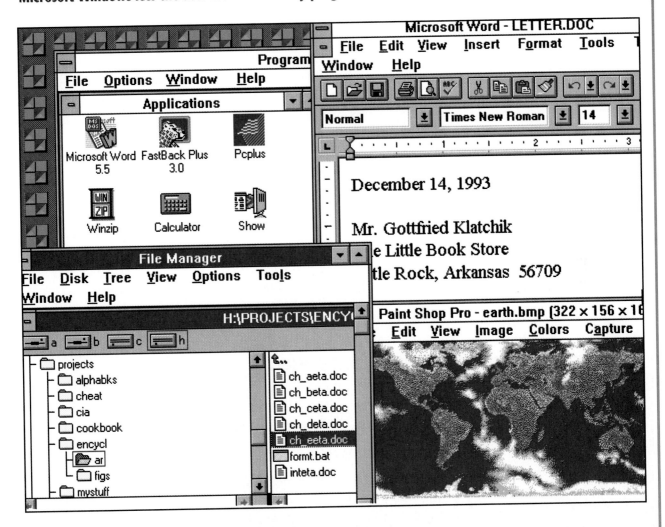

Another big moment in Microsoft history was the announcement in 1983 of a graphical user interface (GUI) for the PC, called Windows. When version 3.0 was released in 1990, the popularity of Windows began to grow, and PCs haven't been the same since. Windows is not an operating system but an operating environment; it sits on top of the DOS, making DOS easier and friendlier to use. A graphical user interface like Windows lets the user select pictorial representations of programs, files, and commands without having to memorize and type in text commands. Windows has a look and feel very similar to the Macintosh, and owes its existence to the popularity of Apple's GUI. Windows is bundled for free on most IBM compatible PCs sold today, and it has helped countless users overcome their fears of using computers.

Along with IBM, Microsoft developed another operating system to replace DOS, called OS/2. Unlike

continues

Microsoft continued

Windows, which can run many programs at the same time in a cooperative process, OS/2 can run many programs simultaneously in a process called preemptive multitasking. With preemptive multitasking, OS/2 allots the same amount of time to each program, preempting tasks if they run too long for their time segment. Windows gives total focus to one program at a time, relying on that program to share resources when possible. However, Microsoft

pulled out midway through the project, and perhaps as a result, OS/2 has not been wildly successful. A preemptive multitasking version of Windows, called Windows NT, is designed to run on networks. (Windows NT is an operating system itself, so it runs without DOS.)

Microsoft's presence in the software publishing field has become an influential one, setting industry standards and leading the way in

market success. Microsoft employs over 14,000 people worldwide, and continues to shape its vision of the future based on the needs of the international community. Also see Access, BASIC, C/C++, DOS, Ergonomics, Excel, GUI, OS/2, PowerPoint, Software, Visual Basic, Windows, Windows NT, and Word for Windows.

GUI

Graphical User Interface. A program that provides an easier, friendlier way of communicating with the computer. GUIs use icons, menus, and dialog boxes to display commands and options.

DOS

Disk Operating System. Special software that tells the computer how to act, how to process work, and how to communicate with the other peripherals.

PROGRAMMING LANGUAGE

Computers cannot understand English, only machine language. In order to tell the computer what to do, instructions must be written so that the computer can understand them. There are several special programming languages including C, BASIC, PASCAL, and more, used to instruct a computer on how to perform a certain task.

Courtesy of Microsoft Corporation

Microsoft corporate offices, located in Redmond, Washington

MIDI

MIDI, which stands for Musical Instrument Digital Interface, was developed in 1982. A standard for cabling and hardware that connect computers to electronic instruments, MIDI also defines the method by which sounds are passed between these devices. MIDI provides a common language so all the components can talk with each other. If the computer has the appropriate equipment, a musician can use MIDI to compose music on the computer, play the music, and edit the composition. In addition, a musician can control various electronic instruments through his computer.

MIDI came about with the manufacture of digital musical instruments, such as electronic keyboards and synthesizers. Such makers as Yamaha and Korg, among others, needed a way to control all instruments in both the recording and playing back of the notes, as well as a way to allow one type of instrument to play notes made by another. MIDI was developed to control these types of specifications. MIDI is used to electronically regulate music through the computer.

MIDI standards are commonly used by musicians creating music for television and motion pictures, and adding sound to multimedia presentations (multimedia combines sound, picture, text, and video). Also see Multimedia and Sound Board.

How Does It Work?

When a musician plays a song with a MIDI keyboard, the note is sent to the computer, along with its length, the amount of attack (velocity of the note), the tempo, pitch, and decay time (the amount of time it takes for a note to fade). These notes are translated into computerized form using the MIDI standard. The musician can then edit the song. For example, using the computer it's easy to change the song from one key to another, or to repeat sections.

A MIDI file contains all the elements of a song: the instruments being played, the notes, the pitch, attack, and tempo. Any of these elements can easily be changed on the computer, and then played back through a MIDI synthesizer.

① **A musician plays a C sharp when the synthesizer is imitating a violin.**

② **A message is sent to the computer.**

Play C Sharp on a Violin

Impact 9000

Impact 9000

④ **When the note is played back, the sound of C sharp on a violin is heard.**

③ **The computer stores the note C sharp and the name of the instrument being played.**

Minicomputer

There are three main types of computers manufactured today: mainframe computers, minicomputers, and microcomputers. Mainframe computers are large, powerful computers typically used in big companies and universities to serve the needs of many users. Microcomputers are personal computers, which serve the needs of an individual. The minicomputer falls in between the other two types of computers.

The first minicomputers were just smaller-scale mainframe computers that served a fewer amount of users than mainframes did. The Digital Equipment Corporation (DEC) introduced the first minicomputer in 1959, called the PDP-1. A minicomputer is usually not as powerful as a mainframe computer, but it's more powerful than a microcomputer. They are not as big as mainframes, but not as small as microcomputers. Unlike mainframes, which can serve hundreds of terminals, minicomputers can serve 4 to 100 users at the same time. Minicomputers are popular among smaller businesses and departments, usually acting as the server for a local area network (LAN). Unlike microcomputers that use only one microprocessor chip, minicomputers may have several microprocessor chips to handle larger amounts of storage and processing power.

Today's minicomputers are manufactured by such companies as IBM, Digital Equipment Corporation, Data General Prime, Wang, Sun, and Hewlett-Packard. Most manufacturers of mainframe computers also make minicomputers. The distinctions among the three types of computers are quickly fading as their functions change with advancements in technology. Also see Central Processing Unit, Mainframe, Microcomputer, Network, and PC.

MAINFRAME

A large, powerful computer used to serve hundreds of users in a company or university setting. Mainframes are capable of storing vast amounts of data and offer centralized processing power.

MICROCOMPUTER

Typically, a microcomputer is a personal computer that can function on its own, and can fit on a desk or be carried around without a great deal of difficulty. However, today's microcomputers are often as powerful as minicomputers. Microcomputers use a single microprocessor chip to handle all of the computer's "thinking."

Minicomputers built in the 1960s and '70s were almost as bulky as mainframes. Today's mini's are smaller and easier to operate.

Modem

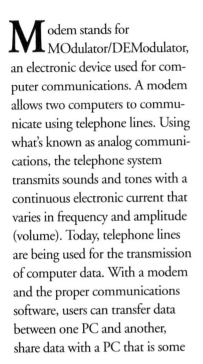

Modem stands for MOdulator/DEModulator, an electronic device used for computer communications. A modem allows two computers to communicate using telephone lines. Using what's known as analog communications, the telephone system transmits sounds and tones with a continuous electronic current that varies in frequency and amplitude (volume). Today, telephone lines are being used for the transmission of computer data. With a modem and the proper communications software, users can transfer data between one PC and another, share data with a PC that is some

distance away, connect to a BBS (bulletin board service) or an on-line service (CompuServe, Prodigy, etc.), buy and sell stocks, download programs, read articles, and more.

The purpose of a modem is to convert computer data into tones and pulses that can be transmitted through a telephone line, and then to change it back again at the receiving end. To send data, a modem changes the computer's digital (binary based) data into an analog (sound based) signal that can be transmitted over a phone line (a phone line can only

transmit analog signals). When a message is received, a modem changes the incoming analog signal (from the phone line) back into a digital signal the computer can understand.

The digital, or binary, codes of a computer involve only two signals, 1's (on) or 0's (off). By changing either the frequency or the amplitude (volume) of an analog signal, a modem can send the 1's and 0's of computer data through telephone lines. A communications program, such as ProComm Plus, manages the actual transmission process between the two

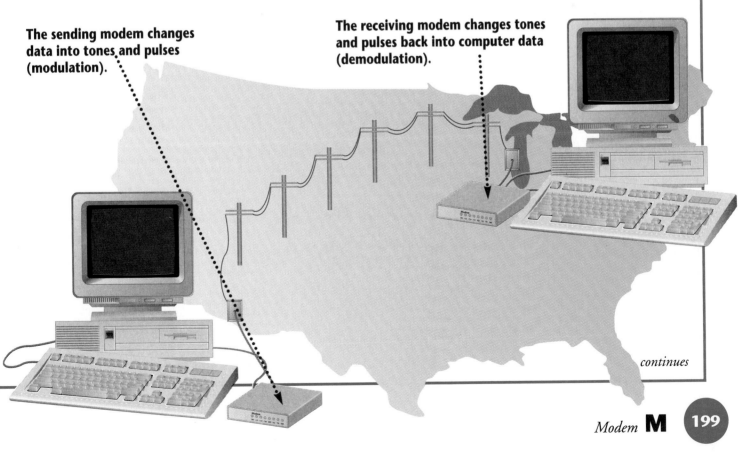

The sending modem changes data into tones and pulses (modulation).

The receiving modem changes tones and pulses back into computer data (demodulation).

continues

Modem continued

computers, determining when to send a character and if a character has been received correctly. The communications program organizes the data to be sent, and then passes that data to the modem, which then converts it to analog signals. In addition, the communications program tells the modem what number to dial, and when to initiate or terminate the call. Through the communications pro-

gram the user can also issue commands to a BBS to upload or download a file, or can type the words for a conversation with another user. The speed of a transmission is measured in bits per second, or bps. Various bps speeds are popular today, ranging from a slow 2,400 bps to 14,400 bps. BPS is sometimes mistakenly called baud, but that's not accurate. Baud is the amount of frequency or volume

changes per second that occur during the transmission. Originally, one change occurred with every bit that was transmitted. But with today's modems, fewer changes occur, so baud rates no longer reflect the actual amount of data being transmitted.

With special software and a fax modem, a user can transmit data to a fax machine. A fax modem

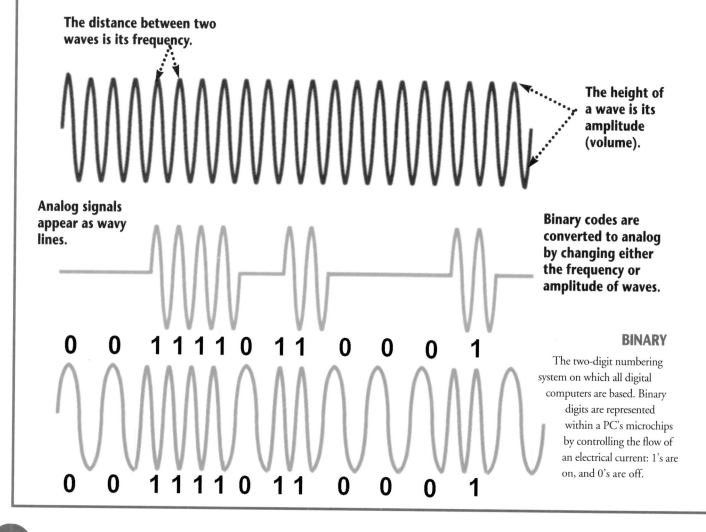

The distance between two waves is its frequency.

The height of a wave is its amplitude (volume).

Analog signals appear as wavy lines.

Binary codes are converted to analog by changing either the frequency or amplitude of waves.

0   0   1 1 1 1   0   1 1   0   0   0   1

0   0   1 1 1 1   0   1 1   0   0   0   1

BINARY

The two-digit numbering system on which all digital computers are based. Binary digits are represented within a PC's microchips by controlling the flow of an electrical current: 1's are on, and 0's are off.

How Does It Work?

A modem is connected to the telephone line and then connected to the PC. A modem changes digital signals from a computer into analog signals that can be sent through a phone line. It also changes incoming analog signals into digital signals that the computer can understand.

The communications software uses a particular protocol to handle the method of data transmission. The protocol is a set of rules that helps to determine whether the correct character was received. If not, that character is retransmitted. Retransmitting a character takes longer than one might expect, since modems transmit only one bit (one part of a character) at a time. In order to transmit data between them, the two PCs involved must use the same protocol. There are many standard protocols included in the communications software available today. Each offers certain advantages, such as better accuracy or better speed.

is similar to any other modem, except that it contains additional equipment that allows it to properly communicate with a fax machine. For example, a user could prepare a report and then fax it to his boss.

A Modem

FAX MODEM

A special modem designed to send and receive faxes.

HAYES

A major manufacturer of modems. Hayes modems are the most popular modems purchased today. Hayes has set many industry standards in the area of computer communications.

BPS

Short for bits per second, a measure of the amount of data a modem can transmit. Common rates range from 2,400 bps to 14,400 bps depending on the modem being used.

DOWNLOADING

When a user receives computer files through a modem from someone else's computer, the process is called downloading.

Using the computer, any type of computer data can be faxed, such as a document, a drawing, or a chart (graph). Likewise, a PC equipped with a fax modem can receive a transmission from a fax machine, making it very easy to keep in touch over long distances. Also see BBS, Communications, CompuServe, Internet, and Prodigy.

PROTOCOL

A set of standards that govern how computers communicate with each other. In order for two computers to talk, they must use the same protocol. The protocol determines how each bit (a 1 or a 0) is sent, and how to detect errors in transmission.

PARITY

The procedure for identifying whether the correct character was received. With even parity, an extra bit is added to the eight bits that make up a character (such as the letter D, which is equal to the eight bits 01000100). This ninth bit makes the total of all the bits an even number. So in the case of the letter D, the ninth bit would be 0, as in 010001000. With odd parity, the ninth bit makes the total come out odd, as in 010001001. After the modem receives the ninth bit for a character, it adds them up and determines whether one of the bits was scrambled. If so, that character is retransmitted.

UPLOADING

When a user sends computer files through a modem from his PC to another computer, the process is called uploading.

Money Management Programs

Money management programs are software programs designed specifically for working with money. They include features that help people balance their checkbooks, manage a budget, keep track of bills and payments, control monies being spent in a business, and more. Money management software falls into two categories: personal finance and accounting.

Personal finance programs, such as Quicken and Microsoft Money, help people organize checking accounts, set up personal budgets, plan for retirement, and pay bills electronically. With a program like Kiplinger's CA Simply Money, the user enters data into a screen that looks just like a check register from a checkbook. Here the user can keep track of transaction

dates, the names of the persons to whom the checks were written, and the amounts of payment. In addition, the user can record deposits to the checking account. After data is entered, the program automatically updates the balance in the account. Another feature of personal finance programs is the ability to make payments by printing out actual checks, and to cross-reference expenses

Kiplinger's CA-Simply Money - Checking 4107579

| File | Edit | Operations | Tools | System | | | | Help |

Date	Via	C	Pay To / Deposit From	Payment	Deposit	Balance
07/11/93	Print	✓	American Home Mortgage C Mortgage Payment	1150.39		2405.59
07/12/93		✓	ATM Withdrawal Cash	140.00		2265.59
07/12/93	Print	✓	First Statewide Visa Visa	241.89		2023.70
07/13/93	Print	✓	County Water Utilities\Water	35.00		1988.70
07/13/93	Print	☐	Jack Simson Materials for Deck Home Repair	337.39		1651.31

| Record | Delete | View... | Home | Balance: | 1648.43 |

| F1=Help | Report | Graph | Find | Notes | Schedule | Advice |

ACCOUNTING PROGRAMS

Geared for small business needs, accounting programs usually include a general ledger, journal, accounts receivable, accounts payable, inventory, payroll, and reports for determining operating expenses and net income.

PERSONAL FINANCE PROGRAM

A program that helps the user keep track of personal monetary transactions. These programs usually include a budget system, check register, report system, and savings planner.

(such as the amounts on the written checks) to an established budget.

Accounting programs, such as Point of Sale, DAC Easy, Acc Pac, and Peachtree Accounting, are used to help organize small business accounting and spending plans. These programs help the user track expenditures, payrolls, inventory, and operating income.

Although keeping track of such details proves a difficult task for most people, money management programs can save time and efforts in organizing finances and account books. These programs allow the user to have more control over his money and where it goes, providing he is diligent in using the program. Also see Applications, Quicken, and Software.

Monitor

A monitor (also called a video display adapter or CRT—Cathode Ray Tube) is an output device that allows the user to see information while working on the computer. Commands and data are visible on the monitor screen as they are being carried out or typed in. A computer monitor looks very much like a television set, and is connected to the computer by a special circuit board called a video adapter. Monitors vary in size, color, and resolution.

Early computer monitors were monochrome (black and some other color, such as white, green, or amber) with very low resolution, but most monitors today offer a full range of color. Today, monochrome monitors are found mostly on portables (laptops or notebook computers) because they are less expensive to produce. Resolution, which refers to the sharpness of the displayed image, has improved dramatically over the years. There are three main types of monitors in use today: CGA, EGA, and VGA. Each is defined by the quality of its resolution. Resolution is measured by the number of dots, called pixels, that can be displayed on-screen. The greater the number of dots, the sharper the image. The dots are measured by how many can fit into one inch (dots per inch, or dpi).

CGA (Color Graphics Adapter) monitors can display a color resolution of 320 by 200 dpi with four colors. CGA monitors, developed in the early 1980s, were the first standard for color display. EGA (Enhanced Graphics Adapter) monitors are an improvement over CGA monitors. They can display a resolution of 640 by 360 dpi with 16 colors. Although EGA monitors are a step up from early CGA monitors, today's standard is the VGA (Video Graphics Array) monitor. VGA monitors are available in three forms: VGA, Enhanced VGA, and Super VGA. A regular VGA monitor can display a resolution of 640 by 480 dpi with 256 colors. Enhanced VGA increases the resolution to 800 by 600 dpi. Super VGA offers a resolution of 1,024 by 768 dpi. With the advent of VGA monitors, CGA and EGA are almost obsolete.

New developments in resolution occur every year. Laptop computers offer an entirely different way to display information on-screen. Some laptops use a plasma display (also called a gas discharge) as a monitor screen. A plasma display uses an inert ionized gas trapped between two panels to create glowing pixel points when electrically charged. Other laptop monitors use LCD screens that translate colors into shades of gray. Also see Output Devices, Portable Computers, Screen Saver, and Video Card.

PIXELS

Also known as picture elements, pixels are tiny dots that make up a monitor screen. Pixels are created by blending three colors (red, blue, and green) in varying intensities to form the color of the pixel

How Does It Work?

Like a television set, a monitor displays its images with tiny pixels, or dots. Digital signals representing the image are first received by the VGA adapter, a circuit board that connects the monitor to the rest of the computer. The adapter runs the signals through a Digital-to-Analog Converter (DAC) circuit, which converts the digital computer information into electrical pulses.

Next, the electrical signals are sent to the electron guns (cathodes) located inside the monitor. The electron guns send out beams that strike a phosphorous coating on the inside of the screen; the phosphorus glows where it is struck by the beam, creating a tiny dot of light. A magnetic field adjusts the beams so they strike the next pixel on-screen, and the process continues until the entire screen has been lit with the image. The phosphorus glow quickly diminishes, so the image is repeatedly scanned across the entire screen, about 60 times per second.

DPI

Dots Per Inch. A monitor's resolution is measured in how many dots can appear on-screen.

BURN IN

A condition that occurs when a monitor screen displays the same image for an extended length of time, leaving a ghost of the image on-screen. This can be prevented by turning down the brightness of the screen, using a screen saver, or making sure the monitor is turned off when left for long periods of time.

Pixel　　**Cathodes**

INTERLACED

Some monitors are interlaced, meaning that the displayed image is scanned onto the screen, every other line with each pass. This allows the monitor to display images quickly, but interlaced monitors often exhibit a noticeable flickering. Non-interlaced monitors display the entire image with each pass, creating a rock-solid display image with no flickering. Non-interlaced monitors are slightly more expensive, but are easier on the eyes—especially when reading text.

SCREEN SAVER

A special program that starts automatically when there has been no activity for a specified period of time (which the user can set). The purpose of a screen saver is to prevent burn-in, where an after-image appears on-screen.

RESOLUTION

The sharpness and clarity of an image on a monitor screen. Resolution is measured in dots, or pixels, per inch.

VGA Adapter card

Morphing

Morphing is the process of gradually changing from one graphic image (picture) to another in a slow blending process. This blending process, when presented at normal speed, makes one object seem to transform into another. When presented at slower speeds, the morphing (changing) process can actually be seen.

Morphing has been used in film, music videos, and commercials with great success. For example, the molten creature in the film "Terminator 2" was changed into various humans and other objects using the morphing process. Michael Jackson's video for his hit song, "Black or White" featured a morphing sequence with one face changing into another. A recent Schick commercial shows a series of men (supposedly with differing toughness in their beards) blending from one to the other with smooth transitions. Another commercial shows a speeding car transforming into a tiger. Even weekly television shows are getting into the act: "Star Trek: Deep Space Nine" features a character called Odo who regularly morphs into objects, such as tables, carts, walls, etc., to catch bad guys. The techniques involved in morphing have been around awhile. The idea of slowing fading one image into another was used in early films (such as "The Wolf Man") to make it appear as if a man were changing into a wolf. Although primitive, the technique, called cross-fading or a slow dissolve, worked well enough. A warping technique developed for correcting satellite images from space was combined with the technique of cross-fading, and morphing was born.

A similar process called tweening is employed in animation. Tweening is the slow change between two similar images, such as from raised arm changing to lowered arm. Tweening is used to indicate motion, by filling in the "gaps" between pictures at different time intervals. The word

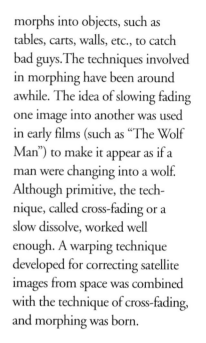

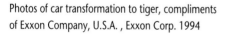
Photos of car transformation to tiger, compliments of Exxon Company, U.S.A. , Exxon Corp. 1994

tweening is a corruption of the word "between" because tweening is used to create the in-between images between one frame of hand-drawn animation and the next. With tweening, animation can be created in less time and with less money than ever before, because each step or change in a figure does not have to be completely hand-drawn.

TWEEN

The in-between images that are inserted between hand-drawn artwork to create full animation. Tweening makes it possible to produce high-quality animation in less time and with less money than traditional animation, where each variation of the image is hand-drawn. Tweens are the images that connect two different poses of the same object. Tweening is the different from morphing, which involves a transition between different objects.

How Does It Work?

M

A special morphing program is used to morph two pictures. The two pictures are converted to computer images (digitized), and then starting and ending points on each picture are identified. For example, to blend the face of a human into that of a miniature collie, the points of the eyes, nose, and mouth on each picture are connected. The process of changing one image into another is accomplished by a series of mathematical formulas whose values slowly change from 1 to 0. The computer uses these changing values to calculate the position of key points in the changing picture, enabling it to slowly blend one image into another. To blend one figure into the next, the original figure's outline is slowly warped along the calculated path.

ANIMATION

A process which simulates motion through the rapid display of still pictures.

CROSS FADING

Also called slow dissolve, this is the blending of two figures through a process that causes one image to slowly fade, while the other image slowly increases in intensity.

Motherboard

The motherboard is the main circuit board inside the computer, and it normally forms the "floor" of the system unit. Plugged into the motherboard in some way are all the electrical components of the computer. Of foremost importance is the central processing unit (CPU) or microprocessor. The CPU chip is considered the brains of the computer; it controls the flow and the processing of data. The math coprocessor is another type of chip that might be found on the motherboard. The math coprocessor helps the CPU perform complex mathematical calculations. Newer CPUs contain an internal math coprocessor.

Memory chips are an essential part of the computer, and they too are found on the motherboard. Memory (RAM) chips are used to temporarily store data while the computer is processing it.

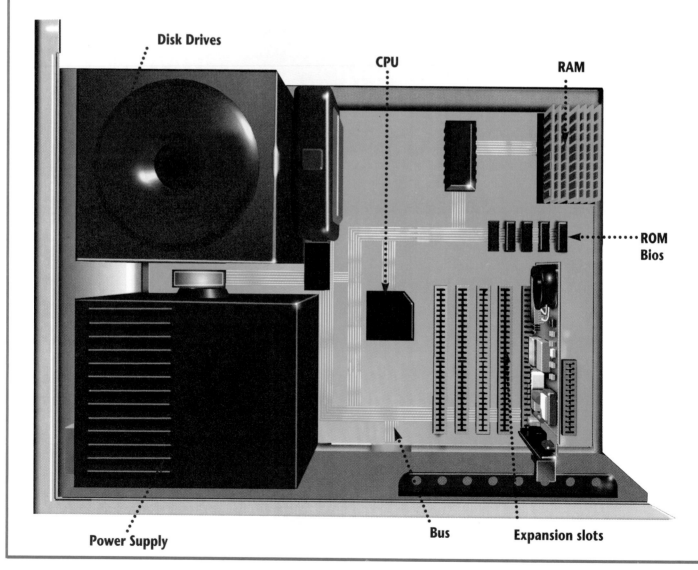

Disk Drives

CPU

RAM

ROM
Bios

Power Supply

Bus

Expansion slots

How Does It Work?

Linking all of the electronic components that are plugged into the motherboard are buses. A bus is a series of interconnected electrical leads that carry signals (such as data and timing signals) from one component to another. These buses are etched into the motherboard itself. The power supply sends power to all the components connected to the motherboard through its bus. In addition, the CPU sends and receives data and instructions from all the PC's components over the motherboard's bus.

SYSTEM UNIT

The main component of a computer, which houses the disk drives, power supply, CPU, RAM, and ROM chips. All of these components are connected to each other through electrical pathways etched onto the motherboard.

BUS

The inner highway of wires connecting the CPU to the PC's different components. Data, address, and control information travels along this bus.

Additional RAM chips can be connected to the motherboard through an expansion slot, a special connector through which peripherals are attached to the computer.

Another type of memory chip found on the motherboard is the read-only memory, or ROM chips. ROM memory is permanent memory that contains the basic information the computer needs in order to work. These instructions are called BIOS, Basic Input-Output System. ROM-BIOS controls the input and output to and from the computer, and helps the CPU manipulate data between RAM and the keyboard, monitor, and other input/output devices. In addition, ROM contains the instructions for system startup.

One important component, the hard disk drive, is linked to the motherboard by a special chip called a controller. The hard disk

MEMORY

Computer memory referes to programs and files stored on disk or temporarily in memory chips. Anytime a program is run or a file is opened, the information is read from a disk (either hard disk or floppy disk) and copied into the computer's memory. The computer's memory is an electronic storage area. From there, the information can be quickly worked with.

stores a user's permanent data, along with applications and operating system software (such as DOS). Usually placed near the hard disk are floppy disk drives, connected in most cases to the same controller. Floppy disk drives read removable disks, which are usually used to store extra copies of files on the hard disk.

Expansion slots are yet another integral part of the motherboard. These slots are used to attach additional circuit boards, called expansion cards, to the computer. Expansion cards are used to add sound, additional memory, an internal modem, or other peripherals to the existing system. Also see BIOS, Bus, Central Processing Unit, Expansion Cards, Floppy Disk Drive, Hard Disk Drive, Memory, Power Supply, RAM, Sound Board, and Video Card.

CHIP

Also called microchip or integrated circuit, a chip is a piece (chip) of a larger section of silicon. A chip is approximately the size of a fingernail, but it performs the same functions as many separate circuits such as transistors (tiny ON/OFF switches), resisters (which change the flow of electricity) and capacitors (which store electricity temporarily).

Motorola

Motorola Inc. is the company responsible for manufacturing the 68000 series microprocessor chips used in Macintosh computers. The microprocessor, also known as the central processing unit (CPU) controls the computer's "thinking" process.

Motorola was founded in 1928 in Chicago by Paul Galvin. At the time, it was known as the Galvin Manufacturing Corporation. The company started out making radio products, the first one being a "battery eliminator" that made it possible for radios to run on household electrical currents instead of batteries. In the 1930s, the Galvin Corporation used the name Motorola in its manufacture of radios for cars. As the name became more closely associated with equipment for "motor cars" and motion, it officially changed its name to Motorola in 1947. Motorola has a history of manufacturing electronic equipment including two-way radios, televisions, and semiconductors. Today, the company is pioneering a variety of electronics for cellular communications, paging and wireless systems, and electronics for aerospace, defense, and automotive industries.

Motorola introduced its first microprocessor, called the 6800, in 1974. But the real impact came when Motorola released a low priced version called the 6502. Its low price and versatility enabled many computer manufacturers to produce their first PCs. The 6502 was used in the Apple II, the Commodore Pet, and the Atari 400 and 800. As a manufacturer of microprocessor chips, Motorola is a competitor of Intel—the manufacturer of microprocessor chips for PCs. The chips designed by Motorola are different from those made by Intel, just as the PC is different from the Macintosh (even though they are both personal computers).

In 1984, when the

Motorola's MC68040 microprocessor (with over 1.2 million transistors incorporated in the chip, yet which is only the size of a thumbnail) is the brain in the most powerful Apple Macintosh computers.

Macintosh computer was introduced, it contained a Motorola 68000 microprocessor chip, which had a 16-bit internal data bus and a 32-bit external data bus (the connector that moves data to and from the CPU), and ran at a clock speed of 7.8 megahertz (electrical cycles per second). The fastest chip up until this time was the PC's Intel 8088 chip, which ran at a clock speed of 4.77 megahertz.

Motorola has since manufactured a series of 68000 chips, each one improving over the last. The

MICROPROCESSOR

Also referred to as the CPU (Central Processing Unit), the microprocessor is an integrated chip on the motherboard inside the system unit. The microprocessor is the "brain" of the computer.

RAM

An acronym for Random Access Memory, this is a computer's electronic memory. RAM is temporary, which means that any data stored in RAM is lost when the computer is turned off.

68020 chip, also known as the "sixty-eight twenty," runs at a speed of 16 megahertz and uses a 32-bit data bus. The 68030 chip is even faster, running at 32 megahertz. The 68040 chip improves on the 68030 chip's power, including a built-in math coprocessor (a special part of the CPU chip that specializes in mathematical calculations). Able to process 20 million instructions per second, the 68040 chip is used in the Macintosh Quadra computers, the most powerful Macintosh computers.

MEGABYTES (M OR MB)

Approximately one million bytes.

DATA BUS

The pathway that data travels between RAM and the CPU. If a data bus has a 16-bit structure, that means it can move 16 bits of data at a time. A 32-bit structure can move 32 bits at a time and is, therefore, twice as fast as the 16-bit data bus.

GIGABYTES

Approximately a billion bytes, or a thousand megabytes.

Motorola's chips continue to increase in power and performance. Its latest endeavor, in conjunction with Apple and IBM, has produced the PowerPC chip, an exceedingly fast chip that is bound to make an impact on the CPU chip market. The PowerPC chip is designed with the capability to handle both Macintosh and IBM-PC compatible software, making computers that use this chip truly unique. Also see Apple Computers, Central Processing Unit, Macintosh, and PowerPC.

PATH COPROCESSOR

Also called a numeric or floating point coprocessor, this is a support chip that increases the speed at which the CPU can calculate mathematical equations.

TRANSISTOR

Tiny ON/OFF switches within a CPU. The transistors form the logical pathways within the CPU, enabling the CPU to process data and follow instructions.

MEGAHERTZ (MHZ)

The measure of a chip's clock speed. One megahertz is equal to one million clock cycles per second.

Mouse

The mouse is an input device that allows the user to point to and select items on-screen. It owes its name to its resemblance to a real mouse—it has a small body and long tail (the cable that connects the mouse to the computer). As the mouse is moved around a desktop, a mouse pointer on-screen moves simultaneously in the same direction. This method of movement is an exceedingly fast and smooth way to navigate around the computer screen. The mouse is used primarily with graphical user interface (GUI) programs to select icons (small pictures which represent files, programs, or commands) and menu commands. It is also necessary to use a mouse with most drawing and paint programs.

The first mouse was invented in 1963 by Doug Englebart at the Stanford Research Institute. In the early 1970s, scientists at Xerox's Palo Alto Research Center (PARC) used the mouse with the development of the first GUI program.

However, mice didn't become widely used until the introduction of personal computers in the 1980s. Microsoft added mouse support to its word processing program and began making mice in 1983. When Apple introduced the Macintosh computer, the first to use a graphical user interface, it came with a free mouse. Since then, the humble computer mouse has grown sleeker and more comfortable to use. Most mice have two buttons that can be pressed to activate commands.

Mouse cord

Mouse buttons

The left mouse button is used most often. Pressing the mouse buttons and moving the mouse around on a desktop performs different pointing and selecting actions that include clicking, double-clicking, and dragging.

Another input device that resembles the mouse is the trackball, an upside-down mouse. With a trackball, the user spins a ball on top of the mouse to move the cursor. A wireless mouse, a regular mouse without a cord, can also be used to perform pointing and clicking actions. Wireless mice use infrared or radio signals to comunicate with the PC. Also see Input Device, Joystick, Pen Computer, and Trackball.

How Does It Work?

Underneath the mouse body is a rubber ball, called a tracking ball. It translates the mouse movements as the mouse is rolled around a desktop into input signals that the computer can understand. Those signals are carried to the computer by the long cable that attaches the mouse to one of the computer's ports. Underneath each mouse button is a tiny switch that records when a button is pressed or clicked, and the interval between clicks. These signals are also sent to the computer through the mouse cable.

Encoder

Tracking ball

Tracking rollers

CLICK

A quick, light tap of the mouse button (usually the left button) without moving the mouse. When pointing to an item, the user can activate that selection by clicking.

DOUBLE-CLICK

Two quick taps of the mouse button, without pausing. A double-click is not the same as two clicks. The double-click interval, which most programs have, controls the amount of time allowed for two clicks in succession.

POINT

A movement of the mouse pointer on-screen so it is positioned directly over an item. The tip of the mouse pointer must be touching the item. A pointing action is followed by an action involving the pressing of the mouse buttons.

DRAG

The action of pressing and holding down the mouse button while simultaneously moving the mouse. Dragging is used in graphics programs to draw lines, circles, and other shapes. It is also used to move items on the screen.

Courtesy of Logitech, Inc.

Multimedia

Multimedia is the combination of text, graphics, sound, video, and animation in a single presentation. Because of its flexibility, multimedia is often used to provide training and instruction to employees in large companies, to teach and introduce new topics of learning in the educational fields, and to provide advertising and information in a shopping mall kiosk (information booth). Multimedia incorporates such computer hardware as CD-ROMs and sound boards to produce innovative and exciting visual presentations.

Multimedia presentations are currently very popular in library and educational settings. A user can open an encyclopedia file on a CD-ROM disc to the word "elephant," and not only does the file contain text describing the environment and habits of the elephant, but it also shows a video of an elephant on the plains of Africa, complete with sound. Such presentations are very effective in gaining attention, allowing users to interact with the computer, and making complex information much easier to understand.

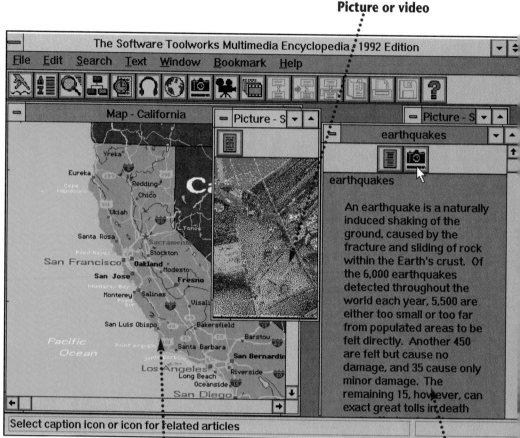

Picture or video

Graphic

Text

To create and view multimedia presentations, a computer must have additional peripherals (hardware) to support the variety of media used. Such a PC usually carries the MPC symbol (for multimedia PC), meaning that it meets the standards established by the Multimedia PC Marketing Council. An MPC compatible CD-ROM drive is of foremost importance. CD-ROMs (Compact Disc Read-Only Memory), are a storage disk used to save vast amounts of data, including sound, animation, video, and graphics. CD-ROMs are the primary source for storing multimedia files. In addition, an MPC must have at least an 80486SX CPU, 8 megabytes of RAM, a clock speed of 25 Mhz, a hard disk with 160 megabytes of free space, a VGA monitor, an MPC compatible 16-bit sound card, speakers, and Microsoft Windows. Although multimedia presentations can run on computers of lesser quality, this system will provide the minimums

necessary to produce high-quality multimedia presentations. Many computers sold today offer all of the multimedia hardware necessary to enjoy multimedia presentations.

Another important part of a multimedia computer is a sound board. Sound boards are special circuit cards that let the computer play recorded music and sound effects. All computers come with built-in speakers that allow users to hear warning beeps; however, additional speakers can be attached to the computer to improve the quality of sound. Also see CD-ROM, Computer Based Training, and Sound Board.

CD-ROM

A storage disk designed to store vast amounts of data. A CD-ROM can store an entire set of encyclopedias and other data. The large capacities of CD-ROM discs make them ideal for the complex storage needs of multimedia presentations. For example, a CD-ROM can store an entire encyclopedia, along with the video, animation, and sound files to make it a multimedia presentation.

INTERACTIVE

A program that allows the user to answer questions, make choices, and control the direction of the program itself.

SOUND BOARD

A special circuit board that plugs into the computer to create and listen to music and special effect sounds.

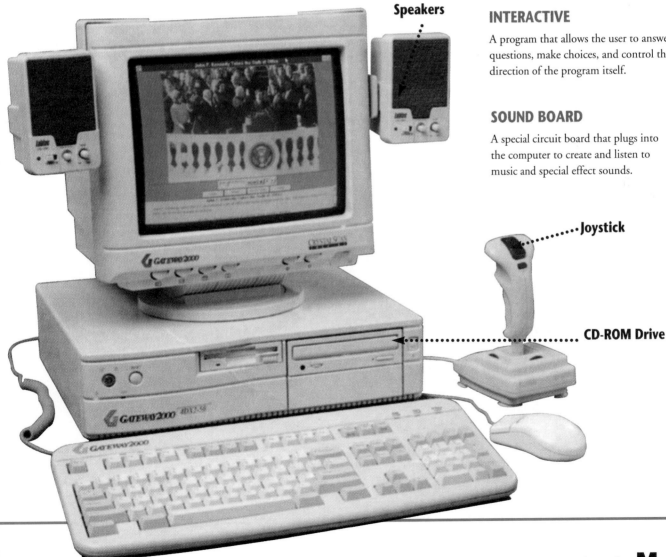

Speakers

Joystick

CD-ROM Drive

Multitasking

Multitasking is the process of running several programs on the computer at the same time. This is not the same as loading two or more programs in memory and accessing them one at a time. Multitasking allows the CPU to process multiple instructions from several programs at once. For example, while using a word processing program to write a letter, a user can access a spreadsheet program to add numbers, even as a drawing program is printing a piece of artwork, and a database program is sorting a long list—all that at the same time.

There are several operating systems that are preemptive multitasking systems, for example OS/2, UNIX, and System 7 for the Macintosh. The new Windows NT by Microsoft also utilizes true multitasking capabilities. Some people classify Microsoft Windows as a multitasking program, however it is not much of one. While it can quickly switch from program to program, it can only concentrate on one running application at a time—Windows depends on the active application to share resources when possible (in other words, to give up some of its time so that Windows can process other tasks).

MULTITASKING

A method of simultaneously processing the instructions for several programs at one time. OS/2, UNIX, Windows NT, and the Macintosh System 7 are all preemptive multitasking operating systems. Windows is a cooperative multitasking system, which depends on the cooperation of the active program to share resources.

CENTRAL PROCESSING UNIT (CPU)

Also called the microprocessor, the CPU is the computer's "brain," controlling all of its functions, processing instructions, and manipulating data.

Also see Memory, Operating System, OS/2, System 7, UNIX, and Windows.

Dear Sirs, I'm writing in response to your ad.

Impact 9000

Impact 9000

When a user is working with a multitasking operating system, he can load many programs at once, but only one of those programs is active (accepting new commands). With a desktop single-user system, there may not seem much of a need for multitasking. After all, what more can one person do? However, some computer tasks are process-intensive—once they are initiated, they take a while to process. Instead of waiting on the computer, the user could switch to another program and start it processing some big task.

In a preemptive multitasking system, the CPU apportions its time so that it spends about the same amount of time processing each program's instructions. Priority can be given to certain programs, enabling them to process their work a bit faster. The active program (the one that the user is currently working with) will continue to respond to commands—although it may appear to process them a bit slower than usual. After all, the CPU is processing many tasks at once, so it won't pay as much attention to the active program as it might if it had nothing else to do.

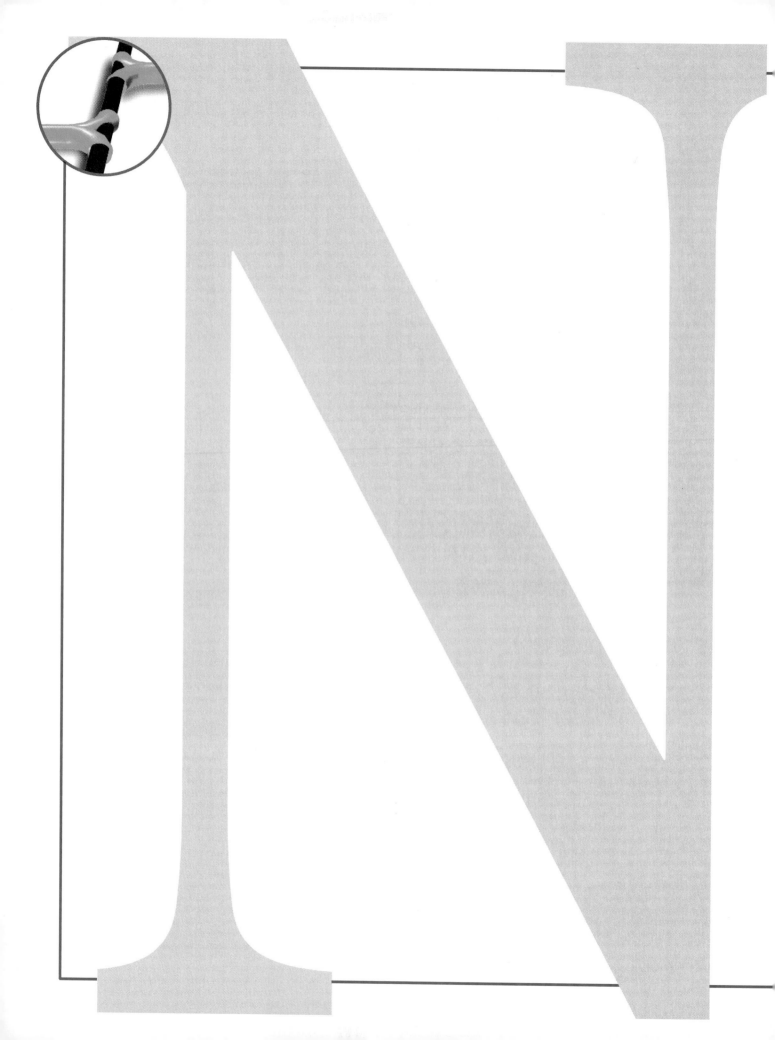

Nanotechnology

In 1959, Dr. Richard Feynman speculated that there were no rules in physics that might prevent the direct manipulation of atoms. Because technology at that time had not progressed to the point where anything Dr. Feynman spoke of could be tested, his theories were treated with indifference and even amusement. In recent years, however, more and more researchers have begun to realize the potential of manipulating atoms to form complex compounds with "nanomachines."

Molecular manufacturing, or nanotechnology as it is called ("nano" from the Greek word meaning dwarf), is the science of manipulating objects at a molecular level to create new objects. In other words, building things from the atom up with molecular machines. It's the ultimate power over nature. For example, with nanotechnology, a material (such as steel) might be made stronger or more flexible. In addition, molecular machines could perform "surgery" where no doctor might dare to go.

Most scientists envision the creation of tiny "nanomachines," machines built from atoms that can manipulate objects at a molecular level. But what does nanotechnology have to do with computers? Using nanotechnology, the tiny ON/OFF switches inside computer chips (which comprise a computer's data and logic circuits) could be replaced with atom-sized switches. This would enable smaller, faster, and

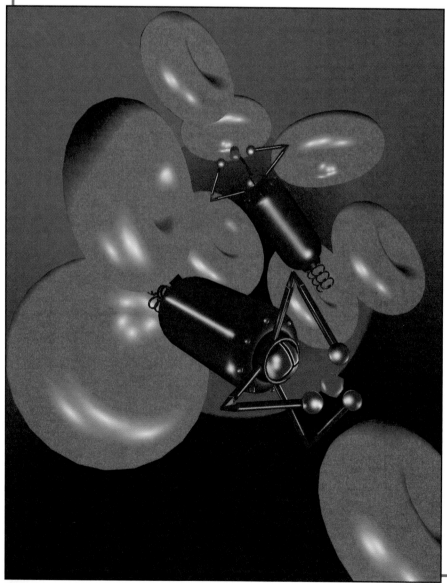

Nanotechnology may someday lead to the development of tiny machines built with atoms that, when released into the blood stream, could cure various diseases.

How Does It Work?

Using nanotechnology, the first atom switch was created: a switch the size of an atom which could be set to "on" or "off." Using such technology, the transistors (similar ON/OFF switches) inside computer chips could be made smaller, therefore making it possible to build computers that are smaller, faster, and more powerful. Researchers at AT&T Bell Laboratories created the first atom switch by applying a small pulse of electricity to an atom, to "bond" it to another surface. When another electrical charge was applied, the atom returned to its former position. In other words, the atom could be switched back and forth. The atom appears as a tiny bump on the surface of the bonding material when the "switch" is turned on. When the atom returns to its original position (the "switch" is turned off), the surface of the bonding material appears smooth.

more efficient computers to be built. Already, Hitachi has designed a way to store a single bit of data using one electron. Toshiba has designed a transistor (the tiny ON/OFF switch inside a computer chip) 2500 times smaller than a human hair. That's half the size of computer transistors used inside an Intel Pentium chip. Nanotechnology is leading the way to smaller and smaller computer chips.

In the late '70s, Eric Drexler (now a researcher into molecular manufacturing) first developed the concept for creating molecular machines. The nanotechnology to perform such a feat is not yet completely functional, but its

time is coming. For example, scientists have already discovered that materials made from smaller particles created using nanotechnology display new characteristics than those same materials in their natural form. For example, researcher Richard Siegal noticed that palladium formed from grains five nanometers wide (five billionths of a meter) was five times harder than normal palladium. Similar studies showed that material could be made more conductive, or could be made to react differently to chemicals, just by varying the size of the grains with which it was constructed. Also see Bit, Memory, and RAM.

Atom switch set to "off"

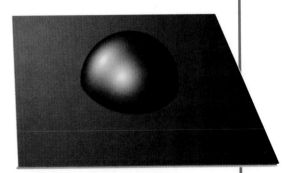

Atom switch set to "on"

ATOMIC MANIPULATION

The manipulation of matter at an atomic level—placing atoms in exact positions.

NANO

One billionth; from the Greek word for dwarf.

PROXIMAL PROBE

A probe precise enough that it can be used to move atoms.

NetWare

NetWare is an extremely popular network operating system (NOS) developed by Novell, Inc. A network is a collection of personal computers and peripherals interconnected by cables or wires, which share programs, data, and other resources (such as printers). At the center of a network is a server, a PC or minicomputer that contains the software to run the network and that acts as a central storehouse and distributor for the shared programs, data, and peripherals. The network operating system runs on top of the regular PC's operating system (such as DOS) as an extra layer, providing network-wide management of these shared resources. The network operating system provides the communications link between all the PCs and peripherals on the network.

It has been estimated that approximately 70% of PC-based local area networks (LANs) use NetWare, probably because of the product's excellent reputation for reliability, hardware and software compatibility, and flexibility with a variety of network configurations. Because NetWare is not limited to DOS-based PCs (there are also versions for Macintosh networks, systems running OS/2, and VAX systems), almost any type of network can use it.

The original NetWare operating system, introduced in 1983, was the first network operating system for PCs. NetWare is now a family of several different network operating systems, including NetWare 2.2, NetWare 3.12, and NetWare 4.01.

NetWare 2.2 is the last version of a network operating system designed to run on a server equipped with a 286 CPU. It can support up to 100 users, 1,000 concurrent open files, and 200 concurrent transactions. Because NetWare 2.2 is based on the old 286 CPUs, it is not sold very much anymore.

NetWare 3.01 was introduced in 1989. The current version, NetWare 3.12, can support up to 250 users per server, allowing up to 100,000 concurrent open files and up to 25,000 concurrent transactions. Netware 3.12 can access

How Does It Work?

NetWare and other network operating systems work in a similar manner. NetWare acts as an invisible layer between the operating system (such as DOS) and the user application. For example, suppose the user has requested a particular file. First NetWare intercepts the request and examines it. If the requested file resides on that user's PC, the request is simply passed down to the operating system, which then retrieves the file and passes it up to the application.

But what if the requested file resides on the network server? NetWare passes the request on to the server, who retrieves it and transmits it to the workstation (the user's PC). At the workstation, NetWare translates the information into a format that the operating system can handle and passes it down to the operating system, which eventually passes it back up to the application. The user is unaware of this process because, in most cases, these requests are handled very quickly.

up to 4 gigabytes (about 4,000 megabytes) of memory, and up to 32 terabytes (about 32,000 gigabytes) of hard disk storage. NetWare 3.12 requires a minimum of a 386 CPU on the network file server, but if the server has a 486 CPU, NetWare 3.12 takes advantage of it.

Netware 4.01 adds additional support for optical disk and CD-ROM drives and for data compression (a process that reduces the size of a file). NetWare 4.01 also has a more efficient file storage system. NetWare 4.01 can support up to 1,000 users connected to a single server.

For small peer-to-peer networks, there is another version called Personal NetWare (which replaces a similar network operating system called NetWare Lite). A peer-to-peer network allows PCs to share files and peripherals without a dedicated

file server. Its starter kit connects two PCs, but it is designed to make expansion easy. Peer-to-peer networks offer no file security, but they are simple to maintain and operate. Also see Network and Novell.

NETWORK

A group of two or more computers that are connected either by cables or communications media (such as modems) for the purpose of sharing programs, files, and peripherals.

PEER-TO-PEER NETWORK

Also called non-dedicated networks, a peer-to-peer network does not use a dedicated file server. Workstations on a peer-to-peer network share files directly, without going through a server. Common peer-to-peer networks include Novell's Personal NetWare, Microsoft's Windows for Workgroups, and Artisoft's LANtastic. However, peer-to-peer networks do not offer any real security features.

1 The user requests a file, which NetWare intercepts and passes to the server.

USER'S PC

SERVER

2 The server retrieves the file and sends it back to the user.

3 NetWare passes the requested file to the user's application.

Network

A network is a group of two or more computers that are linked together by cables or wires, for the purpose of sharing files, programs, and peripherals, such as a printer. Being connected to a network is similar to being connected to another hard drive; the user can access files from other computers on the network as if the files were on his own computer. Network users can share files and peripherals with other users and send and receive electronic mail (with the appropriate software).

There are two types of networks: Local Area Networks (LAN) and Wide Area Networks (WAN). A LAN is usually limited to a single office or building. Several LANs connected together form a WAN, or wide area network. The computers on a WAN can be on the same block, in the same city, or across the world, and can be connected by satellites or by modems and telephone lines. For example, WANs are used to connect different divisions or offices of a large corporation.

A LAN includes a file server, which is the central computer that runs the network's operating system and contains the files and programs to share. It can be a dedicated file server, which means that no one uses the computer, it is simply set up to maintain the network, or a non-dedicated file server, which is a computer that is also being used by someone as a workstation. In the less common peer-to-peer networks, workstations exchange files with each other directly, without the use of a server.

No matter which type of network is used, LAN or WAN, the network needs an operating system.

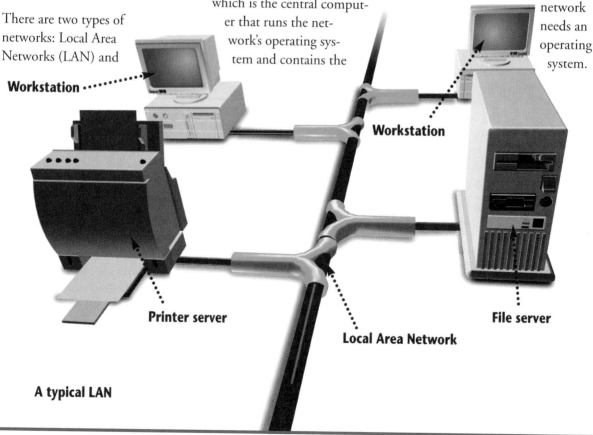

Workstation

Workstation

Printer server

File server

Local Area Network

A typical LAN

The network operating system runs on top of the regular PC's operating system (such as DOS) as an extra layer, providing network-wide management of the shared network files, programs, and peripherals. The network operating system provides the communications link between all the PCs and peripherals on the network. A LAN should also have a network administrator, a person who maintains the network and ensures that everything runs smoothly.

A PC (workstation) is connected to the network by a special circuit board called a network interface card. This card is inserted into an expansion slot inside the system unit. The card is connected to either a cable (a fiber optical cable, or a coaxial cable like the ones used in cable television) or an ordinary telephone wire. Cables offer protection for the data being transmitted over the network, allowing that data to be transmitted over greater distances from the server, with less data error. However, telephone wires are less expensive to install and maintain. Also see E-mail, Internet, NetWare, and Novell.

LAN

Modem

Modem

LAN

LAN

Modem

Wide Area Network

continues

Network continued

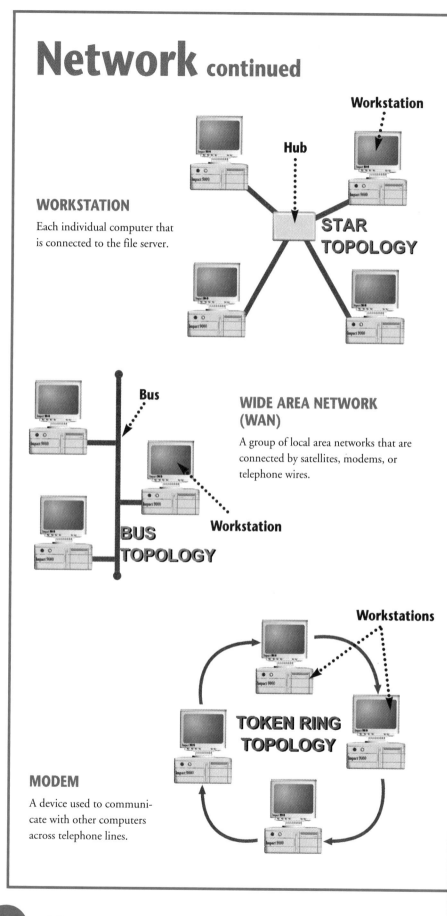

WORKSTATION

Each individual computer that is connected to the file server.

Hub

Workstation

STAR TOPOLOGY

Bus

WIDE AREA NETWORK (WAN)

A group of local area networks that are connected by satellites, modems, or telephone wires.

BUS TOPOLOGY

Workstation

Workstations

TOKEN RING TOPOLOGY

MODEM

A device used to communicate with other computers across telephone lines.

The PCs on a network are connected in various ways, called topologies. There are three basic network topologies: star, bus, and token ring.

In a star network, PCs are connected to a central hub, a computer that is connected to the server. The hub acts as a resource manager and a traffic cop for the network. But if it fails, that part of the network fails. In addition, star networks are costly because of all the cable that's used.

In a bus network, PCs are connected to a central cable called the bus. Bus networks are less costly because they use less cable, however, if the bus fails, the entire network fails. Also, traffic along the bus can get congested, increasing the amount of time it takes to get a file.

In a token ring network, PCs are connected to each other in a kind of ring. Information is passed from one PC to the next, until it reaches its destination. If one PC fails, the entire network can fail. Adding new PCs to the network is difficult, but this topology uses the least amount of cable so it is the least costly.

Norton

Back in the late '70s, Peter Norton was working for Boeing when he heard some pretty bad news: he was being laid off along with hundreds of other aerospace workers. What might have been bad news for Peter turned out to be good news for the computing industry. After accidentally deleting an important file one day, Peter decided to write a program to try to recover it. That program formed the basis of what was to become Norton Utilities.

```
C:\>cd \nu
                          The Norton Utilities 7.0
 Menu   Configuration   Help
      Commands                        Description
     RECOVERY                          RECOVERY
  Diagnostics
  Disk Doctor          * Recover deleted files and repair
  Disk Editor            damaged ones.
  Disk Tools           * Restore formatted disks.
  File Fix             * Protect disks against data loss.
  Image                * Diagnose problems with computer
  Rescue Disk            hardware.
  SmartCan
  UnErase
  UnFormat

     SECURITY
  Disk Monitor
```

Norton Utilities

Norton Utilities is a collection of small, useful programs that enable a user to recover deleted files, repair file allocation problems, repair logical and physical hard disk errors, prepare an emergency startup disk, defragment a hard disk, and improve file access. Norton Utilities was first released in 1982 under the company name, Peter Norton Computing, Inc. There have been many improvements since then. In fact, Norton Utilities is so good that parts of it (the backup program and the defragmenter) are now incorporated into MS-DOS. Norton Utilities also comes with Norton SI (System Information), which is a program that gives a user statistics about his system. For example, with Norton SI a user can find out his computer's performance index, which is a combination of CPU speed and disk speed. There is also a version of Norton Utilities for Macintosh computers.

Norton's programs were unique not only in what they did, but in how they were marketed. Peter thought it would make people feel more comfortable about using his programs if they knew the person behind them, so he used his picture on the cover of his programs and his books so that users could get to know him better. Peter had been writing computing columns for PC Magazine and PC Week since 1982, and in 1983, Brady Books asked him to write a book about the inner workings of the IBM PC. It became a huge hit. What followed were over a dozen more books, all successful—and all with Peter's face on the cover.

Peter ran his business out of his home, hiring another programmer, Brad Kingsbury, in 1985 to take over the programming chores. His products continued to win award after award. Additional products were added: in 1985, Norton Editor was released (a text file editor), and in 1986, Norton Commander joined the line of products.

continues

Norton continued

Norton Commander combines the file editing capabilities of Norton Editor with a complete file viewing system that allows a user to view a file without starting the application. For example, a user could view a Lotus 1-2-3 spreadsheet file without starting 1-2-3. Norton commander is a DOS shell (a program that surrounds DOS and makes it friendly and easier to use). With Norton Commander, a user can copy, move, or delete files; view files; start programs; and create and delete directories.

In 1990, Peter Norton's company merged with Symantec Corporation. With more research and development capital, new products were added, including Norton Anti-Virus (a virus detection and elimination program) and Norton pcANYWHERE (a program that allows a user—such as a technical support person—to dial into a remote PC and run programs, copy files, or run utilities to fix problems).

In 1991, Norton Desktop was introduced. Norton Desktop is a desktop management program that takes the place of Windows Program Manager and the File Manager, making Windows much easier to use. In addition, Norton Desktop has added features, such as Norton Anti-Virus and Norton's Backup utility, in addition to a file viewer, a program launcher, a screen saver, and data recovery programs. Also see Applications, Software, Utilities, Virus, and Windows.

Peter Norton began writing for Brady Books in 1983.

How Does It Work?

When a file is saved to disk, its location is written to a special area called the FAT (file allocation table). Later, when the file is needed, its location is found in the FAT, and the file is retrieved from disk.

When a file is deleted, its location is erased from the FAT, and the associated areas become available to use for saving other files. However, since the file has not actually been deleted from the disk, special utility programs can "retrieve" the deleted file (if used soon enough) and return its name and location to the FAT.

UTILITY

A program that performs a specific task, such as disk management. Norton Utilities allows the user to recover deleted files, repair file allocation problems, repair logical and physical hard disk errors, prepare an emergency startup disk, defragment a hard disk, and improve file access, among other things.

DOS SHELL

A program that surrounds DOS and makes it easier to use by providing menus and simple commands for moving, copying, and deleting files, and for creating and deleting directories. The Norton Commander is a DOS shell.

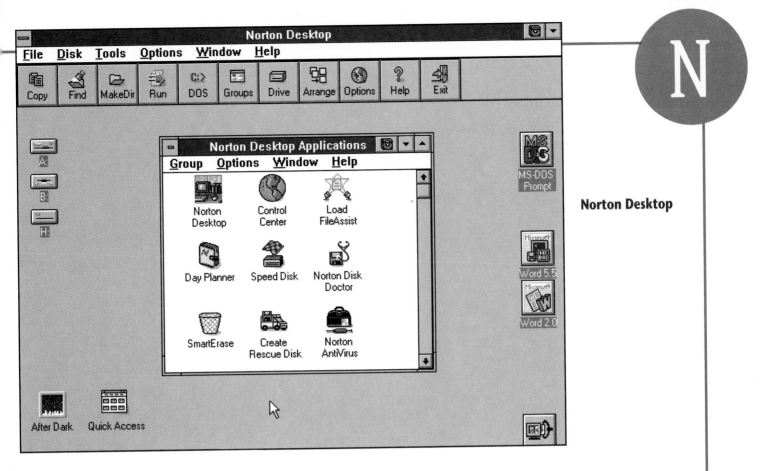

Norton Desktop

DEFRAGMENTATION

Files are often divided into sections and saved onto disks in the first available clusters. This fragments data over the disk, making it take longer for the hard drive to locate all the pieces of a file. Defragmentation reorganizes the data on a hard disk so that all the pieces of a file are located in adjacent clusters, making it easier for the hard drive to

ANTI-VIRUS PROGRAM

A virus is a program that destroys a file's data or the directory structure on a disk. Viruses attach themselves to program files and move with them from disk to disk. Anti-virus programs detect these changes in program files and remove the virus.

FILE EDITOR/FILE VIEWER

A program which allows the user to view the contents of a file created with another application, and/or to edit it. Norton Commander is such a program.

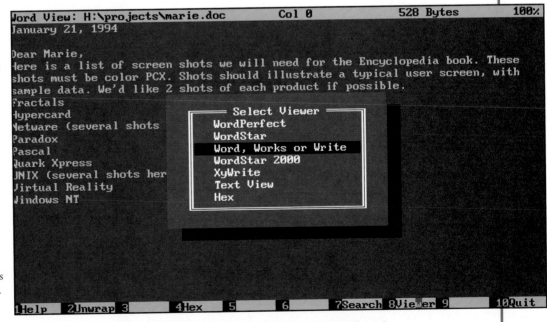

Norton Commander with File Viewer displayed.

Novell

When a person thinks of networks, it is almost impossible not to think of Novell Inc., due in large part to the popularity of their product NetWare, a network operating system. Novell's NetWare runs on top of the regular PC's operating system (such as DOS) as an extra layer, providing network-wide management of shared resources such as printers, programs and files. NetWare provides the communications link between all the PCs and peripherals on the network.

At first, Novell produced only computers and hardware products for PCs. Ray Noorda, who is now president and CEO of Novell, joined the company in 1983 and changed its focus. He thought the idea of connecting computers so they could exchange information was intriguing and challenging, and he eventually turned Novell into a software-producing company instead of a hardware-producing company. They now control about 70% of the network market with three important products: NetWare, Novell DOS (called DR-DOS until Novell merged with Digital Research), and UnixWare (a network operating system for UNIX computers). In fact, Novell is the second largest software manufacturer worldwide, just after Microsoft.

Novell introduced its first network operating system, which was the first network system for PCs, in 1983. NetWare is now a family of several different network operating systems, including NetWare 2.2, NetWare 3.12, and NetWare 4.01. NetWare 2.2 is the last version of a network operating system designed to run on a server equipped with a 286 CPU; as a result, it is not sold very much anymore. NetWare 3.12 supports up to 250 users per server, while NetWare 4.01 supports up to 1,000. A simpler network operating system, called NetWare Lite, allows PCs to share files and peripherals without a dedicated file server.

Novell DOS is a disk operating system that stems from DR DOS, which was developed by Digital Research before Novell bought the company. Although many people have argued that DR-DOS (now called Novell DOS) has been a technological step ahead of MS-DOS (Microsoft Disk Operating System) for the past few years, it has never superseded MS-DOS in popularity. Unlike MS-DOS, Novell DOS 7.0 supports true preemptive multitasking (like OS/2). In 1994, Novell began positioning itself as a formidable competitor to Microsoft by acquiring Word Perfect, Inc. along with the rights to Borland's

Ray Noorda, president and CEO of Novell

Novell's popular networking sofware

LOCAL AREA NETWORK (LAN)

A type of network that is confined to a single area (such as a single building). Several LANs can be connected through telephone lines, creating a wide area network (WAN).

NETWORK

A group of two or more computers that are connected either by cables or communications media, for the purpose of sharing programs, files, and peripherals.

NETWORK OPERATING SYSTEM (NOS)

The software that maintains the network and provides the communications link between all of the nodes (workstations and peripherals). The network operating system runs on top of the PC's operating system, running interference for network requests for shared files and resources. NetWare is an example of a network operating system.

Quatro Pro. With the DR DOS, Unix, and Netware operating systems, along with WordPerfect (one of the most popular word processors) and Quatro Pro (a powerful spreadsheet program) Novell is now a giant in the software industry. Also see DOS, NetWare, and Network.

FILE SERVER

Also called network server. The main computer that runs the network operating system software and that manages the network. It normally has a huge hard drive in order to house all of the programs and files that network users share. Peer-to-peer networks do not use a file server.

The Novell facility in Provo, Utah

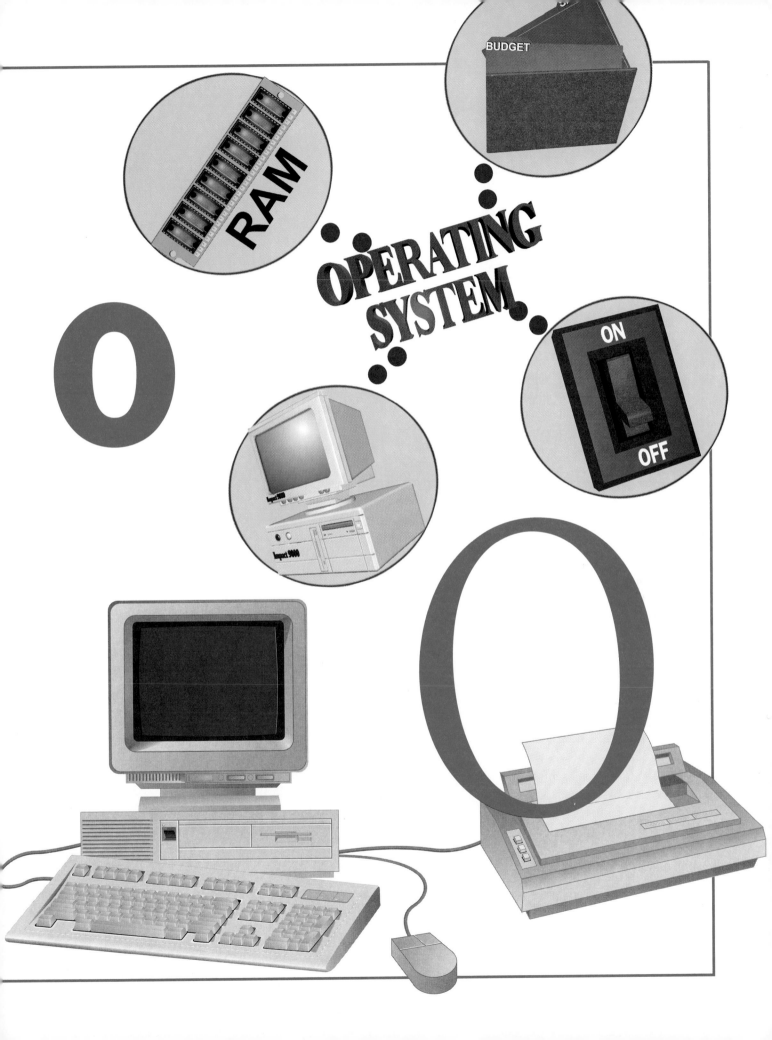

Object-Oriented Programming

Object-oriented programming (OOP) is a programming technique that divides a program into sets of instructions called objects. A program is a set of instructions that tells the computer how to perform a task. Most programs look somewhat like broken English; however, the actual words and the structure of each instruction depend on which programming language is being used. Following the rules of a particular programming language, a programmer writes the step-by-step instructions that tell the computer exactly what to do. BASIC, Pascal, C and C++ are all examples of programming languages. Turbo Pascal (Borland) is the object-oriented version of the Pascal programming language. C++ (Borland) and Visual C++ (Microsoft) are the object-oriented versions of the C programming language.

It's the programmer's job to write the instructions that tell a computer what to do. Each instruction must be very precise, with every step carefully thought out and written. Many parts of a program depend on the results of other calculations. Before the advent of OOP, if a programmer changed one part of a program, it often caused unexpected changes to other parts. That is because non-OOP programs are written in sections that are interdependent. Instructions in one part of the program reference other instructions, and when something is changed, it just doesn't always work.

One thing about object-oriented programming that makes writing programs easier is the characteristic of inheritance. With inheritance, a programmer can create similar objects without rewriting large sections of code. For example, a programmer writing a drawing program could create a rectangle object which is defined as an item with four straight sides joined by right angles—the opposite sides of equal length. A square object could be defined as a rectangle with four equal sides. The square object could "inherit" all the characteristics of a rectangle, with a few unique characteristics of its own. Another trait of object-oriented programming is the characteristic of polymorphism. With polymorphism, each object has the ability to choose the correct internal procedure based on whatever data it receives. For example, if a print object receives a graphics file, it recognizes it and chooses the correct method for printing graphics.

Object-oriented programming techniques are perfect for creating Windows programs, which are usually chock full of objects such as dialog boxes (boxes that request information from the user), icons (pictures that represent a command, such as saving a file), and windows themselves (boxes that contain files, such as a letter or a memo. However, objects do not have to be something that can be seen on-screen (although that's the easiest way to think of them); instead, objects are sections of a program that are independent from the main program. Also see C, Pascal, Programming, Visual Basic, and Windows.

Object-oriented programs use inheritance to pass characteristics form one object to another.

How Does It Work?

With OOP, parts of the program are divided into self-sustaining sections called objects. Each object (section of programming instructions) is responsible for understanding its own function and for handling its own data. That means that with OOP programs, adding new features is easy because each feature is independent of the other features.

For example, if a programmer wanted to write a chess program, he would create separate objects for each chess piece. Each object (such as a knight) would know how it moved on the board and where its current location was. When the player issued a command to the chess program to move the knight, the main part of the program would just tell the Knight object to move. The Knight object would know what its current location was and how to move itself. It would then calculate its new location on the chess board and report that back to the main program. If the programmer needed to add a new piece to the game, such as a Prince, it would be easy because what the Prince needs to know and do would be completely separate from all the other pieces of the game. Adding a Prince would not affect any other part of the program.

CLASS

A collection of objects that share characteristics. For example, the class Auto may contain the two class objects Van and Truck.

Each piece in this chess program is an "Object", with its own functions and data.

OBJECT-ORIENTED PROGRAMMING

A method of programming using "objects" that possess certain properties defining not only what the object is, but also what it does. For example, in a chess program, a Pawn object would be described as looking and moving a particular way. When the user wants to move a pawn, the program instructs the Pawn object to move itself, and the object knows what instructions to issue to the computer to make that happen.

ENCAPSULATION

A characteristic of object-oriented programming. Objects are said to be encapsulated (self-contained) because they contain both data and functions that operate on the data.

INHERITANCE

A characteristic of object-oriented programming that allows the programmer to create a new object that "inherits" some properties from an existing object. For example, a square object inherits some of the characteristics of a rectangle object (they both are made up of four sides).

POLYMORPHISM

A characteristic of object-oriented programming that allows an object to implement the same function differently. For example, a print object will send different signals to a printer to print a graphic (picture) than it will send to print a simple letter.

OLE

O LE stands for Object Linking and Embedding. OLE is a Windows process, and is therefore only available within Windows applications that support it. OLE creates a "connection" between a source object (such as a picture, a chart, or some spreadsheet data) in one Windows application and a destination document in another Windows application. Once the connection is made, the user can use it to keep the source object (the picture, chart, or spreadsheet data) updated without having to import it into the destination document over and over. For example, the user can create a connection between spreadsheet data and a report, between a graphic and a brochure, or between a chart and a presentation, and use this connection to make changes when necessary. The type of connection that's created depends on whether the user chooses to link the object or embed the object.

A link can connect an object (such as a logo) to a document.

Let's say a user links a graphic from Paintbrush (a Windows paint program) to a letter created in Microsoft Word for Windows (a Windows word processing program). Because the graphic is linked to the letter, every time the graphic is updated in Paintbrush, it is automatically updated in the Word letter the next time that letter is opened. In this example, Word is considered the client application because it is receiving information; Paintbrush is considered a server application because it's the one sending information. More specifically, the Word document is considered the destination document, and the Paintbrush graphic is the source document.

When an object (such as a graphic) is linked to the destination document, the graphic is not stored as part of that document. Instead a link or connection is maintained between the graphic and the source document. Because the graphic is not actually part of the destination document, any changes made to the graphic in the original file are not immediately reflected within the destination document; however,

Because the graphic is linked to the letter in Word, the changes are not immediately reflected until the Word document is activated.

Word document (client application)

The user starts the Paintbrush program (server application) to make changes to the linked object, which will take effect when Word is reactivated.

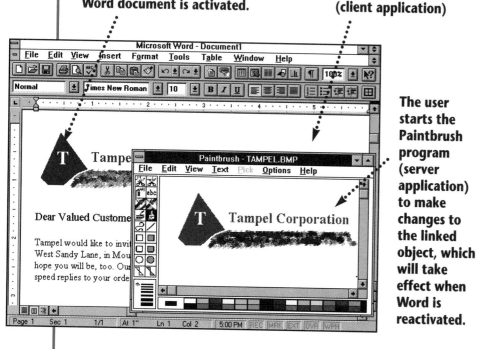

the graphic is updated when the program of the destination document is activated. The link then helps the destination document find the changed graphic and update the linked version of it.

An alternative to linking a graphic (or other object) is embedding. The difference between linking and embedding lies in where the object is actually stored. With embedding, a graphic (or other object) is stored as part of the document. Just as in linking, there is a special connection between the document and the program that created the graphic; however, this time the connection takes a different form. When the user wants to make changes to an embedded graphic (or other object), he doesn't go to the program that created it, but to the destination document. By double-clicking on the object, the user is escorted to the drawing program, where he works within its program window to make changes. When the user finishes making changes and exits the graphics program, he's whisked back to the document—where the graphic already reflects the changes. Unlike a linked object, an embedded object is updated immediately as soon as any changes are made. That's because the user is not making changes to an object that's stored somewhere else, but to an object that's stored within the document.

With embedding, if the user wants to make changes to the object without affecting the embedded

The Embedded object is stored in the Word document.

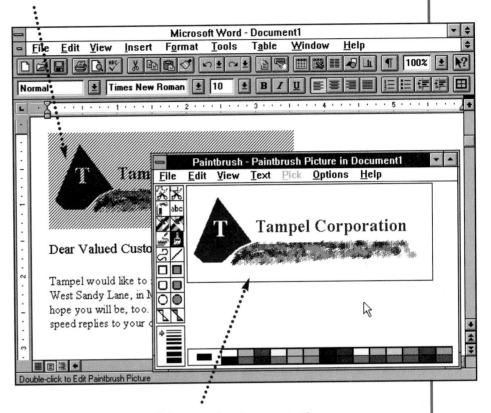

When the user double-clicks to make changes to the embedded object, those changes are immediately reflected in the Word document.

object in his document, he can. Rather than accessing the drawing program through the embedded object, the user makes the changes in the original program and saves them, which doesn't affect the copy of that object that's stored within the destination document. So for example, after embedding the Quarter 1 data into a report, the user can go back to the original file and change everything over to Quarter 2 without affecting the saved report. Also see Windows.

LINKED OBJECT

An object that is created in one Windows application and connected to another Windows application. When the original object is changed, all objects that are linked to it are automatically updated.

EMBEDDED OBJECT

An object that is created in one Windows application and connected to another Windows application. A user can edit the object in the server application by double-clicking on it in the destination document; however, changes to the original object do not affect the embedded copy of that object.

Operating System

An operating system is the program that runs the computer; the program interprets instructions from the user or an application and tells the computer what to do. For example, if the user issues a command to save a file, the operating system analyzes the command, and then issues instructions to the various PC components to carry it out. The operating system is the first program that is run when a user turns on his computer; it makes the computer ready to receive commands. After the PC is properly prepared to receive instructions, the operating system interprets the user's instructions, handles input and output, runs applications, keeps track of the data stored on disk, and communicates with peripherals (such as the monitor, the hard disk, the floppy disk drives, the printer, or a modem). Typical PC operating systems include MS-DOS, PC-DOS, Novell DOS (formerly DR-DOS), OS/2, UNIX, and Macintosh System.

The earliest operating systems were used in the 1950s to handle tape storage on large mainframe computers. But as technology evolved, better operating systems were written to handle more complex chores, such as file management on hard disks,

timesharing (dividing the CPU's time between multiple tasks), and multitasking (processing more than one task at once). Personal computers came on the scene in the late '70s, and different operating systems were developed for them. CP/M (Control Program for Microcomputers) was one of the first PC operating systems, running on the Intel 8080 and the Zilog Z-80, two early microprocessor chips. IBM almost chose CP/M as the operating system for the IBM-PC, but instead they went with Microsoft's PC-DOS.

Today, MS-DOS (Microsoft's disk operating system) is the most popular operating system for PCs, but there are other types too. For example, Novell Inc. produces Novell DOS (formerly DR-DOS). IBM's version of Microsoft DOS is called PC-DOS, which is found on IBM PCs.

OS/2 is a preemptive multitasking operating system (capable of running multiple programs simultaneously) developed through a joint effort by IBM and Microsoft that combines a graphical user interface

DOS Command

MS DOS operating system.

```
C:\>mem

Memory Type         Total   =   Used   +   Free
--------------      -------     -------    -------
Conventional         640K         95K       545K
Upper                155K        105K        50K
Reserved             384K        384K         0K
Extended (XMS)     7,013K      2,269K     4,744K
                   -------     -------    -------
Total memory       8,192K      2,853K     5,339K

Total under 1 MB     795K        200K       595K

Largest executable program size        545K (557,792 bytes)
Largest free upper memory block         49K  (50,560 bytes)
MS-DOS is resident in the high memory area.

C:\>
```

DOS prompt

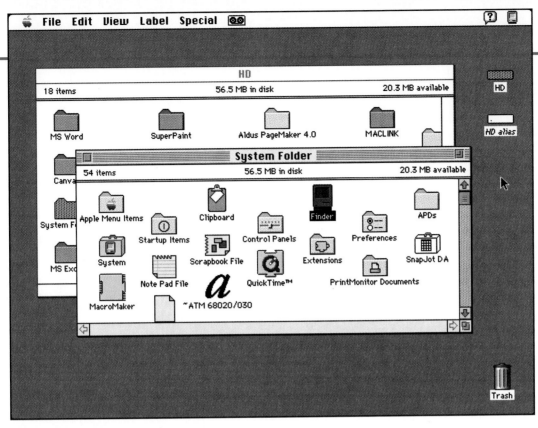

Macintosh System operating system.

environment with powerful memory management features. OS/2 can run OS/2, Windows, or DOS programs with ease.

System 7.x is the operating system found on most Macintosh computers. (Some earlier Macs use ProDOS, which is an operating system for the Apple II family.) Included with System 7 is the Finder, the program that manages the desktop, and MultiFinder, which managers multiple applications on-screen.

UNIX, developed in the early '70s by AT&T, is now owned by Novell. UNIX is a multitasking (capable of running multiple programs simultaneously), multiuser operating system that can run on a variety of computers from PCs to mainframes. As a matter of fact, most mainframes and minicomputers use some form of the UNIX operating system. Local providers (PCs through which a user connects to the Internet, a network of government and university computers around the globe) also use UNIX. There are many versions of UNIX. One version, called A/UX, runs on powerful Macintosh computers.

Different types of operating systems utilize different types of user-interfaces (the part through which the user communicates his wishes to the PC). DOS and UNIX use a command-line interface, which means that the user must type exact commands at a prompt. OS/2 and Macintosh System use a graphical user interface, which allows the user to manipulate icons (pictures) that represent files, programs, and commands. (Windows is not an operating system, but an operating environment that surrounds DOS and provides a friendly user interface.) Also see Boot, DOS, Internet, Microsoft, Novell, OS/2, RAM, ROM, System 7, and UNIX.

continues

Operating System
continued

SYSTEM 7

The most recent version of the operating system that runs Macintosh computers. The System contains a program called the Finder, which runs the graphical user interface.

UNIX

Developed by AT&T and currently owned by Novell, UNIX is a multitasking (capable of running multiple programs simultaneously) multiuser operating system that can run on mainframes and minis, as well as PCs. UNIX is difficult to use, but very powerful.

OS/2

A powerful preemptive multitasking operating system (capable of running multiple programs simultaneously), OS/2 was meant to take the place of DOS. It is the result of a collaboration between IBM and Microsoft.

MS-DOS

The standard PC disk operating system that is produced by Microsoft Corporation.

Managing memory

Managing files

Managing the PC's

Managing system startup

How Does It Work?

One part of the operating system is used only when the PC is started or restarted (booted); that part includes the startup instructions that prepare a computer for use. The core of the operating system, called the kernel, is loaded into memory (RAM) after the startup commands are completed. The kernel contains the instructions that make it possible for the PC to respond to commands from the user or an application.

Once the operating system is loaded into memory, it performs various functions, such as managing memory (loading programs and data) and managing files (saving, retrieving, and deleting files). The operating system also manages input/output by displaying information on the monitor, sending files to the printer or the modem, responding to keypresses or the movement of a mouse or a joystick, reading and writing data to floppy disks or tape cassettes, and reading data on CD-ROMs.

An operating system performs many functions.

OS/2

Operating System/2, also called OS/2, is the result of a joint effort by IBM and Microsoft. However, Microsoft quit the joint venture early on to develop Windows, which was originally intended to be a temporary solution for DOS users who wanted a graphical shell to manage their systems while waiting for OS/2 to be released. OS/2 is a powerful operating system that was originally meant to take the place of DOS. OS/2 supports preemptive multitasking (the ability to process more than one command or task at a time by dividing the CPU's time into tiny processing slots), is compatible with IBM's mainframe and minicomputer operating systems, and has better memory management features than MS-DOS. In addition, its graphical user interface is easier to use than DOS' command-line interface.

The first version of OS/2 was a 16-bit operating system, which meant that data was processed in 16-bit segments (about twice as fast as conventional PCs at the time). OS/2 version 1.x was designed for 286 PCs and up. Although it was intended to replace DOS, not many people were willing to upgrade to OS/2 because the early versions didn't run DOS programs very well, and not many software companies at the time were making OS/2-compatible software.

OS/2 version 2 was released in April of 1992. OS/2 version 2 is a complete 32-bit operating system (on PCs with 386 CPUs and up), which is twice as fast as OS/2 version 1.x, and about four times faster than conventional DOS PCs. OS/2 version 2 runs DOS, Windows, and OS/2 applications all at the same time. OS/2 version 2 has improved memory management capabilities: unlike the artificial limit of 1MB that DOS PCs must endure, OS/2 can manage up to 4 gigabytes of memory directly. OS/2 version 2 also includes an improved file management system that makes file retrieval a breeze.

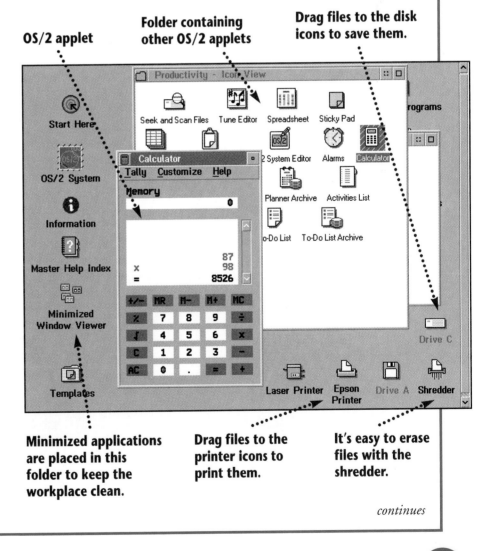

OS/2 applet

Folder containing other OS/2 applets

Drag files to the disk icons to save them.

Minimized applications are placed in this folder to keep the workplace clean.

Drag files to the printer icons to print them.

It's easy to erase files with the shredder.

continues

OS/2 continued

OS/2 version 2.1 supports all Windows 3.1 applications as well. In fact, IBM is fond of saying that OS/2 2.1 is a "better Windows than Windows" because it runs most Windows applications faster than Windows does itself. (Microsoft released its own 32-bit operating system, Windows NT, after OS/2 version 2 was released.)

Like Windows' Program Manager, OS/2 has Presentation Manager to manage its applications and applets (small, built-in applications that come with OS/2). Its files are arranged in folders and subfolders, like in Windows. But unlike Windows, OS/2 combines the program and file management tasks into one unit. (This is similar to Norton Desktop, a shell that sits on top of Windows and manages files and programs more efficiently.) The latest version of OS/2, OS/2 2.1, replaced Presentation Manager with an improved (but similar) interface called the Workplace Shell. Also see Norton, Operating System, Windows, and Windows NT.

OPERATING SYSTEM

The program that is run first when the computer is started. The operating system controls the way input and output is handled and manages applications and peripherals.

MS-DOS

The standard disk operating system for PCs that was developed by Microsoft Corp.

MICROSOFT WINDOWS

A graphical user interface environment that sits on top of DOS and allows the user to communicate with the computer by using icons and menus instead of a command prompt.

How Does It Work?

OS/2 is a preemptive multitasking system, which means that it divides the CPU's time into short time slots, then assigns those time slots to the tasks which are running at the time. A program will be "preempted" for another program when its time is "up".

This system is different than multitasking under WIndows, which depends on mutual cooperation amoung all the running applications. Under Windows, an application is expected to return control to Windows when the application is not really doing anything at the moment.

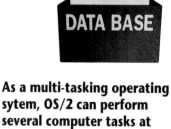

As a multi-tasking operating sytem, OS/2 can perform several computer tasks at the same time, such as searching a database while printing a document and performing calculations.

Output Devices

Once the computer receives input from the user, it processes the data and sends it back to the user in a format he can understand. For example, information is displayed on a monitor or printed out by a printer for the user. This processed data that the computer gives back to the user is called output. Information displayed on a monitor or printed out by a printer is the most common forms of output; however, warning beeps and other noises the computer makes to attract the user's attention are also considered output. Any device that produces output is appropriately called an output device.

Storage devices, such as a hard disk drive or a floppy disk drive, could be considered output devices since they store the output of programs (files). However, they are not usually included in a listing of a PC's output devices, because they also provide input (in the form of stored files) for applications.

A modem (a communications device) also plays both input and output roles, receiving and transmitting data over telephone lines. Input devices are those which accept input from the user, and they include the keyboard, mouse, scanners, touch screens, graphics tablets, and joysticks. Also see Input Devices, Monitor, and Printer.

PRINTER

A peripheral that gives the user a paper copy of text or graphics.

MONITOR

The television-like device the computer uses to display information for the user.

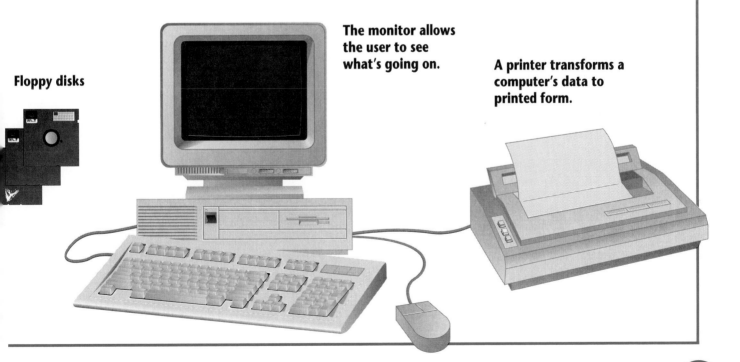

Floppy disks

The monitor allows the user to see what's going on.

A printer transforms a computer's data to printed form.

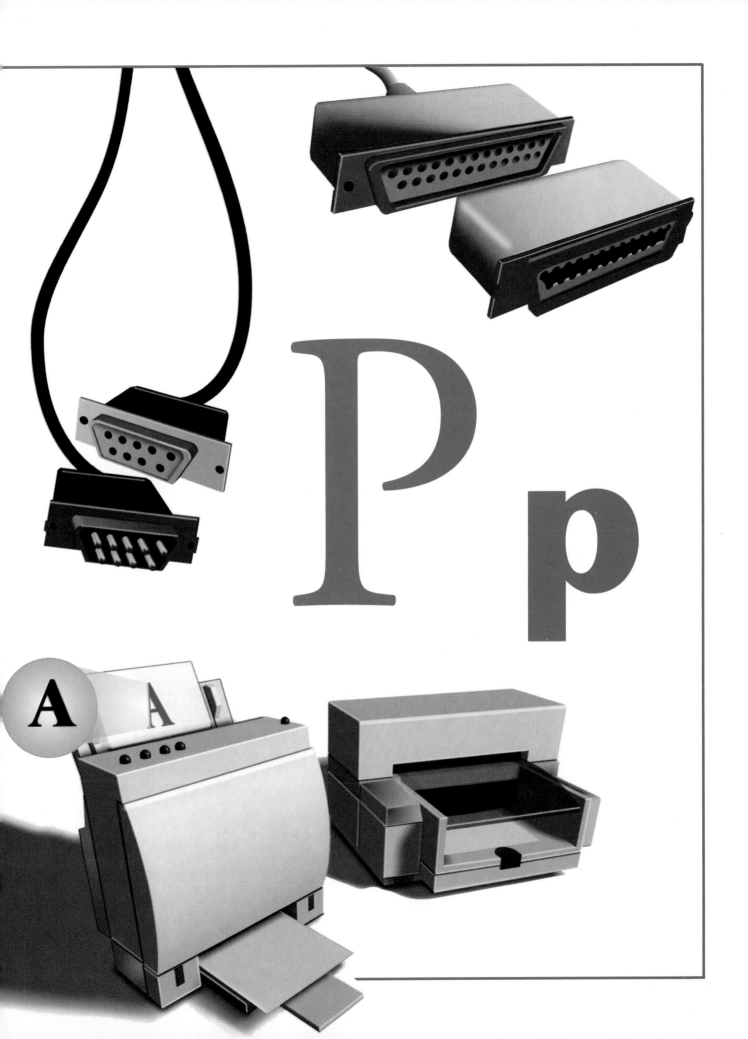

PageMaker

PageMaker is the name of a desktop publishing program made by Aldus Corporation. Desktop publishing programs let the user combine text and graphics into highly detailed page layouts. PageMaker is used to create newsletters, brochures, advertisements, and even books. With PageMaker, the user can manipulate text and graphics on the computer to make professional-looking publications, complete with headlines and columns. (These publications look even more professional when they are printed with a quality printer, such as a laser printer).

PageMaker was one of the first desktop publishing programs made for the computer. Released in 1985, PageMaker helped promote desktop publishing on the computer. The first version of PageMaker was designed for the Macintosh computer. The Mac's graphical user interface (GUI) made programs like PageMaker, in which the user manipulates text and graphics, exceptionally easy to use. Before desktop publishing programs such as PageMaker came along, it took several people to put together a publication: writers, typesetters, layout artists, photographers, and printers worked together to complete the finished product. It was a costly and time-consuming process. Today's desktop publishing programs help speed up the process and bring down the costs of production, making desktop publishing affordable even for the smallest business.

Text can be made to flow between the margins of a column.

Text can jump over a graphic.

Graphics can be placed on top of other objects.

Text can flow around the edges of a graphic.

How Does It Work?

Before it's opened in PageMaker, a text file is usually written, edited, spell checked, and saved in a word processing program (usually only small text passages are spell-checked within PageMaker if necessary). Once the text is prepared, the graphics are designed and the document is assembled. With PageMaker, the user can control where text flows, down one or multiple columns. Text can be made to flow around the edges of a graphic or to jump over it completely. Borders and shading can be added behind graphics or text to add interest.

GUI

Graphical User Interface. A GUI is a graphical way of talking to the computer. Users can select pictorial representations (icons) of files, programs, or commands from a friendly-looking screen.

PAGE LAYOUT

The design and structure of text, graphics, headlines, and columns on a page.

An easy menu system provides quick access to commands.

The toolbox makes it easy to manipulate text and graphics.

PageMaker, now available for the Macintosh and Windows systems, features rulers and grids for setting columns and margins precisely, different layout views that allow the user to zoom in for closer looks, and a toolbox (a collection of buttons that help the user manipulate text and graphic objects). In addition, a template can be created for the left or right-hand pages of a document, and can be automatically repeated throughout. For example, the user can set up a two column format for the left-hand page, and all the left-hand pages of the document will be two-column. PageMaker is a popular program that is simple enough for beginners, yet powerful enough for the demands of professional designers and publishers. Also see Desktop Publishing, GUI, and Macintosh.

ICON

A graphical representation of a program, file, or command. Icons are used with graphical user interface programs.

MENU

A list of commands that the user can select from. Menus are usually drop-down lists, that appear on a computer screen when a menu name is selected.

Paint Programs

A paint program is a special application that uses the mouse to "paint" with the computer, making freehand illustrations and graphics. A painting program uses dots, called pixels, to make an image. By controlling individual dots, the user can create shading and patterns, as well as irregular lines to simulate the effect of a painting or sketch.

Unlike drawing programs that use shapes to build graphic objects and treat each graphic object as a mathematical formula, paint programs keep track of every dot that makes up an image. Each dot can be modified by turning colors on or off. Images made with a paint program cannot be resized and scaled as graphic objects made with drawing programs can. However, drawing programs do not allow the user the flexibility of controlling color and dots.

The very first painting program was written by Bill Atkinson for the original Macintosh computer. It was called, appropriately, MacPaint. MacPaint uses the Macintosh's 72-dot resolution display so that the drawing looks the same on-screen as it does when printed (WYSIWYG technology, or what-you-see-is-what-you-get). Many other painting programs have been created since, including PC Paintbrush for the IBM PC, and SuperPaint for the Macintosh.

Paint programs include a toolbox, which is a collection of icons representing various painting tools. There are usually tools for drawing standard objects, such as rectangles, ellipses, and

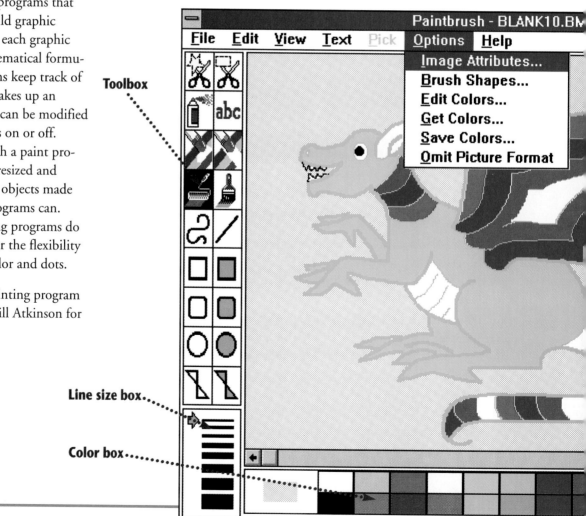

Windows' Paintbrush Program

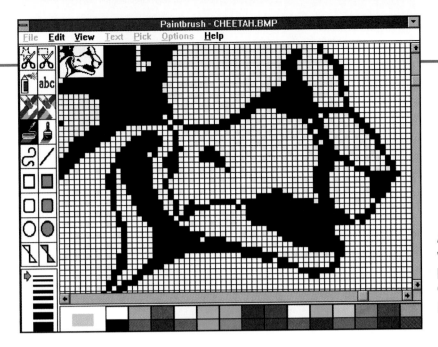

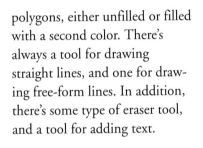

An image created with a painting program is composed of tiny dots called pixels.

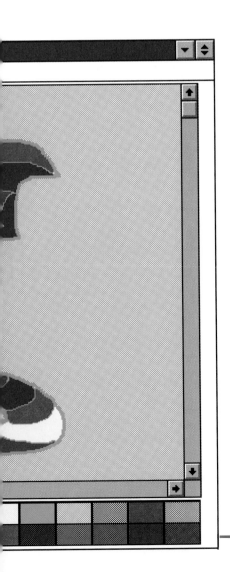

polygons, either unfilled or filled with a second color. There's always a tool for drawing straight lines, and one for drawing free-form lines. In addition, there's some type of eraser tool, and a tool for adding text.

Parts of a painting can be copied by selecting them (drawing a loop around them with a selection tool), and then using the normal Copy and Paste commands. In addition, there is a color box for controlling the color of drawn objects, and a line size box for selecting the thickness of an object's border or the width of a drawn line. Also see Applications, Drawing Programs, Graphics, Software, and SuperPaint.

PANTONE COLORS

Pantone colors come from the Pantone Matching System (PMS), a system used by most printing shops and graphic designers. The Pantone Matching System helps to ensure that the finished color printed by the printer always matches the original color assigned by the designer. There are approximately 500 PMS colors to choose from. Sophisticated computer paint and drawing programs such as CorelDRAW!, Micrografx Designer, Adobe Illustrator, Arts & Letters, and Fractal Design Painter adhere to these Pantone color standards.

PIXEL

Short for picture element, a pixel is a tiny dot on the computer screen. A monitor screen is made up of thousands of pixels. Pixels are turned on or off to form a pattern of a letter or drawing.

Paradox

Paradox is a popular relational database management system published by Borland International, Inc. Database programs are designed to organize large quantities of data, such as address lists, merchandise records, payroll information, and more. Information within databases can quickly be sorted and retrieved, as well as presented in reports and analyzed.

A relational database, such as Paradox, is one in which the user can interrelate data from more than one database file. For example, a database file containing client information can be combined with a database file containing inventory pricing information to create an invoice detailing a client's purchase. In addition, relational databases allow the user to easily add, delete, or rearrange the fields within each record of the database.

Information is entered into a Paradox database through a table, organized into columns and rows. Each row is a record, representing a set of related information about a single person, place, or event. Each column is a field, representing one piece of data that the user would fill in for most (if not all) records in the database.

Paradox was first developed by Ansa Software and was later acquired by Borland. Introduced in 1987, Paradox is noted for its capability to simplify complex database questions into a query by example format—a method of looking up information. Paradox is also known for its special application language, called PAL, that lets the user customize the way in which database information is accessed and processed. For example, an experienced user could create simple boxes into which a less experienced staff could enter, sort, and retrieve data.

In 1993, Borland released Paradox for Windows, which included object-linking and embedding (OLE). Programs with OLE can import data more smoothly from other Windows programs. With object linking, a user can link a file or a part of file from another program to a Paradox database. When that linked data is changed within the original program, the data within the Paradox database will be automatically updated. With embedding, a user can copy all or part of a file created in a Windows

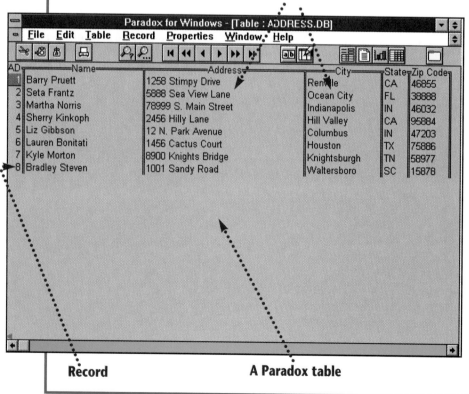

Fields

Record

A Paradox table

How Does It Work?

Relational databases allow separate database files to exchange data and create new files. The way this works is that a user identifies a key field that's the same in both databases. For example, one file may contain a list of client names, and another file may have inventory prices. A key field, such as a product id number, can be used to relate a particular customer's name from the first file to a particular item and its price from the second file to create an invoice.

program, but that data will not automatically be updated when the original is changed. However, the user can access the original program and make changes from within Paradox, rather than having to reopen the file in the program in which it was created. Both methods are especially convenient for users who keep their data in various places other than the Paradox database.

In Paradox for Windows, everything is treated as a simple object, meaning that it's super easy to move, copy, and add data by dragging the data with a mouse. In addition, an object's properties

(whether it contains text or numbers, and how many decimal places those numbers contain) can be easily changed with the click of a mouse.

Paradox continues to remain a popular database program for many types of users. It is a powerful program for experienced users who want to customize it, and yet it is very simple for a novice to learn to use. Paradox is designed to meet everyone's database needs in a straightforward, easy-to-comprehend manner, whether the user wants to track a small list of client addresses, or organize a large number of corporate records. Also see Access, Application, Approach, Borland, Data, Database, and dBASE.

QUERY

A set of criteria that accesses information from a specific part of the database (for example, "Who sold widgets in the month of January?"). Queries locate records in one or more database tables.

DBMS

DataBase Management System. A software program that controls the organization, storage, and retrieval of information found in a database. Additionally, a DBMS can provide security to prevent unauthorized usage.

RELATIONAL DATABASE

A database that allows the user to interrelate data between two or more files.

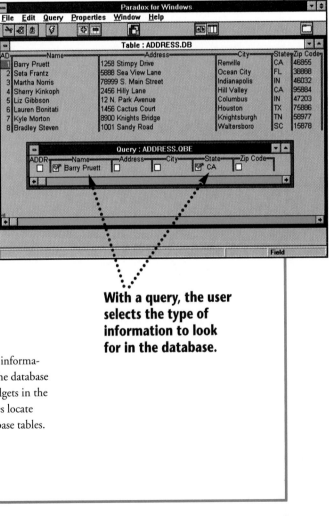

With a query, the user selects the type of information to look for in the database.

Pascal

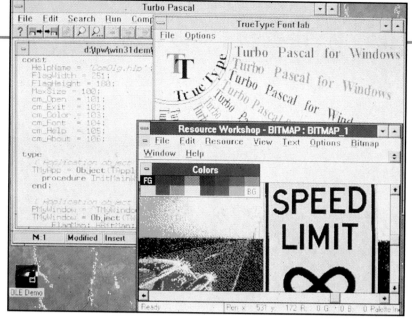

Pascal is the name of a programming language first developed by Niklaus Wirth in the early '70s. Pascal is named after a famous 17th century French mathematician, Blaise Pascal. A powerful computer language, Pascal is taught in schools because its structured programming language helps new students to write logical, well-designed programs. Pascal became very popular for writing commercial applications after 1984, when Borland released its low-priced version, Turbo Pascal.

A program is a set of instructions that tells the computer how to perform a task. Most programs look somewhat like broken English: the actual words and the structure of each instruction depends on which programming language is being used. Following the rules of a particular programming language, a programmer writes the step-by-step instructions that tell the computer exactly what to do.

After these instructions are written, they are converted into a language the computer can understand, called machine language. Machine language is a series of 1's and 0's based on a binary numbering system, which all computers use. With most versions of Pascal, the programming instructions are converted into machine language using

a special program called a compiler. The compiler checks each instruction for certain kinds of errors and displays a message when an error is found.

Pascal is a high-level programming language because it is written in an almost English code that is very easy for the programmer to learn. One of the benefits of using Pascal is its capability to handle procedures and to separate sections of the program that can be reused at any time. For example, a procedure to save a file could be called by any part of the main program when needed. Pascal differs from BASIC in that all variables must be declared; in other words, the type of data that the program manipulates at any given time must be defined. That way, if the program is expecting a number, but gets a bunch of text, an error will occur and the program will stop. This enables the programmer to easily identify problems. Also see BASIC, Binary, Borland, C/C++, and Programming.

Turbo Pascal, the most popular version of the Pascal programming language

COMPILER

Converts a program's instructions into machine language and stores the result in a file. That file can then be used over and over, each time the program is run.

LOW-LEVEL LANGUAGE

A programming language that is similar to machine language, just one level removed from the binary language of 1's and 0's.

HIGH-LEVEL PROGRAMMING LANGUAGE

A programming language that is easier for programmers to understand because it is written more closely to English than to the rudimentary 1's and 0's of machine language. High-level languages require a compiler or an interpreter to translate the program instructions into 1's and 0's that the computer can understand.

MODULA-2

A version of the Pascal language written by Niklaus Wirth in the early '80s. Modula-2 allows the programmer to compile and test each separate procedure before placing it within the main program.

PC

P C stands for personal computer. Personal computers, also called microcomputers, are designed to serve the needs of a single user. Personal computers fit on a desktop and are relatively easy to move around. They are considered stand-alone devices, equipped to handle software and peripherals (other computer parts, such as a printer) without relying on a mainframe computer. In effect, they have the processing power to "stand" on their own. This freedom gives users the option of choosing software that fits their own

personal needs rather than all of the needs of others.

Although there were many personal computer kits being sold at the time, the first PC is generally considered to be the Altair 8800, released in 1975. The personal computer industry really began in 1977 with the introduction of four microcomputers by four different companies: Processor Technology came out with the Sol 20, Apple Computer introduced the Apple II, Commodore introduced the Pet, and Radio Shack came out with the TRS-80. These early computers came with built-in

keyboards, 8-bit microprocessors, and about 16 kilobytes of memory (RAM).

In 1981, IBM introduced the PC, taking the initials from the term "personal computer" as its brand name. The PC used an Intel 8088 microprocessor that was fairly popular at the time, and it used a disk operating system called DOS. The IBM PC made a considerable mark on the personal computer market. As a result, it was heavily copied by such makers as Compaq and Dell, among others. These PC clones are called IBM-compatible computers. The IBM PC and its compatibles dominate the personal computer market today. (Also, the term PC is now generally used to describe the IBM PC or its compatibles.)

In 1983, Apple attempted to regain some lost footing in the personal computer market with the introduction of the Lisa computer, a computer that made full use of a graphical user interface technology (GUI). Unfortunately, the Lisa was too expensive to succeed in the marketplace. The following year,

Apple's Macintosh Color Classic personal computer

continues

PC **P** 253

PC continued

Apple released the Macintosh computer, another type of personal computer that uses a graphical user interface and an operating system other than DOS. The Macintosh has since become the second leading type of personal computer. (IBM PCs and compatibles being the first.)

Behind the industry leaders (IBM, IBM-compatibles, and Apple), there are a few other personal computers available. Commodore, for example, still manufactures less expensive personal computers for the home market. The Commodore Amiga computer offers quality color graphics and sound capabilities. The Amiga uses the same microprocessor as some Macintosh computers, but a different operating system. A variation of the Amiga, called the Video Toaster, is currently used in the production of high-quality videos, TV shows, and commercials requiring special effects. Atari, a brand of personal computers for the home featuring excellent sound capabilities incorporating built-in stereo, is no longer made.

One of Apple's original founders, Steve Jobs, started a new line of personal computers in 1985, called NeXT computers. NeXT computers included high-quality monitors, stereo sound, and a multitasking operating system. NeXT computers were envisioned as high-quality workstations for universities, but are no longer being manufactured.

Although there are not many types of personal computers to choose from today (IBM PC compatibles, Apple, Macintosh, and Amiga), they do come in a variety of sizes, including laptops, notebooks, and palmtops. Also see Apple, IBM, IBM-PC Compatible, Macintosh, Mainframe, Microcomputer, Minicomputer, and Operating System.

A Gateway 2000 personal computer

Apple Macintosh

IBM PC Compatible

PERSONAL COMPUTER

A computer designed to function on its own, which is small enough to fit on a desk or be carried around without a great deal of difficulty. Today's personal computers, or microcomputers, are often as powerful as minicomputers. Microcomputers use a single microprocessor chip to handle all of the computer's "thinking."

MICROCOMPUTER

Another name for a personal computer. A Microcomputer can sit on a desktop and be used by one person. PCs or microcomputers use a single-chip microprocessor as its central processing power.

MINICOMPUTER

Designed as a smaller-scale mainframe computer, the minicomputer is commonly used by several people at once in local area networks or in small organizations or departments within a large corporation.

OPERATING SYSTEM

In order for a computer to process data, it must know how and when. Special programs, called operating systems, are used to instruct the computer in how to perform. Without an operating system, the computer cannot function. Popular operating systems include DOS, system 7, and OS/2.

MAINFRAME COMPUTER

Large central computer designed to meet the processing needs of a large corporation or educational facility. Mainframe computers are the largest computers made today, and they are capable of processing many tasks at one time.

PC Tools

PC Tools is the name of a utility software package made by Central Point Software for both IBM PC compatibles and Macintosh computers. PC Tools combines several popular utilities that enable a user to recover deleted files, repair file allocation problems, repair logical and physical hard disk errors, prepare an emergency startup disk, defragment a hard disk, and improve file access. A utility program is used to manage computer files, diagnose and repair computer problems, and assist in helping the computer run efficiently. Basically, a utility program acts as the computer's maintenance man, fixing up things that go wrong and making sure everything is running smoothly.

PC Tools for Windows includes its own desktop, which sits on top of Windows, combining the program and file management tasks into one easy-to-use program—including the ability to delete, move, and copy files and directories. PC Tools for Windows allows the user to create "virtual desktops" or multiple desktop windows customized for specific purposes. Quick Launch provides quick access to all programs from within any window.

PC Tools also offers virus protection, another important feature for the computer. A virus is a malicious computer program created to vandalize other computer systems. Computer viruses are passed by means of infected program files through floppy disks or modem communications. Upon entering another computer system, they can inflict great damage, including erasing data files, reformatting the hard disk (which also erases data), and even destroying a computer's system files so that it cannot boot or start itself again. PC Tools virus protection feature checks the computer for such viruses and removes them if they are present.

PC Tools can tell the user how much memory is left on the computer's hard disk, how fast the disk is, and other important system information. When the computer's hard disk or even a floppy disk is damaged, PC Tools can help solve the problem. PC Tools can also help recover files that have accidentally been deleted, and can defragment a disk, organizing how the files are stored and making sure all the file's pieces are kept together on a disk and not scattered all over (fragmented). Finally, PC Tools can help users protect data by creating passwords for files that prevent others from opening or changing the data inside a file.

Parts of PC Tools are now incorporated into DOS. Beginning with DOS version 6.0, a version of Central Point's Anti-Virus and Undelete utilities are now included free. Also see Applications, Norton, Software, Utilities, and Virus.

DEFRAGMENT

When files are stored onto a formatted disk, they are stored in clusters. Large files often will not fit into just one cluster, and therefore must be "split up" and stored in several different areas on the disk. The more files that are written and deleted from the disk, the more split up or fragmented all the files become, and the longer it takes the computer to locate each part of a file. Defragmentation is a process that relocates files so they are again stored in neighboring clusters.

BACKUP

Backing up a hard disk involves copying its files to a floppy disk or backup tape. If the hard disk fails somehow, the back-up copies can be used to restore the files that were lost.

VIRUS

A computer program created to do damage to other computers, such as erasing files or reformatting the computer's hard disk drive.

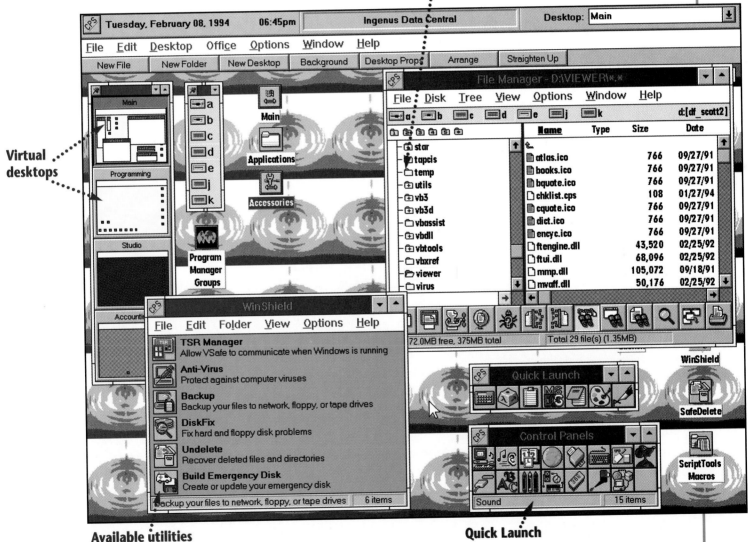

PC Tools for Windows

PC Tools' File Manager

Virtual desktops

Available utilities

Quick Launch

Pen Computing

Pen computers are those which can accept handwriting and other simple hand-drawn symbols as input. Using a pen-like device called a stylus, the user can input text by simply writing it. The computer then translates the handwritten input into a digital display on the screen. Using simple symbols (called gestures) such as an "X" or a check mark, the user can edit the text and enter other commands. Pens are also used in graphics programs to draw finely detailed designs on the computer using an electronic drawing tablet.

The new pen-based computing systems allow the user to input information on a portable notebook-sized screen. Portable palm computers, such as Apple's personal digital assistant (the Newton), use pens extensively to record data. Light pens are used in a similar fashion as the pen stylus; the user presses the tip of the pen to the screen to select specific screen elements.

Pen computing systems are mostly used for inventory, insurance claims, sales, medical claims, and delivery tracking. Also see Input Devices and Portable Computers.

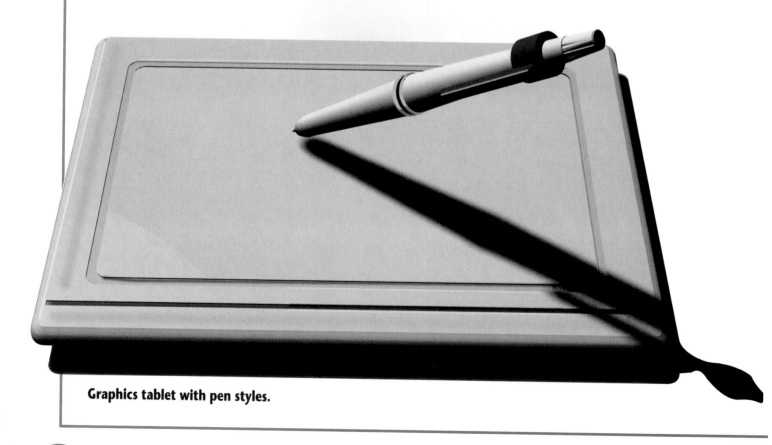

Graphics tablet with pen styles.

How Does It Work?

The touch screens used by pen computers such as Apple's Newton are quite different from regular monitor screens. The touch screen is composed of three layers that all work together to display an image when a pen instrument touches the screen.

The first layer is a mylar sheet with a transparent layer of metal coating the underside. The next layer is a gel containing tiny plastic balls, visible only through a microscope. The final layer is a sheet of glass with a transparent metal coating on the top side. Beneath these three layers is an LCD (liquid crystal display) screen.

As the pen (stylus) touches the screen, the microscopic balls in the gel layer move apart, causing the transparent metal coatings found on the top and bottom layers to touch. The electrical current in that spot is lowered by the contact. The computer notes the area of the screen that has been touched and turns on the corresponding pixel on the LCD screen, making an image or dot appear.

GRAPHICS TABLET

A specialized input device that is used to create drawings on the computer. A graphics tablet uses a special pen that enables the user to draw detailed sketches and artwork, almost like drawing on a real piece of paper.

Gel layer

LCD screen

Mylar layer with metal coating underneath

Glass layer with metal coating on top

PALM COMPUTER

A portable computer that fits into the palm of a user's hand. Most palm computers are used to collect simple data, such as short notes, names and addresses, or sales orders. Other palm computers run full-blown applications stored in special read only memory (ROM) chips.

Portable Computers

Portable computers are computers that can easily be carried around from place to place. Portable computers include laptop and notebook computers, personal digital assistants, and palm computers.

Laptops are small computers, about the size of a briefcase, that are ideal for the user who travels a lot and wants to work on the road or in an airplane. They are called laptops because they are small enough to fit comfortably on a person's lap. They run on an internal rechargeable battery, or can be plugged directly into an electrical outlet. Laptop keyboards usually have small keys that are close together, and sometimes include a trackball (a mouse-like device attached to the keyboard). They have either monochrome LCD screens or color screens; color screens are either passive-matrix (soft color) or active-matrix (crisp, clean color) and use more battery power than monochrome screens. Laptops are almost as powerful as their desktop cousins (personal computers), being fully capable of running the same applications. Because they run off a battery, however, laptops are generally slower. In addition, laptops do not contain as large a hard drive as desktop computers do, and their screens are not as bright and clean.

Laptops and other small computers are sometimes generically referred to as "portables," but in actuality, the first "portable" computers released in the early '80s were rather clunky, weighing from 25–35 pounds, and were often referred to as "luggables." Laptops today are much lighter than those early computers, generally weighing 8–10 pounds.

There is a growing category of smaller, lighter portables called notebooks that usually weigh 6–8 pounds. The main difference between laptops and notebooks is weight; notebooks can be carried in one hand, while laptops cannot. Most companies do not produce laptops anymore, just thinner, lighter versions of them called notebooks. Notebooks are about the size of a three ring binder, have a flip-up display screen, and have a very small keyboard. Like laptops, notebooks fit conveniently into a briefcase. Notebooks are finding favor with computer users because as technology advances, notebooks are becoming even smaller and more powerful than laptops.

Gateway 2000 ColorBook

Courtesy of Gateway 2000

Courtesy of Hewlett-Packard Company

The Hewlett-Packard 100LX palmtop computer can run popular software programs and electronic mail software.

The newest class of portables are sub-notebooks, which weigh 2–6 pounds and are easy to carry around—although their small design makes working on the keyboard slightly difficult. However, even sub-notebooks are capable of running the same applications as a desktop computer.

There are even smaller laptops, called palmtops, that are no larger than a calculator. A palm computer, also known as a hand-held or pocket computer, is a portable computer designed to fit into the palm of a person's hand. Palm computers are battery-operated and are usually made to handle a particular task, such as translating foreign languages, acting as an electronic dayplanner, or functioning as a dictionary. As technology improves, the tasks performed by a palm computer become more complicated and more powerful.

There are several different kinds of palm computers on the market today. Some, such as the Hewlett-Packard

95LX, feature actual keyboard keys that, though much smaller in scale than other laptop keyboards, are used to type in letters and words. Many of these palmtop computers can run actual software programs, such as Lotus 1-2-3 (a spreadsheet program). Another type of palm computer is the notepad or personal digital assistant (PDA), which requires the user to enter data through a touch screen. The Newton MessagePad hand-held computer, made by Apple, uses a pen (or stylus) to write information onto a touch screen. Through its Newton Recognition Architecture, the computer recognizes handwriting and interprets it into the ASCII text that all computers use. With a personal digital assistant like the Newton, users can take notes and make simple drawings, access an electronic address book, and an electronic calendar—all important functions for someone on the go.

Palm computers are very lightweight and are easy to carry around in a pocket or purse, usually weighing less than a pound. With a palm computer, a user can exchange data with personal computers, connect with modems and faxes, and even communicate with other palm computer users. The technology that has brought the computer industry the palm computer is continuing to explore the potential of these tiny computing devices.

Courtesy of Apple

The Newton MessagePad by Apple

continues

Portable Computers

continued

One of the minor problems of using a laptop is transferring files between the desktop unit (personal computer) and the portable unit. A user can either swap floppy disks between the two computers, or he can link the computers with a special cable and use a software program to transfer files. In fact, DOS 6.x comes with a program called Interlink, which serves this purpose nicely. Also, some laptops include internal modems or can be connected to an external modem so that the laptop can easily access files on another computer by utilizing phone lines.

An alternative to the disk swapping or cable connecting techniques of file sharing is the docking system. This is done with a unit that sits on a desktop and a notebook computer. The notebook houses the CPU, and when the user wants to use the full-size monitor and keyboard of the desktop unit, he simply slides the notebook into the desktop unit

and starts working. Currently, docking stations are fairly expensive because they are a relatively new concept; however, the demand for these versatile machines is expected to grow. Also see Apple, Hewlett-Packard, PC, and Pen Computing.

TRACKBALL

How Does It Work

All sizes of portables generally run on internal batteries. There are two different types of popular batteries: Nickel Cadmium (often called Ni-Cad) and Metal Hydride. Of the two, Metal Hydride batteries are more reliable and easier to recharge. However, they are also more expensive than Ni-Cad batteries. Manufacturers are trying to make batteries smaller and lighter to accommodate the popular notebook computers. Currently, batteries usually last from 2 to 4 hours before they need to be recharged.

The Macintosh PowerBook

Courtesy of Apple Computer, Inc.

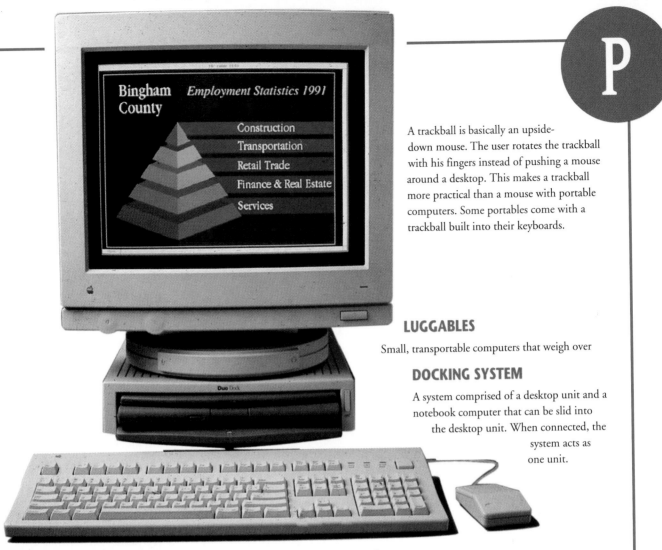

A trackball is basically an upside-down mouse. The user rotates the trackball with his fingers instead of pushing a mouse around a desktop. This makes a trackball more practical than a mouse with portable computers. Some portables come with a trackball built into their keyboards.

LUGGABLES

Small, transportable computers that weigh over

DOCKING SYSTEM

A system comprised of a desktop unit and a notebook computer that can be slid into the desktop unit. When connected, the system acts as one unit.

Courtesy of Apple Computer, Inc.

The Macintosh Duo Dock

Almost a dying breed of computer, a laptop is a briefcase-sized portable computer weighing around 12 pounds. Laptops are being replaced by notebooks, which for the most part are smaller, lighter, and just as powerful. Laptops got their name from the fact that, unlike luggables, they could be used on the lap comfortably.

NOTEBOOK

A 6–8 pound laptop computer that is small enough to fit in a briefcase. It has a flip-up display (some have color displays), and many have built-in trackballs.

SUBNOTEBOOKS

Very similar to notebook computers, but lighter in weight. Subnotebooks weigh an average of 4 pounds.

PALMTOP

A computer about the size of a palm, weighing about a pound. A palmtop computer may come with some applications built-in, or it may serve a simple purpose, such as organizing addresses and appointments. Palmtops are not generally capable of running the same applications as a desktop computer, however this is changing rapidly.

MODEM

A device used to transmit data across telephone lines to and from different computers.

15 pounds and are too heavy and uncomfortable to sit in a person's lap. The first portable computers were "luggables."

LAPTOPS

Ports

DB-25 cable

Ports are the plug-in receptacles located on the back of the computer's system unit that are used to attach peripherals (such as a printer, monitor, keyboard, mouse, modem, or joystick). Cables from each peripheral are plugged into these ports, allowing the connected items to send and receive information from the microprocessor. There are two types of ports: serial and parallel.

Serial ports move one bit of data through the cable at a time. Parallel ports can move eight bits of data, making them much faster than serial ports. All data is measured in bits and bytes. A byte comprises eight bits, and represents one character, such as the letter A. Printers, which require larger amounts of data sent from the computer to the printer, are usually connected to the computer by parallel ports and cables. Unlike parallel ports, serial ports transmit data one bit at a time. Modems, mice and serial printers use serial ports. Because a computer may have many parallel devices, each port is given a name to distinguish the device

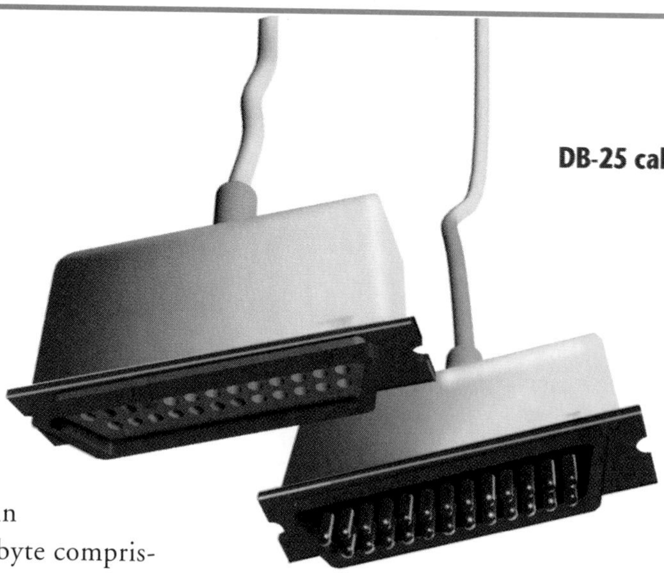

Power supply vent

Power sockets

Game port

Monitor port

IN

OUT

MIC

Keyboard port

Serial ports

Parallel port

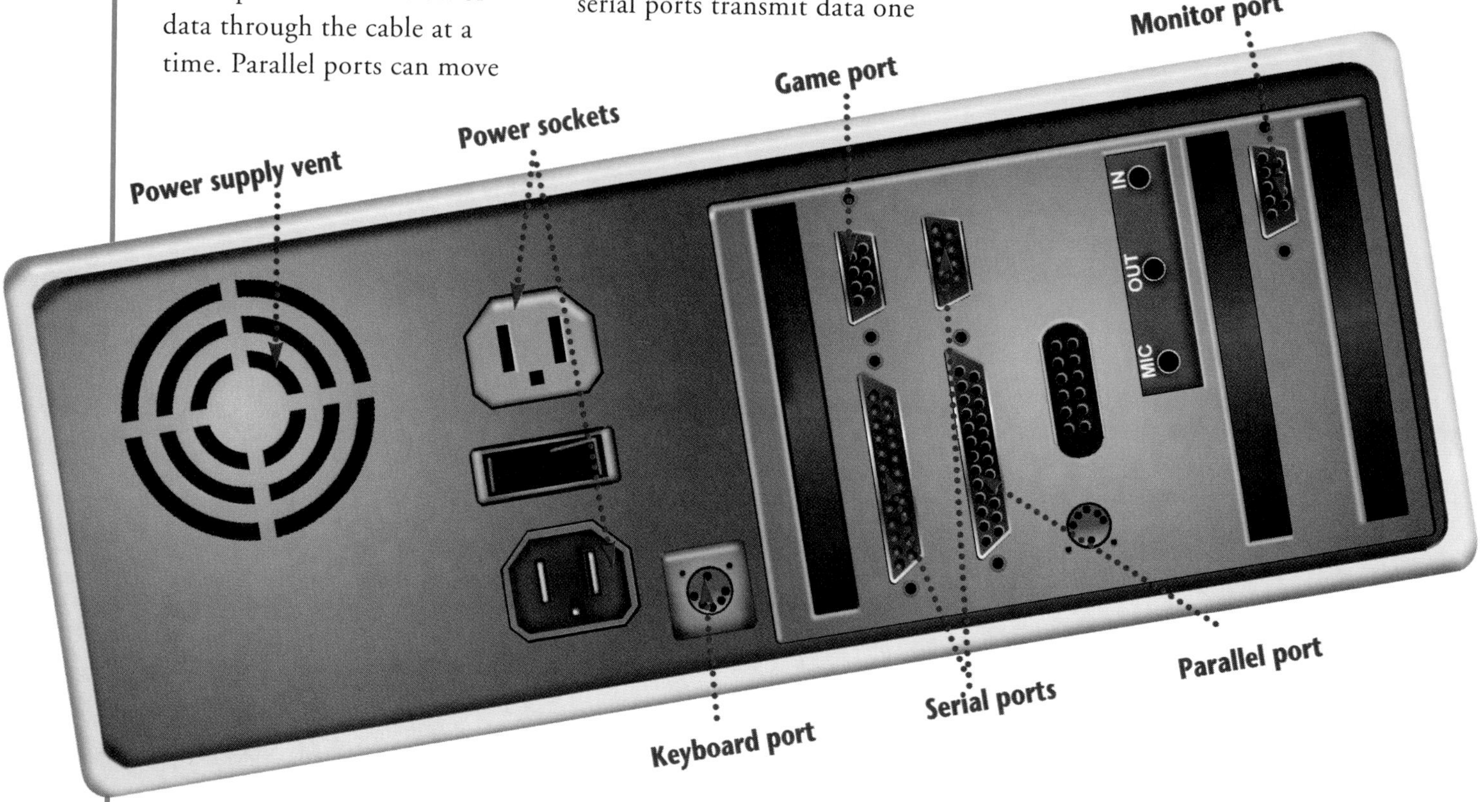

connected to it from other devices. Parallel ports are called LPT1, LPT2, and so on by the computer in order to identify them. These names are internal addresses only, so the user doesn't actually see these as labels on the outside of the computer. Parallel ports are considered female connectors because they contain holes. On the end of the parallel cable are pins that fit into these holes, completing the connection. Parallel ports, used mostly with printers, are called DB-25F ports, large ports with 25 holes. They usually connect to Centronics ports on the printer end, so called because they were designed by Centronics Corporation, the first successful manufacturer of dot-matrix printers.

Serial ports are internally addressed as COM1, COM2, etc. by the computer in order to identify them. Serial ports are considered male connectors because they contain pins. Most personal computers have at least two serial ports, called RS-232 or COM ports. The DB-9 serial port has nine pins, the DB-25 has twenty-five pins. A computer's mouse usually plugs into a nine-pin serial port,

called COM1. Newer computers come with a special port just for the mouse.

Another type of port found on computers today are SCSI (Small Computer System Interface) ports. SCSI ports are made for higher speed peripherals, such as a CD-ROM drive or an external hard drive. It is important to learn about ports in order to hook up a computer and its peripherals correctly. Also see Input Devices, Output Devices, and Peripherals.

DB-9 cable

PERIPHERALS

Other electronic devices hooked up to the computer's system unit. Peripherals include monitors, printers, keyboards, modems, and more.

BINARY

All computers are based on a binary system of 1's and 0's that represent an electrical on/off state. The 1's and 0's represent bits of data that tell the computer what to do.

Centronics cable

Power Supply

The power supply is a box inside the computer's system unit that converts AC electricity from a power outlet to the DC electricity used by the PC. The computer's on/off switch is attached to the power supply box. Power supply is measured in watts. The average PC needs about 200 watts. Some PCs, such as portable laptop computers, run on internal batteries, but they can also be plugged into a conventional outlet.

Because electricity generates heat, the power supply box is equipped with a fan that keeps the box and the other system unit components from overheating. As with anything plugged into a standard electrical outlet, computers are subject to changes in electrical currents caused by storms and power surges. Surge protectors should always be used to protect the computer from damage that may occur as a result of power surges. Also see Safety and System Unit.

SURGE PROTECTOR

Device that usually looks like a power strip, but which protects the equipment plugged into it from surges in electricity.

UPS

Short for Uninterruptible Power Supply. A UPS is usually attached to important equipment (such as a computer), in order to supply it with power even when the electricity goes out. Most UPSs come with built-in surge protection, making them a good value.

Vents

ON/OFF switch

Connection to system components

PowerPC

Motorola PowerPC chip

PowerPC is the name of an innovative new microprocessor chip technology created by the combined efforts of Motorola, IBM, and Apple. The PowerPC chip, scheduled to be released in 1994, is a powerful new chip that will compete with the Intel chips (used with IBM PCs and PC-compatibles) and Motorola's own chips (used with Macintosh computers). The PowerPC chip is designed to run not just one operating system, but many, including DOS, Windows NT, IBM's Workplace OS (which runs Windows, OS/2, and DOS applications), Macintosh System 7, Unix 5.4, and more. However, this versatility comes at a cost: the PowerPC chip will not run existing Windows and DOS applications without help (emulation programs that let the Windows/DOS applications "pretend" they're running on an Intel chip), and that help will slow down Windows and DOS programs.

PowerPC chips are faster than previous chips by Motorola and Intel—faster even than Intel's newest chip, the Pentium microprocessor. The PowerPC can process three instructions per clock cycle (the Pentium chip processes two; most chips process less than one). A clock cycle is like a huge metronome inside the computer; everything is timed by the clock cycle. The more instructions processed during a single clock cycle, the faster programs will run on that computer. This is an important consideration for users who work with graphics programs, such as CAD (computer-aided design) and desktop publishing, because it takes a lot of instructions to display their complex images on the monitor. The PowerPC chip also has fewer transistors inside than other microprocessor chips do, meaning it is less likely to overheat (which makes it ideal for small laptop/notebook computers). The PowerPC sells for half of what a new Pentium chip by Intel sells for. It is anticipated to cause a whirlwind of excitement when it is released. Also see Apple, Central Processing Unit, IBM, Intel, and Motorola.

CPU

Central Processing Unit. The CPU, or microprocessor chip, is the brains of the computer, handling all of the "thinking" and processing that goes on.

MEGAHERTZ

A unit of measurement that indicates the speed of a computer. The larger the megahertz number, the faster the computer. One megahertz is equal to one million clock cycles per second.

PowerPoint

PowerPoint is the name of a presentation graphics program originally developed for the Macintosh by Microsoft Corporation. A Windows version followed in 1990. A presentation graphics program can produce visual images in the form of slides, overhead transparencies, and charts for use in presentations and displays. A presentation graphics program, also known as business presentation graphics, allows the user to enter raw data into the computer and then choose how the data will be visually displayed (as a chart or an on-screen slide, for instance). For example, PowerPoint can help the user design an effective sales presentation, a departmental report, or an instructional presentation for new employees.

PowerPoint features a Toolbar with buttons for changing how text and other objects look. The Tool Palette can be used to add text (such as labels and

captions), lines, and shapes to a slide. In addition, PowerPoint includes a spell checker for checking text and clip art for adding images to slides. With PowerPoint, the user can create charts and then reuse them in other programs. The slides can even be saved as special files that can be taken to a slide service and made into actual slides. Also see Graphics and Microsoft.

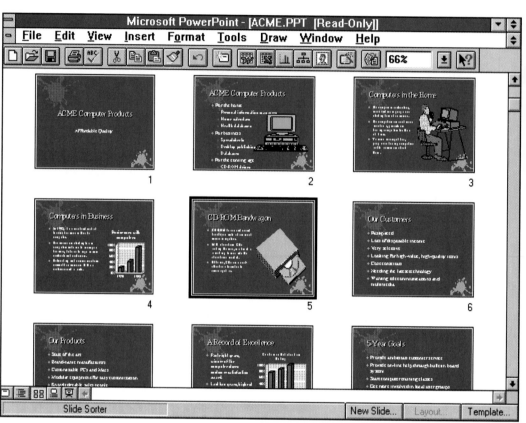

PowerPoint can display data in the form of a slide program on the computer screen.

CHART

A graphical representation of a set of related numbers. For example if one set of numbers is larger than another, its line (or column) in the chart will be longer or higher. Likewise, a lower or shorter line or column indicates a lower set of numbers.

Print Shop

Print Shop is the name of a desktop publishing program created by Broderbund Software, Inc. Desktop publishing programs allow a user to easily combine text and graphics onto a single page. With Print Shop, the user can create all kinds of projects ranging from greeting cards to banners. In essence, it turns the computer into a personal stationery store.

The Print Shop was first released in 1984. Its easy-to-use format and design steps made it a big success among adults and children in the home and educational markets. With the program, users could create all of the types of materials normally associated with a printing company: letterhead, cards, flyers, and more. Available for the Apple IIe and IIc computer, the program quickly sold over 500,000 copies. It is now available in versions for DOS, Windows, Macintosh, Commodore, and Atari systems.

In 1989, Broderbund updated the program, calling it The New Print Shop. This version utilized higher resolution graphics and offered greater flexibility than did the previous version. In 1992, Broderbund introduced The Print Shop Deluxe, an even better version that offered a friendlier graphical interface, scalable fonts and graphics, detailed layouts, and special effects. Today's Print Shop Deluxe is available for DOS, Windows, and Macintosh computers.

The Print Shop Deluxe takes users through a step-by-step process to assemble various projects that include greeting cards, letterhead, signs, calendars, and banners. Users are taught to select layouts, add text and headlines, create special effects (including screen backgrounds and shadows), choose from a library of graphics and borders, and print out a finished piece—all in easy-to-follow steps. The Print Shop Deluxe is perfect for beginners, and is useful for professionals at school or in the office. Also see Desktop Publishing and Graphics.

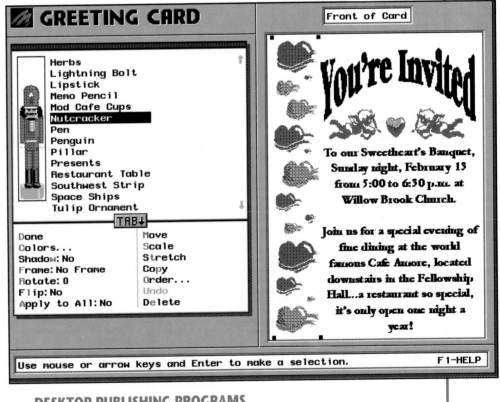

DESKTOP PUBLISHING PROGRAMS

Software programs that allow the user to combine text and graphics to create fully layed-out pages, such as newsletters, flyers, and brochures.

Printer

A printer is an output device that allows the user to see a printout of his work. After a file has been created, a command is entered to send the file to the printer to be printed out. The printer converts the electronic input into a paper printout. There are two types of printers available today: impact and non-impact. Impact printers (whose printheads touch to paper) include dot-matrix and daisywheel printers. Non-impact printers (whose printheads do not touch the paper) include laser, inkjet, and bubble-jet printers.

Although there are many different kinds of printers, they all work to accomplish the same thing—to output a pattern of dots onto a

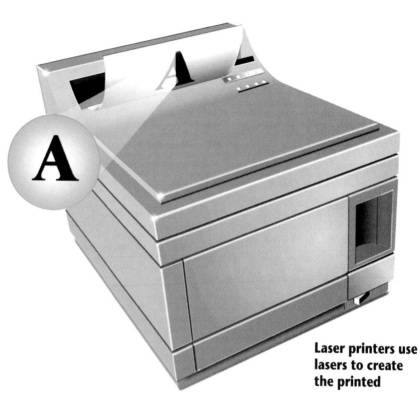

Laser printers use lasers to create the printed

sheet of paper. Whether the output is text or graphics, the printed image is made up of dots. The smaller and closer together the dots are, the clearer the print-out, or resolution, will be.

Some printers come with built-in fonts.

Dot-matrix printers use dots to form letters.

Whether built-in or supplied by a program, computer fonts fall into two groups: bitmapped and outline. Bitmapped fonts, common with dot-matrix printers, are stored in the computer as patterns of dots. For each point size of a bitmapped font, the computer must store a separate set of font characters. This consumes a great deal of disk space. Outlined fonts, common with laser printers, are stored as sets of lines, curves, and points, using a mathematical formula instead of a pattern of dots. Outline fonts can easily be scaled to different sizes and proportions, unlike bitmapped fonts. Also see Output Devices.

How Does It Work?

An impact printer creates characters by impacting an inked ribbon with spokes or pin heads to make an impression on a page. To form a letter or other image, the selected pins press into an inked ribbon, depositing tiny dots of ink.

With non-impact printers, such as a laser printer, no part of the printer touches the page to form characters. Instead, lasers are used to draw an image on an electrically charged drum. Dry ink, or toner, sticks to the electrical charges and as the drum turns, the ink is affixed to the paper by a heating element.

Inkjet and bubble-jet printers use liquid ink to spray characters onto a page. An internal printhead contains a series of little nozzles, or holes, that heat the ink. When the ink bubbles, the bubbles burst to spray the tiny dots onto the paper.

P

Inkjet printers use liquid ink to make the printed image.

INKJET

Uses sprayed ink to form characters on a page. Bubble-jet printers work the same way.

LABEL PRINTERS

Small-scale printers used to make labels for mailing and filing.

Pins

Dot-matrix printer

Label Printer

DOT-MATRIX

Uses a printing head that creates letters by pushing small, blunt-end pins into an inked ribbon.

continues

Printer continued

ON-LINE

When a hardware device, such as a printer, is ready to communicate with the computer it is considered on-line. The on-line state means that it is connected, power is on and it is ready for instruction. Most printers have an on-line light that lets the user know it is ready to print.

DAISYWHEEL PRINTER

Uses a typing element that looks like a hub with flexible character spokes packed closely together. Single characters press against an inked ribbon to form letters.

DEVICE DRIVER

A program that tells the computer how to work with a device, such as a printer, that's connected to the machine.

DOT-MATRIX

Uses a printing head that creates letters by pushing small, blunt-end pins into an inked ribbon.

FONT CARTRIDGE

A removable unit that stores printer fonts. The cartridge can be plugged into many laser and inkjet printers to supplement the built-in fonts.

PRINTER SETUP

Many programs, such as Windows, have a special dialog box for selecting printing options—called Printer Setup. This box or window lists the many options that can be selected, such as paper size, paper orientation, and more.

LASER PRINTER

Uses a laser to transform an image onto an electrically charged drum, which in turn applies dry ink that rubs off onto paper and is affixed by heating.

An Inkjet printer's quality is measured by how many characters are printed per second (CPS) or characters per inch (CPI).

Inkjet printer

Inkjet cartridge

·····Nozzles

······· Printhead

Ink bubbles burst from the nozzles to spray tiny dots onto a page of paper.

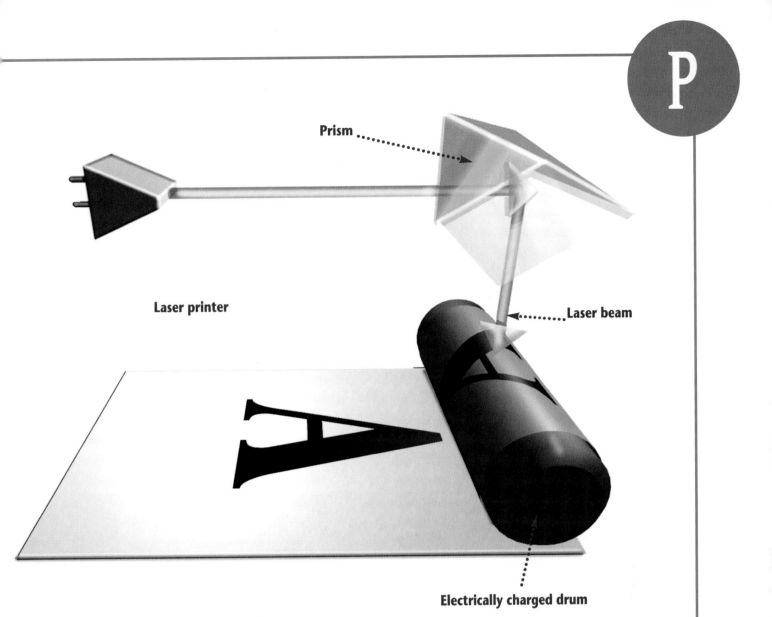

Prism

Laser printer

Laser beam

Electrically charged drum

POSTSCRIPT

A page description language (PDL) invented by Adobe Systems that controls the printing of text and graphics. PostScript is a programming language that tells a printer how to print a page. PostScript is the most commonly used printer language, and it has become the standard for laser printers because of its exceptional graphics capabilities.

PRINTER BUFFER

A temporary holding area for data. When a user issues the print command, the program sends the information to the printer's memory, or buffer. The information is held in the buffer until the printer is ready to use it. Buffers allow the computer to send a file to a printer, so that the computer can continue to process its data without waiting until the printer is actually done printing.

PAPER ORIENTATION

Some printers allow the user to print pages in two directional orientations. Portrait orientation appears as a normal page, with short width and longer length. Landscape orientation prints a page sideways, making the page wider than it is long.

RESOLUTION

The detail or sharpness of a printed image or character. Resolution is measured in dots per inch (DPI).

THERMAL

A type of high-end color printer that uses specially coated, heat sensitive paper to add color to the printed output.

ProComm Plus

ProComm Plus is a communications program marketed by Datastorm Technologies, Inc for IBM PC-compatible computers. Once a shareware program (a program that's initially free, so a user can "test-drive" it before buying it at a very low cost), ProComm Plus is one of the most popular communications programs available today.

With a communications program, a modem (a device which translates computer data into tones and pulses for transmission), and a telephone line, a user can transfer data between one PC and another. For example, the user could share data with a PC that is some distance away (maybe even around the world); connect to a BBS (bulletin board service) and get help with a PC problem; or connect to a pay-for-use on-line service (such as CompuServe) and leave messages for other users, obtain help, buy and sell stocks, download programs, read articles, and more.

ProComm Plus can also imitate a dumb terminal, allowing the user to connect to a mainframe computer. ProComm Plus features an automatic dialing directory, supports unattended file transfers and remote access, and allows "chatting" (communicating through typed messages) while on-line with another computer. ProComm Plus is also available in a Windows version. Also see Communications and Modem.

```
DIALING DIRECTORY: PCPLUS.DIR

     NAME                                  NUMBER    BAUD PDS D P  SCRIPT
  1 Scott Fulton                         9,4750212   2400 N81 F D
  2 ┌─┤ Revise Entry 2├─────────────────────-6824    2400 E71 F D
  3 │         NAME: Compuserve               -5224    2400 N81 F D
  4 │       NUMBER: 9,631-6824                       19200 N81 F D
  5 │         BAUD: 2400                             19200 N81 F D
  6 │       PARITY: EVEN                             19200 N81 F D
  7 │    DATA BITS: 7                                19200 N81 F D
  8 │    STOP BITS: 1                                19200 N81 F D
  9 │       DUPLEX: FULL                             19200 N81 F D
 10 │         PORT: DEFAULT                          19200 N81 F D
    │       SCRIPT:
PgUp│     PROTOCOL: XMODEM                 r Marked   L Print Directory
PgDn│     TERMINAL: ANSI                   e Entry(s) P Dialing Codes
Home│         MODE: MODEM                    Entry    X Exchange Dir
End │     PASSWORD:                          Next     T Toggle Display
↑/↓ │    META FILE:                          Entry    S Sort Directory
Esc │     KBD FILE:                         Notes
    │    NOTE FILE:
Choi└───────────────────────────────────┘

Alt-Z FOR HELP│ ANSI │ FDX │ 2400 E71 │ LOG CLOSED │ PRINT OFF │ OFF-LINE
```

ProComm Plus dialing directory

How Does It Work?

ProComm Plus handles the method of data transmission using a particular protocol. The protocol is a set of rules that helps to determine whether the correct character was received. If not, that character is retransmitted. Retransmitting a character takes longer than one might expect, since modems transmit only one bit (one part of a character) at a time. In order to transmit data between them, the two PCs involved must use the same protocol. There are many standard protocols included in ProComm Plus. Each offers certain advantages, such as better accuracy or better speed.

MODEM

Short for MOdulator/DEModulator, a modem is an electronic device used for communications between computers via telephone lines. Modems convert digital signals into analog signals and back again.

UPLOADING

When a user sends computer files through a modem from his PC to another computer, the process is called uploading.

PARITY

The procedure for identifying whether the correct character was received. With even parity, an extra bit is added to the eight bits that make up a character (such as the letter D, which is equal to the eight bits 01000100). This ninth bit makes the total of all the bits an even number. So in the case of the letter D, the ninth bit would be 0, as in 010001000. With odd parity, the ninth bit makes the total come out odd, as in 010001001. After the modem receives the ninth bit for a character, it adds them up and determines whether one of the bits was scrambled. If so, that character is retransmitted.

PROTOCOL

A set of standards that govern how computers communicate with each other. In order for two computers to talk, they must use the same protocol. The protocol determines how each bit (a 1 or a 0) is sent, and how to detect errors in transmission.

Windows version of ProComm Plus

DOWNLOADING

When a user receives computer files through a modem from someone else's computer, the process is called downloading.

Prodigy

Prodigy is a popular pay-for-use information service originally developed by Sears Roebuck Company and IBM. With a modem, a user can connect to Prodigy and (for a fee) catch up on the latest breaking news, do some shopping, participate in conferences with other users, and even find out what the local weather report predicts. Prodigy is one of several on-line services that are available to computer users who have modems and the software needed to communicate over the telephone lines. However, Prodigy does not allow for uploading or downloading (sending or receiving) of files like other on-line services.

Prodigy is very popular among home users. Its friendly interface and easy-to-use format makes it an ideal tool for the entire family—both children and adults. Prodigy charges a flat fee for monthly use and an additional fee for electronic mail (E-mail) services and for accessing special interest bulletin boards. E-mail, or electronic mail, is one reason a lot of people use on-line services. With e-mail, a user can send messages to and receive messages from another

member, regardless of where that user lives.

Prodigy offers many special interest bulletin boards, where the user can exchange views; read the latest news; get advice on anything from buying a new car to managing finances; find out about the best travel places and rates; get help with his new computer, and more. Children can play games, gather information for a school report, or read exciting stories. Parents can get tips on parenting, exchange healthy recipes, and even do some home shopping. Also see BBS, Communications, CompuServe, and Modem.

Prodigy's many services are easy to access using simple on-screen buttons.

BBS

Bulletin Board Service. An information source and message service (like Prodigy, only much smaller) for computer users. Using a modem, users can dial up BBSs to leave messages and share information.

ON-LINE INFORMATION SERVICES

Fee-based services that allow computer users to access information, buy and sell stocks, download programs, read articles, and more.

UPLOADING

When a user sends computer files through a modem from his PC to another computer, the process is called uploading.

DOWNLOADING

When a user receives computer files through a modem from someone else's computer, the process is called downloading.

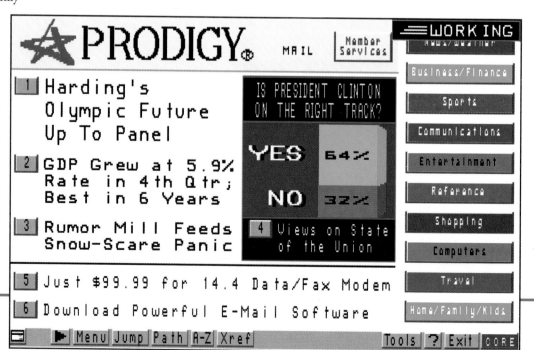

Programming

A program is a set of instructions that tells the computer how to perform some task. Programming is the process of writing these instructions (programs) for the computer to follow. People who specialize in writing programs are called programmers. Programs are written using a programming language that is later converted into a language that the computer can understand.

The English language is not a language the computer knows, nor does it know any other natural language (such as Spanish, French, Russian, etc.). The computer's native tongue, so to speak, is machine language. Machine language is a complex series of 0's and 1's that represent bits of data (a series of on/off states inside the computer). Programmers don't write programs using these 1's and 0's—nor do they need to. Programmers write their programs with a programming language that usually resembles a kind of broken English. These instructions are later converted into the machine language of the computer so they can be run.

has its own commands, and each computer instruction is arranged in a particular way called the syntax. There are standards set by ANSI (American National Standards Institute) for regulating how computer languages, called source languages, are translated. Once a set of instructions

```
  File  Edit  View  Search  Run  Debug  Options                    Help
                          8BALL.BAS
 10    REM Program 8BALL.BAS
 20    REM Simulates an 8-Ball toy
 30    CLS
 40    REM There are 20 messages in the 8-Ball
 50    DIM MESSAGES$(20)
 60    DATA "It is certain"
 70    DATA "Signs point to yes"
 80    DATA "Outlook good"
 90    DATA "My sources say no"
 100   DATA "It is decidedly so"
 110   DATA "You may rely on it"
 120   DATA "Ask again later"
 130   DATA "Better not tell you now"
 140   DATA "Very doubtful"
 150   DATA "Yes, definitely"
 160   DATA "Cannot predict now"
 170   DATA "My reply is no"
 180   DATA "As I see it, yes"
                        Immediate
 <Shift+F1=Help> <F6=Window> <F2=Subs> <F5=Run> <F8=Step>      00001:001
```

A programming statement written in BASIC

Popular computer languages include BASIC, C, C++, and Pascal. Each of these languages

has been written in one of these source languages, it must then be translated into the

continues

Programming continued

machine language that computers can read. There are special programs to do just that, called assemblers, compilers, and interpreters. They translate a source language into actual machine language.

There are two categories of computer languages: low-level languages and high-level languages. Low-level languages most closely resemble the computer's own machine language. They are very difficult to understand, and take a great deal of study to master. When a computer instruction is written in a low-level language, it becomes a single machine language instruction. A low-level language is good for writing fast, memory-concise programs. One such low-level language is Assembler.

High-level languages, on the other hand, are easier to understand because they more closely resemble the English language. High-level languages include BASIC, C, C++, and Pascal. Every computer instruction written in a high-level language is converted into several instructions in machine language. High-level languages are good for writing well-organized programs using fewer programming lines.

BASIC Program

011001

MACHINE LANGUAGE

INTERPRETER

INTERPRETER

Each time an interpreted program is run, it is converted into machine language by an interpreter. This is unlike a compiled program, which is converted into machine language only once.

C Program

COMPILER

COMPILED PROGRAM

A compiled program is converted into machine language only once and is stored permanently in a file.

READY-TO-USE PROGRAM FILE

How Does It Work?

There are several steps a programmer follows to write computer instructions. The first step is to come up with an idea for a program. Secondly, the programmer develops an outline (flow chart) for the program, which helps to organize how the program is written. Thirdly, the user writes the program instructions, following the syntax and structure required within the particular programming language he has chosen. Next, the program is run through a translator program that turns the statements into machine language. Finally, the program is tested, and errors (called bugs) are fixed. After all the bugs have been found, the program is translated into machine language a final time, and the files to run the program over and over are created.

There are two main types of programs written for computers: application programs and operating system programs. Applications are programs that tell the computer to behave as a word processor, a spreadsheet, a drawing screen, or a game. Operating system programs provide the general instructions the computer needs to perform its basic functions such as managing files, running applications, and responding to user commands. Also see ANSI, Applications, BASIC, C/C++, Pascal, Software, and Visual Basic.

BUGS

Errors that appear in programs that cause system problems and failures (crashes).

LOW-LEVEL LANGUAGE

A programming language that is similar to machine language, just one level removed from the binary language of 1's and 0's. Assembler is a low-level programming language.

HIGH-LEVEL LANGUAGE

A programming language that is easier for programmers to understand because it is written more closely to English than to the rudimentary 1's and 0's of machine language. High-level languages require a compiler or an interpreter to translate the program instructions into 1's and 0's that the computer can understand. BASIC, C, C++, and Pascal are all high-level programming languages.

CPU

00100110
01000111
10100000
01010011

140 IF CHOICE = 2 THEN GOTO 210

ASSEMBLER, COMPILER, or INTERPRETER

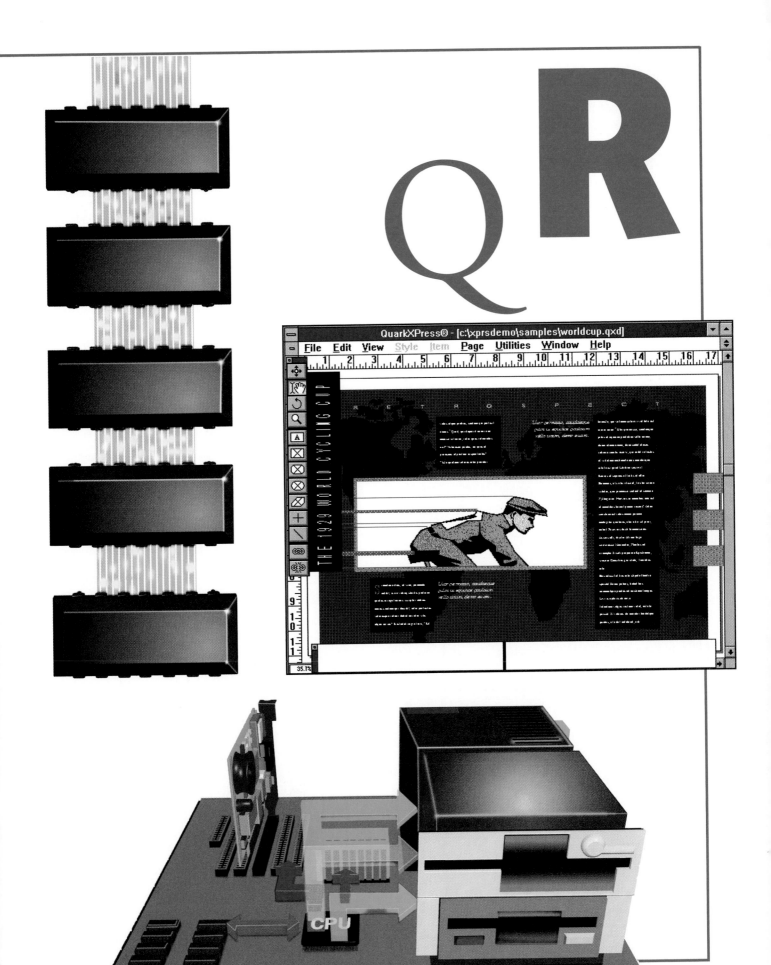

QuarkXPress

QuarkXPress is a desktop publishing program made by Quark, Inc. Desktop publishing programs allow the user to combine text and graphics into highly detailed page layouts. QuarkXPress is a full-featured page layout and production program used to create newsletters, four-color magazines and catalogs, brochures, advertisements, and books. With the program, text and graphics can be manipulated on the computer to make professional-looking publications that incorporate quality typography and design. In fact, this book was designed and layed out using QuarkXPress.

QuarkXPress was first developed for Apple's Macintosh computer. With its graphical user interface (GUI), the arrangement of text and the manipulation of graphics in QuarkXPress was an easy matter. Before desktop publishing programs such as QuarkXPress came along, it took several people to put together a publication; writers, typesetters, layout artists, photographers, and printers worked together to complete the finished product. It was a costly and time-consuming process. Today's desktop publishing programs help speed up the process and bring down the costs of production, making desktop publishing affordable even for the smallest business.

QuarkXPress, now available for both the Macintosh and Windows systems, features a precise measuring system for controlling page layout details, a special method for styling text, automatic trapping (computer techniques that assist in registering colors to prepare the document for a printing press), and seven unique control palettes (special bars that appear on-screen with settings and icons that can be controlled with a click of the mouse). QuarkXPress is a popular program that meets the high-end production demands of layout designers and printing professionals, but it is not well suited for beginners. Also see Desktop Publishing, GUI, Macintosh, and PageMaker.

Page guides

Rulers

Measurements palette

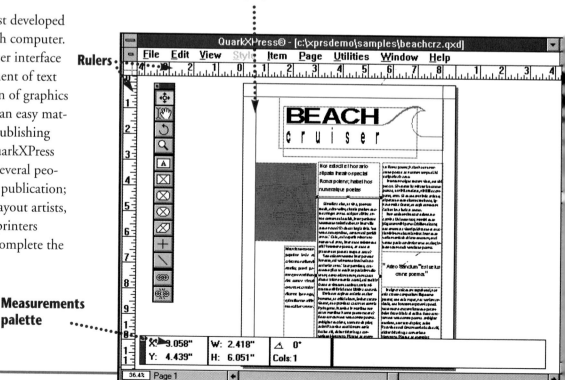

ICON

A graphical representation of a program, file, or command. Icons are used with graphical user interface programs.

Tool palette

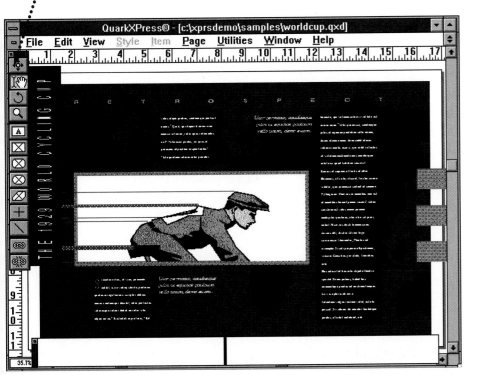

How Does It Work?

Before it's opened in QuarkXPress, a text file is usually written, edited, spell checked, and saved in a word processing program (usually only small text passages are spell checked within QuarkXPress). Once the text is prepared, the graphics are designed and the document is assembled. With QuarkXPress, the user can control where text flows, down one or multiple columns. Text can be made to flow around the edges of a graphic or jump over it completely. Borders and shading can be added behind graphics or text to add interest.

GUI

Graphical User Interface. A GUI provides a graphical way for a user to give a command to a computer. With a GUI, users select pictorial representations (icons) of files, programs, and commands from a friendly looking screen.

TRAPPING

A feature in QuarkXPress with which it prepares a document for printing at a professional printer. Trapping provides a means for the many colors in a color process printing to overlap slightly, preventing loss of color when the two different color objects don't meet exactly.

DESKTOP PUBLISHING

A special type of software program that allows the user to manipulate text and graphics on a single page to create brochures, newsletters, and other illustrated documents. The Macintosh computer helped to start the use of computers for this type of work.

GRAPHICS

Objects created with drawing and painting programs. Graphics are visual images made up of shapes (such as lines and circles) or dots (such as illustrations created with pixels on the computer screen). Just about anything that is not text is designated as a graphic in programs such as QuarkXPress.

PAGE LAYOUT

The design and structure of text, graphics, headlines, and columns on a page.

Quicken

Quicken is a very popular money management program published by Intuit. Money management programs are software programs designed specifically for working with money. They include programs that help people balance their checkbooks, manage a budget, keep track of bills and payments, control monies being spent in a business, and more. Money management software falls into two categories: personal finance and accounting. Quicken is a personal finance program.

Personal finance programs like Quicken help the user organize checking accounts, set up personal budgets, plan for retirement, and pay bills electronically. Data is entered onto a screen that looks just like a check register or an actual check from a checkbook. In the check register, the user can keep track of transaction dates, names of the persons to whom the checks were written, and the amounts of payment. The user enters a category to identify the budget account from which the funds are to be deducted. In addition, the user may enter a memo to help identify the check, and he can record deposits to the checking account. After data is entered, Quicken automatically updates the balance in the account. Quicken also allows a user to make payments by printing out actual checks, and to

Quicken 3 for Windows

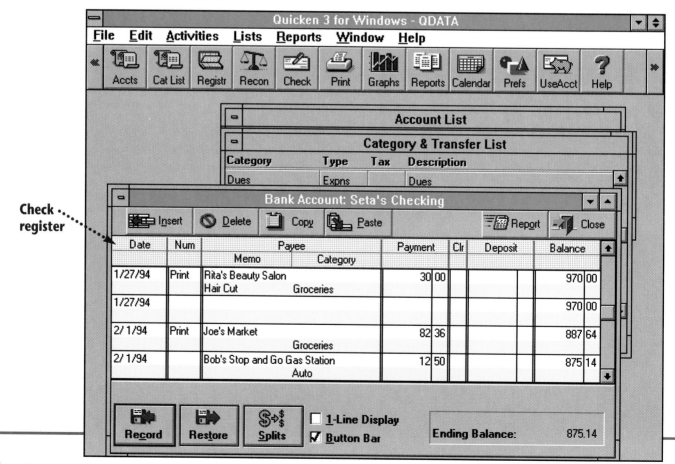

Check register →

ACCOUNTING PROGRAMS

Geared for small business needs, accounting programs usually include a general ledger, journal, accounts receivable, accounts payable, inventory, payroll, and reports for determining operating expenses and net income. Popular accounting programs include Point of Sale, DAC Easy, Acc Pac, and Peachtree Accounting.

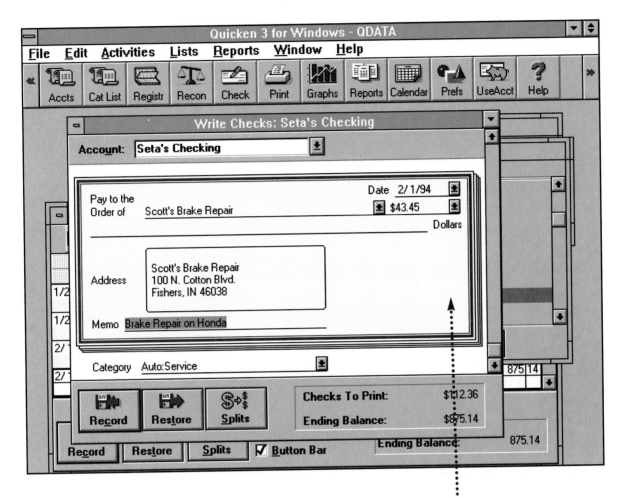

cross-reference expenses (such as the amounts on the written checks) to an established budget.

Quicken can also carry out tax accounting and budgeting, as well as print out reports that help the user track spending and future financial needs. Quicken is an easy-to-understand program that does not require the user to be adept at accounting and accounting terminology. Because of its ease-of-use, Quicken is popularly used as a money management system for small businesses and at home. Quicken is available for both IBM PC and compatibles and the Macintosh computer. Also see Applications, Money Management Programs, and Software.

Checks can be entered in a window that looks like a check.

PERSONAL FINANCE PROGRAM

A program that helps the user keep track of personal monetary transactions. These programs usually include a budget system, check register, report system, and savings planner. Quicken is a personal finance program.

RAM

RAM stands for Random Access Memory, the computer's working memory. RAM temporarily stores data and program instructions so they can be accessed by the computer's central processing unit (CPU), the "thinking" part of the computer that handles the processing of information. RAM (memory) is made up of separate RAM chips plugged into the computer's motherboard inside the system unit. Additional memory chips are often placed on a memory expansion board and inserted into an expansion slot, also inside the system unit.

Data is processed in a computer's memory, so it is one of the most important parts of a computer. Not having enough memory can limit the number and type of programs that can run on a computer. Memory is measured in bytes. Each character, such as the letter A or a question mark, takes up one byte of storage. Bytes can be measured in bigger units of storage: a kilobyte is equal to 1,024 bytes, and a megabyte is equal to 1,048,576 bytes. Most computers today come with a minimum of 4 megabytes of RAM. There are two kinds of RAM: dynamic RAM (DRAM) and static RAM (SRAM). In order to maintain their electrical charges, DRAM chips continually refresh themselves. SRAM chips do not require this refresher charge of electricity because they can retain the charge for longer periods of time. SRAM chips are faster than DRAM chips; however, they also take up more power and are much more expensive.

To speed up processing, some PCs are equipped with caches. A cache is a temporary holding area for the data that the computer uses the most often. Data in the cache is kept current so it's always the most frequently used. Think of a cache as a handy holding bin that keeps important information right at a person's fingertips.

There are two different kinds of caches, made up of different areas

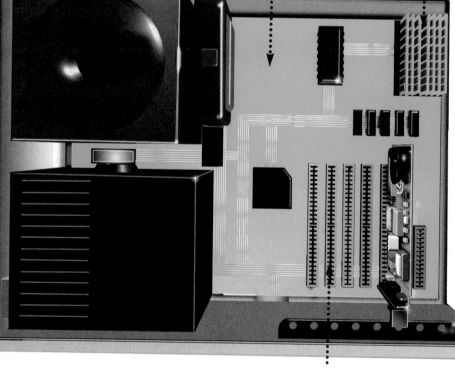

Motherboard

RAM chips

Expansion slots

How Does It Work?

Inside these electronic RAM chips are tiny ON/OFF circuits that represent the data that's currently being processed.

RAM chips

Power is needed to keep these tiny switches set to ON or OFF, so RAM is only a temporary holding area for data. Once the computer is turned off, any data held in the RAM chips is lost. Data that will be reused (such as a letter or a report) must be saved to disk before the computer is turned off. The central processing unit (the brains of the computer) can access data stored in RAM chips very quickly—much more quickly than it can access data stored on a disk.

in memory. A memory cache contains frequently used data from memory (RAM). It's a separate part of memory made up of super fast (and expensive) SRAM chips. Before getting a file out of ordinary RAM, the CPU checks the memory cache first. Because SRAMs are faster, it's quicker to get data from there than from ordinary RAM. A memory cache is different from a disk cache, which is set up in ordinary RAM, and contains the most recently used data from the disk drives. Without spending the extra money on expensive SRAM chips, a disk cache can speed access to files by keeping them in ordinary RAM. Although ordinary RAM chips are not as fast as SRAMs, it's still faster to retrieve data from RAM than to retrieve it from a disk drive, so a disk cache improves system speed. Also see Byte, Cache, Data Storage, Memory, and ROM.

DISK CACHE

A section of ordinary RAM that's set aside. A disk cache holds the most frequently used data from the disk drives for quicker access.

SRAM

Stands for Static Random Access Memory. SRAMs are super-fast RAM chips usually used in caches. SRAMs do not need to have a pulse of electricity sent through them as frequently as DRAM chips do; therefore, they are much faster and easier for a computer to use. However, SRAMs are considerably more expensive than DRAMs (regular RAM) chips.

SIMM

Single In-line Memory Module. A special strip containing additional memory chips that can be inserted onto the computer's motherboard.

DRAM

Stands for Dynamic Random Access Memory. DRAMs make up most of the standard RAM chips found in computers today. A pulse of electricity must be sent through DRAMs regularly or they will lose their data. So the data stored in DRAMs is said to be "dynamic," which is just a fancy word for "easily changed."

ROM

ROM, or read-only memory, is a type of permanent computer memory. Because of their permanency, ROM chips are used to store crucial instructions for the computer's basic input-output functions (such as how to save a file, how to store data in RAM, how to display information on-screen, etc.). These instructions, called the BIOS or basic input output system, are pre-installed into the ROM chips at the time they are manufactured. Unlike RAM chips, ROM chips continue to retain their data even when the computer is turned off. Information kept on ROM chips cannot be erased or changed by the user or by the computer.

The computer's basic input-output system, called BIOS, is a set of instructions that tell the computer how to handle the flow of information between the computer and its peripherals, such as the keyboard (input) or the printer (output). The largest part of BIOS, ROM BIOS, is permanently stored in the computer's ROM chips. One function that BIOS performs happens only when the computer is turned on or restarted (booted). ROM BIOS checks out the computer by performing the power-on-self-test (POST). The computer reads these instructions each time it is turned on and performs a self check of the computer and its components.

In addition to being used on the computer's motherboard, ROM chips are also used in some printers. These

A POST check makes sure all the computer's parts are in working order.

ROM chips

CPU

RAM chips

The CPU does a POST check that reads the ROM chips for startup information.

Motherboard

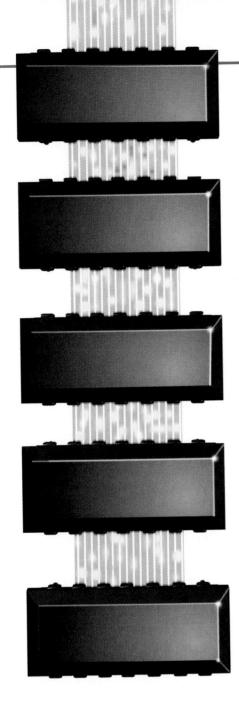

ROM Chips

ROM chips are located inside the printer and permanently store information about fonts (sets of characters of the same size and typeface). Plug-in font cartridges used by other printers have ROM chips inside that keep all of the information that tells the printer how to create type styles.

Palmtop computers, which are about the size of a person's hand, often contain applications (such as Lotus 1-2-3) stored on ROM chips. Because of their small size, palmtops have limited memory so they store many functions on ROM chips. Also see BIOS, Data Storage, Memory, and RAM.

BIOS

Basic Input-Output System. A set of permanent instructions stored in the ROM chips that tell the computer how to manage information flowing between the different computer components.

POST

Power-On-Self-Test. A test the computer performs each time it is turned on to make sure everything is connected properly.

MOTHERBOARD

The printed circuit board inside the computer's system unit that contains chips and wires—the computer's "engine". Plugged into the motherboard are ROM chips containing important instructions.

Safety

Computers are machines and, like other machines, they do from fail from time to time. To avoid frustration when the inevitable happens, there are several precautions computer users can to take to protect their data. One danger against which a user must protect his equipment is a surge in electricity. A surge can occur when lightning strikes nearby, or when power is suddenly restored after a temporary blackout. A basic and inexpensive way to protect computer hardware from power surges is with a surge protector (also called a surge suppressor). It looks like a power strip because it has several outlets; however, a regular power strip won't protect delicate computer equipment from electrical surges. A real surge protector/surge suppressor allows only a certain amount of electricity to flow to the equipment connected to it. If a surge in the electrical power is detected, a voltage sensitive switch absorbs the excess, allowing only the proper amount to continue on

through to the computer equipment. To be safe, users should keep the surge suppressors on at all times. There are many types of surge suppressors available; the better ones also include surge protection for modems and fax machines.

Surge protectors cannot protect against loss of power. Although this will not damage equipment, it can result in the loss of data if the user is working on something when the power goes out. If power outages are a problem, one should consider purchasing a UPS (uninterruptible power supply), which runs on batteries. A UPS is not designed for long term operation (about 10 to 20 minutes), but it does provide enough power for safe shutdowns so no data is lost. A UPS runs on ordinary household current, protecting against power surges until there is a power loss. It then switches over to battery power, which lasts a limited amount of time.

There are also some common sense rules to follow when using computer equipment: keep the workspace clean and free of food and drink. If something is spilled on the keyboard, turn off the computer and allow it to dry out. Do not attempt to clean the keyboard with household cleaners. If

possible, do not smoke around computers; they attract dust and airborne particles like a magnet, and these particles can cause damage to various computer components, especially the magnetic heads used to read and write data in floppy disk drives (which are open to the air). In addition, consider using a screen saver when the computer is not in use. A screen saver can prevent burn-in, a condition that occurs when the same image is displayed on-screen for an extended period of time.

There are a number of things a user can do to protect important data. The easiest way to protect data stored on disks is to keep them in a clean environment at room temperature away from food or liquid, keep the magnetic media covered and protected, and store them away from all magnets. Soft-tipped pens should be used when writing on floppy disk labels. In addition, the write-protect tab or notch can be used to prevent existing data on a floppy disk from being overwritten. Hard disks require different care. A user should defragment the disks occasionally so that files are quickly accessible, and should use an anti-virus program to scan for viruses on the hard disk and any floppy disks.

Electrical outlet

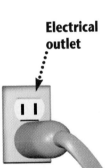

Surge suppressor

Protect a monitor, computer, printer, and modem from electrical surges with a surge supressor.

continues

Safety continued

It is always a good idea to keep a backup copy of all important information on a backup disk or tape. A good utility program will be able to perform a complete system backup and incremental backups as necessary. It will also be able to restore the information from the backup copies to the hard drive, if anything ever happens to damage the original data. Besides a full

backup of the data on the hard drive, it is also a good idea to make a copy of program disks before installing software. A user should keep the original program disks in a safe place and only use the backup copies. In addition, the program disks (and any other important disks) should be write-protected to prevent accidental erasure of data.

Protecting confidential data from the prying eyes of other users is always cause for concern. Although

it may be possible for diligent thieves to crack any security code, the best protection is to use passwords and ID numbers whenever possible in regular computer use, especially on a network. (Network administrators are in charge of security access on a network; discuss any concerns with the network administrator.) If they are placed in a safe overnight, removable hard disks provide another means of preventing unauthorized access. Some computers come with keys that lock the read/write heads in place, preventing access to files. This can become a problem however, if the key is lost or becomes jammed. Some screen savers also provide security when a computer is not in use by requiring that a password be entered before they will restore the screen. Also see Backup, Data Storage, Defragmentation, PCs, Power Supply, Screen Saver, and Virus.

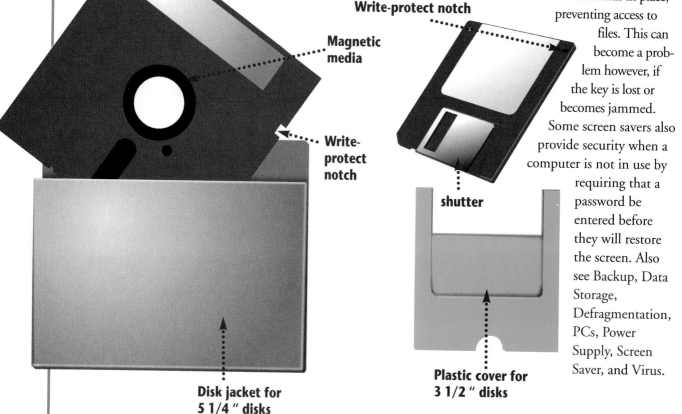

Write-protect notch

Magnetic media

Write-protect notch

Disk jacket for 5 1/4 " disks

shutter

Plastic cover for 3 1/2 " disks

DEFRAGMENTATION

Large files are often divided and saved in several clusters. This fragments data over the disk. Defragmentation reorganizes the data on a hard disk so that all the pieces of a file are located in adjacent clusters, making it easier for the hard drive to locate a file quickly.

ANTI-VIRUS PROGRAM

A virus is a program that destroys a file's data or the directory structure on a disk. Viruses attach themselves to program files and move with them from disk to disk. Anti-virus programs detect these changes in program files and remove the virus.

SCREEN SAVER

A program that displays a moving image when the computer is not in use to prevent damage to the monitor caused by burn-in (a condition that occurs when the same image is displayed on-screen for an extended period of time).

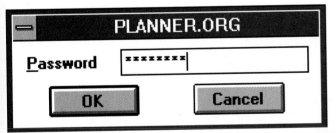

This dialog appears when a user tries to open a password-protected file in Lotus Organizer. The user has typed in a password, which shows up as asterisks.

WRITE-PROTECT

If a disk is write-protected, the data on it can be read but not edited or erased. To write protect a 5 1/4" disk, a tab is placed over the write-protect notch. To write-protect a 3 1/2" disk, the write protect notch is flipped up so that the hole is uncovered.

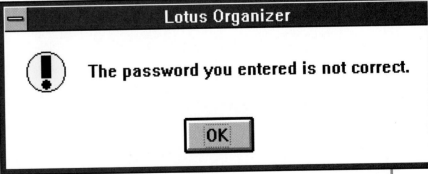

The user has not given the right password and cannot access the file.

Scanner

A scanner is an input device that reads printed information such as pictures or text and, with the help of a scanning program, translates them into digital data the computer can understand. After it's scanned, the image is displayed on the monitor, where the user can edit or print out the image. If handwritten or printed text is scanned in, additional software called OCR (optical character recognition) is needed to interpret the lines and squiggles into actual text characters. This is done by comparing the scanned image of a letter to a table of letters and other characters stored in a file. Using this system, the OCR program makes "its best guess" as to the identity of each text character. The user must then edit the document for accuracy after it has been scanned and interpreted by the OCR program.

There are two popular types of scanners: flatbed and hand-held. A flatbed scanner works (and looks) like a copy machine. The image on paper is inserted in the machine and scanned, converted into signals the computer can understand. A hand-held scanner is much smaller, and is good for capturing small images or pictures that are on irregular surfaces. To use it, the user slowly runs the scanner across the image. It might sometimes be necessary to scan a large image in several small strips because of the scanner's small size. As a result, hand-held scanners do not produce the same quality as flatbed scanners, due to irregularities introduced during the scanning process. However, hand-held scanners are much more affordable than flatbed scanners. Also see Input Devices and Pen Computing.

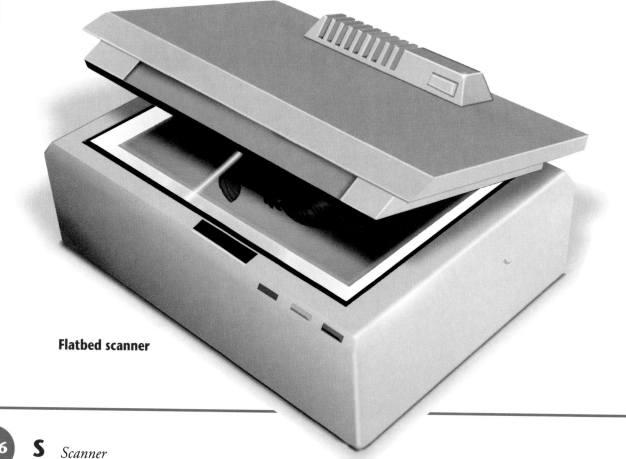

Flatbed scanner

How Does It Work?

In scanning an image, a light is passed over the image, scanning it in thin horizontal strips. The light from each strip of the image is reflected off several mirrors to reach a lens. The lens focuses the light rays onto a sensor array, which registers the strength of the various light beams and translates them into electrical current. The greater the amount of light reflection, the greater the voltage level.

A special microchip called an A-D (analog-to-digital) converter translates the changes in electrical current into a digital signal (such as a byte of data). This data is sent through the cable to the computer, where the scanning program displays the image on-screen. This process is repeated, one line at a time, until the entire image has been scanned in. The image can then be saved and adjusted.

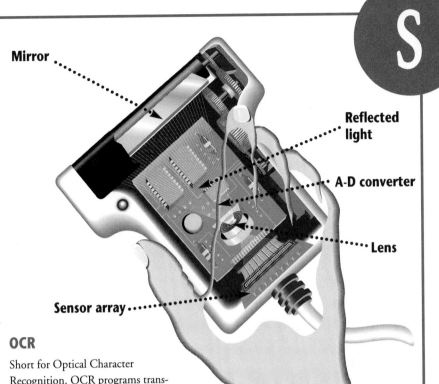

Mirror

Reflected light

A-D converter

Lens

Sensor array

OCR

Short for Optical Character Recognition. OCR programs translate a scanned document into computerized text. Most OCR software cannot interpret handwritten text unless it is carefully printed.

RESOLUTION

The number of dots per inch (dpi) in an image. A common dpi setting is 300. The higher the dpi, the better the image quality. Also, an image scanned with a higher resolution requires more disk space.

BAR CODE SCANNER

Commonly used in warehouses, grocery stores, and checkout registers to scan UPC (universal product code) symbols. The UPC is a series of vertical lines of varying thicknesses. When an item is sold or received into inventory, this code is scanned, identifying the item.

Fish

Impact 9000

Impact 9000

Hand-held scanner

Screen Savers

If a monitor is left on for an extended time, the image on the screen will become "burned in"—that is, a ghost image of the image will remain on the screen. A screen saver is a common utility that prevents burn-in when the computer is not in use. Some screen savers blank the screen altogether and some show moving images.

While they are functional, screen savers can also be quite entertaining. There are hundreds of screen savers available through commercial software and shareware. In addition, some programs such as Norton Desktop and Windows come with their own screen saver utilities. Also see Monitor, Shareware, and Utilities.

After Dark's Aquatic Realm screen saver.

How Does It Work?

While a screen saver is running, it remains mostly inactive, waiting until a certain amount of time has passed without keyboard input or mouse movement. The screen saver then blanks the screen or displays an image that prevents burn-in from occurring. The user can set the amount of time that has to pass before the screen saver becomes active—such as three or five minutes.

The screen saver displays its image until the user moves the mouse or presses a key on the keyboard. When the image disappears, the user is returned to the screen that was displayed before the screen saver started. Some screen savers require that a password be entered before they will restore the screen; this provides added computer security.

Windows comes with its own screen saver, shown here.

AFTER DARK

Popular collection of screen savers contained in one program. After Dark comes in Windows and Mac versions, with specialized add-on packages, such as Star Trek, More After Dark, and Disney.

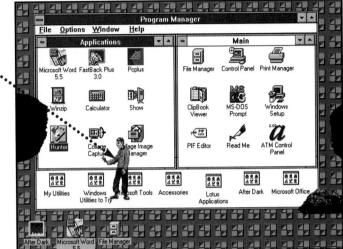

Spock phases out parts of a user's screen in After Dark's Star Trek screen saver.

TSR

Short for Terminate and Stay Resident, this is a type of program that "goes to sleep" after it's activated, waiting for a particular keypress or event to trigger it back into action.

BURN IN

Damage caused to a monitor when an image is displayed for a long period of time. The image is "burnt into" the phosphorous surface of the monitor, creating a ghostly after-image.

SCSI

SCSI stands for Small Computer System Interface, and is commonly pronounced "scuzzy." SCSI is a special interface for transferring data at high speeds between a computer and another device, such as the hard disk drive, CD-ROM drive, tape drive, or a printer. The most common SCSI device is a hard disk, which benefits greatly from the fast data transfer rates. SCSI ports can even be used to connect a computer to a network.

In addition, up to seven different SCSI devices can be connected to a single SCSI port, although only one such device can communicate with the computer (or another device) at a time. On an IBM PC-compatible, a SCSI port might be found connected directly to the motherboard; this type is often used to connect a SCSI hard drive. Additional SCSI ports can be connected through a special circuit board inserted into an expansion slot. Macintosh computers have a single built-in SCSI port, so all the SCSI devices have to be connected to each other instead of to the Mac

itself. (Only six devices can be connected to the Mac SCSI port.) When several devices are connected, they are said to be "daisy-chained." Also see Bus, CPU, Data Storage, Expansion Cards, Hard Disk Drive, Input Devices, and Output Devices.

Tape drive

External hard drive

SCSI devices can exchange data without the help of the CPU.

How Does It Work?

SCSI devices are intelligent and can communicate between themselves without the help of the computer. For example, a SCSI hard disk can back up files to a SCSI tape drive, while the computer is processing other information. SCSI devices communicate using a special control language. Addresses are assigned to each peripheral, and information is sent back and forth using the addresses.

In addition, SCSI devices are in charge of their own file maintenance. For example, a SCSI drive might be told to "save this Sales file." It would then locate an empty space and save the file. Other hard disks require a specific address in which to save a file; this address is determined before the file is sent to the drive to be saved.

PERIPHERAL

Any device (such as a printer, modem, CD-ROM drive, scanner, and so on) that is connected to a computer by a cable and that can communicate with the microprocessor.

PORTS

The various connection holes that allow cables to be plugged into hardware devices. Ports are usually located on back of such devices as drive units, printers, and monitors.

BUS

The "highway" in a computer that transports data between the CPU and its peripherals. A SCSI interface is like a "sub-bus" that allows SCSI devices to transfer data among themselves without the help of the CPU.

INTERFACE

An interface is simply a connection of some kind. A SCSI interface transfers data at high speeds between SCSI devices and the computer.

Shareware

Shareware programs are programs that are made available to users to try before they buy. If the user likes the program and intends to use it, he sends the programmer a small registration fee usually between $10 and $40. There are shareware games, screen savers, word processors, anti-virus programs, and everything in between. There are thousands of shareware programs available on Prodigy, CompuServe, or other on-line services and bulletin boards. These shareware programs have been placed on the on-line services and bulletin boards by their original programmers, in the hopes that someone will download (receive) the file and find it useful. There are also shareware dealers, such as The Software Labs, that will send people shareware programs on disk and only charge the cost of shipping. The user is, of course, still obligated to pay the registration fee for any program he uses after the trial period. When the programmer receives payment from the user, he generally sends the user documentation for the program, technical support, and information on upgrades.

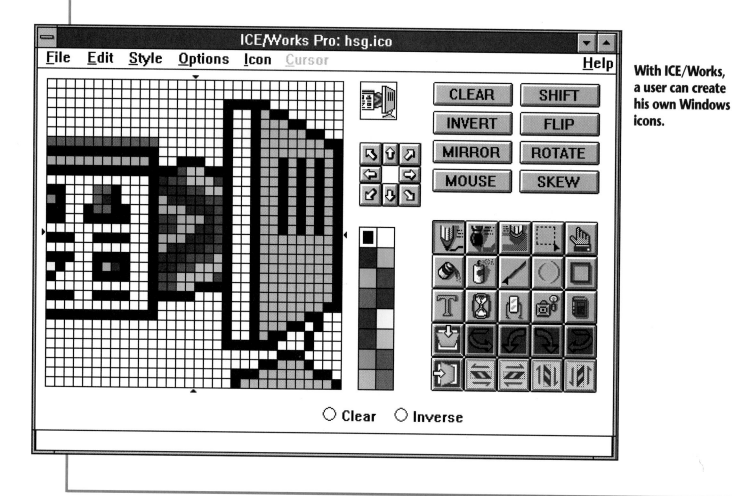

With ICE/Works, a user can create his own Windows icons.

WinZip is a Windows interface for PKZIP and other shareware compression utilities.

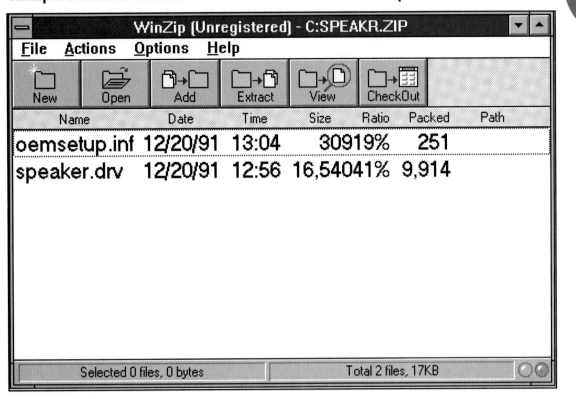

There are other types of software programs that are also available for sharing, but users aren't asked to pay a fee for using them. These products are called freeware and public domain software. A user can simply copy the program and use it. Freeware cannot be sold for profit. Since both shareware and freeware programs are readily available through BBSs and on-line services, it might be difficult to tell them apart. However, shareware programs always present some type of message reminding the user to pay the registration fee after the trial period. Freeware or public domain software programs do not include this message. Regardless, it's up to the user to determine whether or not

a program is freeware, and to be sure to pay for any shareware programs he uses. Also see Applications, BBS, CompuServe, Internet, and Prodigy.

FREEWARE

Programs that are copyrighted by the programmer but may be distributed free of charge to other users.

Super Snakes is a shareware game.

PUBLIC DOMAIN SOFTWARE

Programs that are not copyrighted and are for anyone's use. A user does not have to have the programmer's permission to use the program, nor does he have to pay a fee.

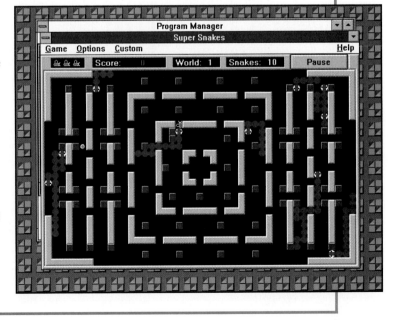

Software

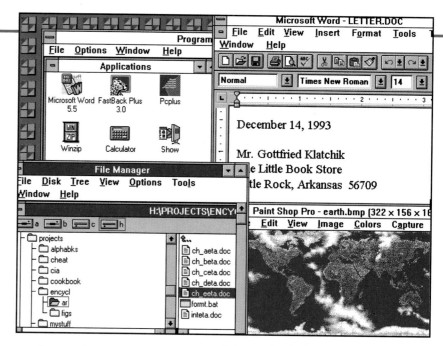

Software is a set of programmed instructions that tell a computer what to do. A computer cannot do anything on its own; it needs to know how to react to the input it gets from a user. Software provides that instruction. Software is the opposite of hardware, the physical components of the computer.

Basically, there are two kinds of software: operating system software and application software. The operating system software, such as DOS on a PC or System 7 on a Macintosh, tells the computer how to interpret commands, manage data, and process input and output. Application software, such as a

word processing program, a spreadsheet program, or a database program, instructs the computer to perform a particular type of task.

Available for any task a user might want to accomplish, there are many types of applications software, such as spreadsheets, databases, money management, desktop publishing, graphics programs,

Microsoft windows is a cross between application and operating systems software.

```
C:\>mem

Memory Type        Total   =   Used   +   Free
----------         -----       ----       ----
Conventional        640K       130K       510K
Upper               155K       100K        55K
Reserved            384K       384K         0K
Extended (XMS)    2,917K     1,241K     1,676K
                   ------      ------     ------
Total memory      4,096K     1,854K     2,242K

Total under 1 MB    795K       229K       566K

Largest executable program size       510K (522,368 bytes)
Largest free upper memory block        55K  (56,288 bytes)
MS-DOS is resident in the high memory area.

C:\>
```

MS-DOS 6.2 is operating system software.

How Does It Work?

Operating system software is automatically loaded into memory when the computer is booted (started). It remains there so it can process commands from both the user and other programs.

Application software is loaded into memory when the user activates the program. This is usually done by typing the name of the program (for example, WP for WordPerfect) or by double-clicking on an icon that represents the program. Once it's loaded into memory, the program sends requests to the operating system software for things it needs, such as files on disk, a calculation to be performed, or information to be displayed on the monitor. If the operating system is multitasking, the user can load more than one program at a time. If not, the application software maintains control over all of the system resources until the user exits the program.

Microsoft Access is database.

word processing, and more. There are specialized programs a user can utilize to perform a specific function, such as figuring taxes, creating a personal budget, managing a small business, and creating graphic art. There are utility programs that help a user manage his files and directories, and keep his data safe from viruses and accidental erasure. There are also numerous games and entertainment packages available, as well as educational programs. In addition to commercial software, shareware and freeware are also distributed through many channels to any user who wants to try them. Also see Application, Database, DOS, Drawing Programs, Hardware, Integrated Software, Money Management Programs, Operating Systems, OS/2, Paint Programs, Screen Savers, Shareware, Spreadsheet, System 7, Terminate and Stay Resident Programs, Utilities, Virus, and Word Processing.

MULTITASKING

A type of operating system (such as OS/2, System 7, and Windows NT) that is capable of processing requests from more than one program at a time. Windows is multitasking, but not in the same way; it depends on the cooperation of the active program to share its resources. If the active program doesn't want to share, Windows can only process its requests and not those of any other program.

APPLICATION SOFTWARE

A program that allows the user to perform a specific task, such as writing a letter, creating a budget, or managing a database.

OPERATING SYSTEM SOFTWARE

A program that tells the computer how to interpret commands and how to manage the data it receives. The user communicates with the computer through the operating system by using specific commands.

SHAREWARE

Software that is distributed to anyone for use on a trial basis. If the user likes the software and wants to use it, he sends the programmer a fee and usually receives more detailed documentation and technical support in return.

Sound Board

A sound board (also called a sound card) is a special circuit board that improves the sound quality of a PC. The sound card is inserted into an expansion slot inside the PC's system unit. Without a sound board, a PC is capable of producing only small beeps and fuzzy sounds. The sound board produces sounds digitally, which accounts for the greatly improved sound capabilities. Sound boards contain sockets for attaching external speakers, so the sound quality isn't distorted by the barely adequate internal PC speaker. Also, a sound board user can purchase a microphone that plugs into most sound boards, allowing the user to record his own sounds. Musicians can connect synthesizers or musical keyboards to a sound board equipped with a MIDI connector. MIDI is a special interface that allows a computer to communicate with electronic instruments so a user can play, record, and edit his own music (with the appropriate software).

Sound is probably an area of personal computing that will be greatly expanded in the near future. Even if a user is not a musician, there are many reasons for purchasing a sound board. For example, many games play stereo sound, which increases the games' realistic feel and improves their entertainment value. Multimedia programs, which incorporate video, text, graphics, animation, and sound into a single presentation, often require the best computer compo-nents in order to be fully enjoyed. Multimedia programs are popular for presentations, training, and education. Many children's software programs utilize multimedia as a means of entertaining while educating. As multimedia systems become more popular, people will want better sound quality than what is currently standard on a PC.

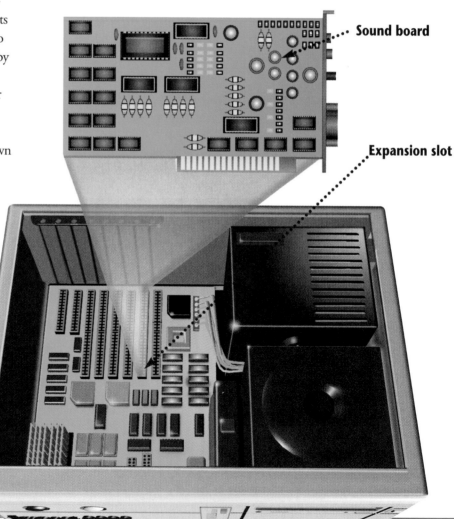

Sound board

Expansion slot

How Does It Work?

When a user speaks into a microphone, a diaphragm in the microphone vibrates, producing a variable electrical current. The current is sent to the sound board through a cable, where it passes through a mixer chip that adjusts its volume.

The analog signal (electrical sound waves) is passed from the mixer chip to another chip called the ADC (analog-to-digital-converter). This chip converts the analog signal to digital information, in much the same way as a modem converts incoming sounds into computer data. This digitized sound is saved to the hard disk in a file that can be reconverted later into analog sound waves and played through a speaker.

Speakers

Audio In: Connect a microphone.

Volume Control

Audio Out: Connect external speakers.

MIDI Port: Connect a synthesizer.

Sound is one of the areas in which Macintosh computers have an advantage over PCs. The latest Macs come with built-in sound capability and ports for connecting microphones and stereo speakers.

With the microphone and the Mac's sound capabilities and software, a user can easily record his own sounds and store them on disk. Also see **Expansion Cards**, **MIDI**, and **Multimedia**.

Microphone

MULTIMEDIA

Programs that combine text, graphics, video, animation, and stereo sound into a single presentation.

Sound board

HARD DISK

MIDI

Musical Instrument Digital Interface. A special interface that allows a computer to communicate with electronic instruments. Using MIDI equipment and special software, a user can record, play, and edit digitized music.

Spreadsheet

A spreadsheet is a type of application that is used to organize, calculate, and analyze numerical data. A spreadsheet can also be used to manage non-numerical data, similar to a database application. The most popular spreadsheets, including Microsoft Excel and Lotus 1-2-3, have several advanced features that allow the user to create charts (graphs), or drawings and insert them in the spreadsheet.

A spreadsheet (sometimes referred to as a worksheet) is filled with columns and rows. The user types data into cells, created by the intersection of a column and a row. Each cell's address consists of the column letter and the row number; for example, cell C5 is the third cell from the left in the fifth row. The row numbers and column letters appear at the beginning of each row or column.

In each cell, a user can enter a value or a formula that references the data in other cells. For example, the user could enter a formula to add the numbers in three cells and display the total. What makes a spreadsheet so valuable is that it automatically recalculates formulas when the user changes a value. For example, if the user changed the number in one of those three cells, the total would be automatically recalculated, along with any other formulas that were using that value.

There are additional features that are common to many spreadsheet programs as well. To make the numbers in a spreadsheet

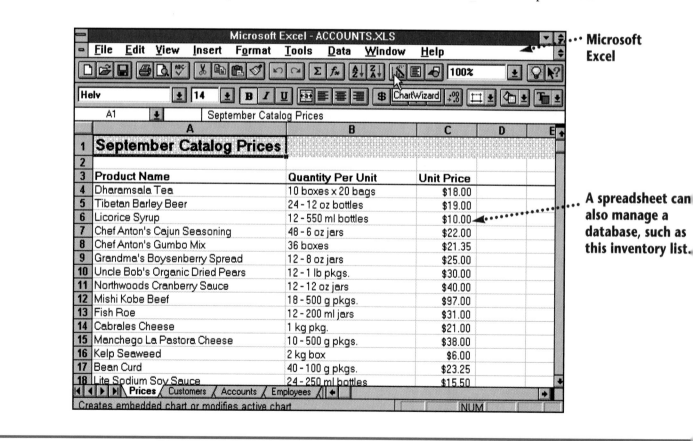

Microsoft Excel

A spreadsheet can also manage a database, such as this inventory list.

more visually pleasing, borders, shading, and lines can be added to cells in almost any spreadsheet. A spreadsheet also allows a user to graph or chart a series of values in order to depict them visually. In addition, a spreadsheet can be used as a simple database manager to organize simple lists, such as clients' names and addresses, product inventory, or investments. Some newer spreadsheet programs group worksheets together in the same file, so the user can easily switch between them. In addition, the user can easily base formulas in one worksheet on data in another worksheet. For example, one spreadsheet file might contain five worksheets, QTR1, QTR2, QTR3, QTR4, and a Year End worksheet, which adds all four quarters together.

The first real spreadsheet was created in 1978 by Dan Bricklin when he decided to try to make the computer do all the recalculating that accounting requires. He and Bob Frankston created the program VisiCalc for the Apple II computer. VisiCalc was an extremely popular program until Lotus 1-2-3 was introduced in 1982 and eventually replaced it in the marketplace. 1-2-3 had the same features as VisiCalc, but it also had database and graphics features that made it more desirable. (Incidentally, the original Lotus 1-2-3 program was remarkably similar to VisiCalc; in fact, the slash (/) that is used to open the Lotus menu was originally used by VisiCalc.)

Just as many people bought Apple IIs so they could use VisiCalc, many people bought the first IBM compatible PCs so

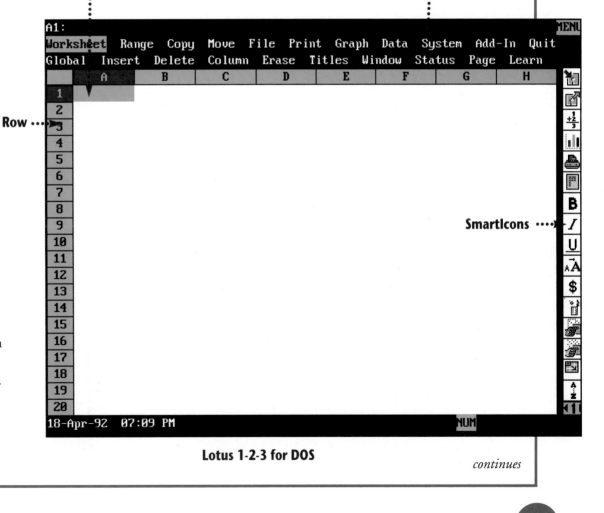

Lotus 1-2-3 for DOS

continues

Spreadsheet continued

they could use Lotus 1-2-3. Lotus 1-2-3 remains one of the most popular software programs of all time, while VisiCalc virtually disappeared from the market in 1984. Since then, several other spreadsheet programs have been developed, the most popular ones being Microsoft Excel for Windows and Macintosh, Lotus 1-2-3 (DOS, Windows, and Mac versions), and Quattro Pro. An innovative spreadsheet that has been fairly popular is Lotus Improv, which works differently than traditional spreadsheets do, allowing users to rearrange data easily to form varying analyses. Also see Application, Excel, Improv, Lotus 1-2-3, and Software.

CELL

The rectangular space that is formed where a row and a column meet. Each cell has its own address made up of the column letter followed by the row number (for example, cell B4 is the second cell over and the fourth cell down).

FORMULAS

The sequence of numbers and symbols that tells the spreadsheet program how and what to calculate.

LOTUS MENU

A special menu system included in Lotus 1-2-3. To use this type of menu, the user presses /, and a list of menu names appears at the top of the screen. When a menu is highlighted, a brief description appears just below this line. When a menu is selected, its list of commands replaces the previous menu listing.

The famous Lotus Menu

Lotus Improv for Windows

	Ytd							
	Qtr1				Qtr2			
	Jan	Feb	Mar	Total	Apr	May	Jun	Total
R. Miller	53,634	63,731	54,629	171,994				0
S. Kinkoph	52,734	56,845	53,934	163,513				0
J. Galloway	49,412	52,072	56,298	157,782				0
J. Fulton	45,290	51,287	54,987	151,564				0
S. Frantz	46,972	49,679	50,592	147,243				0
S. Cooksey	42,689	51,572	47,578	141,839				0
J. Kraynak	43,782	45,278	50,785	139,845				0
M. Show	44,573	46,170	45,961	136,704				

Salespeople

1	Qtr1.Total = groupsum(Qtr1)
2	Qtr2.Total = groupsum(Qtr2)
3	Qtr3.Total = groupsum(Qtr3)
4	Qtr4.Total = groupsum(Qtr4)
5	Ytd.Total = groupsum(Ytd)

How Does It Work?

When using a spreadsheet, the user types data into cells, and then enters formulas into other cells that calculate results based on the original data. When typing a formula, the user specifies cell addresses which tell the spreadsheet program where to find the numbers he wants to use in the calculation. For example, to add the contents of the cells A2 and A3, the user types the formula: =A2+A3. (All Excel formulas begin with an equals sign.)

A function is a preprogrammed mathematical operation. To activate a function, the user simply enters the function name into a formula. For example, in the formula =SUM (A1,A2,A3), the SUM function adds the values in cells A1, A2, and A3.

RANGE

A group of adjacent cells that form a rectangle. If a user names a range, that name can be used in a formula to refer to the range of cells.

FUNCTION

A special type of mathematical operation that has already been written; all the user has to do to use the function is type its name in a formula. For example, in the formula =SUM(A1,A2,A3), the SUM function adds the values in cells A1, A2, and A3.

The formula for the selected cell is displayed here.

A formula is entered into cell D16.

Lotus 1-2-3 Release 4 - [LESSON6.WK4 [RO]]

File Edit View Style Tools Range Window Help

D16   @SUM(D14..D10)

	A	B	C	D	E	F	G	H	I
3			Q1 Income						
4			Bell Audio						
5				Jan	Feb	Mar	Total		
7			Net Sales	$12,000	$19,000	$16,000	$47,000		
9			Expenses:						
10			Salary	$2,000	$2,000	$2,000	$6,000		
11			Int	$1,200	$1,400	$1,600	$4,200		
12			Rent	$600	$600	$600	$1,800		
13			Ads	$900	$2,000	$4,000	$6,900		
14			COG	$4,000	$4,200	$5,000	$13,200		
16			Total Expense	$8,700	$10,200	$13,200	$32,100		
18			Net Income	$3,300	$8,800	$2,800	$14,900		

Currency 0   TimesNewRomanPS 12 01/28/94 2:16 PM   Ready

The result, not the formula, is displayed.

Microsoft Excel - OUTLINE.XLS

File Edit View Insert Format Tools Data Window Help

Arial   10

C5   Midsize

	A	B	C	D	E	F	G	H	I
3				Jan	Feb	Mar	Qtr1		
4	Cars	Compact	1200	1325	1200	3725			
5		Midsize	1400	1256	1400	4056			
6		Full-size	1450	1652	1450	4552			
7		Total Cars	4050	4233	4050	12333			
9	Trucks	Vans	1235	1325	1211	3771			
10		Mini Vans	1200	1300	1352	3852			
11		Total Trucks	2435	2625	2563	7623			
13		Total Cars and Trucks	6485	6858	6613	19956			

Sheet1 / Sheet2 / Sheet3 / Sheet4 / Sheet5 / Sheet6
Ready   NUM

Spreadsheet **S** 311

SuperPaint

SuperPaint is a popular paint program for the Macintosh that was introduced in 1986 by Silicon Beach Software. SuperPaint is now published by Aldus Corporation. A paint program is a special application that allows the user to use the mouse to "paint" with the computer, making freehand illustrations and graphics. A paint program uses dots, called pixels, to make an image. By controlling individual dots, the user can create shading and patterns, as well as irregular lines to simulate the effect of a painting or sketch.

SuperPaint is different from most paint programs because it has two different layers: a paint layer and a draw layer. A drawing program uses objects, such as squares, circles, rectangles, and lines to create a picture. Objects can be connected to each other to form a single group, which can be copied, moved, or otherwise manipulated. In addition, an object can be placed in front or in back of another object to partially obscure its outline.

The drawing layer treats each graphic object as a mathematical formula, as opposed to using the dots to form an image, as it is done on the paint layer. The user can switch back and forth between the layers by clicking on an icon on the screen. The paint

PAINT PROGRAM

A program that allows the user to create bit-mapped objects and edit them pixel-by-pixel (the dots on-screen). Objects drawn in a paint layer cannot be resized; once they are drawn they can only be erased or added to.

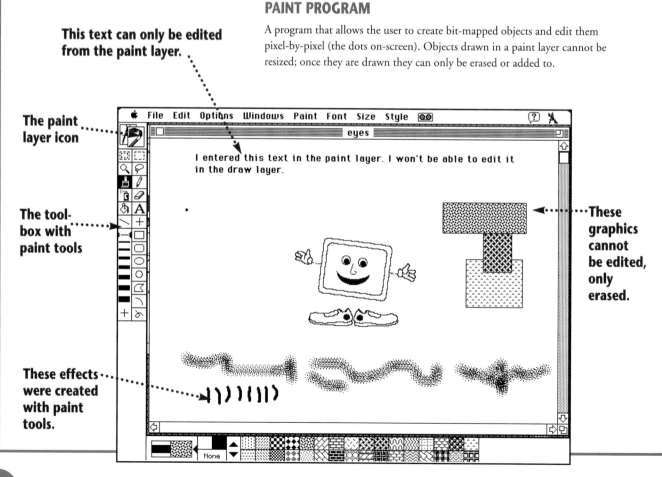

This text can only be edited from the paint layer.

The paint layer icon

The tool-box with paint tools

These effects were created with paint tools.

These graphics cannot be edited, only erased.

How Does It Work?

To create an object, the user clicks on a tool in the toolbox. (To paint, he clicks on the paintbrush; to draw a square, he clicks on the tool with a square on it.) He can choose a pattern or a color from the palette at the bottom of the screen.

Objects created in the draw layer can be selected for editing by double-clicking on them. Handles will appear on the objects, allowing the user to stretch, shrink, or delete the object. Objects created in the paint layer do not have handles; their pixels can be erased or added to, but they cannot be resized.

The layers are like transparent pieces of paper on top of each other: the user can see the images on both layers at the same time, but he can only edit the images that are on the layer that is on top.

layer can produce bit-mapped graphics (pictures composed of pixels), while the draw layer handles object-oriented graphics (pictures composed of lines and curves).

SuperPaint is a more powerful program than MacPaint or MacDraw, and is essential for users who create a lot of graphics.

There are, of course, more specialized and elaborate graphics programs available, such as Adobe Illustrator and Adobe Freehand, which professional graphic artists use. For most Mac users, though, SuperPaint is more than adequate as a paint/draw program. Also see Drawing Programs, Graphics, Macintosh, and Paint Programs.

The draw layer icon

This object has handles, indicating that it can be edited.

The toolbox without paint tools

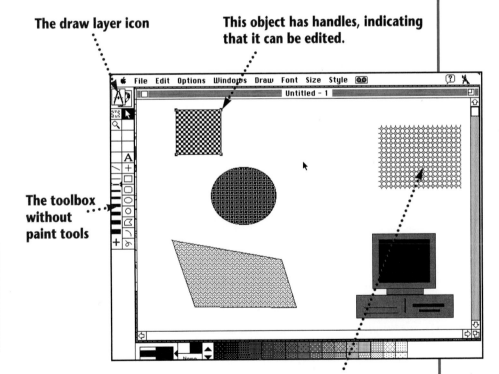

This object was drawn in the paint layer and cannot be selected.

DRAW PROGRAM

Line art can be created with a draw program. Lines can be resized, and objects can be reshaped. Draw programs are good to use for drawing shapes with smooth lines, such as squares and ovals.

System Unit

The system unit holds all of the vital components that allow the computer to process information, store data, and communicate with other parts of the computer. Inside the system unit box is a power supply box that converts the AC electricity from an outlet to the DC electricity that runs the computer. Also inside is the motherboard, the main circuit board in the system unit. Etched into the motherboard is the bus, the electronic pathway over which data flows. All components are connected to this bus, including the expansion slots, into which peripherals (such as the printer, modem, or mouse) can be connected to the computer.

Plugged into the motherboard are various computer components, such as the central processing unit (CPU or microprocessor) chip. The CPU is the "brain" of the computer, processing instructions and managing data. Other chips include RAM (memory) chips, which store data temporarily as it is being worked on. ROM chips contain permanent instructions the computer needs in order to perform its most basic input and output tasks, such as displaying information on a monitor.

Most computers contain one or more disk drives inside the system unit: the hard disk drive and a floppy disk drive (5 1/4-inch, or 3 1/2-inch, or both). Disk drives are used to permanently store data. Also see Central Processing Unit, Expansion Cards, Floppy Disk Drive, Hard Disk Drive, Motherboard, and Power Supply.

BUS

The "highway" in a computer that transports data. There are different types of buses, but they are all used to carry electronic data from one place to another.

CENTRAL PROCESSING UNIT (CPU)

The CPU, or Central Processing Unit, acts as the computer's "brain", carrying out software commands, performing calculations, and conversing with the different hardware needed to operate the computer.

EXPANSION CARDS

Extra circuit boards that a user can connect to the motherboard (through its expansion slots). There are many types of expansion cards, such as modem cards, video cards, sound boards, etc.

Expansion slots

POWER SUPPLY

Converts AC electricity from a power outlet to the
DC electricity used by the PC.

MOTHERBOARD

The motherboard is the main circuit board inside the computer,
and it normally forms the "floor" of the system unit. Plugged into
the motherboard in some way are all the electrical components of
the computer.

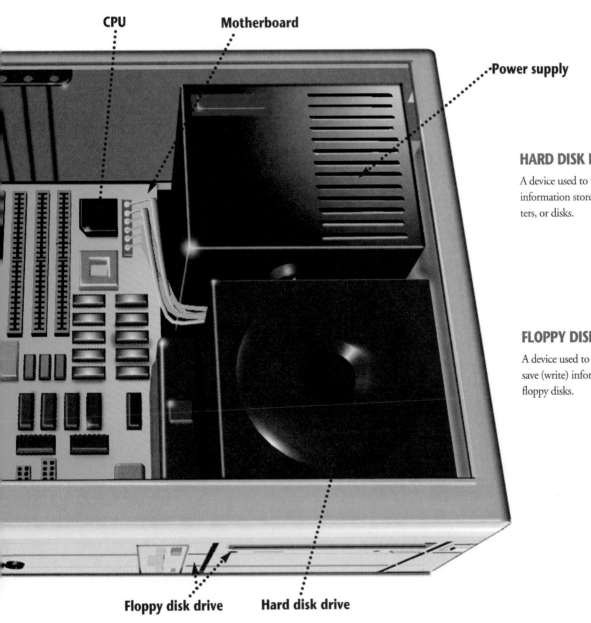

CPU

Motherboard

Power supply

Floppy disk drive   Hard disk drive

HARD DISK DRIVE

A device used to write and read
information stored onto metal platters, or disks.

FLOPPY DISK DRIVE

A device used to retrieve (read) and
save (write) information stored onto
floppy disks.

System 7

The System is the name of the Macintosh's operating system. System 7 is the latest major upgrade (released in 1991) of the System operating system. The System is a graphical user interface (GUI) that allows the user to click on icons and use pull-down menus to issue commands, instead of typing them in at a prompt, like in the DOS and UNIX operating systems. It requires 2M of RAM, but most users need at least 4M of RAM to run normal-sized programs on their Macintoshes and still use System 7's advanced features, such as multitasking (the ability to process instructions from more than one program at a time) and virtual memory (a memory management technique that allows part of the hard disk to be used for RAM storage, enabling programs that need more RAM to get it).

System 7 actually includes two parts (although they do not seem like separate parts to the user): the System software and the Finder. The System manages the computer's processing and disk management chores while the Finder maintains the desktop (the graphical user interface) and manages the applications. The MultiFinder, capable of multitasking multiple applications, used to be an option with older System versions, but it is built into System 7. Now, with the Finder, the user can switch back and forth between any open applications, processing multiple tasks at the same time. The Finder icon is always available in the menu bar of every Macintosh program. To use it, the user clicks on the Finder icon, and then selects the application he wants to switch to.

System 7 contains many nice features, including TrueType fonts. TrueType fonts are outline fonts, which means that they are stored as mathematical formulas that tell the computer how to draw the character. This makes TrueType fonts easy to resize without causing distortions. In addition, TrueType fonts look virtually the same on-screen and on paper.

Another feature, publish and subscribe, is similar to the object linking feature found in Windows. A user can link data across applications, and when one file (the publisher) is changed, the linked file (the subscriber) is automatically updated. For example, a user could link part of a spreadsheet file to a letter, and if the spreadsheet data is later changed, the link will automatically update the letter.

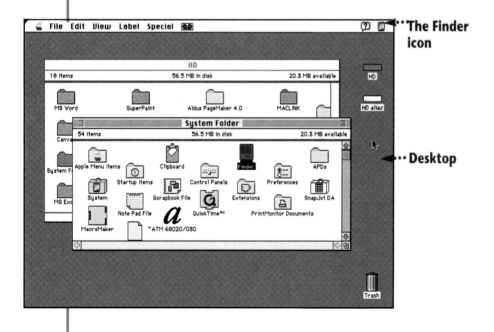

The Finder icon

Desktop

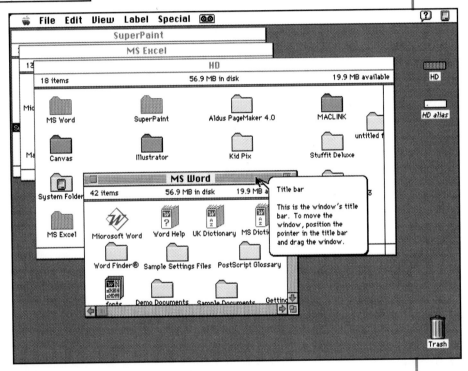

Users can switch to other applications easily with the Finder.

RANDOM ACCESS MEMORY (RAM)

A computer's working memory. Anything stored in RAM is erased when the computer is turned off.

VIRTUAL MEMORY

The computer uses disk space as "extra memory" and swaps information between RAM and the disk.

One feature, balloon help, is wonderful for new users who need to get to know their Mac quickly. When the user rests the mouse pointer on top of an on-screen element, a small balloon of information pops up on-screen. This balloon window contains a brief description of the selected object, along with some hints as to the object's purpose.

While balloon help is great for novice users, System 7 contains several features that make advanced users happy. One of these features is peer-to-peer file sharing, which allows two interconnected Macs to share files without the aid of an actual file server (the main computer that controls a network). In peer-to-peer networking, each Mac is its own file server.

But probably the best feature of System 7 is its 32-bit processing capability. This means that with System 7, data moves between the CPU and other components 32 bits at a time, which is 2 to 4 times that of conventional PCs. Also see Macintosh, Memory, Multitasking, Network, and Operating System.

Balloon help explains concepts to new users.

MULTITASKING

The ability to do more than one task at once. On a computer, this means that the user can have more than one program open at a time, each processing separate tasks, all at the same time. For example, a user could type a letter while the computer is sorting a database, without decreasing system speed.

OPERATING SYSTEM

The program that runs the computer. The operating system is the first program that is loaded when a user turns on his computer. It interprets the user's instructions, handles input and output, runs applications, keeps track of the data stored on disk, and manages peripherals.

Tape Backup Unit

A tape backup unit is a storage device used to store copies of the computer's hard disk files. All hard disk drives inevitably fail sometime, possibly losing all of the data stored on them. Tape backup units and storage tapes (magnetically coated tapes similar in size to cassette tapes) are a perfect way to preserve data. Important files can be copied from the hard disk drive onto a tape for safe storage.

Tape backup units and tapes can easily and quickly store considerable amounts of data onto a single tape. However, data cannot be as easily accessed from a tape backup unit as it can from a hard disk drive. Because accessing the data on tape backup units is so slow, tape backups are used for storing copies of data, but not for storing data that is needed constantly (like the data on a hard disk). Tapes are much more convenient for saving backup copies than floppy disks are, because they hold more data. In fact, an average tape holds approximately 250 megabytes, which is equal to about 180 high-density 3.5-inch disks. Because a tape can usually hold the data on an entire hard disk, a tape backup procedure can be scheduled at night when

no one is around—which makes backing up data more convenient.

A backup tape is either installed just below the floppy disk drives in a spare drive bay, or it is placed outside the system unit in an external tape drive that is connected with a cable. External tape drives resemble external hard disk drives in appearance.

Like floppy disks and hard disk drives, tape backup units also use magnetic particles to write information to a formatted tape. Data is written onto tapes that resemble audio cassettes. Like floppy disks and hard disks, the tape is formatted into parallel tracks where data is stored. The tape itself has a coating of magnetic particles on which data is written. Tape cassettes and drives come in several different sizes and

A Jumbo Trakker 250 tape backup unit by Colorado Memory Systems

capacities. The most popular sizes for personal computers are quarter-inch cartridges (QIC) and digital audio tapes (DAT). Capacities range from 40 megabytes to 250 megabytes for QIC tapes, and from 1 to 5 gigabytes for DAT tapes. Most drives compress the data so they can store more information on a single tape. For example, the Jumbo Trakker 250 by Colorado Memory Systems can store 250 megabytes of data on a 120 megabyte tape because it compresses the data as it is being stored. Also see Data Storage, Disk Drive, Floppy Disk, and Hard Disk Drive.

How Does It Work?

A tiny microchip inside the quarter-inch tape drive tells the tape to start moving. Like an audio cassette player, a capstan traps the tape against a roller so it is kept taut as it moves. Data to be written onto the tape is sent to the read-write head (an electro-magnetic device that realigns the tape's magnetic particles embedded on the tape's coating). Data is recorded onto the tape one formatted track at a time. Once the end of a track is reached—at the end of a spool—themovement of the tape will automatically reverse. Holes punched into the end of a tape tell the drive head to move on to another track. The next bit of data is then stored on a new track.

BYTE

A group of eight bits; equivalent to a single alphanumeric character.

DATA COMPRESSION

A process that makes it possible to store a file in a smaller amount of space than it is normally stored in. To use the file, it must be uncompressed using a similar process.

MEGABYTE

Made up of 1,048,576 bytes, this is equivalent to 500 double-spaced pages of text.

GIGABYTE

Made up of 1,073,741,824 bytes, this is equivalent to a half-million double-spaced pages of text.

Elastic belt

Tape cartridge

Tape

Read-write heads

Capstan

Terminate and Stay Resident Program

Terminate and stay resident (TSR) programs, also called memory resident programs or RAM-resident programs, are programs that keep an application available for use even while the user may be working on another program. Under some operating systems, such as DOS, a user may access only one program at a time. To access a different program, the user must exit the current program, and then load the next one. TSRs are much more convenient. The user does not need to exit one program in order to access the TSR program because a TSR runs all the time in memory, waiting for a specific keypress or event to activate it. TSR programs include utility programs or a computer's desktop accessory.

Calculator

Word processing letter

For example, a person working on a word processing document could open the calculator accessory with a simple keystroke and perform some calculations—even though he is in the middle of a word processing file. Common TSRs include antivirus programs (which stay in memory and guard against system infection), disk-doubling programs (which increase the amount of data a disk can hold by intercepting commands and maintaining their own file management scheme), and desktop accessories (such as a notepad, calculator, dictionary, and appointment book).

232

TSR

Impact 9000

Impact 9000

Dear Sirs,
I am writing in response to your ad. I'm enclosing a check for $232

How Does It Work?

When a TSR is loaded into memory, it shuts down almost all activity, waiting for a particular keystroke combination or an event. One part of the TSR remains functional, and that part intercepts all keypresses before passing them onto the operating system (such as DOS). That way, when the particular keypress combination that activates the TSR occurs, the TSR is aware of it and acts immediately.

While the TSR is active, whatever application the user was working with is "frozen" in memory, but is safe. When the user leaves the TSR, the TSR tells DOS to switch back to the application so the user can continue working.

1MB

640K

System Use

Unused

User Application

TSR DOS

MEMORY

MULTITASKING

A method of simultaneously processing the instructions for several programs. OS/2, Unix, Windows NT, and the Macintosh System 7 are all multitasking operating systems.

····▶ **TRS is always active in memory**

ANTI-VIRUS PROGRAMS

A program that tracks and eliminates computer viruses, destructive programs that can destroy data and disable hard disks. Viruses infect a computer through program files that contain the virus.

The calculator accessory remains in the computer's RAM (random access memory) and is always "on call" at a moment's notice. Without a terminate and stay resident program, the user could only access the calculator by closing the file in which he was currently working and opening the calculator. TSR programs save the user the time of switching between tasks.

TSRs are not as popular as they once were since other operating systems (such as OS/2) and operating environments (such as Windows) allow users to safely run several programs at the same time. (Although Windows does not multitask—process commands from several programs simultaneously—it can safely activate one of several running programs at a time, and allows a user to switch back and forth.) However, even with multitasking systems such as OS/2 and Windows, some TSRs, like anti-virus programs, are always useful. Also see Application, Memory, Multitasking, Operating System, OS/2, System 7, UNIX, and Windows.

RAM

Short for Random Access Memory. RAM is the computer's electronic memory found on chips located on the motherboard. RAM is used whenever a program is loaded and run. The program's information is copied into the RAM chips where it can be interpreted and commands can be carried out. Information stored in RAM is only temporary. As soon as the computer is turned off, all data stored in RAM is lost.

Trackball

The trackball is an input device, similar to the mouse, that allows the user to point to and select items on-screen.

Tracking ball

Resembling an upside-down mouse, the trackball uses a rotating ball that is normally found on the bottom side of a regular mouse. The ball's movement corresponds with the movement of a pointer on-screen. Instead of moving the entire mouse around the desktop to move the corresponding mouse pointer on-screen, only the tracking ball is moved. The ball can be moved with the thumb, fingertips, or palm of the hand.

The trackball also has buttons for performing basic clicking actions used to select commands. Trackballs can do the same computer tasks that a mouse can perform, including drawing pictures, copying and pasting selected items, and dragging on-screen Track-balls are efficient input devices for working in a small area where there is no room for moving a mouse. Because of this feature, trackballs are commonly used with notebook and laptop computers. Usually located in the center or outer edge of the laptop keyboard, the portable trackball is very small, needing only the press of a finger to activate and manipulate it. Also see Input Device and Mouse.

POINTER

An arrow or other symbol that appears on-screen and moves simultaneously with the movements of a mouse or trackball. When a pointer is directly over an icon or menu, selections can be made.

How Does It Work?

When the trackball is rotated by hand or fingertips, two rollers (called motion translator axles) rotate in a corresponding direction. A slotted synchronizer wheel is attached at the end of each roller, through which LEDs (light-emitting diodes) shine. The light pulses caused by the rotation are detected by phototransistors on the opposite side of the wheel. Signals are sent to the PC, and the pointer on-screen is moved a corresponding distance.

Phototransistors

Synchronizer wheel

LEDs

Motion translator axles

DOUBLE-CLICK

To move the mouse pointer over an object or an icon and press the mouse button twice in quick succession.

CLICK

To move the mouse pointer over an object or an icon and press the mouse button.

DRAG

To move the mouse pointer over an object and press the mouse button. While continuing to hold the mouse button down, drag the mouse to the end position and release the mouse button.

MOUSE

A small input device used to point and select items on-screen.

Trackball found on laptop computer

UNIX

UNIX is the name of an operating system that is used with mainframe computers, minicomputers, and personal computers. As a matter of fact, most minicomputers use some form of the UNIX operating system. Operating systems, such as UNIX, tell the computer how to process information; they act as the master control for the entire computer system. UNIX is a multitasking (capable of processing several instructions at the same time), multiuser (networking) operating system favored by large corporations and universities. UNIX is also used in many PCs through which a user connects to the Internet (a network of government and university computers around the globe). There are many versions of UNIX. One version, called A/UX, runs on powerful Macintosh computers. For PCs, versions include AT&T UNIX System V, Microsoft's XENIX, and a variation of AT&T's UNIX called Berkeley UNIX BSD, developed at the University of California, Berkeley.

In 1969, the very first adaptation of UNIX was developed for the PDP-7 minicomputer at AT&T Bell Laboratories. Written in the C programming language, UNIX was originally designed to be used by one person at a time. The name UNIX is based on the abbreviation UNICS, which stands for UNified Information and Computing System. However, newer versions of UNIX improved multitasking capabilities (the ability to run several programs at the same time) making it an ideal operating system for multiple users.

By 1974, UNIX had become a popular operating system for users in the fields of science and in university settings. Because of antitrust regulations, AT&T's Bell Laboratories was unable to market UNIX, so they gave it away free to colleges and universities. In 1979, an enhanced version of UNIX was developed at the University of California at Berkeley. This version, better suited to the engineering and technical fields, was designed for the VAX minicomputer. Microsoft developed an improved version of UNIX called XENIX (which stands for extended UNIX) to run on IBM PCs and other PC-compatibles.

UNIX prompt

UNIX command that lists available files

File name

```
$ls -lf
-rw--- 1 jenful          352     Oct 16 09:08 my.sign
-rw--- 1 jenful         1254     Nov 22 11:01 modem.log
-rw--- 1 jenful       295686     Jan 18 07:02 examples.txt
drw--- 2 jenful         3519     Apr  8 21:04 call_files/
-rw--- 1 jenful        12296     Feb 20 13:00
letterhome.zip
drw--- 2 jenful         2248     Mar  6 22:03 temp/
-rw--- 1 jenful         4210     Nov  2 07:05 list.txt
-rw--- 1 jenful        31810     Oct  3 10:01 network.guide
```

Permissions

Owner of the file

File size

File date and time

How Does It Work?

UNIX is different from other operating systems, such as DOS, because the user does not give it commands directly. Instead, the user types commands into a program called a Shell, which then translates the commands into UNIX. There are many different UNIX Shells available (including the Bourne Shell, Korn Shell, and C Shell), but most of them look and act like DOS. There are differences, however. For example, the DOS prompt is a greater than sign >. With most UNIX Shells, the prompt is either $ or %. The user types a command at the shell prompt and presses Enter or Return. For example, the user could type find, followed by the name of a file, to locate a missing file anywhere on the system. (UNIX is case sensitive, which means that the file name JENNY is not the same as the file name Jenny.) In addition, because UNIX is multitasking, a user can run several programs or commands at one time.

This command will locate all the files called "memo.file" and display them on-screen.

```
$find /usr -name memo.file -print
/usr/georgia/junk/memo.file
/usr/hank/personal/memo.file
/usr/jennifer/procedures/memo.file
/usr/scott/sales/memo.file
/usr/sherry/bookideas/memo.file
```

In Unix, print means to display something on-screen.

Finally, in the early 1980s, AT&T was granted the right to market and sell UNIX. In 1983, they released UNIX System V, a combination of some of the earlier versions of the program. This version introduced UNIX standards, called System V Interface Definition (SVID), that all other variations of UNIX could adhere to. In 1989, AT&T released UNIX System V Release 4.0, which combined XENIX, the University of California at Berkeley's version, and System V into one powerful standard of UNIX. Novell recently bought AT&T's version of UNIX (now called UNIXWare) and continues to market this unique operating system.

Although UNIX is very popular among programmers, as an operating system it is slower, consumes more memory, is more costly, and is harder to master than the more popular DOS operating system. Also see DOS, Internet, Minicomputer, and Operating System.

MULTITASKING

A multitasking operating system such as UNIX is capable of processing more than one task at a time.

INTERNET

An "information highway" composed of interconnected networks across the globe. The Internet connects mostly university, large corporations, scientific, and government networks with a system that allows users to share files and send messages.

NETWORK

A network is a collection of interconnected computers that share files, programs, and peripherals. A local area network (LAN) is connected with cables, usually located within a single building. A wide area network (WAN) is a series of local area networks connected by telephone lines.

SHELL

A user interface that makes a difficult-to-use operating system (such as UNIX or DOS) easier to use and understand. A UNIX shell translates the user's commands into a language that the operating system can understand.

Utilities

Utility programs are used to manage computer files, diagnose and repair computer problems, and assist in helping the computer run more efficiently. Basically, a utility program acts as the computer's maintenance man, fixing up things that go wrong and making sure everything is running smoothly. Most operating systems have many of the utility programs needed to assist with the upkeep of the computer. For example, DOS 6.x includes utilities for managing memory, ridding a system of viruses, defragmenting a hard disk, doubling a disk's storage capacity, backing up files, and restoring accidentally deleted files.

Unfortunately, most operating systems do not offer all of the utilities a user might need to fully maintain

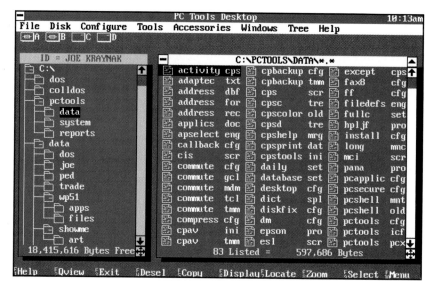

PC-Tools is a utility program that helps the user manage files and directories.

the computer, or the operating system's versions of these utilities are difficult to use or are less efficient. For example, DOS 6.x includes a copy of Norton's backup utility, but it does not allow a user to

backup to tape cassettes. Because of this, many users buy additional utility programs that handle everything. PC-Tools and Norton Utilities are two very popular utility programs. For the Macintosh, Symantec offers both Norton's and its own utility programs.

Utility programs can manage files and directories. This includes the capability to delete, move, and copy files and directories. Such functions help keep the computer's hard disk organized. Utility programs are also useful when a user accidentally deletes files from his disk. A special file recovery feature can help recover deleted files if it is not too late. Another important feature is the utility program's virus

This option in Norton Utilities allows the user to sort his directories.

protection. A virus is a computer program created to vandalize other computer systems. Computer viruses are passed from computer to computer through infected program files (not data files). Upon entering another computer system, they can inflict great damage, including erasing data files, reformatting the hard disk (which also erases data), and even destroying a computer's system files so that it cannot boot or start itself again. A utility program's virus protection feature checks the computer for such viruses and removes them if they are present.

Utility programs can also tell the user how much space is left on the computer's hard disk, how efficiently the disk is running, and other important system information. When the computer's hard disk (or even a floppy disk) is damaged, utility programs can help solve the problem. They can also defragment a disk, organizing how the

files are stored and making sure they are kept together on a disk and not scattered all over (fragmented). Finally, utility programs can help users protect data by creating passwords for files, which prevent others from

opening a file or changing the data inside it. Also see Norton, PC-Tools, and Virus.

With the Norton Utilities program the user can run a diagnostic test that checks the computer for problems.

BACKUP

Backing up a hard disk involves copying its files to a floppy disk or backup tape. In the case that the hard disk fails somehow, the backup copies can be used to restore the files.

DISK DOUBLER

Special program that effectively doubles the amount of storage space on a hard disk by organizing files more ef-ficiently than DOS and by compressing (shrinking them). DoubleSpace, included with DOS 6.x, is such a utility.

DEFRAGMENT

As files are stored onto a formatted disk, they are stored in clusters. Large files often will not fit into just one cluster, and therefore must be "split" up and stored in several different areas on the disk. The more files that are written to and deleted from the disk, the more split up or fragmented the files become, and the longer it takes the computer to locate each part of a file. Defragmentation is a process that relo-

VIRUS

A computer program created to do damage to other computers, for instance erasing files or reformatting the computer's hard disk drive.

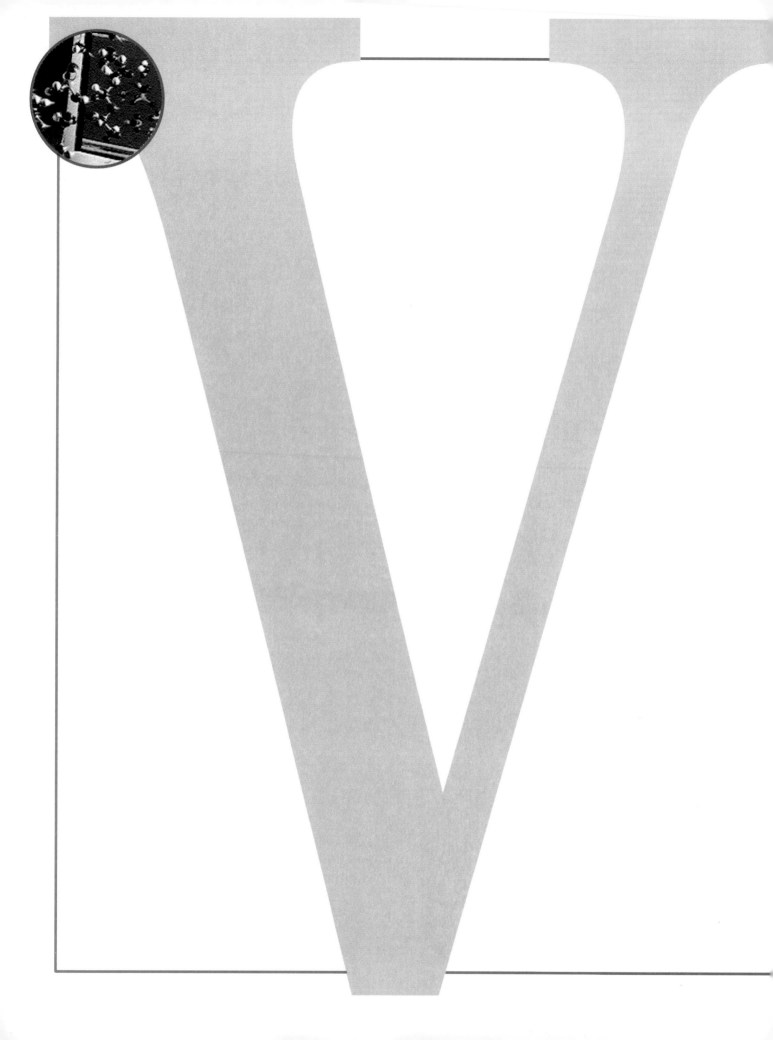

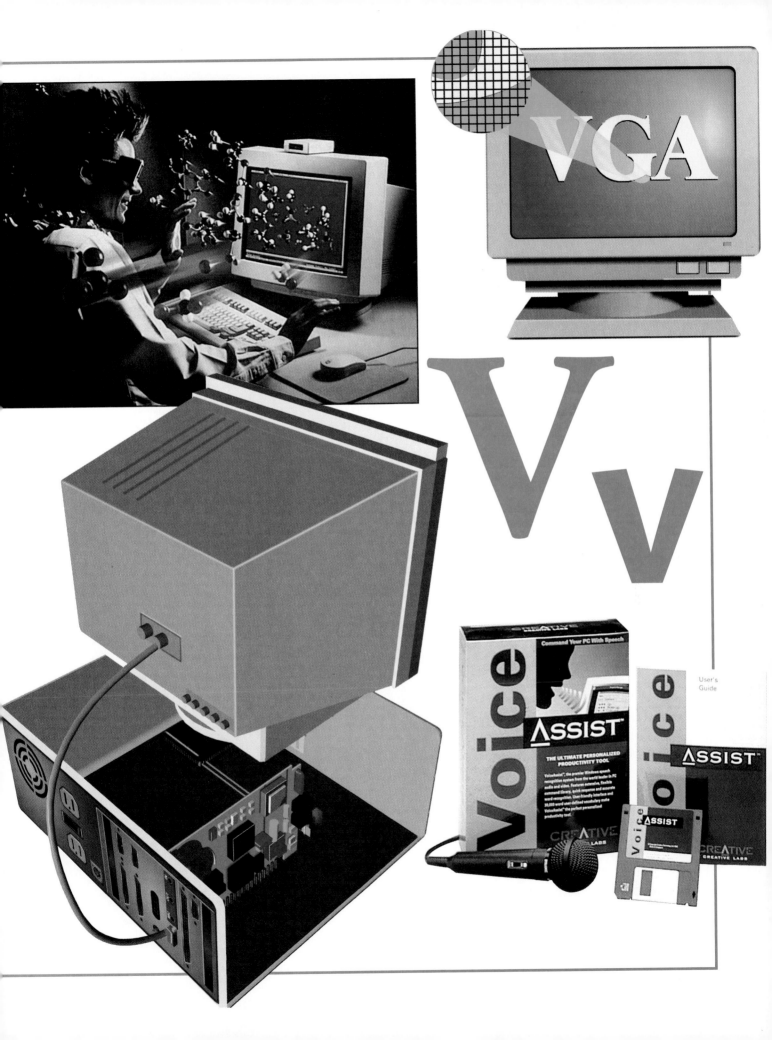

Video Adapter

The video adapter (some times called the graphics adapter) is the special circuit board that connects the monitor to the system unit. Without this video adapter, a user's monitor is useless. Inserted into an expansion slot on the motherboard, the video adapter carries information to the monitor. There are several major types of adapters: MDA, CGA, EGA, and VGA. The type of video adapter will always match the type of monitor in the PC's system.

Early computer monitors were monochrome (black and some other color, such as white, green, or amber), and they were attached to either an MDA or a Hercules adapter. The MDA (Monochrome Display Adapter) could display only text (not graphics), and only in one color. MDA adapters were often replaced with the Hercules adapter, which was faster, had better resolution, and could display graphics. Today, monochrome monitors are found mostly on portables (laptops or notebook computers) because they are less expensive to produce. However, they no longer follow the MDA standard; they usually follow VGA, the standard used in PCs sold today.

There are three main types of color video adapters: CGA, EGA, and VGA, although VGA and its cousins (Enhanced VGA and Super VGA) are the only ones sold today. Each standard is defined by the quality of its resolution. Resolution is measured by the number of dots, called pixels, that can be displayed on-screen—the greater the number of dots, the sharper the image. The dots are measured by how many can fit into one inch (dots per inch, or dpi).

CGA (Color Graphics Adapter), introduced in the early 1980s, was the first standard for color display. CGA adapters can display a color resolution of 320 by 200 dpi with four colors. EGA (Enhanced Graphics Adapter) can display a resolution of 640 by 360 dpi with 16 colors. Today's standard is VGA (Video Graphics Array). VGA is available in three forms: VGA, Enhanced VGA, and Super VGA. A regular VGA monitor can display a resolution of 640 by 480 dpi with 256 colors. Enhanced VGA increases the resolution to 800 by 600 dpi. Super VGA offers a resolution of 1,024 by 768 dpi.

Almost all applications today use some type of graphics, whether its a simple dialog box requesting information from a user, a menu from which a user can select commands, or the display of complex artwork or charts. Windows and OS/2 programs are especially graphics intensive. Displaying graphics on a

How Does It Work?

All of the better systems sold today use either local bus or a graphics coprocessor to speed up the display of graphics. Unlike the normal bus (which connects all the PC's components to the CPU), a local bus is a direct connection from the video adapter to the CPU, allowing for the fastest transfer of data. Local bus video, as it is called, transfers data at the speed of the CPU, and not at the speed of the normal bus (which is set to a slower speed so it can accommodate all peripherals). A local bus video comes built into the motherboard, so it is not something that the user can add.

The other method for speeding up the video display uses a graphics coprocessor. Like a math coprocessor, which processes numbers for the CPU, a graphics coprocessor processes video information. Unlike a math coprocessor, which is usually built-in, a graphics coprocessor is located either next to the CPU on the motherboard, or on a special video adapter called a graphics accelerator. Unlike local bus video, a graphics accelerator can be added by the user.

monitor is a time-intensive process, because the video adapter itself relies on the microprocessor (the CPU) to compute the location of the various pixels to display. The video adapter takes this information and translates it into the appropriate signals to send to the monitor. Also see Expansion Cards, Graphics, Hardware, Monitor, Output Devices, and Portable Computers.

DPI

Dots Per Inch. A monitor's resolution is measured in how many dots can appear on-screen.

LOCAL BUS

A bus that connects the video adapter directly to the CPU so that data can be transferred at faster speeds. A local bus speeds the display of graphics on the monitor. It is built into the motherboard, and is not an option that can be added later by the user.

VIDEO COPROCESSOR

A special microprocessor chip that handles video data so the CPU won't have to. Located either on the motherboard or on a graphics accelerator card, a video coprocessor helps to display graphics faster.

RESOLUTION

The sharpness and clarity of an image on a monitor screen. Resolution is measured in dots, or pixels, per inch.

GRAPHICS ACCELERATOR

A special circuit board that replaces the normal video adapter. A graphics accelerator contains a video coprocessor, which helps to display graphics more quickly on the monitor.

Bus

Video adapter or graphics accelerator

Virtual Reality

Virtual reality is an artificial, three-dimensional reality created by a computer. Virtual reality (VR) involves as many human senses as possible, creating an information-rich environment almost as complex as natural experience. Through the use of special gloves and stereoscopic eyewear, a user feels almost a part of the virtual world. Cyberspace, a term coined by William Gibson in the novel "Neuromancer" refers to this artificially created world.

Using virtual reality, a pilot, a surgeon, or an air-traffic controller can practice his craft without endangering himself or others. Designers can study the forces of nature (water and air flow) on their aircraft and building designs. City planners can foresee future needs for water, electricity, and traffic control before new buildings are constructed. And chemists, geneticists, and molecular engineers can manipulate models to investigate new theories.

Virtual reality dates back to early flight simulators used in WWII to train young pilots. Hollywood got into the act some time later with Cinerama, VistaVision, Sensorama, 3-D glasses, Sensurround, Dolby, and THX stereo, which were all designed to enhance the reality of the movie-going experience. Recently, for the movie "Jurassic Park," the sound was placed on a laser disk (and not encoded on the film) to improve its quality when replayed. This created the effect that the dinosaurs in the movie were right there in the theater.

In the '60s, Ivan Sutherland designed the first head-mounted graphics display and the first interactive computer screen, called the Sketchpad. In the '70s, artist Myron Krueger created Video Place, a user-responsive computerized environment. When a person walked into Video Place, he was surrounded by video images that changed based on his movements. SuperCockpit, a flight simulator developed in 1981, used head-mounted displays to create an artificial world through which a pilot could fly. NASA improved this system with its Virtual Interface Environment Workstation, composed of 3-D stereo sound, head-mounted displays, computer-generated graphics, and a DataGlove. The DataGlove was designed by

Using virtual reality, a new city comes alive.

Courtesy of StereoGraphics

A realistic virtual reality experience involves viewpoint, navigation, manipulation, and immersion.

Jaron Lanier and Tom Zimmerman in order to create a virtual guitar playing experience. Lanier and Zimmerman later founded VPL Research, the first of many VR suppliers.

To be effective, virtual reality involves several techniques: viewpoint, navigation, manipulation, and immersion. Viewpoint is created by simulating the position of the user's eyes within a virtual (computer-created) world. Navigation is the process of moving the user's viewpoint from one position to another within the VR environment. Navigation is normally controlled through special eyepieces that track the movement of a user's eyes, calculating the approximate change in view. Through manipulation, the user's hands join his eyes in the virtual world. Wearing special gloves fitted with electrical connections leading to the computer, the user can reach out and pluck an object off a table. Immersion is the extent to which the user is drawn into the VR world—the measure of how realistic the

continues

Virtual Reality continued

simulation is. However, virtual reality has not yet reached the point where total immersion is possible. The main problem is that the sense of touch is so very hard to simulate with machinery.

Although there are no programs available today that attempt a true virtual reality experience, there are many programs available for fun and entertainment. Among these are flight simulators (such as Falcon 3.0), action-adventure games (such as Shadowcaster), 3-D animation programs (such as Animator and 3-D Studio), and a relatively inexpensive VR creator (called VR Studio). In addition, with popular games such as SimAnt and SimEarth, a user can create his own world and test how that world functions. Various VR simulators are also available as shareware on popular BBSs and information services such as CompuServe. Also see BBS and Shareware.

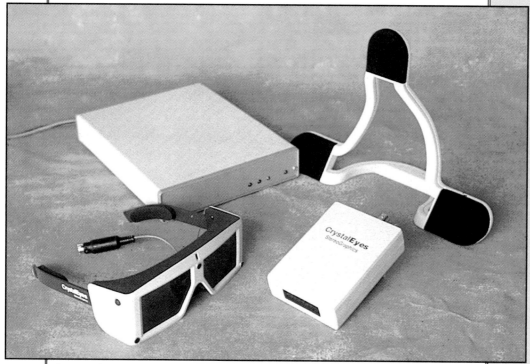

Courtesy of StereoGraphics **Virtual Reality Equipment**

GARAGE VIRTUAL REALITY

Also known as desktop virtual reality, this is the most common type of virtual reality program available. Mostly made up of games that allow the user to experience a scaled down version of a virtual world, garage virtual reality uses the PC's monitor as the window into the virtual world.

How Does It Work?

To create realistic visuals, a headset is used that places a small viewing screen in front of each eye. When the user moves his head, the headset transmits the movement data to the computer, which makes the appropriate changes to the on-screen image.

Creating realistic sound in a VR world is a bit more complicated. Truly realistic sound must come from somewhere in the three-dimensional space of the virtual world. The Convolvotron headset utilizes a complicated set of mathematical formulas to make small adjustments to a digitized sound wave, making it appear as if the sound is coming from various directions.

The most difficult sense to duplicate is the sense of touch. Using a glove-like device, it is possible to duplicate a small range of senses. One such glove employs small air bladders that inflate and deflate, applying differing amounts of pressure to various parts of the hand. Another type of glove uses an arrangement of pistons to apply pressures to the fingers. Still another contains special wires that, when heated, simulate the feel of different textures.

Virus

A virus is a program designed to duplicate itself in order to spread from system to system. Some viruses are harmless, displaying only a simple message; but most are very harmful—destroying data or entire hard disks. Viruses attach themselves to program files and move with them from disk to disk. Anti-virus programs detect these changes in program files and remove the virus. When a virus attaches itself to a file, it lays dormant. However, when a certain date or event occurs, the virus is triggered, becoming active. One famous virus is the Friday the 13th virus (also known as the Jerusalem virus because it was first discovered at the University of Jerusalem in 1987), which is activated every Friday the 13th. What the virus does when activated depends on the virus itself: some reformat hard disks (effectively erasing them), some delete or damage files, and some damage the file allocation table (FAT) so files can't be found and the hard disk is rendered useless.

In the '60s, John Conway wrote a program that could duplicate itself. Soon it became a challenge for hackers (someone particularly skilled in computers, especially computer programming) at

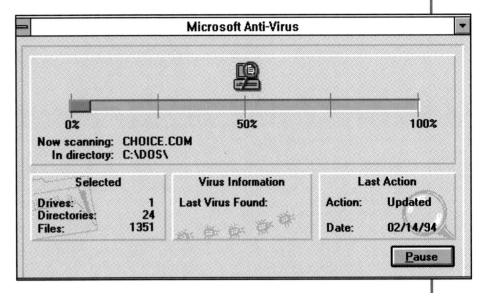

Most viruses can be detected with a good anti-virus program such as the one that comes with DOS 6.x.

colleges and universities around the country to try to write self-duplicating programs—most of which were harmless. The first documented virus was written by Fred Cohen, a USC student in 1983. By the end of the 1980s, viruses had reached epidemic proportions.

Viruses are rare and should be a cause for caution, but not alarm. A user can protect his system from viruses by following such simple procedures such backing up important files frequently, and write-protecting program disks. Some viruses are copied from an infected disk during startup, so it's important to remove all disks

from their drives before starting or restarting (booting) the computer. All files that come from an unknown source should be checked with an anti-virus program before they are copied to the user's hard disk.

Every PC should be equipped with some type of anti-virus program. Most operating systems come with such a program, or they can be purchased separately. Popular anti-virus programs include those by Norton, Symantec, and PC Tools. DOS 6.x includes a version of Central Point's (the makers of PC Tools) Anti-Virus program for both Windows and DOS.

continues

Virus continued

Unfortunately, new viruses are being discovered every day. Users should periodically update their program's list of viruses by following the manufacturer's instructions—this usually involves receiving a file by modem or calling and requesting an update on disk. Also see Files, Floppy Disk, Hard Disk, Networks, Norton, PC Tools, Safety, and Utilities.

Verify Error			
C:\DOS\DBLSPACE.BIN			Update
File has been changed.			Delete
			Stop
	From:	To:	Continue
Attribute:	....	...A	
Time:	06:00:00	06:20:00	
Date:	12/23/1992	09/30/1993	
Size:	50848	64246	
Checksum	02F0	FFE3	

If a file has been changed, its checksum will no longer match.

WORM

Originally harmless, a worm virus does nothing but replicate itself. Eventually, it takes over all the system resources, until the PC is doing nothing else but running the worm virus program. Worms travel from system to system very easily, making them especially dangerous on networks.

TROJAN HORSE

A virus that comes disguised as a friendly program, such as a utility or a game. These viruses are usually quite dangerous, as they are designed to destroy data.

FILE INFECTORS

The most common type of virus, file infectors add virus code to the regular programming code within a program file. When the infected program file is run, the virus infects other program files. That's how the virus replicates itself through a system.

BOOT SECTOR VIRUSES

This type of virus attaches itself to the boot sector of a disk—the part where startup instructions and the file allocation table (FAT) are kept. The boot sector is the part of a disk that is read and loaded into memory each time a disk is booted (started). In addition, its FAT contains vital information about the location of files on the disk.

How Does It Work?

An anti-virus program recognizes the types of changes viruses make to program files. Most anti-virus programs check for viruses when they are first installed, and then they perform a checksum. This checksum is a value derived from the individual bytes that make up a file. If the file's contents are later changed, the checksum won't match and the anti-virus program can warn the user.

While an anti-virus program is running, it sounds a warning if an application tries to change to a program file, which is one way that viruses are spread. Also, if the telltale signs of known viruses are detected, a warning appears. If a virus is detected in a system, the anti-virus program can be used to remove it. However, some viruses can not be removed, and the damaged files must be replaced from copies on backup disks or tapes.

Visual Basic

BASIC stands for Beginner's All-Purpose Symbolic Instruction Code, which is a programming language. BASIC is almost always the first programming language a programmer learns. Visual Basic is an event-driven programming language by Microsoft that is based on BASIC. Event-driven programs react to events, such as a click of a mouse button or the press of a key by the user. They are much more direct and easier for a programmer to write than traditional programs are.

A program is a set of instructions that tells the computer how to perform a task. Most programs look somewhat like broken English; the actual words and the structure of each instruction depends on which programming language is being used. Following the rules of a particular programming language, a programmer writes the step-by-step instructions that tell the computer exactly what to do. After these instructions are written, they are converted into a language the computer can understand, called machine language. Machine language is a series of 1's and 0's based on the binary numbering system that all computers use.

With Visual Basic, the programming instructions are converted into machine language using a special program called a compiler. However, a Visual Basic program is not fully compiled; instead, it's converted into something close to machine language, and then converted the rest of the way whenever the program is actually run. Since Visual Basic programs are not fully compiled, they run a bit slower than fully compiled programs. However, the fact that the Visual Basic program has not yet been fully converted into machine language makes it easier for the programmer to test the program during the writing process.

First released in 1991, Visual Basic took the programming world by storm. Its easy-to-use interface made it simple for beginning programmers to create Windows programs, an achievement once possible only by very experienced programmers. Version 2 was released in 1992,

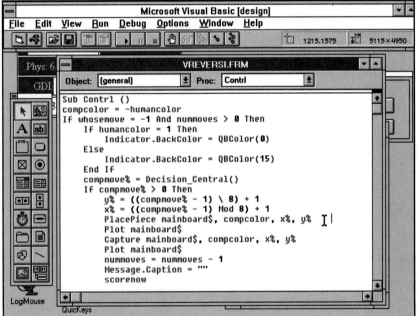

Visual Basic for Windows

continues

Visual Basic continued

and Version 3 was released a year later in 1993. There's even a Visual Basic for DOS, for creating sophisticated-looking DOS programs with ease. Although Visual Basic is not a true object-oriented programming language like C++, it does contain some similar characteristics. Visual Basic uses two primary objects: the form (the windows on-screen) and controls (the buttons, scroll bars, and other items that a user manipulates). Each

object has a pre-defined set of events, such as a click of a mouse button or the press of a key by the user, for which the programmer writes instructions. For example, a button has a click and a double-click event.

However, unlike other OOP languages, Visual Basic does most of the work for the programmer. Instead of writing instructions to create a window complete with scroll bars, a title bar, and mini-

mize and maximize buttons, the Visual Basic programmer simply draws them using the Toolbox. The programmer then writes the instructions for each event associated with the objects he has drawn. Also see Basic, Binary, C/C++, Object-Oriented Programming, Pascal, and Programming.

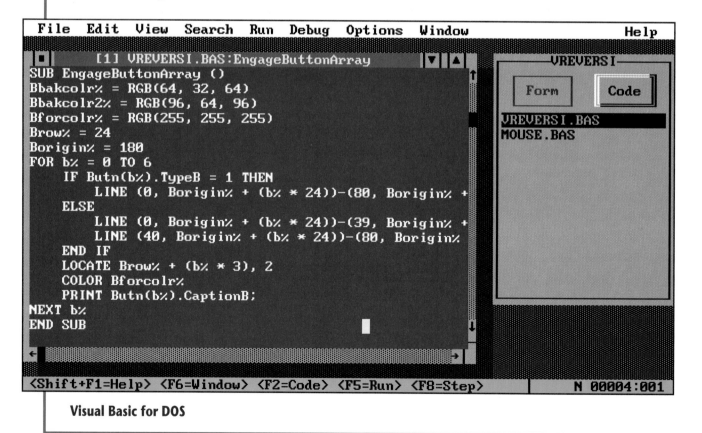

Visual Basic for DOS

How Does It Work?

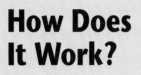

Visual Basic is an event-driven program; the programmer writes instructions only for the events which will occur—this minimizes the amount of writing a programmer must do. For example, the programmer writes the instructions for what the program should do if a user clicks on a certain button or presses a certain key. The event-driven concept is different from other programs written in BASIC, which are procedural. In a procedural program, the program processes each instruction in turn, only occasionally jumping to a different section of instructions and then back. In an event-driven program, the user is in charge. Nothing happens until he triggers an event (by doing something (such as clicking on a button). Then the program responds by processing the instructions related to that event.

VISUAL C++

A version of C++ by Microsoft. Visual C++ is a true object-oriented programming language which combines the best parts of Visual Basic and C++. Visual C++, unlike regular C++, makes it easier for the programmer to create things that the user sees, such as dialog boxes, menus, and messages. It also comes with a help system, menus, and other tools.

INTERPRETER

Each time an interested program (like BASIC) is run, it is converted into machine language by an interpreter. This is unlike a compiled program, which is converted into machine language only once. (A compiled program written with C or C++, for example, is converted into machine language and stored permanently in a file, which is then reused anytime the program is run.)

COMPILER

Converts a program's instructions into machine language and stores the result in a file. That file can then be used over and over, each time the program is run. A Visual Basic program is not fully compiled; it is interested the rest of the way each time it is run.

The programmer draws a form (a window) and adds controls for the user.

Form

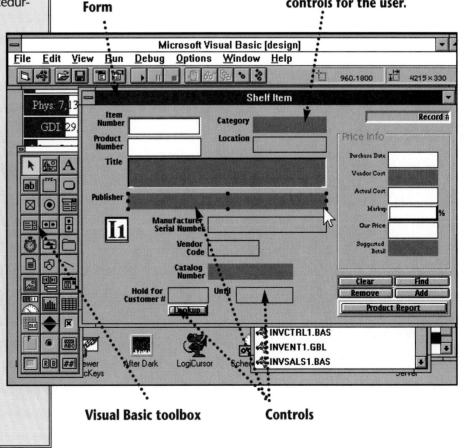

Visual Basic toolbox   **Controls**

Voice Recognition

Voice recognition is the process of converting the spoken word into computerized text and commands. Voice recognition software takes its input in spoken form and, comparing the words against a table of pre-recorded sounds, converts them into their digitized equivalent. This is similar to character recognition software, which interprets written text and commands through a table of recorded letters and symbols. Voice

recognition is far from 100% accurate, however. Most software packages can recognize only a limited number of words, and even then, they sometimes confuse them with other words in their vocabulary.

With a voice recognition program, a user could someday input text into a document by simply speaking it. Currently however, voice recognition software is limited to converting a simple list of spoken commands into specific program instructions. For example, a user could issue the spoken command, "Open Budget spreadsheet" and the voice recognition software

would issue commands to the spreadsheet program to open the Budget file. A user can also record a word that activates a macro (a pre-recorded series of keystrokes that activate commands). For example, the user could record the command "Compute total" to run a macro that would recalculate the totals in a spreadsheet.

Voice recognition software works only with operating systems that come with a built-in set of commands which all programs running under that operating system recognize. These operating systems or operating environments

The voice recognition program matches the spoken words to a pre-recorded pattern.

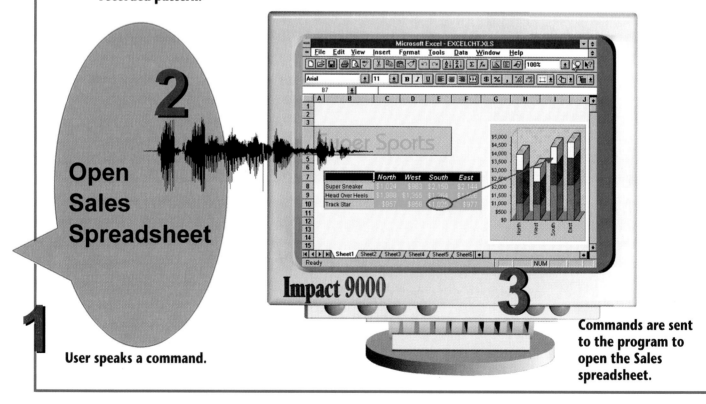

2

Open Sales Spreadsheet

1

User speaks a command.

3

Commands are sent to the program to open the Sales spreadsheet.

How Does It Work?

To add voice recognition to a PC, a user needs to install a sound card, microphone, and the voice recognition software. After installing the software, the user goes through a series of steps to record his voice speaking common commands such as open file, close window, cut, copy, and paste. The sounds are converted to digital information (digitized), and are stored in a file as a digitized sound wave. To activate the command, the user speaks the same words as before. The voice recognition software matches the waveform to one in its list, and sends the appropriate instructions to the correct program.

include Windows, OS/2, and Macintosh System. Macintoshes currently come with voice recognition built-in. The Finder, the Macintosh file management program, supports a lot of standard voice commands such as delete, copy, or move file. Compaq's Presario also comes with a voice recognition system built-in. Also see Communications, Macintosh, MIDI, and Sound Board.

VoiceAssist, the voice recognition program by Creative Labs

To "train" a command, the user selects it from a list, and then speaks the name of the command.

VoiceAssist, the voice recognition program by Creative Labs

NATURAL LANGUAGE PROCESSING

A branch of artificial intelligence research that specializes in the analysis of human speech patterns. Results of this research is used in the development of voice recognition and speech synthesis software.

SOUND CARD

Special circuit board inserted into an expansion slot, which improves the sound reproduction quality of a PC. Popular sound cards include the Sound Blaster and the Pro Audio Spectrum.

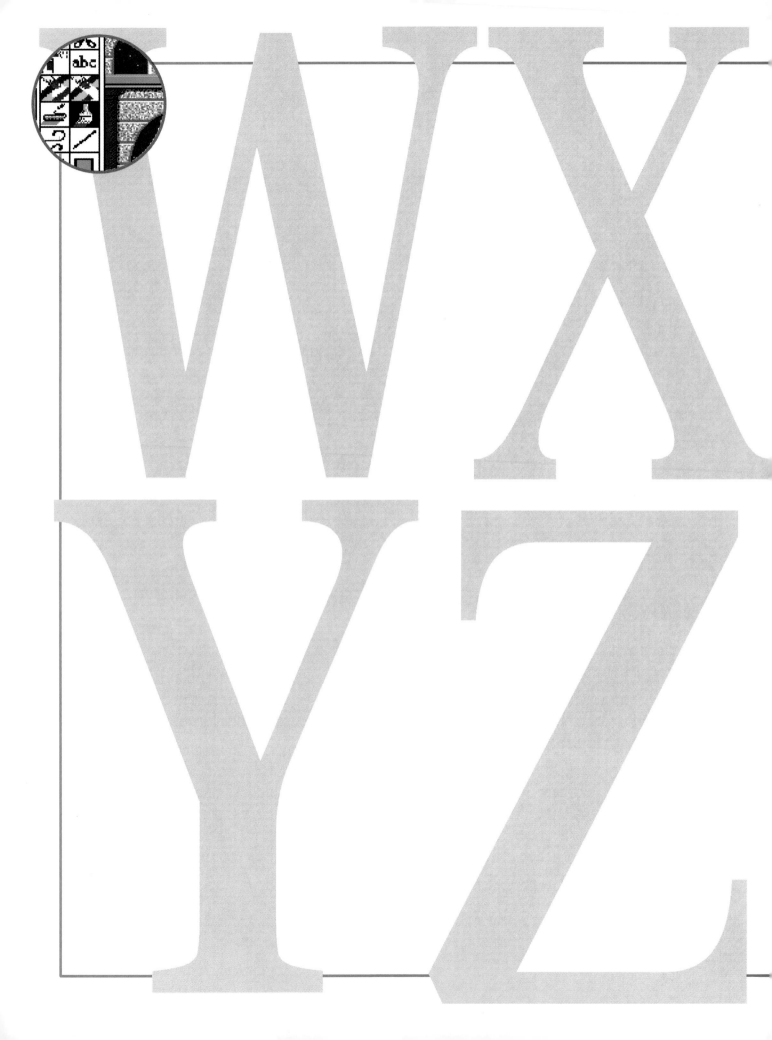

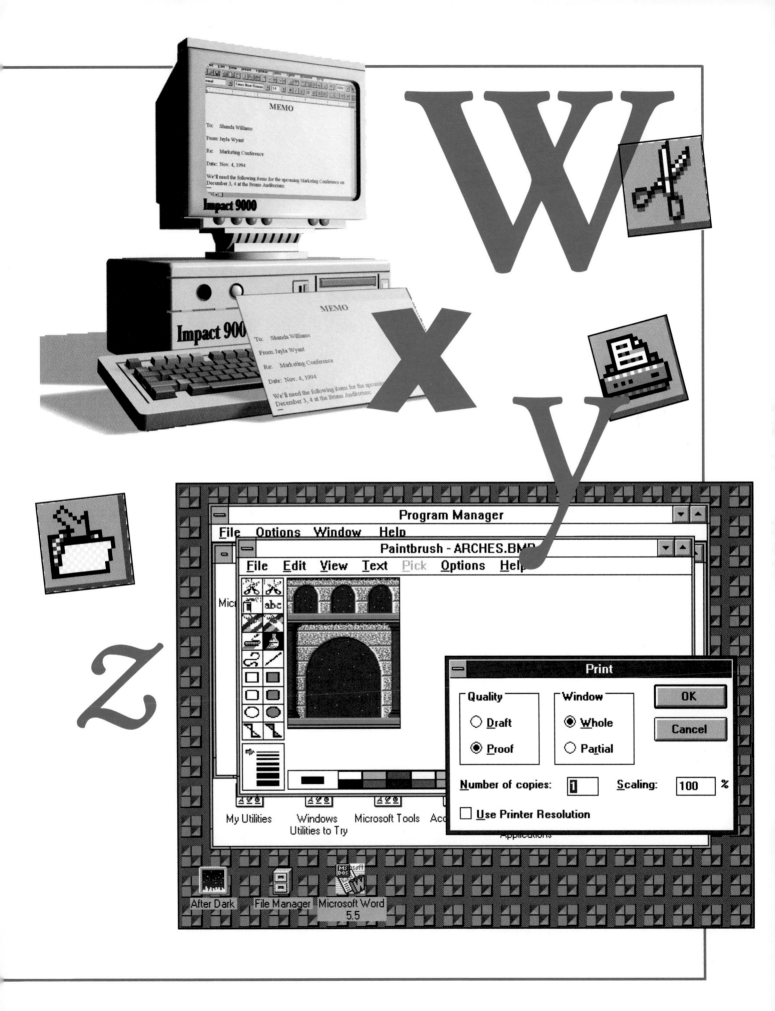

Windows

Windows is the name of a graphical user interface (GUI) environment created by Microsoft Corporation. Windows was created to run on top of Microsoft's DOS, making it easier to use. (DOS is an operating system that tells the computer how to carry out instructions requested by the user.) Windows is not an operating system, but rather an enhancement program (operating environment) that makes the DOS operating system visually appealing and simpler to operate. Windows provides the user with a graphical, friendly interface to carry out computer tasks. Instead of having to type in commands at a DOS-prompt, users can click with a mouse to select commands and programs represented by small graphical pictures, called icons.

Windows has an interesting history in terms of its development. Although Windows is one of the most popular graphical user interfaces (GUI) purchased today, it was not the first. Developers at Xerox's Palo Alto

Microsoft Corporation, located in Redmond, California.

Courtesy of Microsoft Corporation

Research Center (PARC) created the first graphical user interface. Their technology was soon adapted by the developers at Apple who incorporated the friendlier, easy-to-use interface into their Lisa computer. Their version of GUI technology included icons that represented programs, menus that pulled down to reveal lists of commands, and dialog boxes that let the user choose more options. Unfortunately, the Lisa did not fair well on the personal computer market because of its high price tag of $10,000. The following year, in 1984, Apple repackaged its GUI technology

into an innovative computer called the Macintosh. The look and feel of this new visual interface was widely received and generated much excitement in the computer marketplace. Today, the Macintosh is the best selling single brand of computer.

Microsoft began working on a GUI replacement for DOS in 1983, just two years after the first IBM PC was released. Released in 1985, Windows 1.0 featured non-moveable windows, and it was less than impressive. In 1987, Microsoft released Windows 2.0, which allowed the windows to be moved, but was

severely handicapped by DOS' limited 1 megabyte of working RAM. Without the help of special programs (memory device drivers), DOS is restricted to working in a tiny 1 megabyte memory space—a large amount at the time DOS was invented, but not near enough for today's memory-hungry programs. Device drivers did not exist at the time Windows 2 was released.

Microsoft put Windows aside for awhile and began working with IBM on a replacement for the command-driven DOS operating system, one that would also present computer commands, programs, and tasks as graphical elements. In 1987, they released OS/2 (Operating System/2), which improved on DOS's capabilities, and then fol-

lowed that with OS/2 version 1.1 that had a Presentation Manager, called a shell, which made the computer resemble a graphical user interface. (This shell looks a lot like what Microsoft Windows would later evolve into.) OS/2 was not immediately accepted on the PC front because it had a few technical problems and there were not a lot of programs written for it.

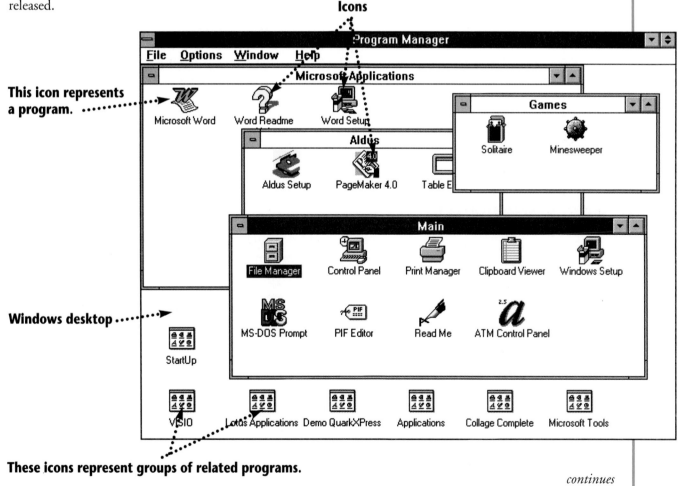

Icons

This icon represents a program.

Windows desktop

These icons represent groups of related programs.

Windows continued

While IBM sought to improve OS/2 with a second version, Microsoft broke away from the joint venture and put all of its efforts behind Windows. In 1990, Microsoft released Windows 3.0, and because of its many improvements, it really impacted the market. Windows could access extended memory (the memory above 1 megabyte), and featured a friendly graphical interface that could run on top of DOS and compete with the Macintosh GUI. In 1992, Windows 3.1 was released, improving the speed at which Windows performed, and adding TrueType font support and multimedia support. Today, Windows is a best-selling product for IBM PCs and PC-compatible computers, with dozens of software products being introduced every day written specifically for Windows. These include Word for Windows, 1-2-3 for Windows, WordPerfect for Windows, and Excel. Windows can also run DOS applications, launched from the Windows interface itself.

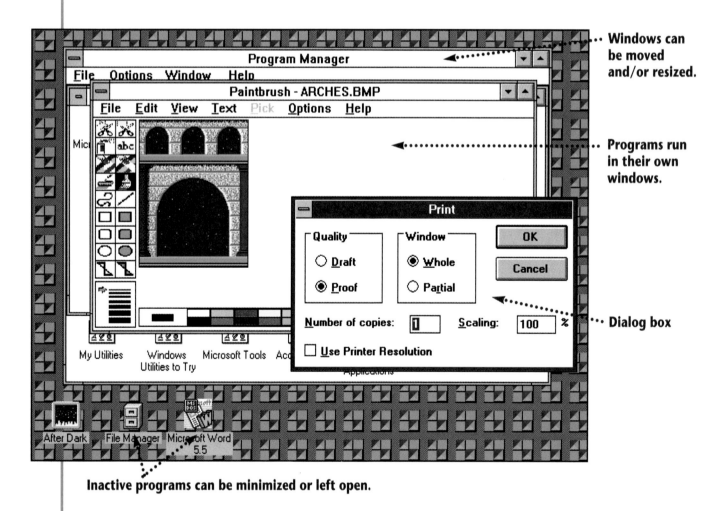

Windows can be moved and/or resized.

Programs run in their own windows.

Dialog box

Inactive programs can be minimized or left open.

How Does It Work?

Windows is not the same kind of multitasking system as OS/2 and Macintosh System. A preemptive multitasking system, such as OS/2, divides its processing time equally between all tasks, preempting those tasks when their allotted time is up. With Windows, the active program has full control over the CPU's time, with the idea that Windows programs will occasionally give up portions of their time for other programs. This usually happens when the program is waiting for something anyway, such as a user's command. Windows can run multiple programs, but only one program is active at a time. Windows NT, a true operating system like OS/2, is the preemptive multitasking version of Windows.

The main Windows program is called the Program Manager. It manages a user's programs, and it's from here that a user starts each application. The Windows overall work area is called the Desktop. Just as a person can access everything found on his office desktop, a Windows user can also access computer programs and accessories—on an electronic desktop, so to speak. The Program Manager (and every other program) sits on top of the Desktop in resizable windows. Program Manager contains program icons that can be opened, moved around, and grouped into program groups.

Typical program groups include the Main group icon that opens up to reveal built-in programs that help the user organize files (File Manager), change the colors and appearance of the desktop (Control Panel), monitor the printing actions (Print Manager), and more. Also found on the Program Manager screen is an Accessories group icon that opens up to reveal handy

A toolbar from Lotus 1-2-3 for Windows, called the SmartIcon bar.

The Main program group in Program Manager

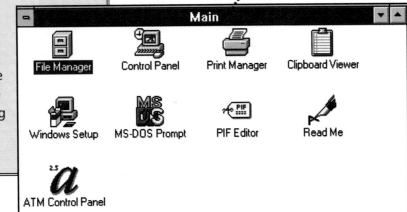

The Main group window has several different options for organizing files, controlling on-screen colors, and even monitoring the printer.

continues

Windows continued

mini-programs called applets, including an electronic calendar, clock, and calculator; Paintbrush (a Windows paint program); Windows Write (an easy-to-use word processing program); and other tools.

Windows has many features similar to the Macintosh. These include icons that represent applications and files, menus that list commands, dialog boxes that let the user select options before a command is carried out, and windows that can be resized and moved around.

Windows is named for the windows that surround running applications. For example, from the Windows Program Manager, the user can start a program that opens up into its own window. That window can be resized, moved around the screen, or reduced again into a little icon. Each application, when started, runs in its own window.

At the top of each window in Windows is a menu bar that lists available menus. When selected, a menu drops down to reveal a list of commands to choose from. Also at the top of each window are minimize and maximize buttons, which are used to

reduce a window to an icon (minimize), or enlarge it to fill the screen (maximize). The similarity of each window in every Windows application cuts down on the amount of time spent learning a new programs.

Another feature found in most Windows applications is the toolbar. Toolbars are horizontal or vertical bars across the top, sides, or bottom of the program window that have square buttons with icons on them. Each button

Pull-down menu   **Menu bar**

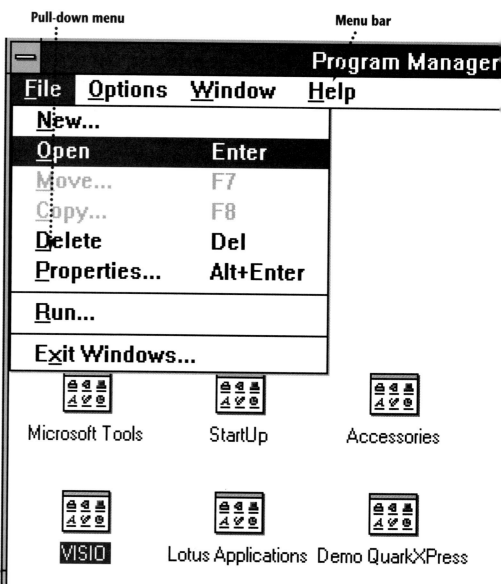

CLIPBOARD

A temporary storage area for text or graphics that are copied or cut from a Windows program. The copied or cut item can then be pasted from the Clipboard into another document or another part of the same document.

GUI

Short for Graphical User Interface. A program that provides an easier, friendlier way of communicating with the computer. GUIs use icons, menus, and dialog boxes to display commands and options.

Minimize button **Maximize button**

represents a different command that can be activated with a click of the mouse. Toolbars save time in selecting commonly used commands.

Windows has come a long way in bringing the graphical user interface to IBM PCs and PC-compatibles. Supported by a wide base of programs written specifically for Windows, many speculate that the command-driven days of DOS (in which users typed in instructions to get the computer to perform) are fading away quickly. With Windows, commands and choices are available with a click of a mouse button, making computing an easier, faster technology to use. Also see DOS, GUI, Macintosh, Microcomputer, Microsoft, and OS/2.

ICON

A tiny graphical picture that represents a program, a file, or a command.

MENU

A list of available commands. Menus commonly pull-down from a menu bar.

TOOLBAR

A bar found on many Windows programs that contains buttons with icons, each representing a common command (such as Print).

DIALOG BOX

A window in which the user provides the computer with the additional information it needs in order to carry out a task. Dialog boxes also offer additional options to choose from.

Games

Aldus

plications

Collage Complete

Windows NT

Windows NT, which stands for Windows New Technology, is made by Microsoft Corporation. Released in 1993, Windows NT looks and acts (for the most part) like Windows 3.1, which is a big plus for users who are already familiar with working in Windows. Windows NT boasts preemptive multitasking capabilities, which means that it splits the CPU's processing time equally among all active programs. This makes it different than Windows 3.1, which can multitask (run more than one program at the same time), but can't multi-process (process multiple tasks) unless the active program "gives up" some of its time to another program. Another nice feature of Windows NT is its built-in security, which protects a user's data.

The original Microsoft Windows was created as a supplemental program for DOS, providing it with the graphical elements it needs to

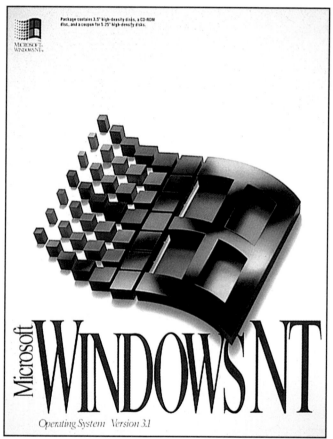

Courtesy of Microsoft Corporation

be friendly and easy to work with. Windows NT does not need DOS, because it is a complete operating system in itself. (Windows is considered an operating environment, not an operating system like Windows NT.) Windows NT can run programs written for DOS, Windows, and OS/2, as well as programs written specifically for it. Windows NT supports computer networks (LANs and WANs), and essentially brings the power of high-end workstations to the desktop computer.

Like OS/2, Windows NT supports long file names—up to 256 characters including extensions; this is much longer than DOS (which limits file names to 8 characters with a 3-character extension). Also like OS/2, Windows NT is a 32-bit operating system (it processes data in 32 bit chunks, about 2 to 4 times faster than DOS). It requires more memory than OS/2 (16 megabytes of RAM—random access memory) and 100 megabytes of space on the computer's hard

disk drive. Windows NT works best on a computer system that uses a 486 microprocessor chip, the new Pentium chip, DEC's Alpha chip, or the MIPS R4000 and R4400 chips. Although Windows NT can run on 386 chips, it is not recommended. The very design of Windows NT is made for high-resolution monitors, specifically the newer Super-VGA monitors.

It may be a year or so before the computer market can gauge how successful Windows NT will be and especially how it will perform. Meanwhile, Microsoft is already working on improving Windows NT—in the fast-paced world of computer technology, new developments come and go in the blink of an eye. Also see DOS, Microsoft, Operating System, OS/2, and Windows.

PREEMPTIVE MULTITASKING

In a preemptive multitasking system, the operating system divides the CPU's time equally between all the programs currently running. This may cause a task to be preempted when its time is up. Windows 3.1 uses a different kind of multitasking called cooperative multitasking, where it is up to a program to give control back to Windows so that resources can be shared.

OPERATING SYSTEM

A program that tells the computer how to process data, how to run peripherals (such as the monitor or printer), and how to interact with the user. Common operating systems include Microsoft's DOS, OS/2, Windows NT, and Mactintosh's System 7.

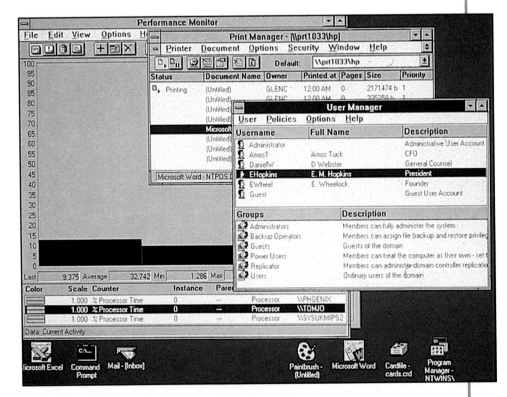

Windows NT looks very similar to Windows 3.1.

Word for Windows

Word for Windows is a word processing program published by Microsoft Corporation. Word processing programs allow the user to work with words to create letters, memos, manuscripts, and more.

(make it bold or italic, for example), add a table, create bulleted and numbered lists, add headers and footers, and number pages. Also included are common utilities, such as a spell checker, grammar checker, and thesaurus. Word

When first introduced, Microsoft Word was written for personal computers running DOS and for the Macintosh computer. Microsoft Word for Windows (often called WinWord to distinguish it from its DOS and Mac cousins) was released in 1989. WinWord utilizes the standard features that all Windows applications use: drop-down menus, dialog boxes, multiple document windows, etc. One Windows feature that is especially nice when creating professional looking documents is WYSIWYG. Using the WYSIWYG format of what-you-see-is-what-you-get, Word presents the user with a screen that shows exactly what will be printed. For example, a newsletter with text and graphics (or any other document) created in the Word for Windows program will print out looking exactly as it appears on-screen. In addition, Word for Windows, like most word processing programs, allows the user to preview a document before printing it.

Word for Windows is a full-featured application that includes not only the capability to work with text, but also a page layout feature for positioning text and graphics precisely within a document. In addition, Word for Windows includes standard word processing options, such as that to format text

for Windows lets the user control the page layout and adjust margins and indents, and even comes with clip art that can be inserted into any document. Word for Windows is one of the most popular word processing programs sold today.

Another important feature of Word for Windows is the toolbar, a horizontal bar at the top of the program window that contains a row of buttons with icons on them. Each icon represents a different command or task that the program can carry out. The latest version of Word for Windows (version 6.0) offers several specialized toolbars, each customized with commands designed for a specific task, such as formatting text, drawing, or adding borders.

Word for Windows toolbar

Word for Windows, like other Microsoft Windows products, includes Wizards, special guides that lead a user through a complicated process (such as creating a newsletter) step by step. Another nice feature, the Format Painter is an icon that allows the user to quickly copy formatting from one set of text to another. WinWord also offers shortcut menus, which appear in the work area when the right mouse button is clicked. Shortcut menus are customized to the task the user is currently working at. For example, if the user is working with text and he activates the shortcut menu, commands relating to formatting or copying text will appear. If he was working on a table instead, a different shortcut menu would appear. Word for Windows has many nice features, including one of the easiest methods around for creating form letters—a complex task in most word processors.

Another WinWord feature is styles. A style is a set of specifications for formatting a section of text, including the font, size, style, indentation, and spacing. Applying a style to text automatically formats the text according to the style's specifications. With the many predefined WinWord styles, a user can quickly create professional looking documents. A user can also define his own styles. Also see Applications, Microsoft, Software, Windows, and Word Processing.

FORMATTING

Commands that affect the appearance of text and the layout of a document. Formatting includes fonts, styles, and positioning of text.

EDITING

To make changes or corrections to a document.

Shortcut menu

Style name

Word Processing

Word processing is the process of using a computer to write and edit text. A word processing program is used to work with text to create letters, memos, reports, or even an entire book like this one. Before the popularity of personal computers, this type of work was performed with a typewriter. However, typewriters were limited in their inability to handle corrections and changes to documents. Because a document created in a word processing program is electronic, changes and corrections can be quickly made on-screen before the document is printed out. The word processing document can also be stored as a file for future use. Word processing programs are the most popular applications used with computers today.

Popular word processing programs include Word for Windows, WordPerfect, and Lotus Ami Pro.

The first computers used in the business world were strictly designed for working with numbers and large lists of information. The task of using a computer to manipulate numbers and data was called data processing. These early computers were quite complicated and difficult to use—giving the terms "data processing" and "computers" a bad reputation in the minds of those who worked with them. These early systems required large staffs to operate them, and they frequently broke down causing many problems with secretaries and other peripheral staff who had to deal with them.

With the advent of simple-to-use word processing programs, software publishers and computer manufacturers had a hard time convincing secretaries that computers and processing were not necessarily bad things. They coined the term "word processing" to differentiate them from the feared data processing equipment from the past. In the early days of marketing computers, they were called "word processors" and referred to as spiffy, jazzed-up typewriters. Over time, the humble computer found its way into every business arena, despite its guise as a word processor.

Today's "word processors" are now recognized as computers, and people use them to create a variety of documents with word processing programs. Word processing programs are used in all areas of publishing, business, home, and education. They have made working with words an easier process for all. Also see Ami Pro, Application, Software, Word for Windows, and WordPerfect.

How Does It Work?

The first step toward creating a word processing document is to type in text. As text is typed, characters are inserted at the cursor or insertion point. When text reaches the end of a line, it automatically wraps to the next line (a process called word wrapping). Word processing programs allow the user to control the appearance and layout of the document, and to rearrange paragraphs and blocks of text. In addition, font styles, sizes, alignment, and margins can all be adjusted to suit the user's needs. Many word processing programs also come with spelling and grammar-checking features to help compose text. When finished typing a document and making any necessary changes, the user can save the document as a file and print it out on paper.

FORMATTING

Commands that affect the appearance of text and the layout of a document. Formatting includes fonts, styles, and positioning of text.

CUT AND PASTE

A feature common in Windows-based applications, that lets the user move text from one location to another.

Menus   **Font size**   **Font style**

Cursor or insertion point   **Word wrap**

Write - ARKSTRY.WRI

File   Edit   Find   Character   Paragraph   Document   Help

Ark Arrives in Two Weeks!

Yes, it's true, Noah's Ark is coming to Willow Brook Church on Saturday, October 31. Noah and his family will be boarding animals from 5:00 to 8:00 p.m. If you are not an animal, come disguised as one. There will be an Ark-boarding party that includes games, food and more fun than a barrel of monkeys. ***Don't miss the boat on this event!*** Come be a part of the excitement! And don't forget to bring an umbrella.

Now, for those of you who are wondering what this is really about--We're having a whiz-bang fellowship for everyone in the family. This event is open to everyone--Invite your friends, bring your neighbors, tell everyone you know to be here! We'll have something for everyone. There will be game booths, prizes, treats, contests, family games, food and a whole lot of fellowship going on.|

However, there is a catch to all this hoopla--You have to come dressed as an animal. In other words, wear a costume. It can be a mammal, amphibian, fish, fowl or insect. Now don't get all hot under the collar, and wipe that grumpy grimace off your face. This is going to be fun. We have no doubt (based on last year's Noah's Ark Party costumes) that you can come up with *SOME* kind of animal costume. You'll be amazed at what you can do with a pair of sweats, a paper bag and/or some items from around the house (did you know that spaghetti strainers can make an excellent pair of bug eyes?). So loosen up, have some fun and *PARTICIPATE*! (Remember--nobody likes a party pooper.) Who knows, you might even win a prize for best costume. (And here's an ominous threat--no one will be allowed on the ark unless you are disguised as an animal. If you show up without a disguise, one will be provided for you--and you won't like wearing a bag shaped like a skunk all night! And we mean it!)

Page 1

WYSIWYG

What-You-See-Is-What-You-Get, pronounced wizzy-wig. This is a way of displaying work on-screen so that it looks exactly the same as it will when printed. Many word processing programs offer this feature.

SEARCH AND REPLACE

To substitute new text in place of old text. Many word processing programs offer a feature that searches for specific text and replaces it with some other specific text.

PAGE PREVIEW

A programming feature that lets the user see how a printed page will look before he prints it out.

EDITING

To make changes or corrections to a document.

DOCUMENT

A memo, letter, report, or other text created with a word processing program.

WordPerfect

For WordPerfect purists, screen elements can be hidden to display a plain typing screen.

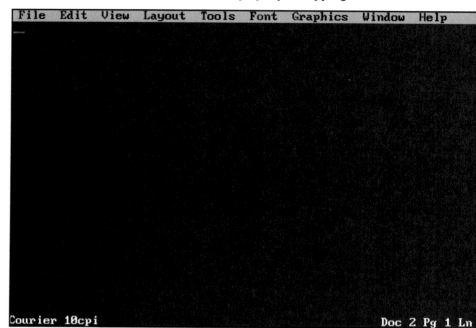

File   Edit   View   Layout   Tools   Font   Graphics   Window   Help

Courier 10cpi   Doc 2 Pg 1 Ln

WordPerfect for DOS has been one of the most popular word processing packages for over ten years. It has come a long way from its introduction in 1980 by the WordPerfect Corporation. It is now available in many formats, including PC (DOS and Windows versions), Macintosh, Apple II, and Amiga. One of its strengths is that WordPerfect files from one version of the program are perfectly compatible with files from other versions. This does have a downside, however, since the WordPerfect versions for the Macintosh and for Windows do not take full advantage of their GUI technology in order to maintain this compatibility between all WordPerfect versions. However, WordPerfect remains one of the most powerful, full-featured word processors around, and it has an incredible following.

In its first versions, WordPerfect users pressed functions keys to enter commands (for example, a user pressed Shift and F7 at the same time to print a document). This method of issuing commands proved popular with fast typists who preferred to leave their fingers on the keyboard when issuing commands. The whole WordPerfect screen was basically blank, with a few numbers at the bottom of the screen to tell the user which column

and page he was on. The lack of a displayed menu of commands made WordPerfect perhaps a bit difficult to learn, but its blank screen and function key command system was preferred by experienced typists. In WordPerfect 5.1, a mouse-driven pull-down menu was added, along with a button bar similar to other word processors. These features made WordPerfect more accessible for casual users. However, experienced users could elect to display the menu and button bar, or to maintain a clean typing screen.

Another feature of WordPerfect is its editable formatting codes (codes that surround formatted text). For example, a start bold code and an end bold code are inserted before and after a section of bold text.

These codes could be displayed and deleted, if necessary, to remove the formatting. Text in WordPerfect for DOS is entered in text mode, which means that the formatting is not always visible (larger text is diplayed in the same size as other text, for example).

WordPerfect for Windows is an incredibly powerful program, with such features as desktop publishing capabilities, graph and table features, an equation editor for scientific equations, mail merge features, book production features (such as tools to create tables of contents, outlines, and indexes), legal document functions (such as line numbering), and the WP Draw program. In 1994, WordPerfect was purchased by Novell, Inc. Also see Applications, Software, and Word Processing.

WordPerfect, shown here in text view, removes all distractions so a user can concentrate on just typing.

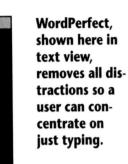

s 1"

WYSIWYG

An abbreviation for What-You-See-Is-What-You-Get (pronounced "wizzy-wig"). The term is used to describe text or graphics that look the same on-screen as they do when printed out on paper.

WP DRAW

A drawing program that comes with WordPerfect 6 for Windows. Art can be created in WP Draw and easily imported into a WordPerfect document.

Button bar

File   Edit   View   Layout   Tools   Font   Graphics   Window   Help

| Marg ▼ | None | | 1 Col ▼ | Left ▼ | Courier 10cpi | ▼ | 12pt ▼ |

File Mgr · Save As · Print · Preview · Font · GrphMode · TextMode · Envelope · Speller · Gramatik · QuikFndr · Tbl Edit · Search

[WORDPERFECT CORPORATION]

[1555 N Technology Way • Orem, UT 84057 • (801) 555-0000 • fax (801) 555-0000]

February 16, 1994

[Addressee]
[Company]
[Street Address]
[City, State ZIP code]

Dear [Name]:

[Type your letter here]

Sincerely,

C:\WPDOCS\LETTER.TEM   Doc 1 Pg 1 Ln 0.5" Pos 1"

WordPerfect 6 for DOS, shown here in graphics mode.

Undo - Reverse the last change made to the document - Ctrl+Z

File   Edit   View   Insert   Layout   Tools   Graphics   Table   Window   Help

Undo	Ctrl+Z
Undelete...	Ctrl+Shift+Z
Repeat...	
Cut	Ctrl+X
Copy	Ctrl+C
Paste	Ctrl+V
Append	
Select	▶
Paste Special...	
Links...	
Object...	
Find...	F2
Replace...	Ctrl+F2
Go To...	Ctrl+G
Convert Case	▶

Indent   Draw   Chart   Figure   Text   QuickFormat   Styles

B I U ▯L ⊞ ▤ ▤L 1.0 100%

mpt response to our travel requests. We really appreciate your a spontaneous vacation this month. We are both looking nd Jim Dude Ranch.

Barb and Walt Winesburg

Times New Roman Regular 12 pt   Select   Pg 1 Ln 2.97" Pos 1.50"

DESKTOP PUBLISHING

Programs that have desktop publishing capabilities are usually able to produce quality graphics and have advanced character style features. They can handle columns of text and usually come with many design tools that a user would need if he was creating a newsletter.

MAIL MERGE

A feature that merges addresses in a database with fields in a form letter. With a mail merge feature, a user could create one letter to send to several different addresses.

WordPerfect 6 for Windows

WYSIWYG

WYSIWYG, pronounced "wizzy-wig," stands for What-You-See-Is-What-You-Get. This term refers to programs that display files on-screen just as they will look when printed out on a printer. Because the appearance of a printed document is so important, WYSIWYG is most closely associated with word processing programs. When a user is working with a word processing document, he often makes changes to the appearance of text. Some text may appear bold, while other text may be italicized, for example. Those changes need to be reflected both in how the document looks on the monitor screen and in how the document prints out from the printer.

WYSIWYG is not confined to word processing programs only. Windows, OS/2, and Macintosh have WYSIWYG technology built-in, so all programs written for them contain this feature as a matter of course. TrueType fonts, introduced with Windows 3.1 and now available on the Macintosh, enable the monitor to display text exactly as it will appear when printed.

Before the development of WYSIWYG programs, users could not always predict how the output of a document would compare with the commands that were entered to format the text. A user could accidentally change the font or the font size of text but not realize it was different until it was printed out. All text looked the same on the screen, regardless of the font it was going to be printed in. In addition, styles like italics and underlining often did not appear on-screen, they were indicated by a different color of text. Users sometimes had to print multiple copies of a document just to fix character formatting errors that they couldn't see by looking at the monitor.

How Does It Work?

True WYSIWYG is a coordination game between the monitor and the printer. This coordination is best handled by a font manager program, which contains matched sets of screen and printer fonts. Even so, there may still be slight differences in the displayed document and the printed document, depending on how those fonts are created.

If the fonts are bitmapped — stored as a pattern of tiny dots called pixels—the size of the dots will vary from monitor to printer, creating a less than perfect result. Outline fonts are stored as sets of lines, curves, and points, using a mathematical formula instead of a pattern of dots. Outline fonts can easily be scaled to different sizes and proportions, unlike bitmapped fonts. This makes it easier for outline fonts to attain true WYSIWYG, since they can be scaled to the resolution of the monitor and printer being used.

One of the earliest companies to experiment with WYSIWYG was Lotus, who incorporated the technology into their 1-2-3 program as a feature called Allways. With Allways, a user could display the spreadsheet or a chart on-screen, change its format, and be assured that the printed result would match what he saw. Most programs today feature some form of WYSIWYG, and some programs (mostly word processors) even allow the user to view his document in different views. There are usually two or three views, including a draft view, a normal view (which is usually the default), and a page layout view (which displays an entire page). Draft view usually means that the WYSIWYG feature is not applied to the document. Using draft view conserves system resources because the on-screen display is less complex than with other views. The normal view displays the document on-screen as it will look when printed out. Also see Font, GUI, Macintosh, OS/2, Windows, and Word Processing.

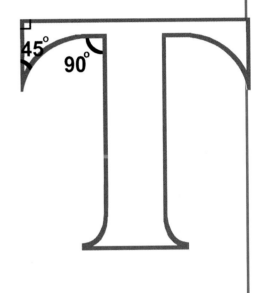

CHARACTER FORMATTING

Changing the style of the text. For example, **bold**, *italics*, and underlining are common character formats.

FONT

The name of the font, the font size, and the font style of text. For example, a common font is 12-pt Helvetica Bold (where 12-pt is the size, Helvetica is the font name, and Bold is the style).

RESOLUTION

The sharpness of text or a graphic that is measured by the amount of dots per inch (dpi). The higher the dpi, the better the quality of the image.